The Celtic Christian Sites of the central and southern Marches

The Celtic Christian Sites of the central and southern Marches

by
Sarah & John Zaluckyj

Logaston Press

LOGASTON PRESS
Little Logaston Woonton Almeley
Herefordshire HR3 6QH
logastonpress.co.uk

First published by Logaston Press 2006
Copyright © Sarah & John Zaluckyj 2006

ISBN 1 904396 57 7
(978 1 904396 57 4)

Set in Gramond and Times by Logaston Press
and printed in Great Britain by
Oaklands Book Services

IN LOVING MEMORY OF

HELEN CHAPLIN
1962 – 2005

and

KEITH NICHOLSON
1942 – 2006

Dear friends, so deeply missed

Contents

Montgomeryshire

Radnorshire

Gwent

Appendix

Acknowledgements

We would like to thank Andy Johnson for his continued interest and support in the preparation of this book — his help and kindness have been much appreciated.

We would like to express our sincere gratitude to our parents Stanley and Pauline Coleman and to the late Barbara and Zenon Zaluckyj for their inspiration, past and present. Love also to our sister Helen and to our special nephew, Fali Mistry.

We owe a debt of deep gratitude to the late Keith Nicholson for the extraordinary help he gave us in the past — his generosity was a rare and wonderful thing that will never be forgotten. Our thanks too to John Tucker of Aston-On-Clun for the inspiration he gave us back in the early 1980s — we believe he ignited our historical writing endeavours.

Our thanks too to our friends for their interest during this project — we promise we will now start talking about something else!

We would like to thank Jan Shivel of The Wellsprings Fellowship for the help she has given so generously — again very much appreciated.

We also owe thanks to Clwyd-Powys Archaeological Trust and Glamorgan-Gwent Archaeological Trust for providing us with print-outs of the Sites and Monuments Record in 2000, which proved to be the backbone for the book. Mention should also be made of Clwyd-Powys Archaeological Trust's Historical Churches Survey which has been made available on the Internet — this superb survey has been used extensively for the sites in this book.

In a similar vein we would like to express our appreciation of Llanerch Press of Wales for re-publishing otherwise hard-to-find texts such as Baring-Gould and Fisher's *Lives of the British Saints* — they have also ensured that many marvellous medieval works are now within the budget of everyone and, for this, they should be warmly congratulated.

Thanks too to Herefordshire Archaeology Unit for their help, past and present, and also to the curator of Brecon Museum in 2004 who generously allowed us to photograph the museum's early medieval stones. Any mistakes/misinterpretations that exist within the text are, of course, entirely our own responsibility.

We would also like to express our gratitude to the churchwarden of Llanhilleth church for her invaluable help when we visited the site in July 2005, and thanks to the churchwarden of Hope Bagot, Shropshire who made us so welcome in 2002.

Grateful thanks to Bob Jenkins and Margaret Price for the loan of various books and journals in the preparation of the work, and thanks also to Marge Feryok for her support and for her help on a site visit.

Many thank yous to Dougie Tittensor for looking after the dogs when we were out photographing around the Welsh Borders for hours on end — the dogs think you are the tops!

All the photographs are our own, with the exception of that on p.114 for which thanks are due to Malcolm Thurlby for its use in this book.

Last, but quite definitely not least, our love to Kay, Jacob, Benjy & Bronwyn for making everything worthwhile.

Sarah & John Zaluckyj
August 2006

CHAPTER ONE

The Arrival of Christianity in Britain

The first written record of Christian links with Britain appears in a story relating to the year 52 AD in 'what is perhaps ... the most impudent forgery in Welsh Literature'.[1] The legend relates that Caratacus, the famous British leader who fought against the Roman advance, and his family were turned over to the Romans and taken to Rome where they were converted to Christianity. Caratacus' family included his father, Bran, and his daughter, Claudia. In about 59 AD, so the story goes, they and Aristobulus, who had been ordained by St. Paul as the first Bishop of the Britons, returned to Wales and introduced the Christian faith.[2] The tale has several major problems, however, not least in that Caratacus was not from Wales, but simply an ally who had led the Silures of south-east Wales and the Ordovices of central Wales against the Romans. An even greater difficulty is created by the fact that Caratacus never left Italy after his capture but stayed in 'honourable confinement'.[3] Then again, Bran was not his father but rather a mythical figure who gained cult status within Wales, and Claudia was not his daughter, rather the child of Claudius Cogidubnus whom the Roman historian, Tacitus, refers to as a British king and who also acted as an imperial legate (provincial governor) probably over Kent, Surrey and Sussex.[4]

Claudia has been identified by some historians with a Claudia Rufina of Italy who married Pudens, a friend of St. Paul. Their four children were educated '"literally" on the knees of the apostles'[5] and all of them became saints. Pudens's house was one of the first in Rome to be used for Christian worship and Claudia and Pudens are said to have received St. Peter. Claudia was connected by adoption to the Rufine family, as was the earliest governor of Roman Britain, Aulus Plautius. He had fought against Caratacus and governed Britain for four years until his return to Rome in 47 AD. Ten years later Plautius' wife was accused of practising an illicit religion, possibly Christianity.[6] As wife of an ex-governor of Britain it could just be that she was practising the faith when in this country, although this is a very tentative possibility.

Another legend which was treated as historical fact for many years, principally because it appears in Bede's work and in the Llandaff Charters, is that of a King Lucius, termed 'King of Britain' (*Britio*), who, in the 150s/160s, requested

1

that the Christian faith should be introduced into his country. Misinterpretation of the world *Britio* meant that the location was ascribed to Britain, when the text actually refers to a Lucius who was prince of Edessa, previously known as *Birtha* or *Britio Edessenorum.*[7]

There is no hard evidence for Christianity in Britain before 200 AD. Irenaeus, bishop of Lyons, writing between 176 and 189 enumerated known Christian churches but did not mention any in Britain. It is probable that if there had been any substantial Christian settlements in Britain at this time, Irenaeus would have been aware of them and noted their existence.[8] However, this does not preclude the existence of small numbers of Christians and the possibility of some communication between individuals and small groups of believers, as occurred in Rome around this time.

In about 200, Tertullian the Cathaginiean, discussing the spread of Christianity, remarked that 'places of the British not approached by the Romans …[were like other regions] made subject to the true Christ.' Tertullian's contemporary, Origen, based in Alexandria, also refers to Britain as being among the places where the Church was 'now established at the very ends of the [Roman] world'. But the references are unspecific and vague — neither writer was concerned to establish the exact locations or numbers of British Christians.[9]

Even so, as an evangelical religion which actively sought to recruit new members, Christianity had some popularity in the face of the materially acquisitional and violent culture of the Roman empire. This resulted in its spread from Rome during the years when the empire was at its peak. The arrival in Britain of Roman administrators and military personnel, some of whom would have been Christian, would have encouraged the spread of the new religion.

It is during the mid-3rd century that Christian individuals finally enter the historical record in Britain. Three people known by name were martyred for their Christian faith during that century: Alban, Aaron and Julius, of whom St. Alban (or Albanus) is the most well-known. His name was later seized upon by the British church to promote the religion and spearhead a growing increase in Christianity's popularity over the succeeding centuries — St. Alban's shrine was duly recognised for its significance by King Offa of Mercia who established a double monastery of monks and nuns at St. Albans in 793.[10] It has been suggested that Alban's name was used so enthusiastically in post-Roman Britain because of the absence of any early, named founding fathers, unlike many parts of the Continent where Churches claimed descent from individual Apostles.[11] Tradition has it that, as a pagan soldier, Alban had been converted to Christianity whilst hiding a priest during an early persecution of the religion. Nineteenth-century historians have suggested that Alban died in about 306 during the Great Persecution of 303–11 under Diocletian. More recent opinion favours a time between 250–9 during the persecutions of the Roman emperors Decius or Valerian,[12] or as early as

*The Roman amphitheatre at Caerleon. It was probably at this site
that the saints Aaron and Julius were executed*

about 209.[13] The earlier dates are now favoured as it is believed that more names
would have been recorded if the martyrdoms had been carried out during the
Great Persecution, a time when the then Governors of Britain, Constantius and
Constantine, would have been sympathetic to Christians. Two other martyrdoms
that occurred in the late 3rd century were of northern bishops: Nelior, Bishop of
Carlisle, and Nicholas, Bishop of Penryhn, near Glasgow.[14]

Gildas considers that the martyrdoms of Aaron and Julius occurred at about
the same time as that of St. Alban but little is known of these saints. They appear
to have lived at Caerleon, just north of Newport in south-east Wales, and the
name Aaron suggests a convert from Judaism.[15] They were apparently soldiers of
the Second Augustan Legion based at Caerleon. As such they would have been
required to worship the Roman pagan gods. Their refusal to do so, and their
refusal to denounce the Christian faith, would have led to their arrest, trial and
eventual execution. As Roman citizens they would probably have been sent to the
nearby civilian town of Caerwent to be tried, only being returned to Caerleon to
be beheaded. It is possible that they were buried in the Roman cemetery on the
ridge which overlooks Caerleon and a funeral chapel or *martyrium* was built over
their graves, to be replaced by a medieval oratory.[16]

In the 12th century Giraldus Cambrensis refers to two churches with 'their
convent and society of canons, at Caerleon, dedicated to Aaron and Julian'. In the
very late 16th century Bishop Godwin of Newport observed that in the memory

of the preceding generation two chapels, named after Aaron and Julius respectively, were said to have existed about two miles apart on the east and west sides of Caerleon. Baring-Gould and Fisher surmise that in the 1900s a place called St. Julian's, then a farmhouse but once a mansion, probably occupied the site of St. Julian's church. They also suggest that the site of St. Aaron's chapel was near to the Roman camp of Penrhos. North-west of Caerleon there was a Cae Aron (Aaron's field) and a Cwm Aron (Aaron's dingle) in the neighbouring parish of Llanfrechfa. According to the Iolo manuscripts Llanharan (a chapelry in Llanilid parish), 6 miles east of Bridgend, was also dedicated to St. Aaron.[17] This suggests that the martyrdoms of the saints did indeed occur at Caerleon, or in the immediate area.

It was in 313 that the Roman emperor Constantine the Great made Christianity the official religion of the empire, changing its status from a minority cult into a religion that anyone in a position of influence would be keen to follow.

In 314 at least three bishops from Britain attended a council held at Arles in southern France: Eborius of York, Restitutus of London and Adelfius, most likely from Lincoln but possibly from Caerleon. It is possible that a fourth bishop or delegation attended from an unnamed location, perhaps Cirencester.[18]

British bishops may have also attended church councils held at Nice in 325 and Sardica in 347, but western delegates were not individually named. The next council for which there is proof of the attendance of British bishops is at Ariminium (Rimini) in Italy in 359, their presence being noted because three of them had to rely on imperial funds to cover their accommodation and travel expenses. By the end of the 4th century the number of bishops in Britain may have reached twenty, with the country's churches concentrated in the *civitas* capitals.[19]

However there is evidence of the survival of paganism in the late 4th and even the very early 5th centuries in Britain, with a strong pagan elite indicated. Indeed, there is some archaeological evidence that 4th-century Britain Christianity was probably more rurally based within the poorer sectors of the community than it was in mainland Europe, where Christianity was popular in towns but not so in rural areas. Dark suggests there may have been more Christians in Britain at this date than is usually supposed because Christians were possibly more conservative in their display of religion than their pagan counterparts. If Christians were worshipping in their homes, which were unadorned with Christian symbolism, or were worshiping in groups with a priest using a portable altar, archaeological traces of them would be almost impossible to find. Wealthy Christians, however, would have had the means to build dedicated rooms for worship and some rooms have been found in Roman villas with Christian wall-paintings and mosaics, although these are few. Wealthy pagans, with a much more visible religion and the means to display cult statues and to deposit votive offerings and hoards, for example, are archaeologically more visible. Consequently their pagan regalia is also more easily noticed. It would seem, therefore, that by c.400 the population of Britain included substantial Christian and pagan communities with the former growing at the expense of the latter. There were probably churches with bishops in the major towns with pagan landowners predominating in the countryside, albeit with 'suggestions of unusually early rural Christianity'. Churches and monasteries had become the main religious foci. This would represent a major shift over the previous 50 years.[20]

Christian monasticism was also taking root, a strand of Christian thought that was to have a large impact on the development of the British Church. The person traditionally associated with this development is St. Antony of Egypt who lived c.251–356. His biographer Bishop Athanasius of Alexandria, who was keen to promote the form of monasticism espoused by St. Antony, wrote his *Life* a year after his death. St. Antony was a moderately wealthy Christian farmer living in Upper Egypt who decided to withdraw from society to follow a religious life, giving away all his worldly possessions. This was not unknown, and across Egypt there were groups of people living in communal houses who had disposed of their possessions and who lived an ascetic life seeking a greater communion with God through prayer and meditation. But Antony went one step further and removed himself from society.

Initially St. Antony moved to the fringes of his village but, in about 305 at the age of 35, he left the settled area of Egypt and sought a solitary life in the desert.[21] He was to spend most of his last forty years in the desert, at a hermitage on Mount Kolzim close to the Red Sea.[22]

It is quite possible that St. Antony could have been dismissed or merely tolerated as just another hermit or crazy man living outside normal society, but instead his idea caught on. He believed that the ascetic should strive for self-knowledge and self-purification, renouncing the pleasures of worldly comfort, food and sex, with the aim of creating a new 'genderless, consistent and singular' identity in which his soul could achieve union with God. It was thought that by working until exhausted, through disturbed sleep and controlling the intake of food, that carnal desire would be controlled; it was certainly known that by significantly reducing calorific intake impotence would be induced.[23] Quite how the urge for food was controlled is unclear, but all monastic diets agreed on the exclusion of meat.

Before long St. Antony was attracting both followers and people seeking advice, with the result that the solitude he sought was in danger of disappearing. In time he became one of the holy men to whom people made pilgrimage, even from overseas. Some of these visitors inevitably stayed and followed St. Antony's example, creating sizeable settlements. Not surprisingly, St. Antony sought ever more isolated locations.

This process was replicated elsewhere in Egypt. In about 315 another follower of the ascetic life had settled on the 'Mount' of Nitria, about 40 miles south-east of Alexandria, and he too became a magnet for others. By the end of the 4th century there were somewhere between 3,000 and 5,000 monks living on Nitria which housed doctors, seven bakeries, and even confectioners! Some monks lived in communities, others alone. As Richard Morris so aptly remarks, Nitria was 'a kind of monastic tern colony'. Other such settlements followed at Kellia — 'the cells' — about 10 miles from Nitria, and Wadi' n Natrun, 52 miles from Nitria. A visitor to the area in 395 observed 'There are so many that an earthly emperor could not assemble so large an army. For there is no town or village in Egypt and the Thebaid which is not surrounded by hermitages as if by walls...'. With these settlements came a new problem — competitive self-abuse. In trying to outdo each other in ascetic discipline, came a sense of pride — one of the seven deadly sins — in how much self abuse one could inflict.[24] In the somewhat later British and Irish monasteries laws had to be laid down to curb some particularly revolting practises.

Those monks who lived in close association with others soon established the basic Christian monastic system. They would work either in agriculture, in crafts or in small industries and their wares were taken, via a steward, for sale in the outside world enabling the monks to support themselves. Although part of a community, the monks often led solitary lives working on their own, during which time they were expected to pray and meditate. Initially the monks lived in individual cells, but as the settlements expanded dormitories and refectories developed. The communities might develop their own bakeries, forges, carpenters' shops, fullers, tanners, shoemakers and weaving shops.[25]

The monastic idea soon spread, through the influence of trade routes, returning pilgrims and Athanasius's biography which was circulating in the West before Athanasius died.[26] By the 350s experiments in monastic life were taking place in Italy and Gaul. One of the earliest western forms of monastery was the small family or house monastery, where aristocrats and other prosperous individuals chose an ascetic Christian life and turned their own homes into religious retreats for family and friends. The use of Roman villas in Britain as house monasteries is known, for example, at Lullingstone in Kent and at Llandough and Llancarfen in south Wales.[27]

By the late 5th and early 6th centuries there was a growth in 'more organized asceticism' in Britain, with the foundation of establishments such as that at Llantwit Major in Glamorgan. Originally known as Llanilltud Fawr after its founder, the highly influential British saint, Illtud, it was built close to a major Romano-British villa, although the monastery's exact location is not known.[28] Llantwit Major became the premier monastic site in western Britain and a highly esteemed monastic school whose list of students reads like a Who's Who of the great age of saints: Samson, Dyfrig (Dubricius), Gildas, Paul Aurelian, and Cadoc.

One champion of monasticism in the West was Martin of Tours. Martin (c.316–397) was a native of what is now Hungary and the son of pagan parents. His father was an officer in the Roman army and Martin was brought up in northern Italy and joined the army, probably as a conscript. It was during this time that he realised that his Christian beliefs prevented him from continuing as a soldier. As an objector to military service he was imprisoned and only released after the end of that particular phase of hostilities. He then became a protégé of the ascetic Hilary of Poitiers and was baptized. It was Hilary who gave him land on which to found a monastery, the first in Gaul. Martin started out as a solitary monk but others inevitably joined him, and he found himself the pioneer of western monasticism, becoming bishop of Tours by popular consent in 372.[29] In Martin's monastery of Marmoutier near Tours the harsh, ascetic life of the eastern monasteries was moderated and the monks, many of whom were from wealthy families, were not expected to undertake manual work; indeed Martin's biographer, Sulpicius Severus, suggests peasants undertook the heavy, manual labour needed to keep the community running.[30] Yet Martin was to become a leading reformer within the Church, believing that the Christian word should be shared equally among rich and poor, urban and rural dwellers, and that God made no distinction in class or wealth. These ideas brought him into conflict with the Gallic bishops and other Christian elite who were of wealthy, aristocratic backgrounds who abhorred the idea that the peasant and the Barbarian should be included. Martin was the champion of the oppressed against their oppressors and insisted on living a simple life, keeping a dishevelled appearance and travelling about on foot, by donkey or by boat, which further annoyed his refined contemporaries within the Church.[31]

One of Martin's closest adherents was Victricius, bishop of Rouen who visited Britain in the 390s.[32] The reason for this visit was not recorded, but it was possibly in order to settle some matter of religious controversy on the island.

Victricius expanded Martin's reforms by preaching to the 'barbarians' of frontier districts. Using Martin's egalitarian principles, Victricius announced that 'men do not differ by nature, but only in time and place, in their occupations and ideas; for difference is foreign to divine unity.' Pope Innocent did not like Victricius' pronouncements and warned that 'Rome condemned innovators, whose presumption violated the purity of the church by seeking favour of the people rather than by fearing the judgement of God.'[33] However, Victricius' and Martin's belief that Christianity was for the people and that all men were equal, was gaining support among other bishops, some of whom were in Britain.

To help the spread of Christianity, Victricius' aim was to convert populations beyond the existing frontiers of the religion by using wandering monks, and to increase the use of venerated shrines to strengthen the religion's hold on the population. Such wandering monks were rare when he visited Britain in the 390s, but by 411 'were common'.[34] With the lack of historical record for Britain for the 4th to 6th centuries, it is difficult to know what effect Martin of Tours and Victricius had on British monasticism. What is agreed is that late 4th-century Britain had a strong Christian Church with differences within it of a magnitude that it was thought necessary to send a bishop of Gaul to settle them.

Pelagius

A British writer and thinker was soon to be at the heart of a wider controversy. Pelagius, a well-respected and established writer in Rome, favoured the humanist and individual style of Christianity that had been embodied in its origins. After the sack of Rome in 410, the teachings of Augustine, bishop of Hippo in North Africa and a hard-line reformer, appealed to Rome which favoured the idea of Original Sin. This deemed that man inherited Adam's sin and that he could only be redeemed by the grace of God. This placed strong emphasis on the word of God being interpreted by a hierarchical clergy, who delivered grace to those partaking in Mass and the sacraments. Pelagius was appalled by this view and sought to re-establish, or at least defend, the more egalitarian and gently individualistic notion of Christianity. In this approach individuals acquired grace through their own good works under their own freewill. With the sack of Rome, the Church feared that this older view might cause the Church to break into hostile factions, just as secular society had done. In Augustine of Hippo's theology, salvation was dependent on sacraments given by an ordained priest who was himself under the control of a bishop, who in turn was under the control of a pope 'in a disciplined hierarchy that might preserve the unity of the church'.[35] Augustine used extreme tenets of Pelagius' more radical followers to have Pelagianism outlawed and banned in 418. Described by his opponents as being 'a most monstrous great Goliath of a man ... with a great solid neck', Pelagius was considered a threat. After 410 he fled to North Africa and from there to the Holy Land. He used lectures, sermons, pamphlets and tracts to spread his ideas, although the extent and true authorship of much Pelagian literature is not known with any great certainty.[36]

Nevertheless, all the known leaders of the Pelagian radicals in Rome were reputedly from Britain and the authors of surviving Pelagian writings were British, the most forceful of whom was an unnamed young man writing in Sicily who is known to history as the Sicilian Briton.[37] A well-educated aristocrat whose preaching for Christian equality dates to about 410,[38] his writings against social inequality are astonishing in their directness:

> One man owns many large mansions adorned with costly marbles, another
> has not so much as a small hut to keep out the cold and heat ... inequality

of wealth is not to be blamed upon the graciousness of God, but upon the iniquity of men.[39]

The Sicilian Briton was not 'a lone idealist, but the spokesman of a movement' and such pronouncements as 'It is the rich, dripping with excessive wealth, whom the will to cruelty leads into acts of such wickedness ...' that understandably made the wealthy elite uncomfortable, if not defensive. However, it was probably the statement 'Abolish the rich and you will have no more poor ... for it is the few rich who are the cause of the many poor ...'[40] that would have struck fear into the ruling Roman authorities and which lead to Augustine attacking Pelagius.

The Pelagian controversy was resolved on the Continent within about eight years. Yet the philosophy was in some respects central to monastic/ascetic belief, in that Pelagianism supported the need of the monk to be able to commune directly with God. Pelagianism, although renounced in Gaul, was considered no heresy within Britain, with Fastidius, a British Pelagian writer, speaking out in favour of a fairer distribution of wealth in *c.*411. Nothing is recorded in Britain during the next decade or so. Then, in about 428, a chronicler, Prosper, who backed Augustine, recorded that the Pelagian heresy had been revived by a British bishop. It is thought some unrecorded incident, possibly the condemnation of a British bishop in Gaul, sparked off a previously latent dispute and the Pope despatched Germanus of Auxerre to Britain,[41] He was supported by Bishop Lupus of the neighbouring see of Troyes. Germanus' main opponent in Britain was Agricola, the son of a bishop, who appears to have been backed by a powerful party of local magnates. The Pelagians confronted Germanus and Lupus at a large public meeting, possibly held at Verulanium because Germanus visited St. Alban's shrine just after the meeting. The Pelagians were 'conspicuous for riches, brilliant in dress, and surrounded by a fawning multitude' so Germanus's biographer, Constantius, reports.[42] These observations do not sit well with the egalitarian precepts of Pelagianism, but it must be remembered that they were the comments of the enemies of this belief.

On one hand it would seem the mission was essentially successful, for by the time Gildas was writing in the mid-6th century Pelagianism was reputedly dead and buried. Yet, John Morris states 'There is little trace of Augustine's thinking in the later writings of the British, and there is no reason to suppose that any considerable body of British opinion welcomed it during his lifetime, though there is ample evidence that Pelagian views persisted.'[43] In support of this Dark notes the existence of a royally commissioned manuscript of Pelagius's works which, from a dedication-inscription, dates it to the late 7th or 8th century with a provenance of production in Wales — suggesting that Pelagius was still considered 'orthodox by the British Church, or else royal commission of such a manuscript would have been unthinkable'.[44]

What the Pelagian controversy does show is that the 5th-century British church was strong and intellectually buoyant enough to entertain ideas which challenged orthodox Christianity, and one might suggest that the social equality, personal resourcefulness and responsibility espoused by Pelagianism and the teaching of Martin of Tours created a climate which favoured the growth of British monasticism.

CHAPTER TWO

The Post-Roman Era

Along with the Picts and the Germanic tribes of north-west Europe, the Irish took advantage of the crumbling Roman administration of Britain, and especially of the weak defences on the western side, to establish themselves on Britain's western promontories, which included Dyfed and Gwynedd. One of the most important areas of Irish expansion was within Dyfed where the settlement was significant enough to render the area's population bi-lingual by the 5th century and 'to form what was virtually a little Irish kingdom'.[1] Indeed Dyfed, with the inland mountainous kingdom of Brycheiniog, were the only two areas where the origins of British dynasties come about through migrations from outside Roman Britain. Dark suggests a 6th century date for the foundation of Brycheiniog, judging from the date of the earliest inscribed stones in the area. He considers that it may have been formed by an Irish sub-group moving from Dyfed into what was a weak borderland area between the kingdoms of the Ordovices and the Silures. That Brycheiniog was part of the late medieval diocese of St. David's and that it is within an area of dedications to St. David strengthens this claim. This kingdom was not an area of a known pre-Roman Iron Age British tribe, yet given its collection of possible pre-9th-century dedications to saints that were prominent in Dyfed, suggests strong links with the west.[2]

The Roman writer Ammianus Marcellinus states that during the 4th century the Irish raids were as formidable as those of the Picts and the Saxons. In the Irish text *Sanas Cormaic*, or *Cormac's Glossary*, it was claimed that since St. Patrick's time the Irish held divided kingdoms with 'the most important halves being in Britain'. Irish inroads were helped by the way Rome ran the outlying areas of their empire. Although forts were established throughout Britain and a network of military and trading roads were set up in Wales, none were established on the Lleyn peninsula or in Dyfed, leaving both areas weak and open to attack. Responsibility for these areas was vested in local British leaders who were established as foederati or protectors under Rome's jurisdiction. A tombstone, which originally stood in the entrance to Castell Dwyran graveyard (north-east of Narberth in Pembrokeshire), dated to about 550 and inscribed 'Memoria Voteporigis Protictoris' indicates just such a local ruler, believed to be the Vorteporius whom Gildas savages in his history as a tyrant of the Demetae (the men of Dyfed). Voteporigis is derived from an Irish name, and who better to keep Irish invaders out of Dyfed than 'an Irish dynasty with Irish subjects'. Rome was not concerned that the native population had been displaced or conquered by another faction in an outlying zone; their concern was that their own interests were being protected. It has also been observed that inscribed stones bearing Irish names are preserved at Llandeilo and that they run in sequence over three generations, demonstrating the secure hold that the Irish had in some Welsh areas.[3] There is also the stone found at Wroxeter, unearthed in the Roman city's eastern rampart, that celebrates Cunorix, probably a sub-Roman military leader of Irish origin as the stone's Latin text has Irish spelling. The stone is dated linguistically to about 460–75. Even if the Cunorix in question was in someone else's employ, or was acting independently as a ruler, it shows that Irish influence stretched far inland as Wroxeter is 5 miles south-east of Shrewsbury in Shropshire.

By the later 4th century Roman power in Britain was breaking down. Not only were the Irish making inroads into Wales and Scotland but the Picts were harrying southern Britain and were even credited with launching a seabourne raid on London. The Angles and Saxons were also settling in the south-east and the east of England. The movement of the Anglo-Saxons into the midlands and as far west as the Welsh borders in the 7th century effectively cut Wales off from surviving British kingdoms of the north, helping to create an insular Welsh church and culture.

The Pictish, Irish and Germanic inroads into Britain were significant enough for the Roman writer Marcellanius to term it the *Conspirito Barbaria* — the Barbarian Conspiracy — of 367, the suggestion being that the groups planned their attacks in concert. However any putative confederation was loosely bound and, if there was any central control, it soon evaporated when the spoils of war beckoned. Four crack Roman units were sent over under the command of Theodosius who restored peace and order. When a subsequent governor of Roman Britain, Constantine III, revolted against Rome in 407, usurped the title of emperor and crossed into Gaul taking with him part of the army, Britain was left ever more vulnerable to attack. This was exacerbated after Rome lost control in Britain in 410. From then on, the country was increasingly ruled by local kings, the leading figure amongst them being Vortigern, who was probably a Romano-Briton. Vortigern has traditionally been blamed for instigating the Germanic inroads by his decision to hire mercenaries to protect the British against the Picts. Vortigern's apparent failure to pay these mercenaries led to the Saxon revolt in 446 and to waves of subsequent Germanic settlers. However it is important to remember that there were already such settlers engaged in trade within Britain, and the Romans probably used others as mercenaries, a tradition that Vortigern followed.

Archaeological evidence suggests that in the post-Roman period in the west and north of Britain hillforts were re-used, principally for high-status domestic settlement, complementing the villa settlements found in lowland Britain. Thus we may visualise the hillfort settlement, with varying degrees of Romanisation in its social and economic make-up, as the residence of the local British ruler or king who governed his people from a site which had probably been in the hands of a ruling dynasty for generations, possibly from the Iron Age. Such a social structure would have encouraged Christianity in these areas to be run on more localised, tribal lines, and it is within this backdrop that the later British church emerged.

The Origins of the Welsh Borderland Kingdoms

In eastern Wales the kingdom of Powys appears to represent the former territory of the Cornovii. Gildas refers to a King Cuneglasus who may have been the British king of this region, one of whose main bases was a hillfort. This was possibly at the Wrekin near Wroxeter where some, albeit ambiguous, evidence exists for use in the late and post-Roman periods. Further archaeological evidence, however, suggests that it might have been Wroxeter itself that was the main political centre (or at least one of them) of the kingdom of Powys in the 5th century.[4]

Of the origins of the other Welsh kingdom encountered in the gazetteer in this book, that of Gwent, the evidence is less clear. The name is derived from the combination of Gwlad ('country of') and Venta Silurum, the Roman name for Caerwent. In this area, as with the neighbouring kingdom of Glywysing to the west, Romano-British sites were sometimes re-used as ecclesiastical foci, notably Caerwent, and also, perhaps, as non-religious settlements. There is no evidence of 5th–7th century secular reuse of late Roman military sites, and the Roman villas at this date no longer had high-level occupation, although some were possibly also used as ecclesiastical foci. It is possible that the use of the name Gwent implies a re-emerging local tribal leadership of the area outside of the immediate environs of Caerwent. The south-east of Wales is an area where one might expect the re-emergence of such a dynasty 'given the strong Pre-Roman Iron-Age kingship of the Silures'. A sub-Roman urban authority based at Caerwent may have controlled the town's immediate environs, but political control was perhaps relocated to the nearby hillfort sometime during the 5th and 6th centuries. Archaeological evidence points to two phases of post-Roman, pre-Viking use at Caerwent. The first was a sub-Roman use of the town with a 5th–6th century cemetery outside of the town's walls, implying a resident population and the survival of Roman law which forbade burials within a town. The second phase is marked by a large cemetery within the town, perhaps beginning in the 6th century, which may have been the precursor of the later monastic site in the area of the present medieval church.[5]

As pressure on Britain increased, so some of the native population moved to Armorica (approximately modern Brittany), where three principalities had been established: Dumnonia (located on the central and eastern coasts of northern Brittany), Cornubia and Venetia, probably occupied by people from Devon, Cornwall and Gwent respectively.[6] The works of Gildas, a mid-6th century historian, has traditionally ascribed this movement of British peoples to the influx of the Angles and Saxons. However it is likely that the Irish penetration had a significant bearing on the movement to Brittany from the western areas of Britain.[7] The Armorican coast was as vulnerable to attack by the Germanic tribes as was the British coast, thus there was nothing to gain by establishing a British colony if the threat was from the Anglo-Saxons alone. Brittany was relatively sparsely populated at that time because of Germanic raids and a corrupt Roman rule which had overtaxed the population to the point that the agricultural infrastructure had been destroyed. Rising in rebellion the population had been cut down and the area left as desert. By 460 the Visigoths were attacking Brittany and had become such a threat that a force of reputedly 12,000 Britons from the region formed an alliance with Rome to fight against them. Even if the number is an exaggeration, that a force of Britons was raised within Brittany suggests there was a sizeable British population. Indeed the area was becoming increasingly self-contained and began looking towards Britain for its religious lead, breaking with Tours, which had traditionally been its diocesan centre, and placing itself under the direction of the bishopric of Llandaff in south Wales. The situation was only reversed when Britanny was returned to the diocese of Tours in 572.

Meanwhile the Anglo-Saxon influx continued in Britain, sometimes peaceably and blending in with the resident British population, but displacing them when warfare occurred in localised areas. The resultant Saxon controlled territories in the south-east and those of the Angles in the east and midlands of England in the 5th and 6th centuries saw the introduction of Germanic/Scandinavian paganism which pushed the British Church into the western areas of Britain.

At what date Wales was converted to Christianity is not known — in Anglo-Saxon accounts there are no references to pagan Britons or to pagan practice or practitioners among the British. It is likely that early Christianity in Wales had some relationship with that of Roman Britain and that the conversion of what we now call the Welsh took place during that period. However, inscribed stones which have inscriptions and letter forms that parallel those of Christian Africa and Gaul, are concentrated in western Wales showing that other influences were also at work, presumably from sea-borne missionaries. The 5th and early 6th century saw the disappearance of the urban-based nature of Romano-British Christianity, whilst changes in burial practice meant the adoption of new sites with a tendency to focus on what was considered a 'holy place'.[8]

Monasticism probably reached the British Isles in the latter part of the 5th century, starting with south-west Britain and south Wales, and reaching Ireland by the early 6th century. At this time, Maelgwn, the king of Gywnedd who had several unholy confrontations with the saints, is recorded as having once vowed to be a monk, although he subsequently had a change of heart. The early Welsh poem, *Marwnad Cynddylan*, also speaks in favour of attacks on 'book-holding monks', proving their presence.

Some monasteries developed into great scholastic centres, of which the most important were Llanilltud Fawr (now known as Llantwit Major), founded by St. Illtud in about 450, and Llancarfan founded by St. Cadoc. Llanilltud Fawr supposedly had 2-3,000 novices although this is probably a later exaggeration. In reality little is known of the church in Wales prior to the Norman Conquest, unlike that of the Church in Ireland. As Wendy Davies states 'Romantic views of a Celtic Church, spanning Celtic areas, with its own institutional structure and special brand of spirituality, have often been expressed, but have little to support them, especially with reference to Wales.' Popular view assigns a power to monastic institutions which is difficult to support in Wales. Later tradition and the inferences made from the spread of dedications has led to suggestions of many more early foundations than probably existed; there is only written evidence, outside of often unreliable charter evidence, of about 35 religious foundations in Wales before the Norman Conquest. To this one might add Presteigne in Radnorshire as a pre-Norman foundation.[9]

As for those foundations which are named, Bardsey (an island 2 miles off the tip of the Lleyn peninsula in north Wales) is known to have had monks, and Bangor-on-Dee (5 miles south-east of Wrexham) had a monastery — indeed Bede states that in the early 6th century this monastery was able to send 1,200 monks to pray for the British forces ranged against the Anglo-Saxons on the eve of the battle of Chester. There was also a monastic community on Caldey Island (off the Pembrokeshire coast) and Llantwit is also recorded as having a 'great monastery'; four others had bishops associated with them: Llandeilo Fawr, Llandaff, Bangor and St. David's.[10] There is very little information about the other early sites. It is not even clear whether they were isolated from lay/secular villages, or formed part of a larger settlement. The *Life* of Samson, one of the few *Lives* that was written within 50 years or so of the saint's death (most were written down post-Conquest), refers to a number of unnamed foundations made by Samson's relatives; these are numerous enough to suggest there may have been many religious foundations which have left no mark and are lost to the record.[11]

Other evidence is less reliable. Whilst the concentrations of early Christian inscribed stones at sites such as Llanwnda (north-west of Fishguard) and St. Edrens (east of St. David's) may suggest a pre-Conquest church or monastic foundation, it may equally be that the stones were brought together at these sites after the Norman Conquest.[12] Evidence for other pre-Conquest churches may exist beneath existing medieval churches.

Undated enclosures around modern churches such as Llanmerewig (3 miles east of Newtown in Powys) and Meifod (north-west of Montgomery) may represent an early cemetery boundary in the former, and a boundary ditch surrounding a monastery in the case of Meifod,[13] but again there is no hard evidence. Both of these sites are included in the gazetteer. What can be said is that most of the early sites are, not surprisingly, close to the coast or sited in valleys and occupy fertile land.

In the southern part of the Welsh Borders there exists a degree of charter evidence for early religious foundations, although here caution has to be exercised. The charters are contained within a collection called the *Book of Llandaff* or the *Liber Landavensis*, a 12th-century compilation that was inspired by Bishop Urban of Llandaff to assert the privileges and rights of the newly-formed see of Llandaff over those of Hereford and St. David's. It was compiled partly in response to perceived appropriation of Church property or rights by the incoming Normans, and it is most likely that some of the charters are fraudulent in their claims that properties were gifted as early as the 6th century to make sure the rival sees could not claim possession. The problem is therefore to sort out fact from fiction. The *Lives* of the saints Dyfrig (Dubricius), Teilo and Oudoceus, who were associated with Llandaff, and the *Life* of Samson are also contained with the book.[14]

The Llandaff charters refer to 36 monasteries in the south-east of 'Wales' — a definition that also includes the southern half of Herefordshire — and a further 38 'ecclesiae', a term which means 'church' but was often used for monastery. Assuming that the number of sites is roughly accurate (if not all the land grants assigned to them), this is probably a higher density than for most other areas of Wales. The south-east region of Wales had a more intensive Roman background to the rest of the country with probably a different tenurial make-up, and it certainly had a higher population on much more exploitable agricultural land. Indeed, only 11 of the 74 sites mentioned in the Llandaff charters are in modern Glamorgan where the topography is similar to that of the rest of Wales. This suggests that the density of foundations in Glamorgan may be more typical of the majority of Wales.[15]

The place-name element 'llan' is popularly thought to signify an early religious foundation. 'Llan' literally means 'enclosure' but, from an early date, was used to denote one surrounding a religious site. With reference to the Llandaff charters, Ray notes that the use of the earlier term *lann* (and later *llan* referred to a church enclosure and also to an estate, usually small, which was gifted to support the foundation. Just such a gift was made by a King Gwrfodwr of Erging to a Bishop Ufelfyw of land at *Bolgros* (usually identified with Preston-on-Wye or Bellamore, north-west of Hereford) in about 610. Ray also observes how the charter records how the bishop, accompanied by his clergy, went around the bounds of the estate sprinkling holy water as 'the holy cross and relics were carried in front of him' and how, in the presence of King Gwrfodwr, the bishop consecrated the ground in the middle of the estate for a church dedicated to the Holy Trinity and the saints Paul, Dyfrig and Teilo. Such a practice was probably observed at the foundation of all sites. 'Llan' names can therefore provide a helpful clue to early Christian sites but cannot in themselves verify the existence of an early church, for such names were also given to properties that simply belonged to an important and wealthy religious foundation. Llandeilo Rwnws and Llandeilo Pentywyn, for example, were properties of the important foundation of Llandeilo Fawr (15 miles south-west of Llandovery). It is more realistic to suggest that surviving llan place-names might echo, albeit faintly, 'ancient patterns of gifting, association and allegiance' and might explain why there are some dedications to saints well away from their 'home' territory, the result of a grant to a distant Christian centre. Others may denote a late revival in a certain saint's cult status. It must also be borne in mind that not all early Christian sites had *llan* names, e.g. Tywyn and Caerwent. In south-east Wales in the 7th and 8th centuries many sites were referred to as *podum* (monastery) and only became 'Llan' in the later and more permanent place-name, e.g. *podum Loudeu* became Llanlowdy.[16]

Apart from the charters, most references to early Christian foundations are of 11th century date, but of their foundation there is no record. The charters do provide evidence for the foundation of some churches, for example at *Bolgros* in 610 and at Garway in 615, which are both in Erging (Herefordshire) by King Gwrfodwr. It is possible that Welsh Bicknor and Llandinabo, also in Erging, were founded in the late 6th century.

In Wales, monasticism was recognised as a distinct vocation from the earliest date and a variety of monastic practices were characteristic, with communal life being the most popular, as opposed to the isolated, hermetical life. Indeed, in the south-east region of Wales there is no evidence that any religious community offered the rigorous, ascetic monastic experience so beloved of the Desert Fathers, although in Wales as a whole a few such isolated communities did emerge in the 6th century. It is possible, for example, that hermits may have lived in the caves at Radyr near Cardiff, and at Bacon Holes in the Gower where finds from the early medieval period have been made.[17]

Within Wales the seat of bishoprics was often sited in a monastery, as at St. David's and Llandaff. By the 9th and 10th centuries no distinction appears to have been made between these two types of communities, and it is likely that the distinction between religious communities with monastic vows and those without became more blurred with time. In the south-east region of Wales mention of abbots ceased after the mid-10th century and the representatives of communities are referred to as priests or *sacerdotes*, suggesting a gradual change from houses with both monastic and secular clergy to only the latter.[18]

There is some evidence that a bishopric existed in the south-eastern area of Wales from the 6th to early 10th century, possibly based near to Kenderchurch (about 9 miles south-west of Hereford); at Glasbury (approximately 3 miles south-west of Hay-on-Wye) or near to Welsh Bicknor (4 miles south of Ross-on-Wye). A bishopric probably existed at Llandeilo Fawr in the 8th and 9th centuries. Although both of these putative bishoprics had disappeared by the 10th century, Davies states that at least one bishop was apparently working in the south-east of Wales between the 6th to 12th centuries at any one time. Unfortunately nothing is known of the origin of any bishoprics in this area or how they correlated to Britain's late Roman religious administrations.[19] Elsewhere in Wales, as well as a bishop at St. David's, there is a record of a bishop at Bangor in about 800 and at Llanbadarn Fawr (Aberystwyth). The number of pre-Conquest bishoprics were thus probably few and widely spaced, although comments by the 6th-century writer Gildas and in the 11th-century *Life* of St. David indicate a large number of bishops (in the latter 118 bishops were reported as having attended the synod of Llanddewi Brefi), but these numbers probably included those who would more usually be termed abbots.[20]

Early inscribed stones at Llanddewi Brefi

British bishoprics were certainly much more fluid in their boundaries as compared to their Anglo-Saxon counterparts but, in organisation, the two Churches were almost the same in that the kingdom-bishopric was the normal unit, although this structure was adopted later in the British Church. However, in early British monasteries many abbots would be chosen from within the local tribe in preference to having a monastery ruled by an outsider. The importance given to the tribal connections of monasteries essentially deprived the bishop of his power of discipline which was usually his prerogative.[21] In the early years, notably during the 6th century, it would appear that once monasteries had been founded in Wales, the church consecrated and priests ordained, that the monks had little need of bishops.[22] Indeed many of the early monks, including Gildas, resisted pressures to accept sees within Britain; after St. Dyfrig (Dubricius) only St. Teilo is regularly styled a bishop. This comparatively reduced status of Welsh bishops is amply demonstrated in the separate law codes of Anglo-Saxon England and those of Wales; in the former the bishop had ealdorman status (an ealdorman being the king's chief administrator of the shire), but in Welsh law a bishop had only the status of a free tribesman. Against this, an Anglo-Saxon bishop could be deposed by his king, but in Wales there is no record of such an event, rather the reverse.[23] In the early 7th century, Welsh monastic communities had *parochia* attached which comprised smaller monasteries dependent on the mother house (the important central monastery/church of the community).

Wales was rather slow in accepting the idea that one kingdom should have its own bishop. The *clas* system — associated with the cantref, or even the smaller commote (secular administrative units) — operated in Wales whereby the mother church had clergy headed by an abbot, in which the clergy were allowed to marry. Laymen were also increasingly the heads of religious communities. By the 9th century the *clas* system was declining, partly as a result of Danish incursions and by the 10th century there is evidence that bishops had become the dominant ecclesiastical figure.[24] There is no early evidence of a hierarchy among bishops in Wales although in the 9th century reference is made to a Welsh archbishop. The idea of a primate of the Welsh church really only developed after the Norman Conquest and under Norman influence, although in the late pre-Conquest era there are signs that ecclesiastical power had become concentrated into the hands of a few major religious foundations and their bishops who were keen to expand the territories of their dioceses.[25]

From the comments of Gildas in the 6th century it is clear that married clergy existed, and this was certainly still the case in the 9th century at Llandeilo Fawr. In Erging there is evidence from the 7th century that sons succeeded to office, and in the 9th to 11th centuries some clerical families can be traced over a number of generations. As late as the 12th century Giraldus Cambrensis complained that sons succeeded to benefices in the Welsh monasteries by hereditary right rather than by election and, by implication, by blood rather than ability.[26]

The size of monastic communities in Wales is uncertain and, although important foundations such as Llantwit, Llancarfan, St. David's, Tywyn, Clynnog and Llanbadarn Fawr may have had monks numbering in the hundreds, if not the thousands, the later saints' *Lives* indicates that most communities were small, numbering around 10 inhabitants, and the charters suggest equally small communities. There were monastic rules and vows, but reports of clergy making long

Early cross-head from Llanbadarn Fawr

journeys in lavish style with large retinues, of in-fighting for clerical offices and of clergy who 'failed to help the poor and teach the people, and lay about in drunken stupor' demonstrates that the ideal was sometimes only that. Some monasteries insisted on manual labour from its monks, although some did not and employed lay people to till the fields and look after stock. The smaller the community the more likely it was to require manual labour of its monks, as these establishments were probably just about self-supporting. In the large monastic communities there would be a division of labour with increasingly complex offices such as that of cellarar (a monk who was in charge of the storeroom), doctor, scribe, steward, cooks, herdsmen and even grave-diggers. The late 11th-century *Life* of St. David presents the most detailed information on the life of monks. Although this work is a very important comment on the way 11th-century clerics were thinking in west Wales, it may also contain the rules formulated by David which had been passed on orally. In the *Life* it is also clear that the monks lived under absolute obedience to an abbot whose permission was needed for all things. Monks were described as being isolated from the world in the confines of the monastery, they lived in common, sharing possessions and were subject to a rule. Manual work was the norm with the monks working out in the fields during the day and, afterwards, there would be prayer or study. In the evening they prayed and worshipped in the church for about three hours; there would be prayers again at dawn. The monastic diet was limited to vegetables, bread, salt and 'temperate' drink, and clothing was cheap with skins being much used. The virtues of chastity, compassion, modesty, charity, patience and humility were all encouraged, a model that accords well with the 'moderately ascetic cenobetic practice' encouraged in late and post-Roman Mediterranean monasteries.[27]

There is very little evidence in the written sources of what early monastic communities actually looked like. However, it is known that the monastery was deemed to be a separate place which was marked off from the outside world by a well-defined boundary. This comprised a bank and ditch and/or a hedge or palisade. The plan of the buildings within the enclosure was usually haphazard, being determined largely by the lie of the land, with the buildings constructed from timber, wattle or stone depending on which was readily available. The church within the enclosure was often of small and simple design and there may have been several churches on the same site; archaeological evidence suggests they were often only big enough to hold an altar with enough room for a small congregation.[28] The much later saints' *Lives* imply the existence of a church or oratory, or both, eating and sleeping quarters and a guest house for visitors but with little evidence of individual cells for the monks; Davies adds there must have been buildings for writing and reading.[29] The smaller the community, one would imagine the less specialisation of buildings.

Scholarly opinion suggests that circular or curvilinear churchyards and monastic enclosures imply an early, pre-Norman origin, possibly deriving from a mixture of native pagan and Irish Christian practice. There are some splendid examples along the Welsh borders of such churchyards, for example at Llansantffraid-in-Elfael (7 miles north-east of Builth Wells), and at Llanmerewig (near Newtown, Powys). Some ecclesiastical sites and burial grounds are certainly known to have made use of earlier curvilinear enclosures, but without excavation it is impossible to determine the date of an enclosure. Even with excavation, only the broadest dates are normally recoverable. Yet excavation has shown that not all curvilinear enclosures denote an early origin, with some constructed as late as the 12th century. Only two church enclosures have been excavated in Wales, one of them at Capel Maelog near Llandrindod Wells, Radnorshire, where radio-carbon dating gave a range of AD 766 to 1020 for its construction. The relationship in time between the enclosure and the majority of graves could not be determined, although the church was later than the enclosure. Early Christian burials are difficult to date. They are often devoid of any dateable grave goods and reliance is often made upon radio-carbon dating organic matter such as surviving bone or wood from the coffin. Such a technique usually provides dates within a 300 to 400 year band which is of little help when more specific dating is needed. To complicate matters, it has also now been recognised that east/west orientated graves are not exclusively Christian. At Abdon, just over the border in Shropshire, an oval-shaped churchyard actually overlaid a 13th-century house site, which warns against automatically assuming circular churchyards date to between the post-Roman and pre-Norman era (the early medieval period).[30] There are also many examples of rectangular or square churchyards with known early origins. There is also some evidence that the larger the size of a religious enclosure, the more important the site.

Excavation has shown that many sites have been deliberately levelled, with parts being raised in the process, whilst the term *podum*, often used for a monastery in the Llandaff Charters, suggests that naturally raised sites or deliberately levelled and raised sites were preferred. Indeed, such sites are described in various saints' *Lives*, as is the miraculous levelling of areas for foundations.[31]

The raised nature of many churchyards has occasioned various theories. One suggests that such mounded sites were initially burial barrows before becoming Christian graveyards. As the round barrow remained the common burial practice over many centuries, it implies a strong impulse behind their construction. Prehistoric man would have been in tune with nature and the cyclical rhythms of the earth and it is possible that they should want to inter their remains in a womb-shaped barrow, perhaps with the idea that they might be reborn as the dead vegetation of winter is reborn in spring. Chetan and Brueton suggest the possibility that such pagan burial barrows became sanctified and Christianised over a long period. Over the centuries the original circle of the barrow would have been eroded by the straightening of roads and boundaries and the significance of the circular shape of the enclosure would have been forgotten as it lost its shape. They also observe there is some evidence that yews were planted on top of barrows and that these were a feature long before the beginning of Christianity.[32] Given the awe in which yews were held in both prehistoric and historic eras (see below), it is not surprising that early Christians would have reused what was an early pagan totem and, by so doing, Christianise it.

Another theory suggests that raised churchyards are the result of thousands of interments over centuries. An average English rural churchyard is estimated to contain at least 10,000 bodies, most of which would have been buried in a shroud, and only a few in coffins. Once decayed, a human body reduces to about 10 lbs in weight which gives a total of 45 tons from 10,000 bodies. One cubic yard of earth weighs about one ton, with the average churchyard covering about 5,000 square yards. To raise this area by 3 feet would require about 5,000 cubic yards of soil; 45 tons of human remains would equate to about 45 cubic yards of soil, a negligible contribution.[33] As the land on which some churches stands may be 5 to 10 feet above the surrounding area (and there are a number of such sites along the Welsh Border), even if the estimate for the volume for human remains was doubled or quadrupled, this is a poor explanation for a raised churchyard.

Yet another factor may have caused some of the raised churchyards. On extensive travels around the Welsh Borders one is struck by the number of gardens, for example, that conform very closely to the look of raised churchyards. It is a timely reminder that the use of tracks alongside the boundary of a site, coupled with the constant use of the site itself can produce a hollowing and raising effect that has nothing to do with ancient barrows or the build up of bodies!

Moccas in Herefordshire is an excellent example of why caution should be exercised in considering whether a circular/curvilinear, raised or large churchyard may imply an early date. It is almost certainly the site of an important early monastery. On early Ordnance Survey maps and on a late 18th-century plan of Moccas Park, made soon after Capability Brown remodelled the park's landscape, the churchyard is shown as being sub-oval and ringed with trees; however, on an earlier and very detailed 18th-century estate map, which pre-dated Brown's changes, the churchyard is shown as being small, rectangular and present only on the southern side of the church. Large churchyards can be useful, however, in

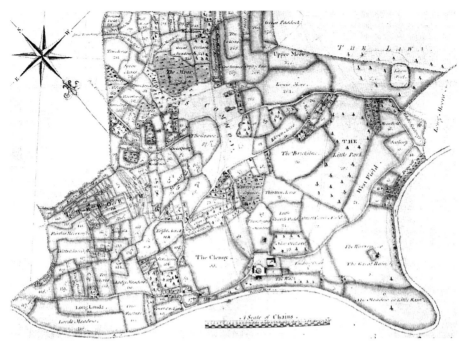

*A survey of the Moccas Estate in 1772 showing the roughly oval shape of the
churchyard enclosure (to the south-east of the main buildings in the lower centre of
the illustration), created as part of Capability Brown's remodelling of the park's landscape,
and nothing to do with any early Christian activity*

identifying sites of early major churches about which no historical records or other
physical remains survive.[34] One such example may be at Llandrinio near Oswestry
which originally had a curved boundary enclosing about 5 acres (and still has a
churchyard of 3 acres) but is not recorded as an important early church.

The presence of inscribed early medieval stones are also indicators of early
sites but, unlike western Wales, the Welsh border area has very few and, even with
these, it is unclear whether the stones originated from the site or were brought in at
a later date for safe keeping. The few examples will be discussed in the gazetteer.

In some cases Bronze and Iron Age burial grounds have been reused for
early medieval cemeteries. Although continuity in use is apparent, the nature of
this continuity is unclear. In some cases it appears that burials were continuous
over centuries whereas, in others, the site was re-used, presumably after a period of
disuse. One suggestion is that the re-use of an older burial site was part of a wider,
post-Roman phenomenon in which 'the past was used to legitimate current social
elites', rather than showing any real continuity in the burial of a tribal or family
group.[35] Just as the Anglo-Saxon elites shamelessly invented the past in their genealogies to secure power, it is likely that their British counterparts were doing much

the same thing in claiming prestige in the form of a very visible landscape features in which to be buried. Such features would have included Bronze Age ritual and funerary monuments, along with Iron Age defended enclosures. Excavations at Trelystan and Four Crosses (south-east and north-east of Welshpool respectively) have provided evidence of such re-use. Roman cemeteries were also re-used in the sub/post-Roman era: in Wales, Caerwent is one of the best known. A Roman urban cemetery outside the east gate was used in the post-Roman period with burials being radio-carbon dated to between the 4th and 11th centuries.[36]

Even if a continuity of burial practice can be established at cemeteries it does not mean that the site developed into a church with a churchyard. Some cemeteries did not achieve ecclesiastical status and were perhaps abandoned in favour of burial close to the relics of saints and martyrs. From Ireland comes evidence of moral blackmail being used to encourage a move away from mixed pagan and Christian kin/tribal burial sites, with the threat that angels 'would not visit those Christians who were buried among evil men'.[37]

One common feature of early sites is the presence of a well or spring, usually in close relation to the church, used for personal and baptismal purposes. The need for a spring may have been a factor in the choice of a site for an early Christian hermit or monastic community, as too the possibility of Christianising a well or spring that may have previously been used for pagan ritual practice. As many wells and springs dedicated to Christian saints were deemed to have healing or divination properties, even into modern times, the link with a pagan past seems quite plausible. Indeed some rites practised under a Christian mantle have such a pagan flavour that making a link is almost irresistible.

Yews are also often present in churchyards, and there are a number of reasons given for their presence. Very old yews cannot be dated scientifically with any accuracy. The tree's habit of hollowing out with age makes dendrochronological dating (dating by tree rings) impossible as the heart wood is missing. However, there is agreement that yews can live for over 1,000 years, with some individual trees reaching 2,000 years or more. The yew in Discoed churchyard near to Presteigne on the Welsh Border has been estimated by some to be about 5,000 years old, which, if true, predates the birth of Christ by some 3,000 years! However this date is contended by other tree specialists.

A rough age for a yew can be calculated from the circumference (girth) of the tree, with a 20 foot (6 metre) girth indicating an age range of 700-1,000 years, and a 23-33 foot girth (7-10 metres) suggesting an age range of 1,200 to 2,000 years. However the conditions of each site clearly affects the size of any tree and the yew is no exception. Very cramped, dry and exhausted soil can curtail the size of yew as can human interference in the form of pruning and lopping which can bring about premature hollowing. The yew is the slowest growing British tree and in some cases old yews appear not to have grown for a century or more, even though they are very much alive. A remarkable feature of the yew is its ability to regenerate even after severe fire or wind damage which would destroy most trees.[38] The phoenix-like ability of the yew, its longevity and apparent invincibility would have undoubtedly impressed the mind of early man, as it still does today. With its thick foliage and wide trunk, the yew also has a unique sheltering quality against wind and rain which would not have been lost to man. If early saints used existing hollowed-out yews for shelter as has been suggested, then the deliberate planting of such a tree at a new Christian foundation may have been a way of sanctifying the site by using a tree which was already held in awe, especially if the tree was already associated with eternal life. When Augustine brought the Romanised Christian mission to Anglo-Saxon England in the late 6th century, the missionaries actively sought to Christianise pagan sites and it is possible that the early British saints did the same. There is a repeated motif in the various *Lives* in which a saint plants his/her staff into the ground which miraculously grows into a tree; this may dimly recall a ceremony which sanctified a barrow or other previously unconsecrated ground.[39]

There are a number of Welsh yews with girths of 33 feet, and therefore at least 1,300 to 1,500 years old, in churchyards with dedications to saints who apparently flourished in the 6th and 7th centuries, strongly suggesting a connection between the two. Similarly aged yews found in some English churchyards may therefore be markers of early saints' cells. Indeed the oldest yews may mark the sites of lost early Christian cells or hermitages which were often tiny, some measuring only 10ft by 13ft (3m by 4m). One of the oldest yews, that by the roadside at Yew Tree Farm in Discoed, Radnorshire, may therefore mark a vanished early church site, but its proximity to another probable early site at Discoed church, with its own ancient yew, is puzzling. Would they have co-existed, or did Discoed church supersede the other site? The survival of such yews long after the putative founding saint may then be partly explained in that no-one would have dared destroy a tree with such saintly connotations, added to the fact that yews are quite difficult to destroy and that there may have been an old reverence for the yew in the collective conscious. There is a reference to a yew in a charter of 1152 referring to the manor of Eastham in Cheshire which was given to the abbot and monks of St. Werburg's; the villagers apparently entreated the monks 'to have a care of ye olde yew' which was then about 400 years old and is still alive today. Is this an example of a yew that was planted by an early saint whose identity was lost, but the idea that the tree was of special and/or religious importance was retained in folk memory? Even more convincing evidence is to be found in the laws of Hywel Dda in 950 when a very heavy fine was levied for felling 'yews associated with the saints'.[40] In Anglo-Saxon England it is interesting how many yews remained when Norman churches were built which suggests there was some similar preservation given, whether by law or custom.

A particular feature of some Welsh churchyards is a circle of large yews. Some 25 examples remain, either intact or somewhat fragmentary.[41] It has been suggested that prehistoric stone circles may be representations of the circles of trees in ancient pagan groves.[42] Perhaps the yew circles similarly remember such sites and became Christianised features of the previous pagan religion.

What of the location of individual yews in a churchyard? Of the 400 or so yews listed in a gazetteer, 70 are aligned east/west, more than 150 are to be found to the south and south-west, with those to the south often being female, those to the south-west being male. Allen Meredith, the authority on ancient yews, notes that the oldest yews are generally found on the north side of graveyards and are usually male, and he considers this side was 'the original position of the yew', deliberately planted there to give protection against evil and to guard the souls of the dead. It may even have been thought that the souls of the dead lived in the tree. There is a long-held tradition that the north side is the 'dark side' and the abode of the devil and the place of evil. Indeed the north sides of many rural churchyards are often bereft of graves because of this belief, and it is only in modern times, with the pressure of land, that burials have been allowed here. A door in the north wall of a church was often known as the 'devil's door' and was left open during baptisms, for example, so that evil spirits could exit. Meredith also observes that yews which are sited east and west in a churchyard may indicate a Celtic planting as they align with the rising and the setting sun and may well hark back to pagan Celtic times.[43]

Set against all this potential reverence for and association with the yew, it is strange that no representations in wood or stone of the tree exist in any British church from before about 1870.[44]

There are several other popular theories about why yews are present in churchyards, the most widespread of which is that they were planted to provide wood for the medieval longbow. This is erroneous as the age of a number of churchyard yews clearly exceeds 1,000 years and it is amongst the slowest growing trees in the world. In 1841 G.A. Hansard observed in his *Book of Archery* 'Is it not absurd to suppose that men would plant within these contracted bounds, a single tree of such slow growth, that in the space of a century its height and substance are scarcely sufficient to supply half a dozen bow staves ...?'. Henry IV, who reigned between 1399–1413, whilst authorising his bowyer to enter private land to collect yew wood 'expressly exempted the estates of the religious orders' which rather flies in the face of churchyard yews being fair game for the raw materials. The fact that churchyard yews have long been regarded with some religious or superstitious awe may also have mitigated against their use for the manufacture of weapons, or indeed for any secular use. The age of the longbow began in Britain with the Norman Conquest and for the next 500 years the quantity of yew needed was enormous. The best wood came from the bole or trunk which would obviously mean the felling of the tree — inferior wood came from the branches. By the mid-15th century (or even earlier) yew wood was having to be imported. By then, many of the few hundred yews in churchyards were probably hollowed with age and of no use to the bowyer, which no doubt secured their survival. The decline of the longbow probably had as much to do with the depletion of yew generally as it did with the advances in firearms.[45]

Another theory that yews were planted in churchyards to deter livestock from grazing has little to recommend it. Although yew berries are poisonous there is debate as to how toxic they are to cattle and sheep. There are reports of horses and cattle dying soon after eating yew, but these are countered by reports of cattle grazing yew with no ill effect. It is probably the quantity that was eaten that was the important factor.[46] As Chetan and Brueton remark drily 'there are far quicker and more effective ways of keeping cattle out of a graveyard than planting a slow-growing tree which may or may not be toxic' — a strong hedge or fence is an obvious answer.

As a slight aside, yew branches were used in Britain and Ireland as a substitute for palm branches in the celebration of Palm Sunday, a festival that dates back to the 5th century.[47]

It would seem, at least in the area covered by this book, that yews are perhaps the earliest evidence of religious practice on a site. If some of the oldest yews do indeed date back 1,000 to 5,000 years then we are dealing with living entities that pre-date many of the prehistoric stone circles and other early monuments. Whatever their true age, it is clear that yews are living monuments of exceptional interest which should receive our continued respect and protection.

Interaction between the Church and General Population

It appears that the general population had limited contact with monks and clerics. Although St. David's biographer, Rhigyfarch, claims David preached to the masses on Sundays and that some heard the preaching of the Gospels in churches, no reference is made to the attendance of church by the laity in any existing source. This may be because there were few churches outside monastic communities before the mid-11th century. It appears that churches were used most often by the general population as places to store valuables and even clothes and food in times of danger. There is no mention of the laity taking communion, and their greatest involvement with the Church was in the ceremonies involved with birth and death.

Burial within churches appears to have been initially restricted to the saint and his immediate followers. It was only by the 11th century that burial rights emerged and, late in that century, that burial within a community's cemetery had become normal — at least for the aristocracy and on making a payment.[48] It is likely that members of religious communities were buried in associated cemeteries from the foundation's inception. In south-west Wales there also are a number of large burial sites which occupy neither the sites of modern settlements nor cemeteries. In the early medieval period, Christians would often worship in the open air under a portable or permanent cross with a priest using a portable altar, and with rivers or springs being used for baptism. Thus the presence of permanent buildings may not have been necessary. However burial in consecrated ground must have been crucial considering the belief in bodily resurrection.[49] Could this perhaps explain the presence of such early Christian burials at places such as Ashgrove?

The available written evidence shows that the primary source of support and income for religious communities was land. In some cases charter evidence makes it clear that this land was often around the church and related buildings so, for example, the community of St. Buddwalan (Ballingham, southern Herefordshire) had 'two and a half unciae of land surrounding the monastery' noted in about 620. At Caerwent the monastery was supported from the fields beyond the old Roman city which were referred to as 'the ager suburbanus' meaning quite literally the suburban estate. Some larger monasteries received part of their income through renders from scattered properties. Renders could take the form of obligations of hospitality or in the form of food or drink.[50] In the Welsh borders it is likely that most religious establishments were small, self-supporting communities as no large and wealthy establishments are recorded.

It was considered that ecclesiastical land/property should be immune from secular taxes from the king or lords — the demands for tax exemption are common in the saints' *Lives* and in surviving charters, although whether they were always exempt in practice is not clear. The right of 'sheltering offenders and the accused from pursuit and from legal process' was also recorded in the saints' *Lives*. This was more than the right of sanctuary within a churchyard because a large area or territory might afford considerable protection depending upon the status of the individual. Communities even began competing with one another for superior powers of protection as a way of a displaying influence and status. If a king or noble violated this protected area by committing murder, assault, rape or abduction then he was liable to compensate the religious house in question — the Saints' *Lives* give examples of land being given in reparation for such violations.[51]

It can be seen that the British Church was far from static, thanks to the work of the early saints and their followers. Baring-Gould and Fisher present a picture of the saints being constantly on the move 'dotting their churches or their cells wherever they could obtain a foothold.' As soon as an abbot had received a grant of land he would establish a few monks to safeguard the gift, then hurry off to solicit another donation of land on which to found a church. St. Columba, for example, is reported as having established 100 churches on his travels.[52]

The British Church sent missionaries to Ireland which spread the faith and, when Christianity became established in that country, Irish missionaries travelled to Northumbria and Scotland to found churches — it was at this time that the important monastery of Iona was founded. British Christianity moved down tentatively into Mercia and to East Anglia, whilst colonists took it across the Channel, from whence it continued its loose circular motion with figureheads of the British Church arriving back in Ireland, Scotland and western Britain from Britanny and Gaul to reinforce the faith, and vice versa.

The introduction of Romanised Christianity into pagan Anglo-Saxon England began in 597 when Pope Gregory the Great sent St. Augustine from Rome with the intention of converting the heathen English. The British Church had been partially left to its own devices after Rome's abandonment of Britain and had become somewhat insular. There are references to British saints visiting Rome and attending synods in the 4th and 5th centuries, and thus the British Church was well aware of changes within the Christian Church as a whole. Indeed there is evidence that the British Church was more aligned to the Eastern Orthodox Church which had begun its break with Rome in the 4th century after it 'rejected the bishop of Rome's claim to be the leader of all Christianity as well as the infallibility of his pronouncements.' The Celtic/British Church even conducted their services in Greek until the 7th and 8th centuries, the language originally used after Christianity broke with Judaism, and the language used by the Eastern Church.[53]

One of the differences between the British and Roman Churches was that the former acknowledged John, the brother of James, as their authority, whereas Rome cited Peter as theirs. The tonsure was correspondingly different, with the Celts shaving a line from ear to ear — the tonsure of St. John — whereas the Roman church shaved the crown of the head as a symbol of the crown of thorns worn by Christ. The Roman Church saw the Celtic Church's tonsure as an extension of druidic practices and thus considered it barbaric.[54] The British Church observed Saturday, the Jewish Holy day, as their day of rest (the Sabbath), the Roman church celebrating their Sabbath on Sunday, the first day of the week and symbolic of Christ's resurrection. In about 604 Pope Gregory upheld the observance of Sunday and 'stigmatized any respect for the Sabbath [Saturday] as Judaizing'. With the arrival of Theodore of Tarsus, a firm protagonist of Roman Christianity, to Britain there was an increasing emphasis on Sunday, with the prohibition of work and the inclusion of fasting. There had been debate amongst British Christians between those who observed Saturday, those who wished to keep Saturday and Sunday, and those who wanted to observe Sunday alone — the shift to the observance of Sunday was gradual. In contrast to Rome in the 6th century, Celtic Christians were allowed to wash their hair and feet, to travel and to collect food on the holy day. Over the next

200 years this attitude changed to that of Rome where all work and travel on a Sunday was condemned.[55]

There were also differences between the Celtic and Roman Churches in the way the Eucharist was performed, the former having more in common with the Eastern Church, and also differences in the observance of lesser feasts and fasts.[56]

The best known difference between the two Churches, however, was the dating of Easter. The Roman church changed its computations for Easter Day twice in the 5th century and again in the 6th (the last serious alteration being made in 1582 with the introduction of the Gregorian Calendar). The Celtic Church considered that the amendments took them ever further away from the original date and meaning of Easter, and thus stayed with the computations based on the Jewish lunar calendar which allowed Easter to fall in the month of Nisan (the seventh month of the Jewish year, equivalent to March/April) when Passover fell on the full moon. As the first Easter occurred on the 14th day of Nisan, 'the Celts celebrated the festival on whatever Sunday fell between the fourteenth and the twentieth days after the first full moon following the spring equinox', even if Easter fell on the day of the Passover. To the Celts the declaration at the Council of Nicaea in 325, which made it illegal to celebrate a Christian festival on the same day as a Jewish one, seemed illogical because Christ had been a Jew and was executed on a Jewish feast day.[57] To them the date of Easter had become arbitrary.

With the scene set for conflict between the British Church and the incoming Roman Church in 597, it is not surprising that it took St. Augustine six years before formal contact was made with the British clergy in 603. The only record of the conference is found in Bede's *Ecclesiastical History of the English Church*, written in the first half of the 8th century when the controversy over the differences between the two Churches had peaked and resulted in much bitterness. Bede seems to infer that two meetings took place between Augustine and the British bishops and learned men from Wales and the south-west, the first at Augustine's Oak, variously identified with Aust on the Severn, Cressage in Shropshire, Down Ampney near Cricklade, Bistre in Clywyd and Abberley in north-west Worcestershire. As Bede states that the meeting was held on the borders of the Hwicce (an Anglo-Saxon sub-kingdom that covered Worcestershire, Gloucestershire and the south-west part of Warwickshire) and that of the West Saxons, Aust or Down Ampney seem the most likely venues. The location of the second meeting is not given, but learned men from a nearby monastery, usually identified with Bangor-on-Dee 12 miles south of Chester, attended the meeting and Chester is therefore usually considered to be the second venue. However it is considered that Bede's references may in fact be to just a single meeting, further complicating the interpretation of the possible venue.[58]

Pope Gregory had appreciated the worth of the British Church in its zeal and devotion and hoped the two could work together in converting the pagan Anglo-Saxons. One of the demands made at the meeting(s) was, therefore, that the British Church should give up customs which were contrary to the unity of the two Churches: a mixture of liturgical practice including the type of tonsure worn by the monks, and the date of Easter. The inclusion of the latter may be a later view of events to put Augustine in an even worse light, because in 603 that controversy was not acute.[59]

Augustine was inexperienced in his dealings with the Britons as he had little or no knowledge of the Church beyond that of his native Rome. He had also been prejudiced against the British Church by Pope Gregory's observation that it had refrained from converting the pagan Anglo-Saxons even though the latter 'eagerly desires to be converted to the Christian faith.'[60] If that had been the case it seems unlikely that the British Church would have been inactive in seeking converts — unless there were real fears of the Anglo-Saxons as the enemy.

Augustine's lack of tact and sympathy with the British delegation disabled any co-operation, his refusal to stand up to greet the British delegation at the start of the meeting being symptomatic of his view of his British counterparts. The British were also suspicious of Augustine's motives and realised the political implications of their Church being placed under the direct control of Rome via a bishop at Canterbury, who was himself under the control of an Anglo-Saxon king. Such a metropolitan authority was also new and foreign to the Britons as they had never had an archbishop or primate.[61] It is likely that the British bishops were concerned that such subjugation would mean that Rome would sweep away the traditions of the earlier saints and supplant a new form of monasticism;[62] and it was the cult of saints and their followers that had been the cornerstone of the British Church's impetus and survival. The refusal to meet Augustine's demands was not a repudiation of the authority of the pope and Rome, rather a personal rejection of the pope's representative. Significantly it was not the pope who insisted on the uniformity of the British Church with Rome, instead the demand came from Augustine who had been disturbed by the liturgical variations he had seen as he had travelled around Britain. The encounter appears to have had no effect on Welsh tradition and Augustine did not seem concerned with the failure of the meeting(s). He made no further overture to the British Church before he died the following May.[63]

The fact that no agreement was reached did, however, lead to resentment between the two Churches. British clergy refused to celebrate divine office with their English counterparts and made 'a point of purifying any vessels they had used for eating or drinking.' Moreover English converts who moved to Wales were expected to undertake 40 days penance before the British clergy accepted them.[64] The situation came to a head in the 660s in the Northumbrian royal household. Its king, Oswiu, used the British calculation for Easter, whereas his wife, a Romanised Christian, observed the Roman date. This led to logistical problems, as one was observing Lent whilst the other was celebrating Easter. This brought forth the famous Synod of Whitby in 664. Bishop Colman supported the British calculation and customs, while Bishop Wilfrid supported Rome's stance. King Oswiu had to chose and came down on the side of Rome which led to Bishop Colman's resigning the bishopric of Lindisfarne and withdrawing to Iona and thence to Ireland where he died in 676, and Bishop Wilfrid's elevation to the bishopric of York. Iona conformed to Rome's demands in 697 but Wales held out until 768 when it finally conformed under Bishop Elvodug of Gwynedd.

CHAPTER 3

The Early Saints

As much of the history of early Christianity along the Welsh border is tied up with the lives and activities of the early saints, it is sensible to try and set out the facts concerning those whose influence was the greatest. This is far from straightforward, for they lived during the Dark Ages, 'dark' because little information was written down at the time and many of the records that did exist were lost in the later ravages by Vikings, Danes and Saxons. In addition, most structures of the period would have been built of wood, leaving little archaeological evidence.

The main sources of information for the British saints are contained in the various *Lives*. These were most usually written down several centuries after the saint had died, and were thus reliant on oral tradition and tales handed down the ages. A few were compiled into the *Book of Llandaff* in the early 1100s. Of the other *Lives*, various copies or versions were made over the following centuries and inevitably changes were made and passages added, mostly fictitious. Some of these *Lives* were based on earlier sources but they are all full of fantastical events, miracles, confounded biographies of similarly named people (notably so in the case of St. Cadoc) and sometimes include stories written for current consumption — trying to establish the rights of one diocese over another, or of Welsh rights over those of Canterbury, or even Welsh pride against English aggression. Despite this, some 'facts' can be determined and their different characters discerned — the mediator Dyfrig; the soldier monk Illtud; the irascible Cadoc; the rigorous David; the healer Beuno. On occasion a fantastical tale is worth recounting here because of the light it can shed on the times.

Other information can be found in some of the early charters that relate to south-east Wales, although care has to be exercised as these were often 'recorded' at Llandaff in the early 12th century when the diocese was trying to increase its size at the expense of Hereford to the east and St. David's to the west. Thus various claims can be made which, at the very least, push a kernel of truth to the limits of plausibility.

There is also the evidence from church dedications. Whilst not all dedications to early Welsh saints mean that the saint was personally involved in the foundation of the church, they do provide an indication of the extent of the saint's cult, in terms of the area in which he, or his followers, presumably worked or were at least known. Again care has to be exercised, as dedications do change over the years with fashion, and thus some dedications may be late, whilst other, early ones, have been replaced. St. David, for example, was by far the most frequently mentioned saint in Wales and was prominent in the south-west of Wales, but he was also invoked in the south-east region as early as the 7th century. It is possible that dedications found in clusters belonged to federated communities which were dependent on mother houses — Davies suggests that such federations (which were within about a 50-60 miles radius or a few days' journey) existed for St. Illtud in what is now Glamorgan, then dependent on Llantwit; for St. David over much of south Wales, dependent on St. David's; for Padarn over most of central Wales, dependent on Llanbadarn Fawr (Aberystwyth); for Tysilio in the east midland area of Wales, dependent on Meifod; and for Beuno in the north-western Wales, centred on Clynnog Fawr south-west of Caernavon.[1] For Beuno there is also a small cluster of dedications in central Powys.

There was also a strong tendency for the veneration of local men from the 7th century. Such local saints might find followers beyond their immediate area and may have even been venerated as saints abroad, as for example were David, Teilo, Cadoc and Gildas. Saints with wider appeal were also venerated, such as St. Michael, as early as the 8th century. However, some could be so local that nothing more than the name is known. A man could be chosen either because of their exceptionally pure and moral character, or because it was known, or believed, that he had founded a church or religious community — the act of foundation alone was sometimes enough to earn them the status of a saint. Thus we have a St. Buddwalan of Ballingham church (7 miles south-east of Hereford) which is recorded in about 620 and a St. Tisoi at Llansoy (about 8 miles south-south-west of Monmouth) recorded in about 725.[2] Were such men of humble origin without the machinery of prestige to record their lives? We will never know. But men they probably were, for the lack of women in the British list of saints is noticeable. There are a few exceptions, for example St. Winifred and St. Melangell; for the most part women who achieved sainthood did so through being murdered whilst trying to flee the attentions of slighted suitors after they had chosen religion over the secular world. It does appear that Anglo-Saxon women had a more constructive role in the church and monasticism where some were abbesses and even founders. It is possible, of course, that some of the obscure names in Welsh dedications may record foundations by female saints.

The early saints, including those in Britain, were not social reformers who set out to change society for the better, but were men who had given up society as an evil to be avoided. It was only later that Rome restricted the use of the term to someone who was long-dead and whose life fulfilled a strict set of criteria concerning good works and miracles. In the 5th and 6th centuries the general population increasingly approved of the saints' example and 'began to see in them a possible protection against the ills that beset ordinary men.'[3] Special qualities such as compassion, charity, outstanding morality and the ability to perform miracles were seen as the prerequisites of a saint. They were seen as a link between man and God. Many were members of the elite within a tribe, often a chieftain's younger son, who had been educated at a monastery. In the later saints' *Lives* there is much more emphasis on miracles (in contrast to the earliest *Lives*, such as that of St. Samson), whilst the most striking quality is that of power rather than humility or compassion; indeed Welsh (and Irish) saints can seem more vindictive than those of other nationalities. In the later *Lives* the emphasis is again not on the saint as healer, as it was on the Continent, but rather on his ability to control nature. Thus St. David is shown bringing warmth to the springs at Bath, and Cadoc narrowing the River Taff so he could pass.[4]

Of the British saints whose biographies exist, almost all appear to have been the sons of kings or of powerful aristocratic families, which parallels the Anglo-Saxon system whereby saints, the founders of the monasteries, and abbots and abbesses were mostly from royal or aristocratic backgrounds. It was also a period of great contact with Brittany, partly due to the spread of the Yellow Plague throughout Britain in around 547, when many left the country to avoid its ravages. As recorded in their *Lives*, several of the saints and their disciples spent a few years in Brittany in the years immediately after the arrival of the plague, returning to pick up the pieces when the plague had run its course.

The earliest saint, St. Dyfrig, was particularly active in Erging (or Archenfield) the sub-Roman kingdom that was essentially a swathe of Herefordshire between the Wye and the Black Mountains and that part of south Herefordshire around Ross and *Ariconium*, a former Roman mining town. His primary foundations were the monasteries at Hentland (or more probably Llanfrother, see below) and Moccas, and the area contains several church dedications to him. But his influence spread into south Wales.

There are a number of churches dedicated to St. Illtud in Wales, mostly in Glamorgan. His primary monastic foundation was Llancarfan (South Glamorgan). In the area covered by this book the early dedications are at Llanilltud (Breconshire), Llanhamlach (with St. Peter, Breconshire), and Llanelltyd (Merionethshire).

Cadoc's dedications in south-east Wales have a tendency to form two clusters: the first around Llangattock-Nigh (also called Juxta)-Usk in Gwent, and the second in the eastern area of the Vale of Glamorgan in the old kingdom of Glywysig and centring on Llancarfan. Cadoc's cult also appears to have spread westwards, along the line of Roman roads through Glamorgan to Carmarthenshire, Pembrokeshire and thence to Ireland.[5] Dedications are also found in Anglesey and as far north as Kilmadock near Callander in Scotland and at Cambuslang in Glasgow. A ruined chapel and holy well at Cadoc Farm in Cornwall remembers the saint two miles west of Padstow on the north Cornish coast, and there are 23 dedications in Brittany.[6]

The geographic distribution of dedications to St. Illtud and St. Cadoc are fairly similar. It has been suggested that this fact, coupled with the area of dedications to St. Dyfrig, indicate a proselytizing of Christianity out from Erging and Brycheiniog into the south-eastern lowlands. The saints' cults had a Romano-British character and the later medieval traditions about local leaders 'indicate the persistence of this "Roman" orientation to a degree not found among the later Celtic saints in other parts of Wales.' Indeed, references to Dyfrig indicate a leader more in keeping with a 'Roman territorial bishop than a recluse of the Celtic type'; those to Cadoc portray a man in a 'strong Roman setting'; and, in the *Life* of Samson, Illtud may be interpreted as combining elements in his learning and divination from 'such diverse sources as the Christian tradition, the Roman aristocracy, and the pagan priesthood'. In a similar vein, Illtud's (and Cadoc's) monastic schools were renowned for their high standards of education and scholarship which contrasted with the great monasteries to the west of Wales which had no great tradition of learning. With this in mind, it is no surprise that the nucleus of the see of Llandaff covered much the same area as that which had the majority of Illtud, Dyfrig and Cadoc churches — it appears to have been a culturally distinct area, even in the 6th century.[7]

St. David and St. Teilo, however, are full-blooded Celtic saints. A mention has already been made of the quantity of dedications to St. David. Teilo's importance is shown in the great number of dedications to him in south Wales and also several in Brittany. The orientation of the distribution pattern of his dedications in Wales is from west to east and they appear to radiate from Llandeilo Fawr ('the great church of Teilo').[8]

The close association of David and Teilo is suggested by the similarity of the distribution pattern of dedications, except in western Pembrokeshire and Cardiganshire where dedications to Teilo are unknown but to David are numerous. The pattern and widespread nature of David dedications suggests that Teilo and David could be viewed as 'evangelists emerging from the remoter western territories to denounce the broader faith of the south-eastern zone'. However, it is a rather big assumption to make from what is residual dedication evidence. It is significant, however, that the distribution of St. David's churches largely determined the extent of the area of St. David's diocese in the Middle Ages (in a similar manner to the way the Dyfrig, Cadoc and Illtud churches determined the medieval diocese of Llandaff.) That Teilo's dedications overlapped with those of St. David partly explains why boundary disputes arose in the Norman era between the bishops of Llandaff, who claimed Teilo as their founder, and the bishops of St. David's. The eventual demarcation of the Norman dioceses in south Wales may well reflect what had been two marked provinces in early Christian times, possibly even culturally distinct in Roman times and in the prehistoric era.[9]

The geographical distribution of foundations dedicated to St. Padarn falls into two groups: those east of the central uplands, and those to the west. The dedications appear to follow or are close to the routes of two north-south orientated Roman roads, namely from the Roman fort at Y Gaer near Brecon northwards to Castell Colleen near Llandrindod Wells to the east of the Cambrian mountains, and in the west from Carmarthen (*Maridunum*) to the Roman stations at Llanio and possibly further north to Pennal in Merionethshire. Indeed Padarn appears to have been more closely associated with what survived of Roman civilization in the southern half of Wales than either St. David or St. Teilo, which may suggest Padarn's activities were the earlier.[10]

Beuno is the most recent of the saints considered here, dying in about 642. Much of his activity is centred on north-west Wales, but he was born near the river Severn in Powys and his earliest foundations lie in the east of the country.

So what can be gleaned about the life and character of each of these saints from their *Lives* and other documents?

St. Dyfrig

St. Dyfrig was born in Herefordshire in about 450 and became a teacher and leader to other saints, to the extent of having a degree of jurisdiction over them. He was the prime missionary in Erging or Archenfield, where it is accepted that Dyfrig was bishop of the sub-Roman community that developed in the region based on *Ariconium*.[11]

At its greatest extent Erging encompassed Ledbury and the Malvern Hills and stretched to the Black Mountains to the west. It originated as a small British kingdom that was relatively stable and was probably ruled by a hereditary British ruling family who emerged after the withdrawal of Roman administration. It is likely that Christianity existed in Erging continuously since Roman times. The kings of Erging have been identified from the Llandaff Charters and ruled from the mid-6th to the early 7th century, when control passed to Gwent and thence to the Anglo-Saxon sub-kingdom of Mercia, the Magonsaete, in the later 8th century. However Erging retained some independence as it had its own bishop in 914.

There are four accounts of the life of Dyfrig, of which the main one is found in the *Book of Llandaff*. This was compiled in about 1150, although the *Life* was probably written a little earlier. There is a fabulous account of Dyfrig in Geoffrey of Monmouth's *History of Britain* which was published in 1147, and a *Life* written by Benedict of Gloucester which combined elements of an earlier version of Geoffrey's *History* and the *Life* in the *Book of Llandaff*. There also exists a condensed version of the *Life* by Benedict of Gloucester made by John of

Tynemouth. Geoffrey's, Benedict's and John of Tynemouth's biographies are generally considered to be of little use, meaning that the main source for Dyfrig is the *Life* in the *Book of Llandaff*, which also contains charters or grants to Dyfrig and his followers. However, caution has to be exercised concerning these charters. The gifts of land made to Dyfrig and his followers would have originally been recorded in the margins of a Book of the Gospels that belonged to the church of Llandaff, and these would record only 'the names of the grantor and grantee, and those of the clerical and lay witnesses to the transfer — little more'. The *Book of Llandaff*'s compiler then added 'colour', sometimes the circumstances in which the gift was made, and often the boundaries of the land concerned 'from his own knowledge'. Finally the text would be written so as to accommodate any claims advanced by the Church of Llandaff to possession of lands that had been given to Dyfrig and his followers.[12]

St. Dyfrig is the first bishop recorded as holding episcopal power in the area that became the see of Llandaff, although he was not the founder of the see.[13] The claims by Geoffrey of Monmouth that Dyfrig was archbishop of Caerleon and also claims by Llandaff Cathedral that he was their first bishop are untrue.

Dyfrig's *Life* in the *Book of Llandaff* is essentially a collection of Herefordshire legends about the saint which the author may have found in an older *Life* used in a church dedicated to the saint, possibly Moccas; to this material the 12th-century 'biographer' grafted information from the *Life* of St. Samson and also added an appendix. The *Life* of St. Samson was written in the early 7th century by a monk from Dol in Brittany and contains the earliest and probably the most accurate information about Dyfrig as it was not influenced by the political motives that coloured the *Book of Llandaff*. The first mention of Dyfrig is when he ordains Samson as a deacon at Llanilltud Fawr (now known as Llantwit Major). The *Life* tells us that Dyfrig later ordained Samson as presbyter and, later still in the work, he is described as spending a greater part of one Lent on Caldey Island where he received Samson and his father and uncle kindly. Dyfrig promoted Samson to cellarer and, when Caldey's first abbot, Piro, died, it was he who suggested that Samson should take his place. The way that Dyfrig is introduced into the *Life* without any preamble, as though it is obvious who he was, demonstrates his historicity and also strongly suggests that he was widely remembered in the 7th century at Llantwit Major and Caldey Island.[14]

Dyfrig's biography was written in a hurry as his body was moved from its original resting place at Bardsey to Llandaff Cathedral in May 1120; lessons containing a biography were needed for Dyfrig's festival on 14 November. The *Life* notes that he was born at Madley in west-central Herefordshire. The *Iolo Manuscripts*, and other late Welsh genealogies, name Brychan of Brycheiniog as Dyfrig's father but this probably comes from a mistake over a confusion in names — indeed his father is not named in the Llandaff *Life*. That Dyfrig had a British

(Celtic) rather than a Romanised name suggests he may have been of native British extraction; it means 'water baby' or 'waterling', a name which may have suggested the miraculous story of his birth.[15]

The *Life* states that Peibio, the king of Erging, was enraged when, on returning from a military campaign, he found that his daughter, Ebrdil, was pregnant and refused to name the father. Peibio tried to drown her by tying her up in a skin bag and throwing her into the river Wye. When this failed, because she was repeatedly washed up to safety on the banks of the river, he tried to burn her on a pyre. When Peibio's messengers went to the pyre the following morning they found Ebrdil sitting there with her newborn son.

The cross at Madley, now by the side of the road, which may mark the site of Dyfrig's birth

Until 1996 a stone cross stood in the middle of the road on the north side of Madley church which, it is tentatively suggested, marked the supposed site of the birth. The place was consequently called Matle 'the good or fortunate place' — however the author of the *Life* may have manipulated a spelling of Madley in available documents to arrive at a suitable birthplace for the saint.[16] The story of miraculous or difficult births and survivals — feature in the stories of a number of early British saints and heroes. It was intended to underline the specialness of the child and their holiness by surviving attempts on his and/or his mother's life, implying they must have been given some special or divine protection.[17] It was part of the mystique, marking them out as special before or just after they were born.

Peibio relented when he saw his newborn grandson and legend recounts how the baby Dyfrig stroked Peibio's cheeks, miraculously curing him of a lifetime's disorder which had caused him to dribble constantly from his mouth — earning him the Latin epithet *Spumosus* and King Driveller by the inhabitants of the area. A monument depicting Peibio and his affliction, described as a picture 'of a king, with a man on each side of him, with napkins wiping the rheum and drivel from his mouth', was said to exist in a Herefordshire parish, believed to be Madley.[18]

As a result of this cure Peibio made Dyfrig the heir of Madley and the whole 'island' which was called after Ebrdil, the saint's mother, *Insulam/Inis Ebrdil* (also known as *Mais Mail Lochou*). There is a suggestion that Ebrdil was 'a saint of very early date (perhaps really a male saint), whose career had been entirely forgotten' and the story was an attempt to connect Dyfrig and this older saint who was worshipped in the district.[19] Baring-Gould and Fisher, however, suggest that Ebrdil was the sister, not daughter, of Peibio.[20] The name Ebrdil (and its variants) features several times in the Llandaff Charters. There is *Lann Emrdil* (or *Efrdil*) north-east of Usk, sometimes identified with Llanerthill,[21] in Monmouthshire (SO 434 045). This is now simply a farm without a trace of a church, clearly another lost early British Christian site. First recorded in *c*.685, it was regranted in about 745 where it is referred to as *Lann Ebrdil*.[22] However this latter name and its position in the list of the *c*.745 grant, between what is obviously Moccas and Bellamore (Bellimoor) makes it more likely that it is Madley that is meant.[23] There is also a *Finnuan Efrdil* close to the River Monnow near to Welsh Newton[24] under *Lann Cinfall* which both Doble and Davies identify with Llangynfyl (SO 495 167). The modern-day Explorer OS map shows a wood with that name and a farm called Llangunville. An alternative name mentioned in the charters is *Merthirchinfall* (Merthir Cynfall)[25] and merthyr names are indicative of very early British Christian sites.

Under *Tir Conloc* in about 575 (which Davies identifies with Madley)[26] *Insulam Ebrdil* is once again mentioned,[27] and a stream called *Euyrdil* is also mentioned in the boundaries for Llandeilo Fawr and this is one of the charters that immediately precedes Dyfrig's *Life* in the *Book of Llandaff*. This charter and the *Life* of Oudoceus, also contained in the book, insist on a connection with Dyfrig and Llandeilo Fawr.[28]

Ebrdil was clearly of some importance for the name to be remembered thus. It has been suggested that, if Ebrdil was a female, she may have been the member of a local tribe and been adopted by Peibio as a result of her son's close association with the king.[29] Peibio appears as a legendary king in Welsh folklore and St. David's biographer, Rhygyfarch, tells us that David cured the king of blindness. Although Peibio was probably an historical figure, there is no indication in the Llandaff Charters that Peibio was Dyfrig's grandfather or was related to him in any way.[30]

The *Life* states that church land, called *Inis Ebrdil*, lay close to, and perhaps even surrounded, *Matle* (Madley), and Doble believes this must have included the *Lann Ebrdil* (the sacred enclosure/church of Ebrdil) mentioned in the Llandaff charters.[31] There is a suggestion that *Lann Ebrdil* was the original Welsh name for Madley. If Ebrdil was the original dedicatee of the church, then it was replaced by

Dyfrig and, later still, in the Middle Ages, the dedication changed to the Nativity of the Virgin. Madley church was rebuilt in the 13th and 14th centuries and today is a lofty church with the feeling of a small cathedral; its scale is seen as far outweighing the size of the village. It is thought that *Insulam Ebrdil* covered approximately the modern parishes of Madley, Moccas, Blakemere, Tyberton, Preston-on-Wye, Kingstone and Eaton Bishop, as well as the western parts of Allensmore and Clehonger.[32] Taken together these cover an extensive area of the central-western part of Herefordshire. *Insulam Ebrdil* is an alternative name for *Mais Mail Lochou*.

The *Lochou* component of *Mais Mail Lochou* has been identified with Llacheu, the reputed son of the legendary King Arthur. One of Llacheu's few appearances in the legend suggest 'his origins lie in a pre-Christian deity associated with fire and water', elements which feature in the story of Dyfrig's birth. Coplestone-Crow

suggests that Dyfrig and Ebrdil were 'Christian successors to a local Celtic deity, elements of whose cult were assimilated into their own legendary origins.' A deity that had the attributes of fire and water would have been an appropriate cult figure in Erging because its wealth appears to have been founded on ironworking and smithying carried on from Romano-British times, evidence of which has been found at the Roman town of *Ariconium* (Weston-under-Penyard) and at *Magnis* (Kenchester). Fire and water were essential elements in the quenching and tempering processes. If Madley was a local focus for the deity's cult in the Mawfield district of Erging, it is perhaps possible that it too was an ironworking/smithying centre, albeit on a smaller scale than *Ariconium*.[33]

There is an interesting absence of a conversion narrative in Dyfrig's *Life* which implies he was brought up in an environment which was already Christian.[34] Nor is anything known about Dyfrig's early education. A rather dubious remark in the *Book of Llandaff* states that he was a disciple of Germanus of Auxerre, but this is unlikely as Germanus died in 448 when, at best, Dyfrig would have been a very young child.

We are on firmer ground when it comes to his adult life. This may be divided into two

A stained glass image of St. Dubricius

parts: the first spent as a missionary and teacher, and the second in his work as a bishop.[35] It is the first part, when his activities were centred on Erging, that particularly concern us. Dyfrig is universally portrayed as a man of great learning and a superb teacher who worked mainly in the area around Hereford and in Gwent. However, a church dedication to St. Dyfrig at Gwenddwr, south of Builth Wells, and to St. Dubricius at Porlock suggests he, or more likely his followers, were active further afield in the west and south-west, perhaps as part of the great missionary expansion which started from south Wales and 'covered the coast of Somerset with churches and monasteries.'[36] Dyfrig's work in Erging is better known than that elsewhere, largely because the Llandaff charters record grants of land given to Dyfrig by the reigning kings of Erging to enable him to found monasteries. It is possible that Dyfrig's earliest foundation was at *Ariconium*. If this is so, this strengthens the case for this town being the original centre of the British kingdom and points to Dyfrig's close association with Romano-British Christianity.[37] *Ariconium* has even been considered the source of the Welsh Christian movement of the 5th and 6th centuries.[38]

As a teacher Dyfrig attracted many students and followers from across Britain who wanted to study at the schools connected with his monasteries. His most famous foundation was at Hentland, in south-east Herefordshire, and this became the centre of his missionary endeavour. Rather than being located near the present church, the monastery may have been at nearby Llanfrother Farm (SO 542 287). A 14th century spelling of Llanfrother is *Hendresroude* which translates possibly to the 'old place of the brethren', whilst the modern name is translated as 'the old sacred enclosure/church of the monks'. The later church at Hentland may have been established by St. Teilo (see gazetteer).[39] The *Life* states Dyfrig had 1,000 clerks under his care at Hentland.[40]

After seven years Dyfrig moved and returned for an unspecified time to *Inis Ebrdil* (his alleged motherland) and then chose 'a spot (*locum*) in a corner of that island, on the river Wye, convenient because of its being well wooded and abounding in fish. Here he remained, with his innumerable disciples, for many years, continuing his teaching …'. This was Moccas, 10 miles north-west of Hentland. According to the *Life* an angel had appeared to Dyfrig in a dream and 'instructed him to build a settlement and a church in the name of the Holy Trinity at … the exact spot to be indicated by his finding there a white sow with young. Immediately on awaking, the saint with his disciples obediently went round the place … and, as the angel had promised, a white sow with her pigs started up from her lair. On that spot he built the settlement and church, and there for many years he lived as a monk … preaching and teaching the clergy and people, and through his teaching, which shone throughout Britain "like a candle upon a stand" … the whole British nation preserved the true Faith without any strain of false doctrine.' The discovery of a sow with her young on the site of a future monastery is a favourite theme in the *Lives* of the British saints; it is also found in a *Life* of Paul Aurelian (Paulinus) written in the late 9th century and the later *Lives* of Cadoc (see under Cadoc), Brynach and Kentigern.[41] The use of the pig appears to be linked with the belief 'that a white sow and her farrow would mark a divinely chosen spot' and is perhaps based on the legend of the founding of Rome.[42] The name Moccas is derived from the Welsh *Mochros* which means quite literally 'pig marsh' or 'swine moor'.

The reason for the move from Hentland to Moccas is not known, but it has been suggested that Hentland was found to be too close for safety to the Anglo-Saxon border of the Mercian sub-kingdom of the Magonsaete and a more remote site was needed.[43] However an alternative theory suggests that it was because of the need for improved communications that Moccas was chosen, because a few miles east ran the Chester to Caerleon road with the main route into the west of Wales readily accessible to the south.[44] As this was a communal monastery and a monastic school, good communications would have been needed. One can be in a 'wilderness' but have an efficient network of roads a few miles away — piety and practicality needed to exist hand-in-hand. However, Moccas did not achieve the same importance as Hentland. One reason for its decline could be that there were several other monastic schools emerging and it is likely Moccas became one of many, suggesting a flowering of the British missionary movement.

Dyfrig subsequently became more active in south Wales at Caldey Island and, at some stage, became bishop of the area (not the see) of Llandaff. Benedict of Gloucester relates that at the battle of Mount Badon, Dyfrig prayed and exhorted the Britons to victory 'as a second Moses on a mountain-top above the contending hosts.'[45] Badon was fought in about 495 between the British and the invading Anglo-Saxons in the West Country, possibly around Bath. Geoffrey of Monmouth gives a fanciful version of what appears to be the same event but is called the battle of Bath. Here Dyfrig accompanies King Arthur and climbs to the top of a hill to exhort the Britons to fight the Christian fight against the pagan Saxons.[46] This is similar to the account of St. Teilo who prayed for victory on behalf of King Iddon and the British against the Anglo-Saxons at Llantilio Crossenny (see gazetteer), although in Dyfrig's case the reference is much less specific and so less believable.

Nine charters are contained in the *Book of Llandaff* which record grants of land to Dyfrig which are mostly in Herefordshire. It states that Dyfrig was given the churches which he then assigned to his disciples, and founded others personally which he then gave away in the same manner. It is an unlikely story but enabled the author to claim for their diocese a large number of churches for the territory which Llandaff claimed as Dyfrig's inheritance. As with many foundations credited to other Welsh saints, it is suggested that many of these Dubrician churches must have been founded at different periods and independently.[47]

Although most of Dyfrig's dedications are found in southern Herefordshire, it is of some interest that he apparently secured a foundation at Penally in Pembrokeshire. Baring-Gould and Fisher suggest that, following the custom of British saints, Dyfrig sought an island to which he could retreat at Lent, eventually securing Caldey Island. Here he founded a monastery and placed Piro in command, although he retained overall control. An early inscribed stone which contains Ogam and Latin script was discovered on Caldey Island which partly reads MAGL DUBR and this has been interpreted as 'the (tonsured) servant of Dubricius'. As founder and abbot of Caldey, Dyfrig would have gained influence over the neighbouring area and thereby probably secured land at Penally. A grant of land to Dyfrig at Penally is recorded in the Llandaff Charters by one Noe ab Arthur, king of Dyfed, in the early 8th century, but is anachronistic as Dyfrig would have been long dead by then. Penally was the birthplace of another important saint considered in this study, Teilo, and Baring-Gould and Fisher note it is 'by no means impossible that Dyfrig may have noticed the clever, pious child, and have directed his early education at Caldey, till he was ready to be sent to Paulinus at Ty Gwyn'.[48] Ty Gwyn was an early monastic school near St. David's in Pembrokeshire.

It is not quite so easy to explain Dyfrig's four dedications in the Gower but that he had a foothold there seems a reasonable conclusion; moreover three of his disciples became founders and abbots in this area. This may have occurred under the influence of St. Cenydd of the Gower whose son, Ufelwy, had been a pupil of Dyfrig.[49] When Cenydd moved to Brittany, his son may have moved to the Gower to take up his father's work and thus introduced Dyfrig's influence into this area.

Dyfrig visited Llancarfan and Llantwit Major on his travels to and from Caldey but, although he had no jurisdiction over either place, he was welcomed at both monasteries and 'invited to exercise episcopal functions at Llantwit, where there was probably at the time no bishop to ordain and consecrate candidates.'[50]

Dyfrig also attended the famous Synod of Llanddewi Brefi in about 545 and it was he, with St. Deiniol, who succeeded in encouraging the reluctant St. David to attend (see below).

In old age, and probably soon after the Synod of Llanddewi Brefi, Dyfrig retired to Bardsey Island off the Lleyn Peninsula in north-west Wales, where he died, perhaps within a matter of months. If we accept the putative dates suggested by Baring-Gould and Fisher for his life, Dyfrig was about 96 years old when he died, a very good age even in modern times![51] Bardsey Island is also known as the Island of 20,000 Saints after the number of saints who are allegedly buried there. It became a major pilgrimage destination from the 5th century, and three pilgrimages to Bardsey were reckoned to be equivalent to one to Rome.[52] Dyfrig was buried at Bardsey but in 1120 his remains were translated to Llandaff Cathedral.

His relics were originally interred in the presbytery and his tomb is considered to be in a recess in the north aisle wall. His effigy was probably carved in 1220 and depicts the saint in episcopal habits with a plain mitre.[53]

The *Book of Llandaff* paints a vivid picture of what happened to the churches and land in Erging not long after Dyfrig's demise. In about 577 the Anglo-Saxons won a decisive battle against the Britons at Deorham which led to the influx of Anglo-Saxons into the Severn Valley and Welsh borders. 'Be it known,' says a charter of *c*.745, 'that great tribulations and devastations took place in the time of Telpald and Ithail, kings of Britain, and this was due to the heathen Saxon race … and it was so extensive that the whole borderland of Britain was almost destroyed … and mainly about the river Wye, on account of wars and frequent daily and nightly incursions, on one side and on the other. After a while, peace having been established, the land was restored by force and vigour (to its rightful owners); but it was swept bare and unoccupied, with men few and far between.'[54] The monasteries in Erging and Ewyas (the small neighbouring British kingdom to the west) were wasted, the monks fleeing and carrying away what they could.

Tradition has it that Dyfrig was instrumental in the founding of the Choir of Cadoc at Llancarfan and to have been its principal before St. Cadoc and confessor to St. Germanus, although it is significant that no mention is made of Dyfrig in the *Life* of St. Cadoc. However it is stated elsewhere that Dyfrig confirmed Cadoc's father, Gwynllyw, in his resolve in old age to lead a hermetical life and ministered to him at his death. Dyfrig has a holy well named after him, Ffynnon Ddyfrig, at Garn Llywyd which is a mile from Llancarfan.[55] It was also Dyfrig who 'fixed the boundaries of the burial place' at Llantwit Major and who prepared its titular saint, St. Illtud, for entry into the monastic world. He also consecrated St. Deniol at Bangor.

Geoffrey of Monmouth adds several fanciful details concerning Dyfrig in *The History of the Kings of Britain*. According to Geoffrey, the saint is made archbishop of 'the city of the legions' (unspecified but probably Chester or Caerleon). Dyfrig also supposedly crowned the 15-year-old King Arthur at Silchester (Berkshire) and Geoffrey later records that Dyfrig was also primate of Britain and legate to the papal see and 'was so remarkably pious that by merely praying he could cure anyone who was ill'. It is also stated that Dyfrig resigned the archbishopric and became a hermit, his long-held ambition.[56] Unfortunately Geoffrey cannot be relied upon as myth and legend colour much of his narrative. The references to the archbishopric and of metropolitan sees are anachronistic as such positions and institutions came about much later and were unknown in Britain in Dyfrig's time.

Dyfrig's stature within the early British Church is undisputed and fortunately records of some of his foundations do exist in the Llandaff Charters, a privilege not generally accorded to other saints.

St. Illtud

Illtud predated many of the major saints and founders of monastic schools and was an effective tutor to many church leaders, being partly responsible for the training of the saints Samson, David, Paul of Leon (Paulinus) and Gildas. He may therefore be regarded as a founding father and was described in the *Life* of St. Samson as the 'most learned of all the Britons in the knowledge of Scripture … and in every branch of philosophy — poetry and rhetoric, grammar and arithmetic; and he was most sagacious and gifted with the power of foretelling future events.'[57] Important areas relating to his cult exist around Brecon, at Llantwit Major and in Brittany.

There are three manuscript sources for his *Life*. The first is an early 13th-century manuscript and the other two are John of Tynemouth's abridgements of the first. The 13th-century *Life* post-dates Illtud's life by about 700 years and contains obvious anachronisms but does at least predate Geoffrey of Monmouth's fantastical history. It may well be based on an earlier *Life*, now lost.[58] Information about Illtud also appears in the *Lives* of Samson, Cadoc and Gildas.

Illtud was born in about 450 and his parents were Bicanus, a soldier who had been forced into exile into Brittany, and Rieinguled, the daughter of a British king. His parents were married in Gaul, where he was also born. He was christened Illtyd meaning 'one safe from every crime', and his *Life* certainly informs us that he was 'blameless in the five stages of life, and was laudable and beloved by all persons.' He was educated by Germanus the Armorican to the age of about 12, when he chose against the religious life and instead moved to Britain to serve under King Arthur, who is said in one source to be Illtud's first cousin, a claim backed up in the Welsh pedigrees. When Illtud was about 22 he became a knight, married a virtuous woman called Trynihid and moved to mid-Glamorgan to serve under King Poulentus (or Paul Penychen) who was St. Cadoc's uncle. Paul chose Illtud to preside over the royal household, being known for his eloquence, tact and intelligence. He was subsequently put in charge of the soldiery too.[59]

A story is recounted that, when Illtud was aged about 26, some of his soldiers drowned in marshy ground. Illtud was not actually present at the time, but the loss of life affected him greatly and the tale continues that Illtud sought out St. Cadoc for direction and who advised him to take up the monastic life. However, if Illtud as a child was educated by Germanus, who died in 474, he would not have sought solace from Cadoc — who died in about 577. It is possible, however, that there is still some historical fact in the story in that Illtud may have lost of group of men under his charge, an event which so upset him that he decided to renounce the secular life. Whatever the precise details, Illtud left Paul's service and travelled to the banks of the Nadauan (the river Dawon or Thaw in South Glamorgan) with his wife and attendants, setting up a rough shelter there. Apparently an angel came to Illtud in a dream and warned him that his love for his wife was a hindrance to his new religious life and directed him to go to a 'certain wooded valley to the west' where he would find an abode. On waking Illtud ordered his wife to attend to the horses. When she returned naked to their shelter he rejected her 'as the poison of a serpent' and instructed her to dress and be gone. Not heeding her pleadings he dismissed her and travelled to the wooded valley at Hodnant ('Fruitful Valley') to seek a place for his devotions. He then visited St. Dyfrig (Dubricius) for advice. Dyfrig told him to pay penance for his past misdeeds and, having shaved his beard and cut his hair, Illtud took the clerical habit.[60]

Illtud returned to the Hodnant valley where Dyfrig, according to the *Life*, fixed the bounds of the burial place, in the middle of which Illtud laid the foundation of an oratory 'in honour of the supreme, and undivided Trinity' (an early dedication to the Holy Trinity). Then he built a church 'of stone materials and surrounded it with a quadrangular ditch.' We are told that Illtud 'lived an ascetic life, bathing every morning in cold water, and rising to prayers in the midst of the night' and generally doing good works. This site appears to have been at Llantwit. It is said in the *Iolo Manuscripts* that a school for saints had previously occupied the site but had been destroyed by pirates, so when Illtud arrived the site was deserted.[61]

The *Book of Llandaff* states that Dyfrig made Illtud abbot of Llantwit which became a famous monastery and, according to the somewhat unreliable Iolo manuscripts, at one time housed 3,000 monks. Dyfrig would have had no authority over him but the *Life* mentions that Dyfrig visited Llantwit at Lent to correct any deficiencies and confirm what should be done, probably simply under the guise of a mentor.[62]

Illtud did not appear to have had any legal right to the land upon which he built his church. King Meirchion 'The Mad' was the landholder, and whilst out hunting, burst into Illtud's hermitage in pursuit of a fawn (some sources say a stag) which had fled there for safety. The king did not move to kill it but was annoyed that Illtud had set up a hermitage without his permission and demanded he hand over the beast. Illtud refused to do so, instead offering him a meal. The king accepted, subsequently grumbled about the quality of the fare, but nevertheless then stayed the night. By the next morning the king had been won round and granted him the land and the right to establish a 'tribal school'. Illtud kept the fawn, tamed it and trained it to draw carriages. According to legend, Illtud's 'Golden Stag' is buried within the vicinity and when discovered great wealth will accrue to Llantwit.[63]

Within a short time Illtud had many followers at his monastery including fifty canons. Amongst those he tutored were the saints Samson, Paulinus (Paul of Leon), Gildas and David. Maelgwn, the badly behaved king of Gwynedd, may also have been educated for a while at Llantwit. Illtud was by this time ordained and was described by Gildas as 'the refined teacher of almost the whole of Britain.'[64]

Illtud's actions concerning his abandonment of his wife deserve some scrutiny. We are told that after living in holy retreat for some years where she devoted her attention to helping widows and impoverished nuns, her life was devout and blameless. After several years she decided to visit Illtud. Travelling to Llantwit she found him, thin and with a mud-besmirched face, working in the fields. He turned his back on her, refused to speak, and did not even offer her the hospitality that it was then customary to give to strangers.[65] During the early period of the church, married partners sometimes did live separately after a few years of marriage, particularly when vows of celibacy were not part of monastic life. Illtud could have therefore continued to live with his wife, or have maintained communication with her without fear of criticism. In his *Life*, the chapter concerning Illtud's first rejection of his wife ends with four hexameters 'expressing the feelings of a rabid celibate towards the female sex'[66] and probably in fact says more about the biographer's misogynistic feelings than Illtud's own views.

Illtud encountered problems with Cyflym, (the 'Very Acute') steward to King Meirchion. Cyflym resented the saint's tax free tenure of the rich pastureland and took every opportunity to vex Illtud. Because of his unpleasant, domineering and wicked behaviour, God caused him to 'melt like wax softened and rendered liquid by the heat of fire.' The king, maddened by the death of Cyflym, armed and took soldiers and 'proceeded together to the holy place to take revenge on the chief, and the inhabitants of the place.' Not surprisingly, Illtud thought it expedient to leave the monastery and spent over a year living in hiding in a cave at Lingarthic on the River Ewenny. The *Life* also states that Illtud left to get away from 'the clamouring people who were an impediment to his prayers.' He did not even tell his fellow monks of his whereabouts. At the cave he spent a simple, contemplative life in the vein of the early Desert Fathers. Illtud was eventually persuaded to return to Llantwit, but the king's replacement steward, Cefygid, was to prove as unpleasant as Cyflym. He had the nasty habit of impounding the monastery's cattle for three days and not feeding them so that they became lean. Cefygid subsequently drowned in marshy ground and the king, once again, marched out on the monastery, only to be swallowed up by the earth at the gates and was never seen again. The *Life* informs us that Illtud was again 'troubled by the multitude of persons coming to him, and disturbed in his prayers, went on that account to the cave of Lingarch.' These two episodes with the stewards and subsequent actions sound suspiciously like garbled accounts of the same event.[67]

Llantwit became the leading centre for learning in the region. On hearing that his native land, Brittany was ravaged by famine and knowing that his granaries were full, he ordered ships, filled them with as much grain as they could carry and set off, landing first at Leon, where he set up Lanildut, then moving on to La Roche Derrien, before travelling inland. He stayed for two years after assisting the inhabitants with seed corn and set up several other foundations during that time.

Despite requests that he should stay in Brittany, he decided to return to Britain where he remained until his old age. His biography tells us that being infirm, he decided to return to Dol in Brittany to die. This clashes with information in the *Life* of Samson, who was in Cornwall when he heard that Illtud was dead or dying, and went on to establish Dol in about 547. Illtud died between 527 and 537, aged between 77 and 87. Welsh tradition has it that he died in Breconshire and that he was buried at Bedd Gwyl Illtud, where he had been living for a while, at Llanilltud south of Brecon (see gazetteer). Illtud's cult in Breconshire centred upon Llanilltyd church, now demolished, although the curvilinear boundary and churchyard still exists.[68]

Illtud's festival is 6th November, the reputed day of his death. He is honoured in Wales for introducing an improved method of ploughing. In one of the *Triads*, (ancient Welsh poems), Illtud is stated as being one of the 'three Knights of the Court of Arthur who kept the Greal [Holy Grail]' – the other two knights being St. Cadoc and Peredur.[69]

There is also a legend that Illtud's mare was mated by a stag at Llanhamlach (see gazetteer), giving birth to an animal of wondrous speed with a horse's hind-quarters and a stag's behind. Giraldus Cambrensis found this local legend which he stated was from much older sources, possibly a lost *Life*, which was read in Llanhamlach church.[70]

St. David

The earliest extant *Life* of St. David was written by Rhygyfarch, the son of Bishop Sulien of St. David's, in the late 11th century, approximately 500 years after David's death. Although a late text, Bishop Sulien was bishop of St. David's for about ten years and knew the traditions about St. David well, and which he undoubtedly passed on to his son. Sulien was indeed instrumental in brokering a meeting between William the Conqueror and two very powerful Welsh princes in 1081 at St. David's. It was here the Welsh princes probably appealed to William 'to uphold the Welsh church against the increasing power of Rome.' Rhygyfarch was present at this meeting and it has been suggested that he may well have written St. David's *Life* at about this time — even for this occasion, and it was thus not just a biography but a political statement concerning the independence of the Welsh church.[71] If the *Life* was written in 1081 it would explain Rhygyfarch's statement that he used old documents in its compilation. St. David's was sacked repeatedly by Vikings between 795 and 1088 and, on the latter occasion, the cathedral was almost completely destroyed and it is doubtful that any documents relating to St. David survived.[72] The chronology of events during David's life is not determinable.

Other *Lives* of St. David exist: one of the early 13th century by Giraldus Cambrensis which expands on Rhygyfarch's text; an abridgement in John of

Tynemouth's collection (referred to below as the *Latin Lives*), and the *Llyfr Ancr Llanddewi Brefi* written in 1346 by an anchorite at Llanddewi and which is an abridgement of Rhygyfarch's *Life* and, like that by Giraldus Cambrensis, contains material from now lost sources.[73]

David was born sometime between 495 and 500 into a ruling family in Ceredigion. David's father, Sant, was the son of Ceredig, the founder of Ceredigion, who in turn was the son of Cunedda whom tradition has it came from northern Britain and conquered north Wales. Other sources state that Sant was the son of Cedig, son of Ceredig.[74] Rhygyfarch's *Life* states that Sant laid aside the rule of Ceredigion to embrace 'the ecclesiastical profession'. Sant was directed by an angel to go and find three things while out hunting: a stag, a salmon and a swarm of bees. When following a stag alongside the river Teifi, he found bees swarming in a tree at a place called *Lin Henlan*, now called Henlann, a hamlet 3 miles east of Newcastle Emlyn. Here Sant took the honeycomb and caught a salmon and was told by the angel to give the stag, honey and fish to the monastery of Maucen to be held for Sant's as yet unborn son. The stag was supposed to signify the future David's power over the ancient serpent, with the salmon proclaiming his abstinence and the bees declaring his wisdom. Maucen's monastery, named after its abbot, but more commonly referred to as Ty Gwyn (the White House) because of its whitewashed stone walls, lay on the slopes of Carn Llidi near Whitesands Bay and St. David's. The monastery is considered to have been either a double-monastery which housed monks and nuns in separate quarters, or had a school which received male and female students. Fragmentary remains are believed to have existed until the turn of the 20th century, largely consisting of an extensive cemetery containing graves covered with slabs and marked by a slate set perpendicularly in the ground. It was here that David's mother, Non, was either a nun or a pupil.[75] Sant fell for Non and thus was David conceived. The *Life* states David was conceived by force — Non's status as a nun meant that consensual relations would have been difficult to explain away!

During her pregnancy Non went into retreat to a cottage on the cliffs above what is now called St. Non's Bay. She was apparently being threatened by her father who wanted to kill the child, but more likely did not relish the scandal caused by her condition. Non duly gave birth to David at St. Non's Bay during which, legend report, she gripped a stone so tightly that her finger marks remained on its edge (these marks were more likely to have been Ogham script). This stone, now lost, was built into the foundations of the altar at the chapel on the site, of which there are still remains, along with a holy well close by. It was converted from a house to a chapel in medieval times with a superstructure being raised on the old foundations; on the east side was an early incised cross stone — still visible today. After the Reformation when pilgrims stopped coming to the chapel it was again converted into a house, and then used as a vegetable garden! The stone which

Non gripped during the pain of childbirth was searched for in the late 19th/early 20th century but was found to have been removed at an unknown date 'from the floor of the footpace on which the alter stood. The marks of removal were clearly distinguishable.' In the 1900s the remains were recorded as being rectangular and approximately orientated north/south, with a substructure constructed from 'rude masses of stone put together without mortar'. In the late 20th century it was noted that the remains did not have any distinguishing features which would aid dating; the earliest written reference to a chapel dates from 1335. However, a report of an early excavation of what appear to be slab-lined graves may indicate early Christian use.[76]

In St. Ailbe's *Life* it is said that Sant had David baptized by Ailbe, indicating that Sant handed the child over for fostering and an education in the religious life. However in the Irish *Life* of St. Colman it is claimed that Colman arrived one night at the house of a British king whose wife had just given birth to a still-born son whom St. Colman brought back to life and subsequently taught, and that this child was St. David. Both Ailbe and Colman are represented in local place-names:

St. Non's Chapel on St. David's Head. One of the purposes of thsi chapel, and for the other seven medieval chapels dotted along the headland, was to offer mariners a place to offer thanks for a safe journey — St. Justinian's Chapel west of St. David's is another example, but St. Non's was the most important. The well just to the east of St. Non's Chapel is called St. Non's Well and kept its reputation as a healing well long after the Reformation. Antiquarians remarked that offerings of pebbles and pins were made at it on 2 March, St. Non's Day. The present vaulting is 18th century but probably replaced an earlier struc-ture. The well was one of the most famous in Wales, especially prized for the healing of eye diseases. In medieval times it was considered that two pilgrimages to St. David's were equal to one to Rome.[77]

Ailbe at Llan Eilw and Fagwr Eilw near St. David's, and Colman at Llan Golman (8 miles north of Narberth) and at Capel Colman (6 miles west-south-west of Newcastle Emlyn), both in northern Pembrokeshire. These places may indicate historical association with these saints, or they may have given rise to the association in the tradition as a way of explaining the place-names.[78]

David was sent for his education to a place called *Yr Henllwyn* — it was here that he spent his childhood. This place appears to have had a number of names and Baring-Gould and Fisher identify it as the same place as Ty Gwyn over which St. Paulinus (also known as Paul Aurelian) was abbot. The Latin rendering of Ty Gwyn is *Alba Domus* which, in the early 20th century, was the name of a farmhouse on the site. Ty Gwyn had been run by Maucen, a disciple of St. Patrick (who is reputed to have founded the monastery), but, in David's time, was run by Paulinus on behalf of David's family, it being a donation to the church by Cynyr, David's grandfather. Others suggest that David was educated at a monastery at Henfynyw just south of Aberaeron, further north up the coast, or under Paulinus at Llanddeusant (about 7 miles south-east of Llandovery in mid-Wales). Whatever the location, David stayed in training for ten years and, according to the *Life* of St. Teilo, formed a strong friendship with that saint. However, David's various *Lives* record that Teilo was David's disciple and joined him after leaving Paulinus's tutorage. To add even more confusion, the *Life* of St. Illtud records that David, Paulinus, Gildas and Samson were fellow disciples under Illtud who taught them — which just underlines how confused the legends of the saints can be![79]

After studying it appears that David established a number of religious foundations; Rhygyfarch claiming that the saint founded twelve monasteries (see below). David took over Ty Gwyn from Paulinus in about 527 and it was at this time that he ran into a dispute with Gildas who was greedy for control of the foundation and

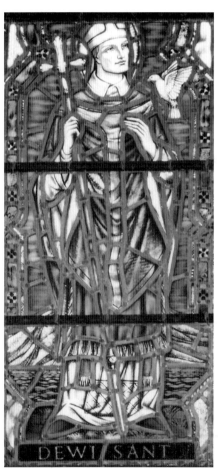

St. David as depicted in stained glass at Strata Florida

tried to depose him. Finnian of Clonard was called in to intervene and decided in David's favour as Gildas was in breach of Celtic/British justice which gave the heir of the founder the right to run the foundation if he was suitable. Paulinus had taken charge of the foundation by proxy on behalf of Cynyr's tribe until a suitable leader was found amongst them; and David was eminently suited. After David's election he put his uncle, Guistlianus, in charge and departed either to find followers or establish other foundations. On his return, David decided to move the site of the monastery inland away from the risk of pirate attacks to the present site of St. David's which was concealed from the sea. Ty Gwyn was abandoned.[80]

The new monastery thrived. The monks undertook most of the manual work, growing crops and living in rather austere conditions likened to those of the Desert Fathers. Indeed David's austerity created problems within the monastery. For example, his steward tried to murder his favourite disciple Aidan, and then with the cook and deacon tried to poison David but failed because an Irish visitor to the monastery, St. Scuthin (or Scuthyn), realised what was happening and the poisoned bread was thrown away to be eaten by a dog and raven who immediately died.

St. David as depicted in stained glass at St. Arvans

Another visiting Irish saint, murdered a boy detailed to wait on him by David in a fit of rage, and took the boy's name of Laicinn as penance.[81]

David does appear to have been somewhat difficult. The important synod of Llanddewi Brefi, which was held prior to 545 and the advent of the Yellow Plague, was called to discuss canons of discipline and was convened by St. Dyfrig. David was called to attend by Paulinus to help resolve disputed matters, but refused. Only after the third visit to ask his attendance by none other than the saints Dyfrig and Deiniol did David deign to attend. On arrival David found the site of the synod unsuitable and instead preached from a mound upon which the present church at Llanddewi Brefi stands. Having made a significant impact, David attended a second synod. Although the date given for this is 569 in the *Annales Cambriae* it is known that it was held prior to the outbreak of Yellow Plague as Finnion of Clonard had to restore peace, and Finnian died of the plague in 548. The Yellow Plague, so called because of the yellowish, bloodless appearance of those affected, became widespread throughout the British Isles, causing many to flee to Brittany. These included many of the Welsh saints. Rhygyfarch does not mention that David fled the plague, but as he is known to have made foundations in Brittany it is likely he left Britain at this time along with Teilo and Padarn. It appears that his mother accompanied him and settled in Dirinon in Brittany where she eventually died and was buried.[82]

From the pattern of scattered dedications it is possible that David worked with St. Teilo on his return to Britain to re-establish a strong church within the south of Wales. David apparently recruited some survivors of Dyfrig's followers to help him. There is no record of the level of mortality of the Yellow Plague but it is likely many died. One may perhaps draw a comparison with the effects of the Black Death in the mid-14th century where at least a third of the population was killed, and for some decades afterwards there was plentiful land which was either free of tenure and going to waste, or available at much lower rents than before. There is also a tendency for people to look more to the church through a combination of fear and the need for support and comfort after such a trauma. If the effects of the Yellow Plague were anywhere near as severe as those of the Black Death, David and Teilo and the other surviving saints may have found that acquiring land for their foundations was relatively easy.

As no chronological records exist for David we cannot say when his foundations were established or whether individual monasteries or churches were set up before the plague or afterwards, if David himself was personally instrumental in their foundation or whether they were founded by his followers. In Rhygyfarch's *Life* there are claims that David founded Glastonbury, Bath and Crowland although it is known the latter was founded by the 7th century Anglo-Saxon saint Guthlac. David was also linked with the foundation of monasteries at Repton and Leominster. Repton (Derbyshire) was first recorded in the early 8th century and was Anglo-Saxon monastery and it is unlikely that David had any part in its foundation, not least because it is hundreds of miles away from his area of known activity. His involvement with Leominster is at least possible, although again it is a fair distance from south Wales. Leominster was traditionally thought to be a 7th-century Anglo-Saxon foundation but the work of Joe Hillaby has shown that the layout of its monastic precinct has similarities with earlier British monastic foundations. It is just possible that the later Anglo-Saxon foundation was in fact a re-establishment of an earlier British monastery, but whether St. David had any hand in it is debatable. Rhygyfarch also lists Colva, Glascwm (both in Radnorshire), Llangyfelach in the Gower and Raglan in Monmouthshire as those established by David. It is possible that Rhygyfarch gave David such a widespread list of foundations in an attempt to prove Gildas' prophecy that St. David should have hold of all Britain.[83]

In 1836 it was noted that there were 53 dedications to St. David but not a single ancient dedication to him in north Wales.[84] It is suggested that St. Beuno was David's counterpart and there are more churches and chapels dedicated to Beuno in north Wales than to any other saint.

There is little doubt that because of the respect shown to him by others and the kingly authority of his tribal connections and the number of his apparent foundations, that he was firmly in charge of ecclesiastical life in Dyfed. However the implication that he held power throughout south Wales may be the result of propaganda to ward off interference from Canterbury in the early Norman period. David died some time between 574 and 589. He was interred at St. David's but some of his relics were later stolen and taken to Glastonbury.[85] This does not appear to have detracted from the importance and growth of St. David's, which became one of the most important bishoprics in Wales. Indeed, David is the only Welsh saint to have been canonised by Rome, probably in the early 12th century.

St. Teilo

Teilo was a major saint who became a very influential churchman in south Wales during his lifetime. He was the motivating force behind the establishment of Llandaff and paved the way for it to become a major episcopal see after his death.

Teilo's 'biography' or *Life* is contained in the *Book of Llandaff* and all other versions of it are derivative, some being only partial. This Llandaff *Life* was composed in the form of a sermon to be read out at his festival. It is evident from comparison that the writer knew the material contained in the *Lives* of St. David and St. Padarn, but the version of St. David's *Life* was a different one to that which now exists. Another less detailed *Life* of Teilo was written by Geoffrey, brother of Bishop Urban of Llandaff. However the earliest mention of Teilo is recorded in the *Book* of St. Chad, a gospel-book written in about the early 8th century which became the property of the church of St. Teilo for some time and during which a various historical entries were made in the margins. Written in Welsh, they record gifts and agreements made 'on the altar of Teilo' (initially thought to be that at Llandaff, but more recently considered to have been at Llandeilo Fawr — literally 'the great church of Teilo' — in Carmarthenshire). The book became known as the *Book* of St. Chad as it passed from Teilo's church sometime after 850 to Lichfield Cathedral, whose first bishop was St. Chad. Although the book does not detail anything of Teilo's life, it shows that in 9th-century Wales, when the marginalia was added, he was credited with the foundation of the monastery at Llandeilo Fawr and that a cult of St. Teilo existed centuries before his biography was written in the *Book of Llandaff*.[86]

Teilo was born at a place once called *Eccluis Gunniau/Guiniau* near Penally, close to Tenby, where the family had an ancestral claim to land. Teilo was originally called Elios because 'his learning shone as the sun', but this was corrupted to Eliud, a fairly common name at the time. Teilo was a pet name formed by the addition of the prefix to- or ty-. His father was Ensic and his mother Guenhaf. In

1988, excavations of a British chieftain's homestead at Penally on the Trefloyne Estate (a name which is thought to mean 'homestead of Teilo's grove' from Tref Llwyn Teilo) uncovered traces of pottery and coloured glass of a type from Gaul and the eastern Mediterranean dating from the 5th to 7th centuries and equating with Teilo's lifetime. Fine metalwork and quantities of animal bones were also found which suggest feasting and imply Penally was a place of some importance at this time.[87]

It is unclear where Teilo was educated and by whom. His *Life* states he was trained under St. Dyfrig at Hennlan (Hentland in Herefordshire) and that he moved for further training to Ty Gwyn under Paulinus where he became a close friend of St. David. However the link between Dyfrig and Teilo is uncertain and the Herefordshire connection unlikely. It is possible that Teilo was under the older saint's charge at Caldey Island but whether before or after his tutelage with Paulinus is not known.[88]

When St. David went to what is now the area of St. David's to found a monastery, Teilo accompanied him and founded a church a few miles away 'on land that belonged to him as a member of the tribe of Ceredig'. However, Llandeilo Fawr and Llandaff were Teilo's primary foundations. Both places were major centres by the time of Teilo's death, and during his lifetime Llandaff became 'the most powerful, influential, and best endowed monastery in South Wales'. The power of Llandaff grew by degrees due to his work and by the time Oudoceus

St. Teilo's Well at Llandeilo Fawr in Carmarthenshire.
This well is on the edge of the churchyard and set back underneath it

(Teilo's nephew) succeeded him it had in effect become a bishopric. Yet it is interesting that the two monastic centres in south-east Wales that survived as centres of classical, as well as Christian, learning to Norman times were Llantwit Major and Llancarfan, and that no such tradition survived with Teilo's monastery at Llandeilo Fawr or, indeed, with David's at St. David's.[89]

Donations of land were gifted to Teilo by King Iddon in what is now Monmouthshire and the kings of Dyfed with Llandaff lying between these two areas. Teilo did not exercise any control over Dyfrig's churches in Erging nor held any authority over the foundations of Llantwit Major, Llancarfan or Llandough — only if these places were without a bishop at any time might Teilo be called in to perform ordinations. At this time there were no dioceses of Llandaff or St. David's, governance was in the hands of the abbots of the monasteries and 'confined to the *llans* that belonged to them'. There are 37 St. Teilo churches listed in the *Book of Llandaff* and, interestingly, they are all outside the present diocese of Llandaff. Twenty-five of these have retained the place-name element *llan* and 14 have kept the name Llandeilo, 'Teilo's monastery'. That Teilo was the founder and original patron of Llandaff is considered incontrovertible. For a long time any bishop of the diocese was known in Wales as Esgob Teilo, 'Teilo's bishop', the church at Llandaff was Eglwys Deilo, 'Teilo's church', and even the later *Book of Llandaff* was referred to as Llyfr Teilo, 'Teilo's Book'.[90]

In about 547 the Yellow Plague hit the area. The death rate in the region and in his monasteries was so high that Teilo was forced to flee to Brittany with many of his clergy lest they all die. Crossing Cornwall they were well received by King Geraint, who obtained a promise that Teilo would return to hear his confession before he died. During a seven year, seven month stay in Brittany, Teilo set up several foundations and worked alongside Samson, who established the monastery of Dol in about 554. Teilo was granted land for foundations by his brother-in-law Budic, who was regional king of the area at the time, but needed support as his own political position was unstable. When Teilo was about to leave, he asked that Budic hand over his son, Oudoceus, to be taken back to Britain and educated, which Budic obviously did as Oudoceus succeeded Teilo as bishop of Llandaff. On arriving in Britain he probably landed in Falmouth harbour, thence went to Geraint's palace at 'Dingerein'. Geraint was dying and Teilo was able to minister to him as he had promised. The only place-name close to *Dingerein* is below Cardigan in west Wales, and it may be that the author of the *Life* heard of a tradition between Teilo and a Geraint and turned a Welsh king into a Cornish ruler.[91]

Teilo then set about trying to reorganise church possessions in the aftermath of the plague's ravages, and induced some of St. Dyfrig's followers to join him. As a result of his actions, several grants of land were given to Teilo in a variety of interesting ways and for a number of reasons. In 577 Teilo and his clergy were present to give vocal and moral support to King Iddon at a battle with the Anglo-Saxons near White Castle in Monmouthshire, 5 miles east of Abergavenny. For their support, Iddon granted Teilo land to build on at Llantilio Crossenny, (see gazetteer). In another case the king of Demetia (Dyfed) killed one of Teilo's men in a rage, whilst the man had taken sanctuary in a church and was clinging to the altar. For this murder committed in such a holy place the king had to compensate Teilo with the gift of an estate in Carmarthenshire. (Elsewhere Teilo was granted land at Trefgarn (5 miles north of Haverfordwest) by King Aircol Lawhir. He had lost control over his wildly drunken and rowdy household at Lydstep near Tenby to such an extent that members were murdering each other! Teilo sent two of his disciples who successfully restored order. Teilo was also called in by St. Cadoc to help settle a dispute with King Arthur on the banks of the River Usk (see further under St. Cadoc). Cadoc granted him a villa at Merthyr Tegfedd, now Llandegveth (about 3 miles north of Caerleon), for his assistance.[92]

Teilo also consecrated many bishops, amongst them his nephew Ismael, whom he sent out to found new churches in the districts he had given them.[93]

Teilo died at Llandeilo Fawr in approximately 580 and there were immediate disputes over where his body should be interred, with the churches of Penally, Llandeilo Fawr and Llandaff all claiming his remains. The *Life* states that to solve this problem, Teilo's body miraculously multiplied by three to satisfy the claims. However, as miracles subsequently attended Teilo's tomb at Llandaff, it was decided that this was his true resting place. His supposed tomb on the south side of the presbytery was opened in 1830 and revealed that it had been opened almost a century before and an inscription dated 1736 left which stated that it was indeed Teilo's tomb.[94]

An interesting tradition associates Teilo with a Llandeilo near Fishguard in Pembrokeshire. In the 1900s Baring-Gould and Fisher described how a piece of skull, reputedly from the saint, was in the possession of the Melchior family who had owned it for generations. Their farmhouse stood near a holy well dedicated to St. Teilo. Water drunk from the skull and administered by the eldest son of the tenant, (another source says by an heir of the Melchior family), would effect a cure, whereas water drunk directly from the well would not. This story has surprising pre-Christian overtones, when severed heads were often associated with sacred wells in the pagan Celtic religion. When the skull fragment was examined in the 1900s it was found to be the brain pan from a young person's skull, and so not from St. Teilo who died in old age. The site still drew people to it as late as 1900 when the waters were considered to cure whooping cough and pulmonary illnesses.[95]

February 9th is St. Teilo's day. There were various relics and a shrine to the saint at Llandaff Cathedral before the Dissolution. There was also a large statue of St. Teilo in one of the niches in Hereford Cathedral's chapter-house which was later destroyed. Teilo is celebrated in the *Triads* as being one of the three 'Blessed Visitors of the Isle of Britain' along with David and Padarn.[96]

Dedications to Teilo in the area under study are Llantilio Crossenny, Llantilio Pertholey and Llanarth in Monmouthshire; Llandeilo'r Fan and Llywel (along with saints Lywel and David) in Breconshire; and Llandeilo Graban in Radnorshire. There are a number of extinct Teilo foundations, mainly out of the area of this study with the exception of Hentland where there was a Teilo church 'in the same cemetery' as a St. Dyfrig church.[9]

St. Cadoc

There appear to have been three individuals of religious note bearing the name Cadoc (also spelt Cadog and Catwg) whose lives have been confounded, leading to inconsistencies and anachronisms in the different accounts of the saint. The three were the son of Brychan, the son of Gwynllyw, and a third who appears as a bishop but is otherwise unknown. The man to whom the legends apply, and with whom we are concerned, is the son of Gwynllyw.[98]

Cadoc was a contemporary of the saints Gildas, Samson, David and Paulinus. He was born in about 497 or shortly afterwards, and killed in about 577. His biography or *Life* was written approximately 500 years later by Lifris (also known as Lifricus or Leofric), the son of Bishop Herwald of Llandaff in the mid to late 11th century. Therefore, as with all the saints' *Lives,* there is considerable scope for alterations and inaccuracies. Lifris' *Life* of Cadoc now exists in a 13th-century manuscript in the British Museum. Another 14th-century *Life* of Cadoc was written by John of Tynemouth who used Lifris' biography as his basis. A *Life* of Cadoc also existed within France, but was lost, although a subsequent biography by Albert le Grand probably used the lost *Life*, as well as other sources.[99]

As with so many of the early saints, Cadoc was not a poor, inspired man but the son and heir to a regional king. There is at least a degree of authenticity in his ancestry which is often lacking with those of other saints. His father was Gwynllyw, king of Gwynllywg in an area of south Wales that borders Monmouthshire. Cadoc's mother was Gwladys, daughter (or possibly the grand-daughter) of Brychan. His parents were later converted to Christianity and the monastic way of life by Cadoc and both became celebrated as saints; Gwynllyw establishing St. Woolo's in Newport. Despite a glowing account of Gwynllyw's deeds in his own *Life*, Cadoc's *Life* describes his criminal methods in garnering his wealth, such as using his guards to rob and plunder. He had even abducted Gwladys from Brychan's court at Talgarth, although some versions say the marriage suit was legally conducted. It was not long after her abduction that Gladwys became pregnant with Cadoc.[100]

At about the age of six or seven Cadoc was sent to Tathan, a hermit, at Caerwent where the latter had a college 'that had been founded by Ynyr, king of that portion of Gwent'. Cadoc stayed there for about 12 years and was schooled in the classics and theology. He soon showed an ability for performing miracles and cursing adversaries. In one example, he was refused fuel by a servant who said, spitefully, that he could only have the live coals that he could carry away; the boy Cadoc thus used the lap of his habit to carry the red hot coals to Tathan, and was unharmed by the act. Cadoc then cursed the servant who was consumed by fire. As the flames died down, the fire was replaced by a fountain and the area became a small marsh as a permanent reminder of the events.[101]

In Albert le Grand's *Life* of Cadoc it is said that the saint's father decided to make war on a neighbouring king after Cadoc had left Tathan and expected his son to lead his men, but Cadoc's devout Christian outlook made him refuse military service. He deserted his homeland and moved into Morganwg where he roamed amongst the marshes which was part of the territory of his uncle, Paul or Pol Penychen, a sub-king. After disturbing a herd of hogs in a valley, Cadoc was threatened by the swineherd and according to Lifris' *Life*, God put the man under a spell, paralysing his right arm and blinding him until he made a representation to Paul, who granted Cadoc the valley of marshy land. Significantly, Paul had offered the rule of his kingdom to Cadoc if he gave up the religious life, but Cadoc refused asking only for the remote valley. The *Life* gives a vivid picture of the site chosen by Cadoc: '... in that valley there was no dry place, it being a watery moor, producing nothing but reeds, and it was full of various kinds of reptiles and snakes ...'. Such a watery wilderness was an approximation of the austere landscape sought by the Desert Fathers. The *Life* reports that an angel appeared to Cadoc and told him that he would find a cleared, level area for an oratory, and he would 'see a bristly white old boar leaping, being affrighted at the noise of thy footsteps; and there thou mayest lay the foundation of thy church in the name of the Holy Trinity; afterwards in the place where the boar will again stop, thou mayest build a dormitory, and again, where, in his progress, he will make a third stopping, there thou mayest construct thy refectory.' The use of a pig in the choice of a site has already been encountered in Dyfrig's *Life*.[102]

Cadoc was joined by others, probably fellow students from Caerwent, and gradually the monastery of Llancarfan was constructed. Cadoc built a large mound of earth 'to make therein a very handsome cemetery, to be dedicated in honour of God, where the bodies of the faithful might be buried near to the church. The mound being completed, and the cemetery also constructed therein, he made, through impassable places, four large footpaths across four declivities of the rising grounds, which surrounded his residence ...'. That the cemetery appears to have been constructed at the same time or even before the monastery may seem unusual, however cemeteries often preceded churches/monasteries at this early date. Baring-Gould and Fisher note that Cadoc's original foundation may have been a little to the south of the present Llancarfan church, in a field that, in the early 20th century, was called The Culnery and in which there were traces of ancient buildings — today only a well survives. At Llanvithyn (about ½mile north of Llancarfan) Cadoc built 'another mound in the form of a round city, and on the mound ... [built] what in the language of the Britons is Kastell Cadoc (The Castle of Cadoc).' Such a fortification perhaps echoes the saint's royal background.[103]

Cadoc left Llancarfan, heading first to Ireland where he studied for three years. He then went to Llanspyddid, west of Brecon and then in the territory of Brychan, to study Latin under Bachan, a celebrated rhetorician from Italy. Brychan subsequently granted Cadoc land at Llanspyddid for a religious foundation. Leaving this in the charge of Bachan, whom he had made abbot, Cadoc returned to Llancarfan where he found his monastery destroyed. There is no explanation for the destruction but Cadoc set about its rebuilding.[104]

It was at about this time that he is also said to have founded a monastery at Llangadog Fawr 9 miles south-west of Llandovery. While there he was troubled by one Sawyl Benuchel whose stronghold was on Pen-y-Ddinas. Sawyl stole Cadoc's supplies of meat and drink and, as Sawyl and his men lay sated over their spoils a little way off on a hilltop, possibly Carn Goch, Cadoc ordered his monks to shave half the hair from their heads and beards and slash off the lips and ears of their horses. If this is an accurate portrayal of Cadoc, it yet again suggests an aggressive, cruel streak, not of a saint full of grace. After this assault 'Cadoc and fifty of his clerics assumed their ecclesiastical vestments, and marched in procession to the hill to meet, and, if possible, to mitigate the resentment of the freebooter'. According to Cadoc's *Life* the earth then opened up and swallowed up Sawyl and his men. Cadoc then sang the *Te Deum* and blessed his men. It has been noted that both the form of the blessing and the 'mutilation of the men and beasts is truly Celtic in character', indicating an early source for the story which certainly pre-dates the 11th-century *Life*. Intriguingly, situated below Pen-y-Ddinas is Llansawel. The church is supposedly dedicated to St. Sawyl Felyn ab Bledri Hir, but it has been suggested that this is the Sawyl who harried Cadoc. Perhaps the local rogue turned saintly in old age.[105]

Cadoc was on good terms with Gildas, the renowned historian and saint. The two men used to visit Steep and Flat Holme in the Severn estuary during Lent for prayer and meditation, broken only by visits to one another.[106] When Cadoc was in Scotland in the late 520s, he left Gildas in charge of Llancarfan. During the year that he was away (though some versions suggest the period was longer), Cadoc reputedly founded a monastery in Strathclyde.

Cadoc is also supposed to have travelled to Rome via Brittany and then on to Jerusalem. It is likely that his visit to Brittany occurred during the outbreak of the Yellow Plague in 547 when many of the saints fled Britain.[107] He has a number of churches dedicated to him in this region.

Over the years Llancarfan became very large and powerful with Cadoc ruling as abbot and prince over a wide area. Many people were fed at Cadoc's tables each day, the numbers being made up of 100 workmen, 100 poor men, 100 widows, 100 clergy and 100 soldiers — indicating that the monastery was not only looking after the weak and the poor, but it was also being defended as a stronghold. Cadoc does not appear to typify the modern idea of an early monk and saint who would meet aggressors with a crucifix; from his retinue it would seem that Cadoc would meet them at the head of a small army. Llancarfan was renowned for its scholarship and learning and, being close to the south coast of Wales, had good communications with Brittany and Ireland.[108]

Cadoc was out of the country when the Synod of Llanddewi Brefi took place and was enraged that it had been conducted in his absence. He was even more infuriated that David had been given such prominence and determined to 'fast against' this saint, only abandoning such action when it was shown that 'his conduct was contrary to the principles of Christian charity'.[109] Because of this animosity, one wonders whether there was some earlier rivalry between the kingdoms belonging to the fathers of Cadoc and David of which we have no record.

Cadoc appears to have had considerable secular power. Three of King Arthur's soldiers were allegedly killed by one Lawhir who sought sanctuary with Cadoc, who kept him for seven years. This was an extraordinarily long time and went against custom. As a result, David, Teilo and Dochu (possibly Oudoceus), together with other clergymen and judges, were called to mediate between Cadoc and Arthur on the banks of the River Usk. A proposal of one hundred cows per man in compensation was accepted, 'for from ancient times the judgement among the Britons was of this kind'. However Arthur insisted the cows should be of banded colour, red at the front and white at the back, which arrangement Cadoc achieved by a miracle. The cows were then driven into the Usk and Arthur's men, Kai and Bedwyn, drew them by their horns to the river bank, where they immediately changed into bundles of fern. On seeing this Arthur begged pardon from Cadoc for his insulting behaviour and granted the saint the right of refuge of seven years, seven months and seven days. The cows were subsequently found safely in the stalls of their owners. The site of the meeting has been identified with Tredunnock, 'fern homestead', and the ford as Rhyd Gwrthebau, 'Ford of Responses'. (See Tredunnock in the gazetteer).[110]

King Maelgon (Maelgwn, King of Gwynedd who died of the Yellow Plague in about 560), sent troops to collect tribute from Cadoc's steward, and also abducted the steward's daughter. Cadoc's neighbourhood was thrown into turmoil by this behaviour and he assembled a force to pursue and attack Maelgwn's troops, killing some and injuring many more. Maelgwn reacted by marching to the borders of Gwynllwyg, intending to lay waste to it. Cadoc was alerted and went to intercede: 'a pillar of a cloud preceded him, which also covering all the tents ... and the day was as a dark night to them, so that no one was able to see another. Then in the middle of the darkness, the holy man appeared before the tent of the king'. Not surprisingly Maelgwn was compliant, asked forgiveness and proceeded to ratify the refuge which had been granted by Arthur and announced that he had chosen Cadoc as his confessor 'before all others ... among South Wales men'.[111]

Cadoc's *Life* tells us that Maelgwn never again offended the saint and even warned his son, Rhun, who habitually thieved on a large scale, to keep clear of Cadoc and his people. However, whilst out on a plundering spree in his area, some of Rhun's men tried to burn down the saint's barn because the steward had refused them a drink of milk. On hearing it was Cadoc's property, Rhun, who had been playing dice in his tent with his eunuchs, was sent blind by the smoke from the barn which had miraculously drifted straight into his tent. He sent for Cadoc and made his apologies and his eyesight was restored. Rhun increased the refuge already granted and gave Cadoc his messenger, as well his own sword, spear and shield. Cadoc subsequently gave the sword to the ruler of Glamorgan 'with half part of the fish of the river Usk, that he [Cadoc] might have seven of them for food during Lent at Llancarvan'. He also gave the messenger's horse with its trappings to the king for 'one half the fish of the river Neath, so that he might have at Llanmaes during every Lent both boiled and roast food and provisions.' Whether true, it shows that Cadoc's biographer was not afraid to show the saint as a bargainer.[112]

Cadoc was so revered in his father's kingdom that in later years when another Rhun, this time the son of Brychan, had laid waste to Gwynllywg and had been subsequently defeated in a series of battles, no-one dared execute him as he was a nephew to Cadoc; the latter secured his release and gave him refuge. It is said that after his father's time, Cadoc appointed a regent, Meurig, for the kingdom of Gwynllwg, but details of this are confused.[113]

It is possible that in old age Cadoc returned, with other saints, to Ireland in about 564 to help King Ainmire revive Christianity, and was in turn granted land there on the banks of the river Liffey. Cadoc returned to Llancarfan. After about ten years he decided to retire and placed Elli, his disciple, as the new abbot with instructions that he should report to him annually. Lifris' *Life* has Cadoc being taken off in a white cloud from Llancarfan 'and immediately in the twinkling of an eye descended from the cloud in the city of *Beneventum* ...'. Cadoc was re-named Sophias by this community 'for they saw that he was full of divine wisdom, and because it was by that name, it was before ordered by the angel that he should be called.'[114]

The location of *Beneventum* is something of a mystery. It has been variously identified with the place in Southern Italy of the same name; *Benevenna* (Weedon) in Northamptonshire; Caerwent in Gwent; or Llanspyddid near Brecon. Baring-Gould and Fisher observe that it is unlikely that Cadoc, who was overcome with age, would have travelled so far to Southern Italy, and, significantly, add that there is no record of Cadoc being bishop or martyr in the 6th century at that Italian church. They also remark that Cadoc would not have expected Elli to have travelled that far to present an annual report. Of Weedon in Northamptonshire this is most unlikely location as it was part of the embryonic and pagan Mercian kingdom which would not have welcomed a British cleric. Caerwent is perhaps a possible contender considering Cadoc's schooling there under Tathan, yet no tradition connects Cadoc and his death with Caerwent.[115]

Llanspyddid near Brecon does have several aspects to recommend it. Close by is the Roman town of Y Gaer which has been identified with *Bannium*, although some have identified this latter with Abergavenny (*Gobannium*). In relation to Y Gaer, Baring-Gould and Fisher observe that the hill on which the Roman town is sited is called Y Fenni, and the wood on its slope is named Coed Fenni, whilst the farm beneath is Fenni Fach and postulate that the ancient name may have been *Bannium* or *Benni* with the addition of *Venta* or *Ventum* which is descriptive of bare uplands. In an ancient source King Brychan of Brycheiniog is said to have been born at *Benni* and, in the early 19th century, the name Caer Bannau was used for what is now simply known as Y Gaer.[116]

However Henken observes that Baring-Gould and Fisher's reasoning does not allow for any imagination in the story or in its embellishments, and that they have taken the story too literally by seeking historical locations. Another historian, Hywel D. Emanuel, while accepting the *Beneventum* story is a fabrication, attempts to understand why Cadoc's biographer, Lifris, would want his saint connected with an Italian monastery. In the 11th century the Benedictine monasteries of Benevento, and particularly Monte Cassino, were renowned for their learning; by making Cadoc head of Benevento in the 6th century, Lifris would have been 'claiming for him the primacy over a province which had developed by Lifris' own day into the acknowledged centre of western European learning.'[117]

If we discount the *Beneventum* story as propaganda and accept that Cadoc was seeking retirement, a small, quiet location would have been sought, and the monastery at Llanspyddid, where Cadoc had been happy as a young man, seems the most likely location. The peace did not long, however, because an invading force overran the place, killing and plundering in their wake. One of the horsemen entered the church and killed Cadoc who was at the altar. This occurred in about 577. Such an action has the flavour of a pagan action and Anglo-Saxon forces were making headway in western areas at this time. Cadoc was initially buried on site and a church built over his sepulchre. Initially Britons were not allowed to enter the settlement as its citizens were concerned that they would remove Cadoc's remains and put an end to the attendant miracles. In time this was relaxed and monks from Llancarfan were allowed to take Cadoc's body for burial. However even Llancarfan was not safe as a marauding band drove the monks out and they fled with the saint's remains to *Mammeliat*, which Rees has been identified with Mamhilad in Monmouthshire (see gazetteer).[118]

During his lifetime Cadoc was one of the leading figures in the early British monastic movement, heading a monastery which, at its largest, reputedly held 2,000 brethren and was renowned for its teachings. Indeed, it was one of Cadoc's regrets that, although he greatly admired Virgil's works, he would never meet the pagan poet in heaven.[119] Llancarfan was well-positioned on the Roman road system which encouraged communication within Britain and abroad. It eventually became part of the bishopric of Llandaff.

St. Padarn

Padarn's *Life* was written up in the early 13th century, about 600 years after he lived. The original was written in Wales and possibly contains elements which pre-date 720. As such it may include genuine historical tradition. However an ecclesiastic in Vannes in France came across the *Life* and altered and adapted it for polemical reasons. Padarn has thus been confounded with Paternus, first bishop of Vannes (in Brittany) and Bishop Paternus of Avranches (552–65) which latter is roughly contemporary with the Welsh Padarn.[120]

St. Padarn was born of a noble family in the late 5th/early 6th century and died in about 550. He was born in Brittany: his father was Petran and his mother Guean. His uncles were obliged to leave Brittany, probably because of the political ambitions of one of them which misfired. They married the daughters of King Meurig ab Tewdrig of Morganwg, although Padarn's father had married Geuan earlier in Britanny.[121]

Padarn's father left his wife and the baby Padarn and, joining holy orders, travelled to Britain and then to Ireland to follow the holy life. From an early age Padarn was inquisitive about his missing father and chose to copy his devotion by following the Church from the earliest opportunity. Padarn's mother was also of a strong religious persuasion but she missed her husband's company. As soon as Padarn was old enough, he left Brittany in the company of several monks on a mission to Britain in order to find his father and ask that he return to his mother, although this departure may also have been necessary because of political difficulties. The mission was headed by St. Cadfan.[122]

On arriving in Britain Padarn was reputedly trained at Llantwit Major under St. Illtud and then travelled to Llanbadarn Fawr, now a suburb of Aberystwyth, where he became head of a monastery of reputedly 847 monks. (Another document refers to just 120 monks. The reality is that no-one can be sure of the numbers of monks that inhabited the large monastic foundations.) Padarn then visited his father in Ireland but was unable to persuade him to return to his mother. During this visit Padarn was called upon to make peace between two warring kings in which in reputedly succeeded merely by the 'grace of his countenance'. On his return from Ireland Padarn 'built monasteries and churches throughout the region of Ceredigion ... [and] became a lamp in doctrine and practice throughout Britain.'[123]

Padarn's main work, however, centred on Llanbadarn Fawr which became an important centre of learning in Wales, akin to monasteries in south-eastern Wales. It was probably a short-lived diocese in its own right (which was incor-

St. Padarn as depicted in stained glass

porated with that of St. David's soon after 720) and extended for 125,000 acres and encompassed the western part of Radnorshire, part of Breconshire (north of the River Ithon) and the northern half of Cardiganshire.[124]

Padarn is reported to have lived in Wales for 21 years and ruled over three churches: Llanbadarn Fawr, Agam's Cross, which has been identified with Llangorwen (2 miles north-east of Aberystwyth), and a solitary retreat identified with Nant y Mynech in Snowdonia. Padarn is said to have stayed for seven years at each place.[125]

According to his *Life*, St. Padarn had dealings with the King Maelgwn of Gwynedd who is described as 'the great tempter of the saints'. He ordered his two heralds to 'try Saint Padarn in some malicious manner'. They therefore filled their bags with moss and gravel and took these to Padarn and, pretending they were filled with the king's treasure, asked if they could leave them in Padarn's safe-keeping. The saint obliged. Sometime later the heralds returned and, taking up the bags and emptying them, 'saucily exclaimed that the royal treasure had been stolen and gravel and moss had been put in their place'. After threatening ruin on the whole building if the treasure was not restored, Padarn protested, saying the bags had not been touched and suggested trial by boiling water to prove his innocence. He was unharmed when he placed his hands into a boiling cauldron, unlike the heralds who were scalded and died with their souls fleeing 'in the form of ravens over the channel, which unto this day is called by the name one of them, that is Graban.' Maelgwn was struck blind and laid so low with illness that he begged Padarn's pardon for the affront, which Padarn granted and also restored the king's eyesight. Maelgwn then granted the saint land between the rivers Rheidol and Clarach.[126]

Tradition has it that Padarn, with St. David and St. Teilo, visited Jerusalem some time after the Maelgwn incident and that they were received by the patriarch and ordained. Padarn received a tunic (also referred to as a choral cape) in recognition of his beautiful singing voice and also a staff as gifts, (the staff was a sign of episcopal jurisdiction). When the three saints returned to Britain they supposedly divided south Wales into three dioceses between them. Different accounts of this Jerusalem visit occur in the separate *Lives* of all three saints and it is likely that the legend was fabricated later at St. David's to help it obtain primacy from Canterbury. The inserted version in Padarn's *Life* appears to postdate that in St. David's *Life* and was done in order to attempt to restore the see of Llanbadarn Fawr after it had been merged with St. David's, following a period of civil unrest when the inhabitants of Llanbadarn Fawr had murdered their bishop. This merger happened after 720 and Baring-Gould and Fisher note that as there is no mention or indication of Llanbadarn Fawr being merged with St. David's in the legend of the saint, this suggests the presence of a very early, pre-720 Welsh *Life* which was used when the post-Conquest *Life* was compiled.[127]

Padarn's servant was murdered in woods near the Aberystwyth Llanbadarn monastery and, on finding the man's decapitated corpse, Padarn restored the head to the body and brought the man back to life — an example one suspects of a later medieval embellishment which served to display the saint's miraculous powers. The servant's murderers were in the charge of Eithir who governed the area, and as compensation Padarn was granted land free from any tribute between the rivers Rheidol and Paith extending to the coast. In the spirit of Christian forgiveness Padarn told Eithir that he would be 'honourably buried in the cemetery of this place, where thy solemnity will be for ever celebrated by this community'.[128]

Padarn does seem to have been quite a 'human' saint, as evidenced by the following story in his *Life*. St. Samson, Padarn's first cousin, when visiting Padarn's monastery near Guenot (France), was advised by a malicious monk to order Padarn to present himself immediately as a token of submission. The monk presumably thought that Padarn would refuse or meet Samson in his own time, whereas Padarn rushed to meet Samson half-shod as he was in the middle of dressing. The monk sneered and was immediately struck down dead but was revived by Samson who was touched by Padarn's obedience and from then on permanently relieved Padarn's diocese of any taxes due to him.[129] The story gives a glimpse of Padarn as a person who is overjoyed at seeing his relative and does not feel that he had to stand upon ceremony.

According to the *Life*, Padarn had dealings with the legendary King Arthur whilst at Llanbadarn Fawr near Aberystwyth. It was here that Arthur, who is described as 'a certain tyrant' demanded the cape (tunic) which Padarn had received as a gift from his trip to Jerusalem, but Padarn refused him, saying that the cloak was only for the use of those in holy orders. Arthur departed angrily but returned a while later raging at the monastery but was swallowed up to his neck in earth and was forced to ask Padarn's pardon, which was given and Arthur was released. He then accepted 'Padarn for his perpetual patron' and departed in peace. An entrenchment called Llys Arthur was noted by Rees in the mid-19th century in Llanbadarn parish. Interestingly, Arthur is often portrayed in the *Lives* of the Welsh saints in such unflattering tones, quite unlike the heroic character he became in the later medieval romances. As Baring-Gould and Fisher observe, the fact that he is portrayed as 'wholly without heroic qualities [shows] that the *Life* was composed before Geoffrey of Monmouth had thrown a false glamour over this rather disreputable prince.' Padarn died in about 550 and was said by Elgar the Hermit to be buried on Bardsey Island.[130]

St. Beuno

The *Life* of St Beuno is extant in a 1346 manuscript written at Llanddewi Brefi by an anchorite. Written in Welsh, and found in Jesus College MS. 119, it is a paraphrase or abbreviated translation of a lost Latin *Life* of unknown date and, so embodies traditions which are much earlier.[131]

Beuno was the major saint of north Wales, and his work comparable to that of St. David in the south. However, his early days lay in eastern Wales. His father was Bugi and his mother Peren (also spelt Beren or Perfferen). There appears to have been a close family relationship to St. Cadoc, with some sources claiming Cadoc was cousin to Beuno. The *Life* states that Beuno's parents lived at 'Banhenig' near to the River Severn in Powys. The identity of 'Banhenig' has not been established, but Trelystan (3 miles south-east of Welshpool) has been suggested. Just north-east of Trelystan church and on a scarp is Badnage Wood (earlier called *Badnich*) and, within the chapelry, is a dingle called Cwm yr Henog. Another case has been made for Llanymynech (about 11 miles north of Trelystan) which has a St. Bennion's Well.[132]

Bugi and Peren are described 'inoffensive persons, and their lives were virtuous'. They were also aged and childless until one evening they were instructed by an angel to have intercourse which would result in a son being born. Thus was Beuno conceived, probably in the later 6th century. When old enough he was sent for his education to Caerwent and, following that, he took holy orders and became a clergyman. The king of Gwent, Ynyr, became a follower and gave Beuno three estates in Eywas (the western part of Herefordshire). Beuno built a church on the lands given to him at Llanveynoe, near Longtown. Beuno lived there for a while with his followers, but left three of them in charge of the place on being called away to his father who was gravely ill. After his father's death the *Life* states that

Beuno established a church in his father's township and lived there for a while. It is said that Beuno planted an acorn by the side of his father's grave which grew into an 'oak of great size, height, and of a fine form, and on that tree grew a branch which reached the ground, and from the ground again upwards as high as the boughs of the tree, and there was a part of this branch in the ground, as it is at present [14th century]; and if an Englishman should go between that branch and the body of the tree, he would immediately die, but should a Welshman go, he would be nothing worse.' It shows that the anti-English sentiment was raw when this *Life* was written. However there is also a tradition that all trees growing on St. Beuno's land were sacred and to fell any would bring about the death or grievous harm of the perpetrator. It is a tradition repeated by Leland in the mid-16th century. Henken observes that Beuno's trees 'are here protected by the same threats as protect the fairy trees, and it may well be that it was in the beliefs concerning fairy trees that Beuno's tradition started.' Interestingly he is the saint most associated with the miracle of 'a staff sprouting and growing into a tree.'[133]

Beuno was also granted land at Berriew by Mawn, brother to King Brochwel of Powys. His establishment there was large, as testified by the size of churchyard around the existing Victorian church (see gazetteer). A stone called Maen Beuno stands at SJ 203 013 and is said to mark the spot where the saint preached. Legend has it that this was Beuno's first pulpit and that the incised cross on the stone was sketched there by the saint with his thumb.[134]

The *Life* records that whilst at Berriew and out travelling by the River Severn, Beuno heard 'a voice on the other side of the river, inciting dogs to hunt a hare, being that of an Englishman … And when Beino heard the voice … he immediately returned, and coming to his disciples, said to them, "My sons, put on your clothes and your shoes, and let us leave this place, for the nation of this man has a strange language, and is abominable … they have invaded this place, and it will be theirs, and they will keep it in their possession."' These were incoming Anglo-Saxons which puts the xenophobia in some context — although it is probably more of a comment by the Welsh biographer of the contemporary post-Conquest political situation than an accurate reflection of events in the late 6th/early 7th centuries. Beuno left one of his disciples in charge of Berriew, giving him his cross, and departed for Meifod, where he stayed with St. Tysilio. Receiving a grant of land there from Cynan, Brochwel's son, he is said to have founded a church. The churchyard and precincts at Meifod are very large, much greater than at Berriew, and tradition has it that there were three churches or foundations (see gazetteer). There may well have been some tension between the two saints at Meifod, but, if so, this was relieved when Cynan granted land at Gwyddelwern, 3 miles north of Corwen, to Beuno, who moved there and founded a church. This establishment should have worked well but Cynan's grandsons (erroneously termed nephews in the *Life*) arrived and imperiously demanded food and cajoled

Beuno into killing a young ox. It was likely that the youths were claiming food and shelter as a right which could be applied to secular households but from which the churchmen felt themselves exempt. The meat would not cook and the youths claimed the saint had bewitched the food. This angered Beuno who laid a strong curse upon them. As Baring-Gould and Fisher remark pertinently 'Verily, it was a risky thing to interfere with these old Celtic saints, who wielded the keys of the kingdom of Heaven in a very arbitrary fashion.' Nevertheless Beuno still felt it expedient to leave the area, heading to the banks of the river Dee to seek another site, but failed to find one. It is possible that the youths had petitioned their elders to refuse the saint's requests.[135]

It is then that Beuno left Powys for good. He travelled to Flintshire in the kingdom of Gwynedd and approached a chieftain called Temic, son of Eliud, who gave him land on which to build a church. Beuno spent the rest of his life in north-west Wales founding several churches and monasteries, notably that of Clynnog, 9 miles south-west of Caernarfon.

Beuno is unique among the Welsh saints in that he is reputed to have raised at least six people from the dead. Amongst them was his niece, St. Winifred, who had been beheaded. We might concede that he was respected as a healer for such legends to exist.

The year of his death is not given, but 642 has been suggested as Low Sunday, the day on which Beuno reputedly died, fell on 21 April in that year, and it is in keeping with the chronology of his association with King Ynyr of Gwent and Cynan of Powys. There is a tradition that after his death a dispute arose between the churches of Clynnog, Nevern and Bardsey as to who should bury his remains. During the altercation the whole assembly fell asleep and, on awakening, they found three identical coffins. Each party was satisfied, but as late as 1849 it was still believed in Clynnog that the original body of the saint was buried in the parish.[136]

Montgomeryshire

BERRIEW – St. Beuno
(SJ 187 008)

The presence of the yews, the shape and size of the churchyard and the hagiographical link to St. Beuno are evidence of this being an early foundation.

St. Beuno's church lies at the centre of Berriew, 5 miles south-west of Welshpool. The early history of Berriew has been mentioned in the biography of St. Beuno (see p.69). Briefly it is said that one of the princes of Powys gave land at Berriew to Beuno to establish a church and this was for a while the saint's early home.[1] In the first half of the 7th century he heard the voice of a Saxon huntsman on the other side of the River Rhiw and, fearing the place was going to be taken over, he left Berriew. St. Beuno was one of the most important saints of north Wales, to the extent that he is sometimes compared to St. David in the south.

The church at Berriew was rebuilt during the 19th century. The fairly large, sub-oval churchyard has curving boundaries. Sections to the south are walled, but to the north the boundary is formed by the back of timber-framed buildings, which includes the Lion Hotel. This is a good example of pressure on land within an important centre and the desire to live as close to the church as possible. The houses bordering the churchyard appear to be of early 1600s date onwards, but they are likely to be replacements for earlier structures. The churchyard is raised by up to 6½ feet to the south above the lane that borders it, and is raised on the other sides to a lesser degree. The churchyard is fairly flat and would have allowed room for further buildings within the enclosure. There are also old yews to the south-east and in the south-western corner, two on the western boundary close to the River Rhiw and another yew north of the church.[2]

A glacial boulder on the north side of the west path in the churchyard apparently marks 'the meeting point of the three townships of Berriew, Cil and Lower Vaynor.'[3]

Part of the curving and raised churchyard enclosure

BETTWS CEDEWAIN –
St. Beuno (SO 123 968)

A probable early St. Beuno foundation, with a near-circular churchyard, set dramatically on a hill top.

St. Beuno's church at Bettws Cedewain is about 3½ miles north-north-east of Newtown town centre. It was probably once a capella or subservient church to Berriew, Beuno's main foundation in the area.[1] It is reputed to have been founded by the saint and the location of the churchyard and its form indicate an early medieval date.[2] It is likely that St. Beuno established it during the early part of his life, before moving further into Wales to Clynnog.

The structure of the church is late, the tower being completed in the 16th century and the chancel and nave were reconstructed in 1868, although it is possible some medieval masonry was retained in the north wall. The church is on a hill and is reminiscent of a defensive site, for which it would be eminently suitable. At some time between 1254 and 1272 it was one of the appropriated churches of Strata Marcella monastery, and once it belonged to Llanllugan monastery, (see p.95).[3]

The churchyard is of medium size, markedly curvilinear and slopes to the south. It is raised by about 3½ feet to the north-west and east, as much as 10 feet to the west and there is a drop of about 33 feet to the valley of the Bechan Brook on the southern side.[4]

The village buildings to the south are grouped as near as possible to the church, as at Berriew. They do not form the boundary on this occasion but their backyards and accesses abut the boundary. The centre of the village borders about half of the churchyard and is highly nucleated and gives the impression of great age and cohesion.

CARNO – St. John the Baptist
(SN 963 965)

The church contains an early inscribed stone.

The inscribed stone

Situated approximately 12 miles west-north-west of Newtown, the church of St. John the Baptist was completely rebuilt in 1867. There is no record of an early or Celtic dedication and indications are that it was set up by the Knights Hospitaller in the early 13th century, but whether they founded a church from new or replaced an earlier church is not known.[1] Thomas Pennant states that the church 'belonged to the knights of St. John of Jerusalem, who are said to have had a house near it. As one part of their business was the protection of their fellow creatures from violence, it is very possible that they might have had a station in these parts, which were long filled with a lawless banditti.'[2] It is thought likely that the earthwork of Caer Noddfa next to the church was the grange established by the Knights.[3]

There is an early inscribed stone in the west end of the church, nearly 5 feet tall, 1½ feet wide and 6 inches deep. It was found in 1960 about two-thirds of a mile north-north-west of the church at SN 958 973, being used as a gatepost. Its proximity to a location called Capel Peniel on a 1963 Ordnance Survey map has been noted, 'Capel' suggesting a possible early church which is now lost.[4] The stone is dated to between the 7th to 9th centuries[5] and is inscribed with a simple stylised circular cross with crude linear decoration within the circle. It is roughly shaped and is crooked at the base, and has a couple of sockets or holes a few inches in diameter in the front surface. This stone suggests an early Christian foundation within the vicinity of the church.

GUILSFIELD – St. Aelhaiarn
(SJ 192 165)

Dedication evidence, coupled with the evidence of two wells, one unusual, suggest an early site.

Haslam states that Guilsfield (3 miles north of Welshpool) has 'Architecturally one of the richest medieval church interiors in the county',[1] a richly deserved accolade. The repaired medieval roof timbers are admirable, the Tudor panelled ceiling over the chancel especially so.

The church is dedicated to the 7th-century St. Aelhaiarn who was brother to saints Llwchaiarn and Cynhaiarn. Their father was Hygarfael, a regional prince of Powys in the Shrewsbury area, and who was probably based in Llanerfyl parish, several miles west of Guilsfield. The church was, in the past, dedicated to Tysilio as a result of it being under the authority of the *clas* church of Meifod, and also to St. Giles (culled from the parish name of Guilsfield, which itself derives from the Welsh *cegidfa* meaning 'the hemlock field'), and to All Saints. Aelhaiarn was a pupil of St. Beuno. There is another church dedication to him at Llanaelhaiarn in Merionethshire which was subservient to Gwyddelwern, Beuno's church. It is therefore to be expected that his parish at Guilsfield would come under Meifod's jurisdiction as Beuno remained there for a while. In similar vein, when Beuno finally left Powys, Aelhaiarn accompanied him and set up another church near Beuno's main monastery at Clynnog.[2]

Beuno was wont to walk four miles to pray on a stone in a river, and Aelhaiarn followed him one day out of curiosity only to be torn to pieces by wild beasts. St. Beuno 'gathering up his Bones, and praying, he set Bone to Bone, and Limb to Limb, and the Man became whole again, only the part of the Bone under the Eyebrow was wanting; the Saint, to supply that Defect, applied the Iron of his Pike-staff to the Place ...'.[3] This is why Aelhaiarn is also sometimes known as 'the saint with an iron eyebrow'.

The earliest written record of the church is in a taxation record of 1254 when the church was valued at the low rate of £2 as it was dependent on the church at Llandrinio, but by 1291 the value had risen dramatically to £20 by when it may well have become independent.[4] The church is recorded as '*Cap'lla de Kegidua*' and '*Ecclia de Beygidia* (Kegydia)' respectively, names which, interestingly, bear no relation to St. Aelhaiarn. Pennant tells us that in the late 18th century the church was known as St. Giles, and at one time belonged to Strata Marcella abbey.[5]

The churchyard is rectangular in shape and has distinctive curved corners and is raised by about 3½ feet or more above the exterior ground level. It is fairly level and has 22 mature yew trees running around the boundary (with the oldest to the south) which might suggest an early medieval site — however a document exists that refers to the planting of yews in the late 17th/early 18th century. In addition, a grave exists under one of the oldest trees by the southern path commemorating a Richard Jones who died in 1707, aged 90 'who had planted the yew with his father.'[6]

St. Aelhaiarn's well is at the roadside. Baring-Gould and Fisher described it in the early 20th century as 'an oblong trough of good pure water ... in which the sick were wont to bathe, and there are seats of stone ranged along the sides for the accommodation of the patients awaiting the "troubling of the waters", when they might step in, full of confidence, in expectation of a cure.' The 'troubling of the waters' is explained as the sudden but irregular welling up of 'the crystal water ... full of sparkling bubbles' followed by a lull and a welling up elsewhere in the tank. In 1900, following a diphtheria outbreak in the village, the well was walled round and roofed over. It was also locked and made inaccessible by the Parish Council.[7]

Francis Jones records another holy well in Guilsfield Without parish called Trinity Well where, as late as 1910, people visited on Trinity Sunday and drank

The interior of the church

water sweetened with brown sugar — white sugar was not acceptable. Earlier still people from Meifod, Llandyssilio and Welshpool gathered around the well on Trinity Sunday to sing hymns.[8] Although it cannot be proven that these wells were hallowed in the early medieval period it is likely they have a long history, possibly stretching back into prehistory. A healing well, and particularly one that behaves unusually such as Guilsfield's well, would have not been unnoticed by early man. Wells with a tradition of healing and or divination are more likely to have pagan associations — we know that the Iron Age Celts set much store in them and it was only a matter of time before they were Christianised.

LLANDINAM – St. Llonio
(SO 026 886)

Evidence of an early site from the dedication, the topography of the site and a general sense of place indicate this was an early site of importance.

Llandinam is about 4½ miles south-west of Newtown. The church of St. Llonio is situated dramatically on a spur of land at the top of the sloping river terrace above the Severn, and is to the north-west edge of the settlement. It is claimed that a church was founded here as early as 520 and that it became a *clas* foundation and still had its own abbot until the late 13th century. It was the mother church of Llanwnog and Llanidloes, but in a taxation record of 1254 it is given a surprisingly low value of £1 6s. 8d., which rather belies its *clas* or mother church status.[1] However, even with the shortest of visits, the presence of this place works into the memory. Its impressively elevated position and general topography speak of an early and important history. It is interesting that Baring-Gould and Fisher equate the 'Dinam' element of the placename with the Breton word 'Dinan' meaning 'a little fortress'.[2] This is an excellent description of the site which would have made a superlative defensive position.

The church was restored in 1864–5 when most of the walls were rebuilt. Only the north wall of the chancel was left which may date to the 13th century, as may the tower.[3]

The titular saint, St. Llonio, or Llonio Lawhir ('Long-i'-the-Arm) had two brothers who were also saints, Lleuddad and Llyfab. He was born in Brittany and came to Wales with Saints Cadfan, Padarn and others. According to the somewhat dubious Iolo Manuscripts, St. Llonio was a monk of Bangor Illtud, which places him at Llantwit Major, and later a monk at Bardsey; he also became a confessor to St. Padarn at Llanbadarn Fawr. A 16th-century ode to Llonio is found in the Llanstephan Manuscript 53 in which the poet, Huw Arwystli, recalls how he was asleep one May Eve in the church at Llandinam when he, a 'poor despised cripple', was endowed with the gift of poetry. Through this medium of poetry he relates the legend of St. Llonio, recalling how the saint in his early life helped his father fight the pagans 'with great slaughter', but afterwards became a 'righteous confessor' and leaving his homeland settled on a 'delightsome hill on the verdant bank of the Severn' at Llandinam. One Gwrai, whom Baring-Gould and Fisher consider was the son of Gildas, granted Llonio land 'as far as the cock-crow travelled in circumference' and Llonio proceeded to light a fire to denote his possession. He was subsequently granted further land by Maelgwyn Hir (thought to be Maelgwn Gwynedd, the king of Gwynedd who often fell foul of the saints) which extended along the River Severn to Abermule (about 10 miles to the north-east), and was, thus, quite an extensive area. From this a small area

The view from the churchyard

was granted to Gwrai by Llonio who then 'set the bounds of the remainder for his sanctuary' at Llandinam where he stayed for a considerable length of time. The date of his death is unknown and the only church that is certainly dedicated to him is at Llandinam. The church of Aberhafesp (about 4 miles due north-east) is sometimes ascribed to him, but the usual ascription is to St. Gwynog of Llangwnog, son of Gildas. However Baring-Gould and Fisher point out that Aberhafesp's church may be a Llonio dedication as it was part of the land granted to the saint by Maelgwn and was part of the ecclesiastical district 'which owned Llandinam as the mother church.'[4]

The churchyard at Llandinam is fairly large and of a long, triangular shape which slopes south and is determined by the spur of land on which it is built, although the enclosed area is raised above the surrounding land in some places. High Welsh hills rise on all sides except due north which is part of the flat river valley. The north-west boundary is many feet above the adjoining land, although the slope of the ground accentuates this. A modern extension has been added to the north-eastern side and the old boundary can be seen clearly as a grassy bank, several feet high and partly lined with trees. When an entrance was cut through this bank within recent years an archaeological watching brief was conducted and found 'clean clay deposits overlain by modern dumping'. To the south-west of the churchyard a scarp drop of about 3½ feet exists which may be the remains of an earlier boundary, near which is an ancient yew, conservatively claimed to be 800 years old. There is another large yew tree to the north-west of the church. Very close to the south-west of the church is another scarp which 'represents the edge of the platform on which the church is located.'[5]

LLANDRINIO – St. Trinio, St. Peter and St. Paul (SJ 295 170)

A dedication to an early saint, a large churchyard and two incised stones suggest a pre-Norman site of some importance.

Llandrinio is 6 miles south of Oswestry and is set in a flat, pastoral landscape. It is dedicated to the saints Trinio, Peter and Paul. The latter two were added in 1309 when King Edward II granted Llandrinio a three-day fair on the feast day of St. Peter and St. Paul[1] — 29 June, which is also the feast day of St. Trinio. Very little is known of the putative founder, St. Trinio or Trunio. He was first cousin to St. Padarn, St. Samson and St. Cadfan, and it is thought that he travelled to Britain from Brittany in the company of the latter. If so he pre-dates St. David, St. Teilo, St. Melangell and St. Beuno. We are therefore perhaps looking at the approximate years of 475 to 550 for the foundation of this church. Trinio has no other dedications, otherwise the only potential information is in a tale related by Walter Mapp. This concerns a person whose name is doubtfully read as Trinio Faglog who lived in the 5th century near Llyn Syfaddon (the town that was, according to legend, lost under what is now Llangors Lake, see p.209) near Brecon and whose mother was reputedly a fairy.[2]

The church is mentioned in a taxation record of 1254 where it is called '*Ecca de Llantneio*' and had a low value of £2, although it was referred to as having dependent chapelries at Llandysilio, Welshpool and Guilsfield (itself an indication of former high status). In 1291 it had risen in value quite dramatically to £9 and was called '*Ecclia de Landrineaw*'.[3]

The present church is of several different styles and dates. It probably began as a small single-celled structure consisting only of a nave in the present chancel, with extensions added westwards during the Norman and later periods. The building is of interest to the enthusiast as it shows several periods of building.

The churchyard covers approximately 3 acres, is very flat and lies just west of, and very close to, the River Severn. It is possible that the churchyard covered 5 acres at one time, which would have made it as extensive as that at Meifod, because 2 acres of glebeland (the land devoted to the upkeep of the incumbent e.g. vicar of the parish) was separated some time before 1683. It is suggested that this land was on the other side of the present main road when the shape of the churchyard would have been curvilinear, whereas it is now polygonal.[4] Clwyd-Powys Archaeological Trust suggest that a 'supposed Dark Age sanctuary' is attested by the abnormally large size of the churchyard.[5] Certainly the enclosure's size suggests this was once a very important religious site. It is raised by about 1 foot to the east and by about 1½ feet to the west. West of the actual church the ground level rises somewhat but whether this is a natural or man-made feature is uncertain. However there is a faint scarp on the southern side which might be the remains of an earlier boundary. There are also several mature yews on the north and western sides of the church which form a semi-circle[6] — again signifying an early site.

Inside the church are two pieces of a broken stone, probably a sculptured cross-slab, with a suggested date of the 9th or early 10th century. One piece on the inside of the east wall of the porch has had its main face worked away and was reused for an inscription of 1729 — the intact areas show upright bands of decoration incorporating angular key patterns and plaits.[7] The second piece is built into the north wall of the church and shows a similar design. The original site of the cross-slab is not known, although the reworking of the stone in the early 18th century suggests it was on the site.

In the parish there is the Trinity Well where, in common with several other parishes in the vicinity, it was customary to drink sugared water on Trinity Sundays. There was also a Bennion's well within the parish, which is probably linked to St. Beuno.[8]

LLANERFYL – St. Erfyl
(SJ 035 097)

The home of a very ancient yew and an early Christian gravestone commemorating a 13-year-old girl.

Llanerfyl is 5 miles north-west of Llanfair Caereineon. The church was rebuilt in 1870, with some of the 14th-century roof structure and other 15th-century structural elements remaining within the church.

St. Erfyl was reputedly the daughter of St. Padarn, which again demonstrates the fact that early clergy were not celibate. She was a contemporary of St. David, living during the first half of the 6th century. However it has been suggested that she was a relative of St. Cadfan, but this is supposition based on one interpretation of the inscription on the early Christian gravestone (see below). To add to any potential confusion, her name is variously spelt. Little is known of her history, and Llanerfyl is the only dedication to her, so she may have been sedentary as was St. Melangell.[1]

The early gravestone has been dated to the 5th or early 6th century by Nash-Williams, and to the 4th to 5th century by Leslie Alcock.[2] It bears the following interrupted or worn inscription in Latin: HIC(IN) TUM-(U)LO IA/CIT R(U)STE/ECE FILIA PA/TERNINI AN(N)I(S) XIII IN PA(CE).[3] This translates approximately to 'Here in this tomb lies Rosteece, daughter of Paturnus, 13 years in peace', (as in 'aged 13, rest in peace'). It is unusual in that it actually records the age of the deceased person and Fenn and Sinclair suggest that this stone may be a 'tenuous link with the sub-Roman Christianity in Powys, its clergy travelling along disused Roman roads like Sarn Helen…'.[4] The stone was found beneath the ancient yew to the south of the church, but was moved inside against the west wall of the nave in the 20th century for protection. It is over 4 feet tall, 1½ feet wide and 8 inches thick and is cracked and fissured. The script is carved on one side in seven horizontal lines 'of good style fairly deeply incised Roman capitals.'[5] It is not known whether it was originally placed beneath the yew, or whether it had been moved there from elsewhere.

This stone has romantically been taken to be the gravestone of St. Erfyl using her original name, as it was common to take a new devout name when entering holy orders. It could equally be the grave of a younger sister. The Paternus or Padarn mentioned may not be St. Padarn, as the name was not unusual, but could be that of a wealthy man whose family were able to afford a carved stone to remember their daughter. That the stone was found underneath the oldest yew on the churchyard is significant. This yew has a girth of about 35 feet and is on the southern side of the churchyard close to the porch. It is a female yew and its age has been estimated at about 1,600 years, which dates approximately to the time

The ancient yew in the churchyard

of St. Erfyl. A common motif in the stories of the saints is of a tree growing from a staff planted by the saint, and such is the case with St. Erfyl and the yew at Llanerfyl.[6] The proportions of this yew are quite staggering with a huge split trunk and massive branches spreading out close to the ground. It is propped up on its west by a stone pillar and on its east by thick wooden prop. There are several other very old yews in the churchyard to the south and the east.[7]

The original shape of the churchyard was sub-oval but it was enlarged in the 1930s. It is set on the edge of a scarp above the valley of the River Banwy. The boundary is circled by a wall and the site is raised, more so to north and west, where the churchyard level is at least 6½ feet above the surrounding land, less so to the south-east which is raised about 1½ feet. On the eastern side of the churchyard there is a line of yew trees above a scarp which is the original boundary of the church enclosure.[8]

St. Erfyl's Well, Ffynnon Erfyl, was situated about 400 yards north-west of the present church. It was renowned for its cures and parents would carry water from the well to the church to be used for the baptism of their children. The district's young people used to meet at the well on the afternoon of Wake Sunday and also on Easter Monday to drink its water which was sweetened with sugar, and would afterwards dance in a suitable area close by. Baring-Gould and Fisher report that in their time (the early 20th century) the well had been drained.[9]

LLANFAIR CAEREINION –
St. Mary (SJ 104 064)

There is no known British saint associated with this church but the large, curvilinear nature the churchyard and the presence of a holy well suggest this an early foundation. The Mary dedication may be a Norman usurpation of a formis er British dedication, as at Llangurig.

The first documented record of the church is in 1239 when the bishop of St. Asaph granted a portion of it to the nunnery at nearby Llanllugan. However St. Mary's was reputedly founded under the *clas* church at Meifod. It was given the high value of £20 in a 1254 taxation record but was valued at £17 in 1291.[1] Both records refer to the church as '*Ecclesia de Llanveyr*' which shows the St. Mary dedication (Veyr is presumably Fair, meaning Mair, the Welsh form of Mary) is at least 13th century.

The earliest part of the church structure is the fine 13th-century south doorway which was retained during the 1868 rebuilding, along with the 13th-century font. The ground plan of the earlier church was kept, but much of the building was sadly demolished because it was in such bad repair. An 1883 report intriguingly states that 'the walls showed that they had been patched up at different times ... for ancient carved stones were thrown into the masonry in several places

The holy well between the church and the river

as common stone'[2] — which begs the question of the date, the origin and the whereabouts of these carved stones.

The church is on raised ground dramatically overhanging the River Banwy which runs to the north-west. The churchyard is also raised internally, sloping upwards within the boundary. The enclosure was originally curvilinear, but an extension, added in 1902 to accommodate the holy well to the north-west of the church, has altered the original shape. As with many well sites, St. Mary's Well has

Looking up at the church tower from the steps leading to the holy well

been much altered — there is a steep set of modern concrete steps down to the well and recent landscaping around it. However it may be one of the earliest aspects of the site, with pre-Christian associations and healing powers attributed to it. People used to resort to it for the cure of various illnesses. It was also used locally for domestic water supply, having its own pump, and as late as 1910 its waters were believed to have healing properties.[3] The Welsh name for the well is Ffynnon Fair and it was also called Ffynnon Yr Eglwys. In 1954 Francis Jones noted that it still retained some old masonry,

There was also another holy well within the parish, Ffynon Madoc, which was a mineral spring of some repute.[4]

LLANFYLLIN – St. Myllin
(SJ 142 194)

Given the unique dedication to St. Myllin, the evidence of an earlier raised and sub-circular church enclosure, it is likely that this was an early medieval foundation.

Llanfyllin lies 12 miles south-east of Pennant Melangell. The church, which is dedicated to St. Moling or Myllin, was rebuilt in about 1706 in local red brick with stone decoration. It was restored in the mid-19th century when the nave and chancel were rebuilt.[1]

The churchyard is raised above the external ground level, especially to the north-west and north-east, and by about 3½ feet to the south-west; there is also an early boundary bank visible as a gentle scarp which rises to nearly 6½ feet on the eastern and southern sides of the church. It is thus considered that the earlier churchyard was a 'sub-circular raised enclosure' and was extended southwards at different times during the 19th century, giving the churchyard a more rectilinear shape. There are several mature yew trees within the enclosure, the oldest not surprisingly being on the southern side on the old boundary scarp line.[2]

The titular saint St. Moling or Myllin/Mylling (the Welsh version of his name) was 'a famed ecclesiastic and politician of the seventh century' and is termed a bishop and confessor. This is his only dedication in mainland Britain.

St. Myllin's Well

He was Irish and distantly related to the first Christian king of Leinster and was probably born in County Kerry. He was given religious training and set up a monastery at Ross Bruic, now called St. Mullins, in County Carlow. He was subsequently appointed Bishop of Ferns in County Wexford. Whilst he was there he diverted a water-course to supply his residence, a work which took seven years, but as Baring-Gould and Fisher remark a 'great number of miracles are attributed to him, most of them absurd.' He worked politically in Ireland, representing the people of Leinster, and succeeded in outwitting the king in getting tributes reduced which had been financially crippling. He reached old age and died at St. Mullins in about 696. There is no record of him visiting Wales and the reason for the church at Llanfyllin being dedicated to him is unknown.[3] Local tradition, however, has it that St. Myllin was buried in the earlier church under the altar.[4]

A quarter of a mile north-west of the church, crossing the main road and up a steep winding path is St. Myllin's Well (SJ 138 196). The well is near to the top of the hill in a short cave-like structure which is stone-lined and arched over. St. Myllin allegedly baptised converts in this well and it was used for divination and for health cures — people who were ill would tie rags to the bushes by the well to effect a cure. On Trinity Sunday people would visit the well to drink sugared water provided by local maidens with the men returning the compliment by providing cakes and ale at the inn 'at Tynllan'.[5] At the entrance is a board which states 'St. Moling (Myllin), the first to baptise by immersion in Britain, used this well in the 6th century.' This is debatable considering there is no record of Myllin ever visiting Britain, and that he died in the late 7th century, but the fact that Llanfyllin has such a strong association with the saint suggests there may have been some contact, more likely through a disciple. When there is a single dedication to a saint away from his country of origin, there must have been a good reason.

LLANGADFAN – St. Cadfan
(SJ 012 103)

The shape of the churchyard and a holy well indicate an early site.

About 14 miles west of Welshpool, and dedicated to St. Cadfan, some of the church fabric is of possible 15th-century date but it was restored in 1868. Interestingly the church is not in the village centre but south of it on the other side of the River Banwy. It was first mentioned in a taxation record of 1254 as '*Capella de Llankaduan*' and as '*Ecclia de Llangadvan*' in 1291 where it was given a value of £6 10s.[1] — Cadfan's name is clear in both spellings.

The titular saint Cadfan was a later 5th-/early 6th-century saint who was the leader of a large group of Britons, which included St. Padarn and St. Trinio, who left Brittany where they had settled to return to Wales. The migration was probably prompted by family and local leadership frictions, and several of the group, including Padarn and Trinio, were related to Cadfan.[2] This means that St. Cadfan may have slightly pre-dated St. David.

On arriving in Wales, Cadfan established a church at Tywyn in Merioneth-shire and the one at Llangadfan, and went on to become the first abbot of Bardsey, then called Bangor Gadfan. When the other Bangor, or centre of learning, at Bangor Fawr was destroyed by Anglo-Saxons in about 610, Bardsey became a retreat for fleeing clergy, and we are told that 20,000 saints were buried there, clearly a slight overstatement![3]

Ffynnon Gadfan

Cadfan is regarded as a patron of warriors, so it would appear that he led a military life in his earlier days in Brittany. He reputedly travelled between his church at Tywyn, which is said by some sources to have had three altars and was the major site of the two, to Llangadfan, a distance of nearly 40 miles by land, during his missionary endeavours, and supposedly had a preaching station at Bryn yr Eglwys about six miles from Tywyn, which he used en route. The church at Tywyn has a pillar stone, 7 feet long and about 10 inches wide at its broadest, and part of the inscription is believed by some to read (in English translation) 'Beneath a similar mound is extended Cadfan, sad that it should enclose the praise of the earth. May he rest without blemish', although this is disputed. If the inscription is accurate then it suggests St. Cadfan was buried at Tywyn, but traditionally he is said to have been laid to rest at Bardsey. The date of his death is unknown, although his half-brother, St. Winwaloe, died in 532, and Cadfan was at least two years his senior.[4] Cadfan's feast day is 1 November.

Holy wells dedicated to Cadfan at Towyn and Llangadfan were held in great repute. At Tywyn the well was renowned for the cure of 'rheumatic, scrofulous, and cutaneous disorders' and a bath-house was built which was supplied by the well, but the baths were filled in during the 1894 restoration. The well at Llangadfan, Ffynnon Gadfan, is a most atmospheric place and was once covered by a building. When the road, which separates the well from the churchyard, was built, it had to be carried over the well and 'care was taken to construct an arch above it'[5] presumably to allow the waters to flow and be accessible. The holy well is approximately 100 yards from the church gate, along the lane to the north. It now lies in an annex to a garden and has a very interesting 'monolithic' gate-post through which access is still available. The substantial stone tunnel is about 3 feet tall and a few feet long, running a little below the road surface, and has stone steps dropping steeply to the water's surface which is several feet below ground level. Its well-cared for but natural state is a refreshing change from the conversely over-restored or the neglected condition of many holy wells. Close to the well in the same 'complex' is a large, fairly roughly hewn stone trough, date indeterminate. Whether this was a simple cattle trough, or was used for baptisms, is a point of speculation.

The small churchyard is the only visible aspect of the site that is early. It was once sub-circular although it was extended to the west in 1910.[6] The original boundary of the churchyard is unusually pronounced and most memorable. The path from the present churchyard wall leads from the outer iron gates to a solidly-built stone lychgate which was the former entrance. The original boundary runs in both directions from it and is raised by about 3½ feet in places and is still prominent in its shape with a partial ring of trees to its interior. The remaining earlier boundary is enclosed by a stone wall around the perimeter, adjoining pasture to the south and a farmstead to the east and is raised by up to 5 feet above the surrounding land on the north, east and southern sides.[7]

LLANGEDWYN – St. Cedwyn
(SJ 188 241)

An early carved stone outside the church.

The church lies 7 miles south-west of Oswestry at the side of the B4396. It is dedicated to St. Cedwyn, whose father was Gwgon Gwron and mother was Madrun, who was at one time married to King Ynyr of Gwent. This places Cedwyn as a contemporary of the saints Teilo and David, and may give an approximate date for the foundation of the first church. One of the two townships within Llangedwyn parish is called Scrwgan and is believed to mean Esgair Wgan, 'the Ridge or Hill of Gwgan' and appears to remember St. Cedwyn's father, identifying a possible family connection within the area.[1]

The church is an attractive Victorian rebuild in a Norman style, with one outstanding reproduction Norman doorway incorporating an ornate chevron canopy. The churchyard is slightly raised and butterfly in shape, but was once probably elliptical. Part of a possible original boundary survives in the south-east side of the enclosure. On the east there is 'a low, spread bank' about 1 foot high on which grow three yews which represents the earlier boundary, and to the south is a natural scarp up to 6½ feet high which, it is thought, 'almost certainly functioned as the earliest boundary on this side.'[2] The site is low-lying.

Against the external, east wall of the chancel is a small carved stone which may be of 6th-century date. It is a ring-cross of simple design, perhaps even originating from the site. Indeed it is probably the same cross-incised stone that was found built into one of the walls of the church and reported in *Archaeologia Cambrensis* in 1894[3] and is one of the few artefacts which may be considered contemporary with our period of study.

The inscribed stone outside the church

LLANGURIG – St. Curig
(SN 909 799)

Reputed site of an early small chapel founded by St. Curig in the 6th century.

This is a striking church on a site allegedly dating back to the 6th century containing stained glass windows that graphically but erroneously depict the story of the founder, St. Curig.

Llangurig is about 5 miles south-west of Llanidloes, the church lying on the north-western outskirts of the village near to, and slightly above, the flood plain of the River Wye. The fabric of the church is partly medieval with Victorian restorations of 1877–78 which, considering a mid-19th-century description of the church as being 'very rude and rough' both within and without, was clearly needed. Llangurig was a *clas* church, dedicated to, and allegedly founded by, St. Curig who died in about 550.[1]

Curig is often styled Curig Lwyd ('the Blessed') and sometimes Curig Farchog ('the Knight'). His legend has been muddled with that of St. Cyriacus, a boy-martyr of Tarsus, because of the Normans fondness for re-dedicating churches. Thus accounts of St. Curig in the Middle Ages are at times nonsensical; at one moment, for example, he is referred to being a child-martyr but then is described as an adult founding Llangurig. The Victorian stained glass windows in the church depict St. Curig's mother (in fact St. Julitta, the mother of St. Cyriacus) receiving a box of land deeds whereas Curig's friend, the nun Elidan, who lived in the area during Curig's lifetime, should have been depicted.[2]

St. Curig was probably a native of Brittany and a pupil of St. Illtud at Llantwit Major. His parentage is unknown. He seems to have led the life of a missionary, having dedications in Carmarthenshire, Caernarvonshire, Glamorganshire and Denbighshire. Within the area covered by this book there was a St. Curig's Chapel at Langstone near Llanmartin in Monmouthshire (now destroyed), and Baring-Gould and Fisher observe that in their day Llanilid (or Crai) in Breconshire was dedicated to St. Julitta[3] which may have formerly been a Curig dedication.

Tradition has it that after St. Curig landed in Britain at Aberystwyth, he rested on top of a hill (still called Eisteddfa Gurig — 'Curig's Seat') above Llangurig. He was taken with the fine prospect of the Wye Valley before him and was inspired to set up 'a humble cell and chapel' here.[4]

There is a legend that also places Curig's uncle, who we are told was a monk, at the site. King Maelgwn Gwynedd's men set upon the uncle's servants who were returning from Ceredigion with supplies for their master. The robbers' hands became stuck fast to the sacks and they were dragged by their horses to Curig's uncle's cell at Llangurig where the saint loosened their hands by prayer. Maelgwn was furious and sent men to fetch the monk, but they were rendered blind which incensed the king even more and he personally set out on the monk's destruction, but he too was sent blind as were the rest of his men. In desperation they sought mercy from the monk who prayed to Curig and their sight was restored. Maelgwn then gave 'large and ample lands ... to the monk and Ciric for ever, free from rent or *gwestfa* (food-rent) to king or bishop for ever.'[5] Whether this was Curig's uncle or Cyriacus's depends on which legend is chosen, and the fact that the uncle is also called Maelgwn only confuses the story further.

A description of the boundaries of the grant is given which are interesting as they show that what is now understood as Llangurig parish, or much of it, originally belonged to 'three different principalities.'[6]

Several poets in the late medieval/early modern era mention St. Curig. The 15th-century poet, Huw Cae Llwyd, describes how King Maelgwn came across the hermitage on the Wye and tried to deceive a nun living there of her possessions and in compensation 'gave as an offering pasture land of great price to the sacred enclosure.' In the 16th century Huw Arwystli (see also under Llandinam) also alludes to the nun on the banks of the Wye and refers to grants to Llangurig comprising 'three lands like a golden strand, three in one ring.' A 15th-century bard, Lewis Glyn Cothi, makes reference to 'the brave knight Curig's coat of mail' showing that in Wales, at least in the Middle Ages, Curig was believed to have been a soldier at some stage in his life.[7]

The only clear points to emerge from these legends are that Curig may have been a soldier who was converted and became a monk; that he lived at the same time as the 6th-century king of Gwynedd, Maelgwn; that he had a monk's cell at Llangurig which later became a church; and that a nun, called Elidan lived close by on the banks of the River Wye; and that he was held in high enough esteem to become a bishop.[8]

It is possible that trouble from Maelgwn Gwynedd may have been a factor in Curig leaving Wales for Brittany, for it is suggested that the Breton *Life* of Kirik probably represents that same person as the Welsh Curig. Unfortunately it gives no details of his time in Wales but describes how he moved to Brittany with St. Tudwal, probably travelling through Devon and Cornwall, as there is a possible dedication to the saint in each county. Curig arrived in Brittany between 520–535 and set up a monastery there with fourteen other monks, and subsequently established a chapel in a valley surrounded by dense woods where he stayed in solitude for two years. St. Paul Aurelian met him at this retreat and persuaded Curig to accompany him to his monastery at Occismor. Curig agreed and stayed there for many years working for St. Paul who, it appears, consecrated Curig as a bishop. Curig died on 17 February whilst on missionary work in Brittany and was buried at Locquirec. The year of his demise is not known, but it was probably shortly before 550.[9]

Although the Normans re-dedicated many of St. Curig's foundations to St. Cyriacus and St. Julitta, there is no evidence to suggest that all churches dedicated to them jointly or individually were previously dedicated to Curig; some indeed may have been new foundations. However Baring-Gould and Fisher note that 'in purely Welsh districts the Curig churches are undoubtedly to be attributed to S. Curig and not to Cyriacus ...'.[10]

Various low disused channels and earthworks are visible in the pasture to the south of church. Some of these may be due to the meandering of the river, others look man made. Without excavation it is impossible to date the visible remnants, but some may relate to the early medieval period and the time of the earliest church on the site. The fact that this pasture is next to the river may, however, suggest otherwise, as the area would have been flooded numerous times over the centuries which would mask any very early features under alluvium.

The church was owned by the Cistercian abbey of Strata Florida (Cardiganshire) some time after 1164. In 1254 the church was recorded as 'Ecclesia de Lankiric' and given a surprisingly low value of £1 6s. 8d.[11]

The churchyard is D-shaped and has some curving to the northern side. The enclosure slopes downwards from the main road to the north and has a stream running along the western boundary. The church itself is built on a level platform. The boundaries facing the Wye are walled and the churchyard is about 6½ feet higher than the external land to the west and south.[12]

In the mid-18th century a coin hoard dating from Henry I or Henry II's reign was allegedly found in the churchyard, but no other details are known.[13]

LLANGYNOG – St. Cynog
(SJ 053 261)

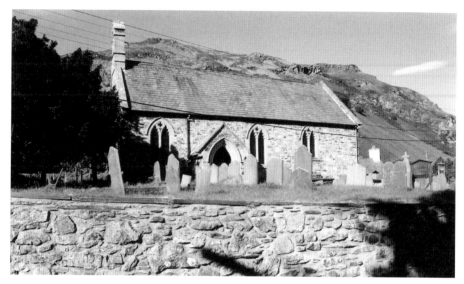

Indications are that this is an early medieval site, taking into account the dedication, the sub-circular shape of the churchyard,[1] as well as the magnificent yew.

The church is in the centre of Llangynog, some 6 miles west of Llanrhaeadr-ym-Mochnant. The area was once quarried heavily for its lead and slate, and long-disused spoil heaps that overhang the natural crags which rise steeply, almost surrounding the small village, are slowly naturalising to form a striking and imposing landscape.

The church is dedicated to St. Cynog, eldest son of Brychan of Breconshire; his mother was Banadlined who was probably local to Llanrhaeadr-ym-Mochant (see p.99). Although Cynog had strong associations with Breconshire, he also had connections with this area as his half-brother, St. Dogfan, established an oratory at or near Llanrhaeadr-ym-Mochnant where he is patron saint of the parish church.

The church was rebuilt completely in the late 18th century and was restored in 1894. It is a plain utilitarian structure with Victorian ornamentation and has a simple attractive design.

The churchyard is noticeably raised with a stone boundary wall and a drop to the surrounding land of 7 to 8 feet and more in places. There are no obvious extensions to the churchyard, so this may be the original shape. There is a very old yew in the south-west corner — is this an example of an early saint's planting? The proximity to the important church at Pennant Melangell is probably significant.

LLANLLUGAN – St. Mary
(SJ 058 023)

The presence of a holy well, the probable dedication to Llorcan Wyddel, the presence of the yews and the shape of the churchyard strongly suggest that Llanllugan was founded in the early medieval period. It is also the site of a small 12th-century nunnery.

This entry should be viewed along with that for Llanwyddelan (see p.104) from which it is about 1¾ miles north-west, as the crow flies.

The church of St. Mary is about 4 miles south-west of Llanfair Caereinion in a beautiful and remote spot. The present dedication may have been a Norman imposition and perhaps linked with the Cistercian nunnery which was founded here before 1188 and survived until the Dissolution of the Monasteries in the mid-16th century. It was a daughter house to that at Strata Marcella abbey[1] which is about 2½ miles north-east of Welshpool. However there is evidence that the site is much older and was dedicated to a 6th-century Welsh saint, Llorcan Wyddel.

The church is included in a poem of Cynddelw (*c.*1150–1200) which refers to St. Tysilio's churches:

> A church he raised with his fostering hand,
> Llanllugyrn, with a chancel for Mass.[2]

It is generally thought that the church is indeed one of St. Tysilio's foundations. The 'Llugyrn' element of the name has been treated as a Welsh noun rendering the meaning of 'The Church of the War Horns.' However Baring-Gould and Fisher suggest the name is a Welsh assimilation of the Irish name Lorcan and believe the person in question is Llorcan Wyddel, whom St. Beuno is reputed to have raised from the dead[3] as discussed under Llanwyddelan. Indeed the church is traditionally described as being founded by Llorcan Wyddel in the 6th century and it is suggested that the original dedication may have been to Llorcan.[4] It is likely that Llanllugan and nearby Llanwyddelan were under St. Beuno's control through Llorcan, in the same way that Guilsfield and Llanaelhaiarn were under his disciple Aelhaiarn. Medieval fantasy has both Llorcan and Aelhaiarn being raised from the dead by Beuno. One wonders if the zealous medieval scribe meant they were awakened to a religious life from a profane existence, rather than physically resurrected from the dead? Fenn and Sinclair suggest that Llanlugan's absorption into the *parochia* of Meifod may reflect the tension that existed between Tysilio and Beuno when they were at Meifod in the 6th century which led to Beuno's departure for north Wales.[5]

The church structure is largely of late 14th- to early 15th-century date, but its design gives the impression of the church's earlier importance, as the ghost of an extra entrance and additional building can be seen when examining the north wall. The location of the 12th-century nunnery is unknown, but a site to the south in a meadow by the River Rhiw has been suggested, although it is possible that the lost building on the north side of the church was part of the nunnery. The nunnery is assumed to have been a small community — in 1377 an abbess and four nuns were recorded.[6] The church does have a rather odd, truncated look to one side and it is possible it has been shortened in length.

An undated charter for Llanllugan nunnery came to light in Shrewsbury in the 19th century and is now is held at the Glamorgan Archives.[7] It was quite a find as medieval charters relating to Powys are scarce. The charter is tentatively dated to about 1216–17, and gives details of a portion of land given by one Maredudd ap Rhobert. The land concerned either covers the extent of the manor, or at least the township. This area was seized by Maredudd c.1216 and the grant obviously must post-date this seizure which brings the 1188 date of the foundation of the nunnery into question. It is possible, of course, that Maredudd's charter merely confirmed land belonging to the nunnery, or that the latter was transferred from another site to Llanlugan.[8] In 1539, and on the eve of the Dissolution, Leland describes the nunnery as 'a veri litle poore nunneri.'[9]

The present churchyard has been extended southwards down the hill by some yards, but the original may have been curvilinear. There is a curving scarp rising up to about 2 feet to the south of the church which is thought to be the original boundary. This continues outside the present boundary near to the west gate, and there is also some embanking inside the churchyard wall on the north side which may be original. An old yew, now felled, was recorded as being near the south-west corner and a yew to the south-east which in 1994 was recorded as no longer growing.[10] Do these indicate a pre-Norman planting?

The well near the church

Across the lane from the church is a well that is accessed by a short flight of steps. The structure looks quite early and substantial, more so than many holy wells. A sprite called the Bwgan is said to have lived near the well on the Lower Lliw. A tree grows above the well and the Bwgan is said to live amongst the tree roots and when the water flow subsides he is angered and 'is then up to all kinds of tricks' being a mischievous spirit.[11] The well may have been used for baptisms in the past, as well as for water supply.

LLANMEREWIG –
St. Llwchaiarn (SO 157 932)

One of the best preserved near circular and embanked churchyards, reputedly sited on a prehistoric enclosure.

St. Llwchaiarn's church at Llanmerewig (about 3 miles north-east of Newtown) was mainly rebuilt during 1833–45 with a distinctive thin tower, the only 13th-century remains being the roof timbers and a little masonry. It is an unusual and striking site.

It is said that an otherwise unrecorded saint, Merewig, reputedly founded the church in the late 6th century, but it is thought more probable that it was founded by St. Llwchaiarn who was a monk at Bangor-on-Dee.[1] St. Llwchaiarn lived in the early 7th century and came from a royal family in the commote of Caereinion in Powys and had two brothers who were also saints, Aelhaiarn and Cynhaiarn. The family home was at Llystinwynnan, which is thought to be Llysin in the parish of Llanerfyl. He was therefore local. His grandfather was a prince of part of ancient Powys which included the Severn Valley above Shrewsbury and one of his sons was the esteemed Cynddylan who is the subject of an ancient Welsh poem. In the British defeat near the town of Tren (perhaps somewhere near Shrewsbury) against the Anglo-Saxons St. Llwchaiarn's father, Caranfael, was killed. The sons were thus deprived of their inheritance and took to the religious life 'like so many others of the Welsh saints under similar circumstances.'[2]

St. Llwchaiarn was trained at Bangor Iscoed, now called Bangor-on-Dee, 5 miles south-east of Wrexham. His legend is contained in an obscure early 16th-century poem by the local poet Sion Ceri called *Cywydd Llwchaiarn, Filwr a Sant, o Llamyrewig* — 'a poem to Llwchaiarn, warrior and saint, of Llanmyrewig'. The poem appears in 16th- and 17th-century manuscripts. It states that Llwchaiarn was first cousin to St. Beuno (of whom he was apparently a disciple) and that Llanmerewig was celebrated for 'the miracles wrought there', and contained a statue of the saint 'in a niche, vested in episcopal habits, with hand up-raised in blessing'. It appears that Llwchaiarn was buried at Llanmerewig. When he first arrived at the site he had heard bells ringing on a hill on the banks of the River Severn and it was on this ridge that he built the church. Having prayed here for nine months and nine days in a hair-shirt and kneeling on a stone until his knees were bruised, he was granted nine petitions, of which three were for the benefit of his people. He is described as being 'a great deliverer, a saintly warrior like unto gallant S. George' and he too supposedly killed a dragon single-handed.

The name Llanmerewig is explained as coming from the story of the saint who, with his pastoral staff, caused a hind to leap into a pool, which gave rise

Part of the raised circular/oval churchyard enclosure

to the parish name Llam y Ewig — the Hind's Leap. As well as Llanmerewig, Llwchaiarn is also the patron of Llanllwchaiarn church (SO 124 925) which was rebuilt in 1815 and is in a small hamlet about a mile north-east of the centre of Newtown. Unlike Llanmerewig it is on flat land close to the River Severn and has quite a large, roughly triangular-shaped churchyard. Although both parishes adjoin, the churches are on opposite sides of the river. It is said in the 16th-century poem that great offerings were made at these churches and the saint's territory 'as a sanctuary, was not inferior to Bardsey'. He is also the patron of two churches on Cardigan Bay. St. Beuno's churches of Berriew and Bettws are neighbours of Llwchaiarn's churches in Montgomeryshire, which would tend to support the view that Llwchaiarn was his disciple. His brother founded Guilsfield, and worked locally (see p.76). St. Llwchaiarn's festival was celebrated at both his churches in Montgomeryshire on 12 January.[3]

The most interesting point about Llanmerewig is the churchyard, which is the best example of a raised, oval/circular churchyard of the sites we have visited. The churchyard does not appear to have been altered since its foundation. An earthen bank about 11 to 12 feet wide and up to 3 to 4 feet tall runs around the inside of churchyard wall[4] and is so pronounced that it is visible above the walls upon approaching the site. Davies considers there is every reason to suppose the enclosure is pre-Conquest and may represent an early cemetery boundary.[5] The RCAHMW consider it to be a 're-used prehistoric hill-top enclosure',[6] an opinion we share. A partial ring of eight yews exists just within the boundary on every side but the south, and this only adds to the sense of the place.

LLANRHAEADR-YM-MOCHNANT – St. Dogfan

(SJ 123 260)

The dedication to St. Dogfan, the putative nearby oratory of St. Dogfan, the possible early courses of stonework in the church tower, and the early cross-slab all indicate an early site.

St. Dogfan's church is in the centre of the settlement. A great fair used to be held at Llanrhaeadr annually on St. Dogfan's day and, early in the 20th century, it was still held on 23 and 24 July.[1]

A possible early Christian cemetery has been found about 1 mile south-east of Llanrhaeadr-ym-Mochnant at Meusydd, where about 40 graves arranged in rows were revealed by cropmark evidence. Although not dated, Clwyd-Powys Archaeological Trust consider that this may pre-date the *clas* church and burial ground at Llanrhaeadr. Moreover, the Meusydd cemetery is close to the prehistoric ritual and funerary complex at Maesmochnant, which may reflect 'some form of continuity or reuse of a pre-existing pagan burial ground,' as has also been suggested at Pennant Melangell (see p.111).[2]

Llanrhaeadr-ym-Mochnant (which means 'The Church near the waterfall in [the commote of] Mochnant')[3] appears to have been the centre for the religious operations of St. Dogfan, (spelt also Dogwan or Doewan) In later years it was a *clas*, or mother church, governed by a lay abbot, and, until some time between the 9th and 11th centuries, it may have been the main or even the only church within an area synonymous with the cantref.[4] St. Dogfan was reputedly the son of Brychan of Brycheiniog, and half-brother to Brychan's eldest son Cynog whose mother was Banadlined (or Banhadlwedd). She was probably local to Llanrhaeadr for there are three townships in the parish which contain the name of Banhadla, and Banhadel was a prince of Powys at this time.[5] As Brychan's son, Dogfan is placed right at the beginning of the era of the 'Age of Saints'.

A class of monks of St. Dogfan is said to have existed, possibly as early as the 6th century until after 1291, but the site of the monastery is unknown.[6] It may have been on the present church site. St. Dogfan apparently had an oratory at a site tentatively identified by place-name evidence near Buarth-yr-e (SJ 098 319 on private land) as it appears on modern maps, or Buarth yr Hendre, five miles north-west of Llanrhaeadr. In the early 1900s Baring-Gould and Fisher reported that evidence of the site of the church and graveyard were still visible. Stone remains have been found on or near this site during informal field-walking by local historians. No formal excavation or identification has taken place but the fact that the site is in a dell called Cwm Doefan (Dogfan) and there is a

Ffynnon Ddoefon (Dogfan's Well) in the same dell, lead Baring-Gould and Fisher to observe that 'it has been reasonably conjectured to have been the site of the original oratory founded by Doewan [Dogfan].' It is said that the cloud-berries that grow on the wild hills called the Berwyn Mountains in this parish were called Mwyar Doewan (Doewan's berries), and whoever brought a quart of these ripe berries to the parson on the morning of St. Dogfan's festival day (13 July) 'had his ecclesiastical payments remitted for the year.'[7]

The cross-slab in the nave which may date to the 9th century

The parish church is set in a large, irregularly-shaped churchyard which slopes gently down to the River Tanat. The size of the church enclosure is, in itself, indicative of an early and important foundation. Changes in levels of the churchyard may indicate an earlier boundary between the church and river, although there is no obvious evidence of this. The northern boundary, which has the main entrance, is built up around the edges like that at Berriew, and again indicates pressure upon desirable land within the settlement.

The church structure is built of local stone and mainly of mid- to late-medieval date and was originally a 'long single chamber of uncertain date' and is, indeed, described as having 'an undated early core'.[8] Within the nave is a rectangular cross-slab 'commemorating Gwgam son of Elstan' found in the fabric of the church when the building was being renovated in the 1850s. It has a Latin cross with a long shaft with a ring carved around the cross and an inscription along the central arms of the cross. There is interlace-type patterning carved to either side of the cross shaft. Although the Sites and Monuments Record suggest a date of the 11th century, an information board within the church states that there are indications that the cross-slab dates to the 9th century and was re-used and carved more ornately in the 11th century. The inscription reads CO (CORG) OM FILIU(S) EDELSTAN — interestingly the 10th century Anglo-Saxon king Athelstan is known to have had a Welsh godson known as Elystan Glodrudd who became a prince of

Powys. Elystan is a Welsh version of Athelstan. It is appears then that St. Dogfan's church received the body of a man called Gwgam who was a bishop and a prince — a cross before his name shows that he was a bishop. It is said that Gwgam and his brother were sent to King Athelstan's court for their early schooling which would date the carving to the 10th century, or very early 11th.[9] Clwyd-Powys Archaeological Trust also mention the preserved fragments of 'a Romanesque shrine possibly dedicated to the patron saint, St. Dogfan.'[10]

The church guide suggests that the base of the tower is of a possible pre-9th century date and, even from a cursory view, there is a noticeable difference between the first seven courses of stone running up from ground level to the rest of the stonework of the church. It is of a darker grey stone and the blocks are larger and more crudely worked. If the base is of pre-9th century date — and there is really no way of being certain — then it is a rare example of pre-Norman remains. (Clwyd-Powys Archaeological Trust state that the base is of unknown date.)[11]

Leaving the churchyard by a gate close to the river and following the riverbank for 300 yards, the ruins of a water-mill are to be found which are reputed to be those of Dogfan's Mill. This may be just an anecdotal name, although an element of truth often resides behind local legend, for corn-grinding facilities would have been required in the parish at the time of the monastery. Crossing the river near the mill and following the footpath uphill for about 100 yards you reach a site known as Dogfan's Well close to the path, now just a slightly reedy damp depression in the pasture. In common with many well-sites now, it is unfortunately more noticeable for its ungainly modern pipe than any ancient feature.

The lower courses of the tower which appear to be of much earlier construction compared to those above

LLANWNOG – St. Gwynog
(SO 022 938)

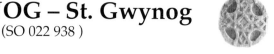

The dedication to St. Gwynog (the probable son of Gildas), the size and shape of the churchyard and the presence of old yews suggest an early site.

Four miles south-east of Carno, St. Gwynog's church at Llanwnog is at the centre of the small village. The walls of the church contain medieval stonework, some of the squared red sandstone possibly having been robbed from the Roman fort at Caersws about 1½ miles to the south-east, although this is unproven. The church was heavily restored in 1863.[1] The rood loft and screen dating to about 1500 are outstanding pieces of woodwork.

The foundation appears to be early. The titular saint, Gwynog, was probably the son of Gildas. Gildas trained under Cadoc and there was friction between him and the young St. David. This would place Gywnog as David's contemporary, born at the beginning of the 6th century or a little before. Gildas placed his son with St. Finnian of Clonard in Ireland for his training, Finnian collecting him and one other disciple from Llancarfan on route for home; this was probably before 525. On completing his training, Gwynog then travelled to Wales. There were once several churches or chapels dedicated to him, but they have all now disappeared, including Llanwynog in Herefordshire which was under the jurisdiction of Clodock; a small chantry chapel of Capel Gwynog mentioned in the parish of Caerleon in 1548; a Capel Gwynog in the parish of Llanfachriath in Merionethshire where legend has it when St. Gwynog visited 'a crystal spring … burst forth near the church, whose water was efficacious in various ailments'; and chapels near the church of Llangwm Dinmael in Denbighshire which were dedicated to St. Gwynog and his brother St. Noethan/Nwython (with whom he is often linked) and which were referred to as being converted to a mill and kiln a long time ago. The only church with a dedication remaining to him is at Llanwnog and this appears to have been the most important.[2]

St. Gwynog's stay in Wales was cut short as his father, Gildas, had a quarrel with the princes of Powys, in particular with Cuneglas, whom he described as 'a bear, the rider of many, wallowing in the old filth of his wickedness, a tawny butcher.' This was sometime between 540 and 544 and, not surprisingly, Gywnog felt it expedient to leave Wales and went to Britanny. In a 15th-century stained glass window in Llanwnog church he is styled as a bishop, an office possibly held in Brittany, conceivably of Vannes. This part of Brittany was plunged into conflict between 550 and 580 by the ruling family, who indulged in murder, fratricide and feuds to gain power. He seems to have been used politically by the different factions, and consequently became unpopular and was exiled from the area and died in about 580, about three years after taking over as bishop.[3]

It is claimed that the church was founded in the 6th century as a daughter establishment to Llandinam (several miles south) but the first clear mention of the church is in 1254 where it is called 'capella de Lanwennic' and had a very low value of 13s. 4d.[4]

The earliest visible feature at Llanwnog is the churchyard which is quite sizeable and is described as 'originally curvilinear' being visibly curved to all sides except the south which is straight and the result of a 19th-century extension to the churchyard. The earlier southern boundary is clearly visible within the churchyard as a scarp which is between 5 feet and 6½ feet high and has a slight curve to it. It is raised by about 3½ feet to the north and east and more so to the west.[5]

The proximity and concentration of buildings near the church indicates an important and desirable centre. The churchyard also has a number of old yews, some of which are of great age. Three are on the north side, two are in the south-west corner, another is in the south-eastern corner and one is close to the west wall of the church — there are also two yews on either side of the eastern path which are described as of 'considerable age'.[6] One has a measured girth of 25 feet[7] which, by Bevan-Jones' reckoning of girths of 23-33 feet having a tentative age range of 1,200-2,000 years,[8] suggest that at least some of the yews have an early medieval origin and may have been deliberate plantings by an early saint — St. Gwynog perhaps?

LLANWYDDELAN –
St. Gwyddelan (SJ 083 012)

An atmospheric hill-top church with a fragment of an early Christian stone and purportedly named after St. Beuno's disciple in the 6th century.

This site should be viewed along with the entry for Llanllugan (see p.95).The church of St. Gwyddelan is about 6 miles north-north-east of Newtown. There is some contention over the identity of the titular saint. There is one other church dedicated to St. Gwyddelan at Dolwyddelan in Carnarvonshire, and early writers have supposed that the dedications are to St. Gwendolina. However the name Gwyddelan means 'the little Irishman'[1] which rather mitigates against Gwendolina. Gwyddelan is said to have been a convert of St. Beuno's to whom the latter gave land for a hermitage at Llanwyddelan.[2] Baring-Gould and Fisher suggest that Gwyddelan may actually refer to Llorcan Wyddel whom Beuno is reputed to have raised from the dead after he was killed by his wife. Beuno set up a church on land given by King Cynan ap Brochwel at 'a place which received its name from the Scot whom Beuno raised there from the dead.' Beuno's disciples often appear to have founded churches in the vicinity of those founded by their master, and close by are Berriew and Bettws Cedewain, both Beuno churches.[3] The position of the churchyard is such that the site could easily have been used for an earlier pre-Christian fortification, being on the incline of a steep hill and commanding wide-ranging views of the hills and valleys.

The church is a late structure, possibly being altered or rebuilt in 1641, and rebuilt completely in 1865.[4] Haslam suggests that the north and eastern walls may be on the old foundations.[5] There is a fragment of an early Christian stone but the visitor must be warned that it is very small and weathered. It is set into the outside of a south-east buttress and measures approximately 1½ feet wide and about 6 inches tall. It has a small area of geometric patterning in one square to the centre of the horizontal side — the Sites and Monument record description is 'a pecked ornament consisting of a panel of two cord twist, a panel of key-pattern and associated lines.' It possibly dates from the 9th century,[6] much later than the supposed foundation, but if it was originally found within the church boundary it would materially add weight to this being an early medieval site.

The original, smaller church enclosure was on top of the knoll on which the church is sited. The old boundary is visible as a scarp within the churchyard, higher than the present south-eastern boundary and closer to the church. This original churchyard was oval-shaped and quite small but an extension to the south-east was added in 1938.[7] If viewed from the south-east at the bottom of the churchyard the raised nature of this inner half of the churchyard can be seen.

The fragment of stone with an early Christian carving on the outside of the south-east buttress

MEIFOD –
St. Tysilio and St. Mary (SJ 155 132)

Meifod is the premier early Christian site of the northern area of this guide and a *clas* or mother church of the region. It has the largest churchyard of any of the sites we have visited, has a reputed foundation going back to *c*.550 and was supposedly the burial place of the Dark Age princes of Powys.

The village is about 16 miles south-west of Oswestry. The first church was reputedly set up by Gwyddfarch whose father was probably a south Italian prince prince. According to legend Gwyddfarch was a hermit or anchorite who had his rocky bed on the hilltop of Gallt yr Ancr, 'the Anchorite's Hill' (SJ 145 128). The site is still called Gwely Gwyddfarch and is about half way along the top of the hill which stands dramatically to the west and south-west of the village. On the first level ground below the summit of the hill overlooking the village there are remains of what appears to be a collapsed structure about 1½ feet tall with the suggestion of an entrance. The remains of Gwyddfarch's rocky bed were described by Baring-Gould and Fisher as 'a trench some eight yards in length.' — are these the same features?[1] The walk to the top of this hill is highly recommended for the superb view gained over Meifod where the size of churchyard can be fully appreciated. Gwyddfarch founded his church/oratory called Eglwys Gwddfarch in the valley which he could see from his hermitage.

His status upon his arrival was as a hermit, but he became abbot of Meifod and it was his presence which encouraged St. Tysilio to flee to Meifod for

The possible site of Gwely Gwyddfarch on the heights of Gallt yr Ancr

The views from Gwely Gwyddfarch over Meifod

protection. Tysilio was the son of Brochwel, Prince of Powys, who had helped to establish St. Melangell at Pennant Melangell. This would logically date him as her contemporary and a generation after St. David, to about 600. Tysilio was also first cousin to St. Asaph, to whom the area's cathedral is dedicated, and to St. Deiniol (see Llangarron, Herefordshire, p.283 and Itton, Monmouthshire, p.331). From an early age Tysilio wished to enter the church, but this was contrary to his father's will, who was determined to train him as a soldier. Tysilio informed his brothers in advance of his intentions, before he fled to Meifod one day when out hunting. Brochwel was furious and sent soldiers to bring him back. They criticised Gwyddfarch for converting Tysilio, but he answered gently and produced the runaway, dressed as a tonsured monk. The men could not persuade him to return and fearing to break his claimed sanctuary, left him and returned to Brochwel, who allowed him to stay. Tysilio did not trust this decision and travelled on to *Inis Suliau* on the Menai Straits where he stayed for seven years and founded the church at Llandyssilio. He then returned to Meifod, but was alarmed by Gwyddfarch who had decided to leave and travel to Rome in his old age, leaving Tysilio without his protection. Tysilio dissuaded him from attempting the journey at his time of life by suggesting that he dreamt of Rome as a substitute. Taking him on a 'long mountain trudge', Gwyddfarch became exhausted, and, at Tysilio's bidding, lay down to sleep. On waking Tysilio asked him how he would complete the distance to Rome if such a walk had tired him so much. Gwyddfarch gave up the idea of travel, saying the he had dreamed of a magnificent city, and that would suffice. Not long afterwards, he died, reputedly on the rocky bed on the hill and Tysilio became abbot.[2]

The battle of Chester in 615/6 saw the British heavily defeated by the Anglo-Saxon King Aethelfrith of Northumbria. Brochwel, who had assembled a large force, managed to escape with about 50 men, but died soon after. He was succeeded by his son, Iago, St. Tysilio's brother, but he died within two years without an heir. Iago's widow, Haiarnwedd (Haiarnmed), decided, after consultation with the 'chief men of Powys', that she would marry Tysilio and set him up as Iago's successor. Tysilio objected, and Haiarnwedd took offence, and, assuming the regency of Powys for herself, harassed the monks of Meifod and seized the monastery revenues. To protect the monks of Meifod from further problems, Tysilio fled to Brittany where he became known as Suliau and established a monastery with some of his followers. After a few years when it had grown, two of his monks from Meifod appeared to inform him that his sister-in-law had died, and invited him back to return. He decided not to go, gave them a Book of the Gospels and his walking staff as gifts, and told them to return to Meifod and continue without him. Tysilio remained in Brittany until his death aged about 75 in *c*.650.[3]

A 12th-century poem by the bard Cynddelw gives an outline description of Meifod at this time. In contrast to its origins under Gwyddfarch, when it had been a very simple oratory with little wealth, Tysilio's monastery had 'fine cloisters and spires, its priests and choir, its offerings and gold-enclustered crozier ... "the sepulchre of kings".' The churchyard at one time reputedly contained three churches. The first was Gwyddfarch's, the second was Tysilio's, and the third was St. Mary's, consecrated in 1155. The present church probably incorporates structures or occupies the site of St. Tysilio's, as his church 'excelled the other two, and his festival day was that observed here to the last.'[4] According to 17th-century records, Gwyddfarch's church/oratory stood just outside the wall of the present churchyard to the west.[5] In 1631 it was used as a cottage and its churchyard as a garden, as was a second church on the site. In 1701 the compiler of another terrier, or document, records seeing the ruins of two churches. Clwyd-Powys Archaeological Trust state that the outline of Gwyddfarch's church/oratory was certainly one of those churches visible in 1631 and that glazed floor tiles were uncovered when the red-brick Congregational Chapel was built in the early 1880s; they also note that part of the adjoining plot is still called 'Gwydffarch's cemetery'.[6]

The third saint associated with Meifod was St. Beuno who stayed for 40 days and nights with Tysilio, setting up a church whilst he was there with land granted by Cynan, Tysilio's brother.[7] The position of this church is not known, but possibly St. Mary's church was a rebuild and re-dedication of Beuno's church.

Meifod was the most important church of Powys, with daughter churches which included those at Welshpool, Llanfair Caereinion, Guilsfield, Llanllugan, and Alderbury in Shropshire. It was also the favourite burial place of the princes of Powys, whose residence was reputedly at Mathrafal[8] (SJ 132 148) about 2¼ miles south-west of the church where there are the earthwork remains of a castle, which is probably post-Norman. The interment of these Powys princes, however, is only properly authenticated as from the 12th century,[9] Thomas Pennant stating that Madoc ap Meredydd, prince of Powys, was buried at Meifod in 1160, as was the noble Gryffydd Maelor in 1188.[10] Madoc is said to have built St. Mary's church, although it is thought it may have been begun as a consequence of a bequest in 1137 by Gruffydd ap Cynan.[11]

Meifod's past importance in the old kingdom of Powys is reflected in the very large size of the churchyard. Thomas Pennant states that in the 1773 it consisted of 'not less than nine acres, and yields to the minister as many pounds, as a pasture.'[12] However Clywd-Powys Archaeological Trust state that it originally covered 5.44 acres. There are visible encroachments in areas that were previously part of the earlier churchyard by cottages to the north-east, whilst to the west there is the Congregational Chapel and its yard and other houses. There is only one church on the site now. There is a scarp bank just within the southern boundary which is a natural river terrace, but it is suggested it may have been used as an earlier boundary.[13] There is also a raised track across the centre of the churchyard running north-east to south-east, the original purpose of which is not known, but as it reportedly stays dry during floods it was possibly a raised walkway between buildings that have now disappeared.

The most immediate and striking feature on approaching the west door of the church are the remains

The early carved cross-slab inside the church

109

of two Romanesque arches from the time of the consecration in the 12th century. The remnants of the old church stare out from the newer structure; inside the picture is similar but more complete with Romanesque arches revealed in the south nave wall during the 1871/2 renovation to the church.

Within the south transept is an ornately carved early cross slab of indeterminate date. A crucified Christ is depicted in a circle at the top which also incorporates a Maltese-type cross, below which is a Latin cross 'encircled with knot-work.' Nash-Williams suggested that because of introduction of Viking features, for example the 'Viking knots and animals of the local Celtic-Norse tradition', a 9th to 10th century date was possible. However, another doyen of archaeology, Ralegh Radford suggested it may have been the tombstone of one of the princes of Powys, possibly Madoc ap Maredudd (Meredydd) who died in 1160.[14] The Sites and Monuments Record postulates a late 9th- or early 10th-century date. Although its original location is unknown, it is thought likely that it was associated with the early *clas* church of Meifod.[15] The slab has been broken in two diagonally towards its bottom and has been cemented together — it measures nearly 5 feet in height, is about 10 inches thick and tapers from the top to the bottom. The work is inspiring in its delicacy and reminiscent of the carving to be seen at Llanhamlach and Llandefaelog Fach, both near Brecon.

PENNANT MELANGELL –
St. Melangell (SJ 024 265)

Important reconstructed remains of a saint's shrine and reputedly founded in the very early 7th century by a female saint.

This site is in an awe-inspiring setting in Cwm Pennant along which runs the young River Tanat which rises in the dramatic valley head. Pennant Melangell is about 2½ miles north-west of Llangynog along a no-through road. The flat bottom of the narrow valley is surrounded by the wooded slopes of mountains which frame three of its sides, the highest peak being 611 metres, or just under 2,000 feet. As Thomas Pennant remarked in the late 18th century 'This valley is exceedingly picturesque : inclosed by hills on all sides, except its entrance; watered by the Tanat, which springs not far off. The upper end is bounded by two vast precipices, down which, at times, fall two great cataracts; between them juts out the great and rude promontory of Moel ddu Fawr, which almost divides the precipices into equal parts: and all together formed a fine and solemn retreat for devotees.'[1] The valley has several clusters of features dating from Neolithic times.

Saint Melangell (or Monacella in the Latinized form) was probably the grand-daughter of Tudwal Tudclud, and her father's name is given in the earliest pedigrees as Cyfelch (with variations in spelling); her mother was Ethni Wyddeles. Melangell's uncle, Rhydderch Hael, was the victor of the battle of Arderydd in 573.[2] She was therefore probably active at around 600, about a generation after

111

The reputed site of St. Melangell's tomb

the saints Teilo and David. Pennant Melangell is the only church dedicated to this saint and shows that she did not travel and establish foundations as so many other early saints were wont to do.

Baring-Gould and Fisher suggest that her legend was possibly written by Matthew of Westminster (a name given to a composite record), and was transcribed from two sources. More recent scholars disagree, suggesting that parts of the legend may date back to the 14th century or earlier, albeit that much is a later gloss. The legend states that St. Melangell was the daughter of the Irish King Iowchel and that he had wanted her to marry a nobleman of his court against her wishes. Thomas Pennant relates that the 'princess had vowed celibacy. She fled from her father's dominions, and took refuge in this place, where she lived fifteen years without seeing the face of man.'[3] In 604, Brochwel Ysgythrog, prince of Powys was out hunting hares in the valley, and during the chase one of the hares ran into a thicket where Melangell was praying and sheltered within the folds of her gown, facing the dogs from its place of protection. Brochwel urged the dogs to attack it, but they would not and retired howling. The prince was impressed and questioned Melangell, and decided to grant her the rights to the land of Pennant in perpetual 'asylum, refuge, and defence.'[4] She spent 37 years in solitude at Pennant, keeping a colony of tame hares about her, and setting up a nunnery which also became famous as a place of sanctuary for the oppressed. The rights granted to her by Brochwel were respected and maintained by his family for the benefit of her successors, although we do not know for how many generations this continued. She was reputedly buried at Pennant, and a shrine was set up. Thomas Pennant records that she died in 'a good old age' and that her 'tomb was in a little chapel, or oratory, adjoining to the church, and now used as a vestry-room. The room still is called Cell-y-bedd, or the Cell of the Grave; her relics, as well as her image, have been long since removed; but I think the last is still to be seen in the church-yard.' It is likely that this latter was the 14th-century effigy reputedly of Melangell which is now in the church (see below). Records of offerings exist detailing donations given at the shrine in 1535, and shows that devotion of this saint was long-lived. Melangell became the patroness of hares which were called Wyn Melangell — 'Melangell's Lambs.' Thomas Pennant records 'Till the last century [17th century], so strong a superstition prevailed, that no person would kill a hare in the parish; and even later, when a hare was pursued by dogs, it was firmly believed, that if any one cried "God and St. Monacella be with thee," it was sure to escape.'[5] Modern stone sculptures of hares are to be seen in the church.

The church lies within a scattered hamlet and overlies part of a middle Bronze Age cremation cemetery dated approximately to 1,200 BC, suggesting a continuity of use from pagan to Christian times. Within the Tanat valley, the only possible religious remains yet found that may date to the period 700 BC–AD 400 are three 'Celtic' heads carved in stone that are set into the front of a mid-17th century house at Glantanat-isaf in the south-east corner of the Tanat Valley.[6]

The churchyard at Pennant Melangell is approximately curvilinear. There are six large yews, with five to the south, east and western sides of the churchyard having girths of up to 13 feet (4 metres) and forming the remnant of a ring around the church. Some are on raised mounds which may be the result of the build up of soil when graves were dug. There is also a low mound to the north-west of the church which indicates the site of another yew.[7] The boundary of the churchyard was 'traditionally held to demarcate the *noddfa* or sanctuary'[8] in which people would claim the protection of the church against arrest, harm or other threats. The earliest fabric of the church is 12th century, but it has been altered, with sections dating from the 15th, 17th and the 19th centuries. The lychgate has some early interest as monolithic stones support the corbelled arches and there are traces of a possible mid-16th- to mid-17th-century verse painted on the inner, south-east facing wall over the arch.[9]

It is suggested that the church and shrine were built in stone on an earlier church site under the patronage of a nobleman, Rhirid Flaidd, in the later part of the 12th century. The apse was constructed to house the reputed grave of St. Melangell. At some stage the doorway from the chancel was blocked, and an outside entrance installed in the north wall of the apse, which was itself eventually blocked. This structure fell into disrepair and was replaced by a square room in 1751 which was first used as a vestry-room and later as a schoolroom. A large, unhewn slate slab set above a stone-edged grave was kept within the structure throughout this time and can been seen today set in the cobbled floor of the reconstructed apse. In 1958 the Cell-y-Bedd was repaired, and the foundations

The shrine at Pennant Melangell

to the earlier apse were found. The shrine was reconstructed and placed within the Cell-y-Bedd and a new floor was laid. The latest restoration programme, which began in 1989, was the most thorough to date and combined extensive archaeological excavation and the recording and demolition of the 1751 building. Six or seven medieval floor layers were found within the apse. On the north side of the church the level of the ground was reduced and several graves were found, some of which were below the foundation levels of the present church and some were found 'capped with quartz pebbles.' Evidence of seven different building phases was also discovered. A second stone-covered grave, besides that attributed to St. Melangell, was found below the apse footings. The apse was rebuilt in the style of the original 12th-century structure with the door from the chancel re-opened.[10] The result is most satisfactory, giving the visitor the impression of walking into an original apse with St. Melangell's grave positioned against the far wall, which is as close to an early saint's resting place as it is possible to get. This would, of course, have been the objective of the original structure.

It is thought that the ornate Romanesque shrine was probably broken up during the Reformation, and parts were used as building material in the south porch, the south side of the chancel, the south and west walls of the church and in the lychgate. In 1989 the shrine was reconstructed as close to the original design as knowledge permitted and was placed in its original position within the chancel. The recreation of the earlier site makes Pennant Melangell a highlight amongst the sites covered in this book, and focuses one's attention on the effect that a saint's shrine would have had upon pilgrims. The carving and design of the shrine are delicate and unique amongst the sites we have visited, and it is 'reputedly the earliest surviving Romanesque shrine in Northern Europe.'[11] The shrine became particularly popular during the Middle Ages. From the 15th-century poems of Guto'r Glyn it appears that pilgrims were travelling long distances to seek remedies for illnesses and the site was 'also seen as a final resting place for former pilgrims.'[12] A 14th-century stone effigy against the south wall of the chancel is supposed to represent St. Melangell — on either side of her waist are purportedly two carvings of hares.

The rood screen dates from the 15th century and is worthy of close inspection, not only for its delicate carved tracery but also for its depiction of the story of St. Melangell. Along the top section there is a depiction of Brochwel hunting, with Melangell in the middle holding a crosier, and hares and dogs are also shown. Thomas Pennant however states that the 'legend is perpetuated by some rude wooden carvings of the saint, with numbers of hares scuttling to her for protection'[13] and one wonders if he is referring to another carving. The screen also has what Clwyd-Powys Archaeological Trust describe as 'a rare carving of the Green Man the woodland spirit of Celtic myth included by the medieval woodcarver in recognition of his ancestors' pre-Christian beliefs.'[14]

The church is positioned on a faint terrace with the ground sloping away to the south — Clwyd-Powys Archaeological Trust consider this slight terrace may be a natural river terrace.[15] There are no marked burials on the north side of the church, a side avoided in past centuries as it was considered the dark or evil side, and only criminals or other 'outsiders' were buried here, which may account for some of the unmarked graves found in the 1989 excavations. A hollow on the north side near a yew tree, which was planted in 1978, is thought to have held a cockpit; the remains of another were found outside the lychgate in what is now the carpark. In times past ball games were played against the north wall, and the church enclosure was also used for fairs. Such activities were suppressed by the early 19th century. There was once a small mound near to the site of the putative cockpit within the churchyard, although it is now destroyed. It is thought that it may have been a Dark Age preaching mound of the type usually associated with St. Germanus, although it may have been an earthwork connected with the cockpit.[16] If the former, it may have been the predecessor to the medieval preaching cross.

There is some evidence that Pennant Melangell started its Christian life as an enclosed cemetery without a church but continued the funerary tradition from a pagan cemetery dating back to the middle Bronze Age. Such evidence of continuity is rare. It is also rare to have a church that still has the reputed grave of its founder, as well as their shrine. Hints of religious activity in the local landscape are found in the holy well, Ffynnon Cwm-Ewyn, which is on the hill above Pennant Melangell. At the head of Cwm Pennant, and up the lane from the church, is a farm called Tyn-y-cablyd (SJ 016 266) which name derives from Maundy Thursday, a day when traditionally people from a higher social standing gave gifts to — and washed the feet of — the poor.[17]

Gwely Melangell (SJ 023 262), or Melangell's Bed, is in a cleft of rock at Craig y Gwely, less than a quarter of a mile south of the church on the opposite side of the valley. Her festival is on 31st January but at Pennant Melangell it was observed on May 27th.[18]

The church is orientated towards pilgrims, those needing personal peace and time to reflect and to meditate. Pennant Melangell is indeed a very special place.

TRELYSTAN – St. Mary
(SJ 263 039)

The church has links to the family of St. Beuno, has an early enclosure and, albeit somewhat later, was the burial place of Edelstan the Renowned in 1010.

The church of St. Mary, Trelystan is in a remote location about 3 miles south-east of Welshpool. It is near the putative homestead of St. Beuno's parents called *Banhenig* (see also p.68) (possibly now remembered in the name Badnage Wood just to the north-east of the church), and may have been founded by Beuno at his father's township when the latter died. However Baring-Gould and Fisher prefer the possibility of this happening at Llanymynch.[1] We prefer Trelystan as the candidate because of the similarity in the name of Badnage with *Banhenig*, and the fact that the site is listed as having a low circular earthwork within the churchyard which is considered to be of probable Dark Age date.[2] The dedication to Mary is likely to be a Norman re-dedication.

The first documentary evidence for the church appears in the 11th century with a reference to the burial of one Edelstan the Renowned in 1010.[3] It would appear that Edelstan is synonymous with Elystan Glodrudd who was the founder of one of the royal tribes of Wales. He figures in later genealogies of many Welsh families and of the English Cadogans. The name Elystan/Edelstan is the Welsh rendition of the Anglo-Saxon name Athelstan and appears to be directly connected with King Athelstan who had dealings with Wales. Hwyel Dda, his contemporary, initiated an anglophile policy and a number of Welsh princes bore Anglo-Saxon names in the 10th and early 11th century and attended the Anglo-Saxon courts, a process that continued for most of the 10th century. Elystan/Edelstan was very likely amongst them. In a 16th-century pedigree it is recorded that Edelstan's wife was the great-grand-daughter of Hywel Dda. In a late source known as Harley MS. 1973, it states 'Elstan Glodrith or Edelstan the renowned, born in the Castle of Hereford, anno 933 and in the 9 year of Edlistan [Athelstan], King of the Saxons, who was his godfather, was Earl of Hereford, lord of the country above Offadich, between Wye and Severn, in the time of Edilred [Aelthelred], King of the Saxons. He dyed and was buried at Chapel Trest Elistan in Caursland.' In another source it states that Edelstan was killed in a 'civil brawl' at Cefn Digoll, Montgomeryshire which Radford and Hemp identify as Caer Digoll, a circular earthwork on the Long Mountain above Trelystan. It is thought that he was killed under the nationalist revival under Gruffydd ap Llywelyn who had his first victory over the Anglo-Saxons in 1039 probably near Buttington a few miles north of Trelystan. As Radford and Hemp remark, after this victory it is likely that Llywelyn turned on his anglophile countrymen and 'a Welsh chieftain established on Cefn Digoll, on the slopes of the Long Mountain, would be an easy and natural victim.' The reputed burial cross-slab of Edelstan's son can be seen at the church of Llanrhaeadr-ym-Mochnant (see p.99)[4]

Trelystan church is most unusual and, on first view, appears to be typical of what one would expect of a 17th-century Welsh-border's domestic dwelling (minus the bell turret, of course). However the external black and white exterior, which is 19th-century brick and timber work, encases a 15th-century timber frame and arch-braced roof which can be seen within the church. It is thought that an early wattle and daub structure was replaced by the timber-framed church in the 15th century and that Strata Marcella monastery had acquired it in the 13th century — the adjoining land called 'Monks Field' was certainly acquired by the monastery in 1229.[5]

The churchyard is quite small and nearly rectangular; it has probably been extended to the south-west and north-east. Within the church enclosure is the remains of an earlier boundary visible as a low circular bank, most obvious on the north-west and north-eastern sides and is as high as 3½ to 4 feet, although there are traces of it on the other sides of the church. There also seems to be low platform or slight mound under the church.[6] The Sites and Monument Record suggest the earthworks represents the 'remains of a Dark Age churchyard enclosure bank' which measures about 165 feet by about 132 feet and which is, significantly, 'respected by [the] layout of graves and gravestones.'[7] There are six yews of some age around the western side of the church with the biggest by the south porch, and a further two yews near the south-east gate, with another which has been felled.[8]

Radnorshire

Llanbadarn Fynydd

Llananno

St. Harmon

River Wye

Llanbister

River Ithon

River Lugg

Llansantffraed Cwmdeuddwr

Nantmel

Llanbadarn Fawr

Discoed

Llanyre

Capel Maelog

Llandegley

Llanfihangel -nant-Melan

Old Radnor

Disserth

River Edw

Glascwm

River Arrow

Llansantffraed-in-Elvel

Cregrina

Colva

Llanfaredd

Rhulen

Llanbadarn-y-Garreg

Bryngwyn

River Wye

Aberedw

Llanddewi Fach

Llandeilo Graban

Llanstephan

Llowes

Boughrood

ABEREDW – St. Cewydd
(SO 080 473)

The shape of the churchyard and its position next to two rivers and a stream are suggestive of an early site.

The church of St. Cewydd is 3½ miles south-east of Builth Wells, situated at the top of a steep bank above the boulder-strewn River Edw, which flows with a fast current, almost a torrent after heavy rain. Appropriately, this is one of the few dedications to the Welsh rain saint.

The site is probably an early one. St. Cewydd was brother to Meilig of Llowes, and son of Caw from Strathclyde in Scotland, whose family were driven out of their lands and fled to Wales. He trained under St. Cadoc, thus is an approximate contemporary of David. We are also told that he had a son, St. Garrai of Llanarrai (now Llanharry) in Glamorganshire, but this is unproven, and the relevant entry is in the Iolo Manuscripts, which can be unreliable. St. Cewydd has two other dedications, the second being at Disserth also in Radnorshire, and the third just across the border in Herefordshire at Cusop. His name is also connected with a farm west of Builth, Cil Cewydd, in Llanfihangel Bryn Pabuan parish near Brecon, which was reputedly his retreat, and he is also linked with a mountain track called Rhiw Gewydd ('Cedwydd's hill-slope') above Llandeilo Graban over which he may have passed to visit his brother at Llowes. There also used to be dedications to him at Lancaut (referred to as *Lann Ceuid*) in the Llandaff

121

Charters near Chepstow, and one at Llangewydd near Bridgend, which have both disappeared. In the parish of Llanymawddwy (Merionethshire) a brook, Cewydd, and a township, Cwm Cewydd, are named after him. It is possible that the saint also had a dedications in Somerset and two in Pembrokeshire.[1]

St. Cewydd is regarded as the Welsh counterpart of St. Swithin, the rain saint; in some sources they share the same festival day, but different churches celebrated it on different days in July. Just as with St. Swithin, the weather could be determined for the next forty days depending on whether it rained on St. Cewydd's feast day. It is not known how Cewydd became the Welsh St. Swithin, but Baring-Gould and Fisher suggest it may have derived from a 'general pre-Christian belief regarding the meteorologically prophetic character of some day about that period of the year.'[2]

Abercdw church is a substantial and attractive building of 14th-century and later date, having an unusual screen with delicately carved ogee tracery. The churchyard feels spacious and is bounded on the south and east by the River Edw, although much lower down in a deeply cut valley. A small stream comes in from the north and meets the Edw just east of the church, a short distance to the west, and beyond the B road, flows the River Wye, a fitting watery location for the rain saint. The church enclosure is quite large and sub-oval and, because of the river and stream, the ground falls away beyond the churchyard on these sides. Within the enclosure there is a gentle south to north slope. The northern boundary is definitely curved and a lane borders this side. There are three old yews on the north side of the church and a younger yew to the south.[3]

BOUGHROOD – St. Cynog
(SO 128 393)

Early dedication and a curvilinear churchyard.

The church is about 8 miles south-west of Hay-on-Wye at the centre of the dispersed village and close to the Wye, which flows a couple of hundred yards to the west. The location, dedication and shape of the churchyard is considered suggestive of an early foundation. The church conforms with distribution of other Cynog dedications as they are mostly in the kingdom of his father, Brychan, who probably had a 'palace' not far away at Talgarth. The church appears in a taxation record of 1291 as *ecclesia de Boghred* with a fairly low value of £3 6s. 8d.[1]

The church was entirely rebuilt in 1854 and no earlier features remain. The churchyard however is large and curvilinear and is 'on level ground on the edge of a river terrace'. The ground within the enclosure is about 3 feet higher than the road surface, and the ground slopes gently up to the wall on this side. While the difference in ground level on the roadside may be due to hollowing through use, the western and southern boundaries which adjoin fields are about 1 to 2 feet higher than the external land. There are no variations in the surface of the churchyard to indicate that it has been extended or altered from its present boundaries with the exception of the southern entrance. Here the boundary has been extended outwards and there is an internal scarp bank running up to about 3½ feet high which records the original perimeter line.[2] If the present churchyard is roughly coeval with the original size of the enclosure, there would have been sufficient room for other structures, but whether there were any is pure speculation.

The curving churchyard boundary with the internal ground level sloping up to the walls

BRYNGWYN – St. Michael
(SO 186 495)

The church contains an early pillar stone and a mysterious carving of two dancing figures.

The church of St. Michael at Bryngwyn is in an elevated position within a small settlement adjoining Bryngwyn Common, 5 miles north-west of Hay-on-Wye. The dedication may be one of the early St. Michael dedications (see under Moccas p.291) although this cannot be proven. It may be significant that it is called *ecclesia de Bringwin* in a 1291 taxation record (where it is given a fairly healthy value of £5 6s. 8d.) and it was only in 1535 that it appears with its present appelation.[1]

The nave and chancel may be 13th century in part but the church was restored in the Victorian period. On the south side of the chancel is a columnar pillar stone dated by Nash-Williams to between the 7th and 9th centuries.[2] Over 5½ feet tall and approximately 1½ feet wide, it would appear originally to have had a rounded top but a large chunk is missing from the top left corner. The stone originally stood in the churchyard, south of the chancel and near the dancing figures. Howse records that it was still there in 1949 and suggests this may have been its original position, although in the Sites and Monuments Record its original site is stated as unknown.[3] It has Ogam lettering (barely visible with the naked eye but just discernable if a photograph, taken of the stone on a very long exposure, is closely examined) which has not been deciphered and a large, deeply-incised cross, with smaller but deeply carved crosses in the angles. At the end of each arm and in the centre of the large cross are circles with a smaller circle carved in each which are referred to as 'ring and dot devices.'[4] The five crosses are supposed to represent the five wounds of Christ. Howse quotes an historian who suggests it may be pre-Christian with the incised cross 'of curious design being an early Christian addition.'[5] Do we then have a pagan artefact that was Christianised? A pillar stone can be found in the porch at Llangasty Tal-y-llyn, but the Llangasty stone looks phallic and no attempt has been made to Christianise it. The presence of Ogam script on the Bryngwyn stone suggests an early Irish presence, stones with Ogam lettering also occurring at Trallong and Defynnog in the Usk valley. The line of Irish communication seems naturally to stretch across south Wales from Pembrokeshire where Ogam inscribed stones are more common, through Carmarthenshire and into south-east Radnorshire through the fertile valleys which have evidence of man's occupation from the prehistoric era.[6]

There is also an interesting stone at the south-east corner of the chancel by the path from the main gate. It has two figures carved at right angles to each other, which Haslam describes as female,[7] their heads pointing together, one on each surface of the wall into which they are set. Each side is about 18 inches long and 8 inches wide. However in the early 19th century the Radnorshire historian Jonathan Williams described the figures as being male and female.[8] We would agree with the latter. The figure on the south wall appears to be wearing a full length skirt and holding their hands on their hips. The opposing fugure looks to be wearing trousers or cullottes, reminiscent of the carving of a figure on the door-surround at Kilpeck in Herefordshire ascribed to the 12th-century Herefordshire School of Sculpture. They are termed dancing figures. The dress of figures looks early, but no date for the carving has been given.

Within the porch to the right is a carved coffin lid having a large cross, and simple but well-carved figures of a chalice and a missal, dated to the 12th century. It was recovered from the chancel floor during renovation and mounted in its present position. A Burgundian coin of 1384–1404 was also found under the floor during restoration and Howse suggests it was probably dropped there by 'one of the Earl of Warwick's soldiers from Pain's Castle.'[9]

The churchyard is described as 'D-shaped' — the rounded part being the western side of the boundary. The enclosure is raised by up to 4 feet on the southern side above the external land, although there is little height difference on the northern and eastern sides. On the west, south-west and north there is internal embanking against the perimeter wall up to a height of 3 feet, and it is particularly noticeable to the south-west corner. North of the church there is a 'shallow scarp running east to west' which is unexplained.[10] In shape and form it is a suggestive of an early curvilinear site.

Bryngwyn is described by Howse as 'one of the best small churches ... and commanding a magnificent view' — all we would add is that on a sunny summer's day the place nears perfection in its idyllic setting.

The pillar stone inside the church

CAPEL MAELOG – St. Meilig
(SO 063 607)

Remains of 12th- or 13th-century foundation resited in Llandrindod Wells, but excavation of the original site tells of an unusually shaped early church.

The current remains near the lake in Llandrindod Wells were moved there in the late 1980s, after excavation in an area which is now an eastern suburb of Llandrindod revealed the remains of a medieval church and enclosure. This was at SO 069 613.[1] In the early 1800s Jonathan Williams had reported that 'in the middle of a cornfield, were dug up the foundations of a very ancient chapel called Llanfaelon, and supposed to have belonged to some monastic edifice, but no account of it exists', — unfortunately Williams did not give the location of the remains.[2] Its location was then forgotten.

The name Capel Mealog appears to be a fairly recent invention and the church was known in 1291 as Llandemaylon/Llanvayloir which are anglicisations of the Welsh name Llanfaelon. In 1517 the last reference to the church was as Llanvaylor and in 1533 when the *Valor Ecclesiasticus* was compiled it was not mentioned, which either means it had ceased to exist as a church, or was, at least, of such little value that it was not listed.[3] Interestingly Llanvailon survived as an alternative name for a farm close by called Bongam Isaf until the early 18th century.

It was thanks to T.E. Morris in the early 20th century that the position of the church was re-established. In 1917 he described the site as occupying the central position in an approximately 2.5 acre field. 'The Chapel enclosure', he wrote, 'is easily traceable, the mounds forming the remains of the northern, and especially of the southern boundaries being definitely marked, and almost suggesting a small encampment within which the Chapel had been built. It was bounded on the east by a steep declivity, at the foot of which a brook flows, containing a number of stones which may have once formed part of the masonry of the Chapel. The western boundary of the enclosure, about 125 ft. in length, now forms a part of the hedge dividing the [next] field ... It is thought that access was obtained to the Church through the land now forming this field. The part of the hedge bordering on the enclosure is stronger than the remainder, inasmuch as its foundations there appear to be of stone. The northern boundary of the enclosure is about 110 ft. in length and the southern about 154 ft.'[4] Morris explains that the name of the nearby Gorse or Gorst farm is an anglicisation of the Welsh word *Gors* meaning 'a bog' and gives an idea of the wild terrain encountered by the early church builders.

Between 1984–6 Clwyd-Powys Archaeological Trust thoroughly excavated the site when it came to light as the area was being prepared for a housing development. They found a number of phases of activity, starting with scattered flintwork dated to prehistoric times, followed by evidence of a possible secular settlement from the late Roman and post-Roman eras. Ploughmarks were found under the banks on the north and south sides which showed agricultural activity on the site before the church was built. The first evidence of religious activity was the presence of a small inhumation (burial) cemetery which pre-dated the first stone church. This comprised at least 20 graves which were 'divided into eastern and western groups by a cross-ditch'. An 'exceptionally large and elaborate burial' was aligned on the subsequent axis of the church and it is suggested that this may have been the grave of the founder. The grave was edged with small upright slabs on its upper edges and contained 'a scattering of large white quartz pebbles'. It is thought conceivable that a wooden church accompanied this earliest cemetery although no evidence was found. The site was enclosed by low earthern banks around the crown of the hill.[5]

When the first stone church was built the cross-ditch was filled in and a building, comprising a small nave about 15 feet wide and 21 feet long and a chancel measuring about 6½ feet by 10 feet, was erected. This church appears to have only had earth floors and the stone walls were not mortared or plastered. Some time later the chancel and the nave's west wall were demolished and curving apses replaced both ends. The chancel arch was also removed 'giving rise to a church plan which appears to be unique in the British Isles, with a single chamber rounded at each end.' Only a few churches were known to have had western apses and the only surviving church in Britain to have one is Langford in Essex. Building material gathered from the foundations of both apses contained reused squared masonry and big fragments of Roman tile and brick and it is likely they were looted from the Roman fort at Castell Colleen less than 1½ miles to the north-west. Britnell considers it is possible they were used for window openings or string courses. Large shallow pits were found at the corners of the church and it is thought they were perhaps quarry pits for clay to bond the walls which still stayed unplastered. Crushed Roman brick was mixed with earth for a new floor and a 'partial rectangular setting of stones indicated the position of a free-standing altar in the eastern apse.' Evidence was also found to suggest that the church had a stone roof at some stage and that some of the windows had leaded lights.[6]

Over 350 graves were found within the church enclosure. Most of them surrounded the eastern end of the church and lay to the east of the original cross-ditch, indicating that this boundary continued to be respected. Those that underlay the church foundation or floors were considered to belong to the pre-church cemetery. A few graves were found within the church cut through the nave floor, and were probably of people of a higher social standing. Several burials were also found cut through the chancel floor, probably the remains of clergy. Some clusters of graves were thought to represent family groups.[7]

Although the date of the early cemetery and building of the first stone church is uncertain, the later church is thought to have dated from the 12th or early 13th centuries which strongly suggests a pre-Norman date for the earliest phases, supported by its dedication to the 6th-century St. Meilig. At some time in the early 16th century the church went out of use. The cemetery stopped being used 'before memorial stones became common, and before graveyards were commonly walled. The church remained small and underdeveloped, its plan fossilized in the fashion of earlier centuries.'[8] Most churches underwent rebuilding and modifications in the 14th to 15th centuries and again, often radically, in the 19th-century Victorian rebuilds, but Capel Maelog missed these and left the ghost of its 12th- or 13th-century layout.

COLVA – St. David
(SO 200 531)

The site is probably mentioned in David's *Life*, and has a partial ring of yews.

The church of St. David, 11 miles west of Kington, is 1,250 feet above sea level, 'one of the highest old sites in Wales'.[1] It is one of a group of four St. David dedications in a small radius in the mid-Wales uplands and fits in well with the monastic ideal of being detached from worldly distractions by remoteness. The fact that Glascwm and Colva are amongst the few sites actually mentioned in St. David's *Life*, although some of the information contained in this section is spurious, adds weight to the idea that Colva is an early dedication, either founded in the 6th or 7th century, or in a later St. David cult movement.

The fabric of the church is old, but not early. Some of the structure is 13th century.[2] There are several old wall-paintings, including one of a skull and crossbones over the font. The design of the church is refreshingly simple, an example of uncluttered rural Welsh church architecture. It has been noted that Colva (with nearby Rhulen) were chapelries attached to Glascwm which would explain why there are no medieval tax assessments for these first two churches.[3]

The churchyard is rectangular and slopes quite steeply north to south; the church is terraced into this slope. The enclosure is raised by up to 6½ feet above the roadway and there are no obvious signs that the churchyard has been extended. The boundaries are walled in places, with large stone blocks clearly visible on the exterior wall to the west; there is an obvious build-up of soil against all the internal boundaries. The churchyard is medium-sized, but as Colva was subordinate to Glascwm, and not known as a major site, there would presumably not have been the need for building space within the enclosure. There are six large yews in a curve to the south of the church, with two on the western perimeter bank.[4]

CREGRINA – St. David
(SO 124 521)

One of a cluster of possible early dedications to St. David but also with tenuous associations with David's mother, Non; also has two ancient-looking yews in the churchyard.

The church of St. David's lies about 6 miles south-west of Builth Wells on a spur of land above the River Edw, which restricts the site. The church's first mention is in 1291 when it is called *ecclesia de Crugrima* and given a low value of £2 13s. 4d.[1]

The churchyard is polygonal and the only earthwork noted in the enclosure is a scarp bank which runs diagonally across the south side and may be a natural feature. There is no indication that the enclosure has been extended although it is accepted some changes to its original form have probably occurred. The shape is not definitive, but the setting is suggestive of an early site as it is quite remote. On the southern boundary of the chuchyard there is 'a hint of a more curvilinear bank or possibly an infilled ditch externally.' On the northern boundary there is a sizeable drop down to a hollowed-out roadway and there is obvious internal embanking on this side. As to the church, the nave may be 13th century, the chancel possibly 15th century with known restorations in 1903 and 1958.[2] The church is painted white and has an old wooden screen and a Norman font.

It is one in a noticeable but small cluster of St. David churches in this area of uplands, those at Colva and Glascwm being mentioned in St. David's *Life*. It is possible that Cregrina was linked with this group at an early date. It was certainly a subservient church to Glascwm and called *Craig Furuna* in earlier documents.[3] It is suggested that St. David's grandmother had her church here where, Non, St. David's mother, may have been born; Non too is also said to have had a church here called 'Llan Non.'[4] This would seem unlikely as Non was associated with Pembrokeshire as was her mother who was married to the king of that area of Wales; however it might explain the cluster of David dedications in this area.

There are two mature yews opposite the west wall of the church. Both have sizeable girths and the one nearest the church has a hollowed trunk.

DISCOED – St. Michael
(SO 276 648)

Discoed has some circumstantial evidence to suggest an early Christian site which replaced a pagan precursor: the raised nature of the churchyard, its partial curvilinearity, the presence of the ancient yews and the well — without a charter or an early inscribed stone this is about as good as the evidence gets.

The church of St. Michael is situated at the centre of the hamlet 2 miles west of Presteigne. The church was partly rebuilt in 1869 but the nave and chancel are not on the same axis and it is possible they stand on old foundations.[1] The medieval shell of the building still survives, but with Victorian windows and doors.[2]

The shape of the churchyard is sub-triangular, or irregular in shape. However there is a slight scarp to the north of the church which may be an earlier boundary. This suggests that the churchyard was once smaller and more rectangular but with a more curved eastern boundary. To the east the churchyard is about 6 feet higher that the external ground level and to the south about 2 feet.[3] The size and shape of the churchyard indicate an early site.

The ancient churchyard yew to the north of the church is the most interesting feature in terms of establishing Discoed as an ancient site. It is a male and its girth has been estimated at 37 feet.[4] It is split almost in two with an enormous, partially intact, divided trunk which shows new growth in the missing sections between the two remaining halves. The tree bole has a completely different appearance when viewed from opposing angles — on one side it looks nearly intact, whilst on the other it is fragmented and hollowed. It has been estimated by some experts to be 5,000 years old[5] which would pre-date Christianity by several thousand years, whilst Bevan-Jones suggests a more conservative date of about 1,400 years, although he allows for the possibility of it being between 2 and 5,000 years old. He observes that hollowing and consequent partial loss of trunks in very old yews makes it far more difficult to estimate an age based purely on girth as the chance of the variability in the growth of the girth is increased, so decreasing the accuracy of estimating an age.[6] A second, female yew to the south-west of the church has a girth of about 22 feet and an estimated age of 1,400 years, and may well coincide with the establishment of a church. Perhaps this was a Christian purification of the site, if the yew on the north side was an old tree in the early medieval period which had pagan associations. Whatever the actual ages of these yews, the male yew looks substantially older than the female and we would suggest it has a pre-Christian origin — it is, after all, on the north-side which is considered by Allen Meredith to be the original position of deliberate plantings to protect against evil.[7] The north side was long held to be the 'dark side' and the place of evil (see section on yew trees pp.24-27). It is possible therefore that the female yew was planted by an early founder/saint at Discoed to Christianise the site or at least to neutralise the pagan aspect presented by the older male yew. The presence of another ancient yew at Yew Tree Farm on the roadside has been mentioned (see p.25) and it is interesting to speculate that this, too, was an early Christian site, indicated today only by its ancient yew and proximity to a spring.

Discoed also has a moss-covered spring nearly 2 feet deep by the main entrance of the churchyard, just in front of the wall.

The dedication to St. Michael may well be an early one as he was a popular saint in the Welsh borders from the 8th century, but, given the age of the yews, we suggest Discoed was founded by an earlier British saint whose name is now forgotten.

DISSERTH – St. Cewydd
(SO 034 584)

Indications in the dedication, setting and physical characteristics of the site suggest it is early, and there is a well which has hints of pagan observance.

The church of St. Cewydd at Disserth (also spelled Diserth) is about 4½ miles north of Builth Wells, cradled in a bend of the River Ithon. This is the second Radnorshire church dedicated to St. Cewydd (for his history see Aberedw p.121). There are very few properties in the immediate locality and the place-name 'Disserth' seems most apposite, as translated it means 'deserted or desert place' which were areas 'so beloved of Celtic saints as offering suitable sites for their churches.' It has been noted by Fenn and Sinclair that churches at places named Disserth (of which there are a few in Wales) tend to be close to churches with St. Brigid dedications — in this case Disserth is in the parish adjoining Llansantffraed (in English, 'the church of St. Bridget') -in-Elvael and they remark that this topographical connection may suggest that the cult of St. Brigid was introduced into Wales in the early 7th century. They also observe that the Irish culdees (wandering saints who sought pefection in solitary places) inspired a similar movement in Wales 'which may be commemortated by dedications to St. Ffraid and their nearby Diserths.' The hidden nature of the site would also have helped protect the inhabitants from raiders and marauders in the same way that the founders of St. David's, Llandaff and Bangor chose riverside hollows for protection.[1]

Haslam remarks that the 'church stands very much as a Victorian architect, called in for advice, might have found many of the Radnorshire churches.' At

Disserth, however, there was no restoration and the fabric takes one straight into the parish life of *c*.1700.'² Disserth church is therefore a rare and rather wonderful survival among the small, country churches of mid-Wales. It has a full set of bench pews, a centrally placed three-decker pulpit in old church style and there are the remnants of 15th-century wall paintings uncovered in 1954. There are also the remains of a rood screen — the timberwork within the church is very becoming in a simple vernacular way. The nave and chancel are as one, are whitewashed externally and probably of 14th-century date; the squat, battlemented tower is reputedly of *c*.1400.³

The churchyard is a rather irregular shape with rounded corners, perhaps bordering on curvilinear. Most of the boundary is walled, against which there is some soil build up internally, as with many putative early sites. The interior of the churchyard does not appear raised, although this may be because of its position next to the River Ithon and the result of potential flooding. It is noticeable that many riverside sites do not have raised churchyards or visible early boundaries. Indeed, there is no sign of an earlier, relict boundary within the churchyard despite some irregularity in the ground surface of the enclosure north of the church,⁴ but perhaps the existing churchyard has remained unchanged.

There are a number of yews along the boundary, four to the east, three to the west and south. Although they are not deemed to be of great age,⁵ their presence may be significant for an early site.

There is also a well within the churchyard (but after searching we were unable to find it — it is probably very overgrown and hidden) called Ffynnon Gewydd after St. Cewydd. It was customary in the past to dress the well on New Year's Day with mistletoe, a practice still observed in the late 17th century. In 1698 the antiquarian Edward Lhuyd reported meeting a woman who told him that on every new year's day she filled her pitcher, then dressed the well with mistletoe 'for she who came first after midnight to the well, which must be dressed, would receive its fruits and be as a queen.'⁶ A similar custom was observed in Herefordshire at Dinedor at the Holy or Holly Well, which now feeds a garden pond in a private boarding kennels. The first water drawn from this well in the new year was called 'the cream of the well' and it was thought to bring good luck and possibly even beauty to those who obtained it, drank it or washed in it. It was competed over and if it was presented to a neighbour 'as a pledge of good fortune; a pecuniary compliment is expected in return.'⁷ In Ireland during Beltane celebrations the first water drawn from a well after midnight on 1 May was termed 'the purity of the well' and this water would be kept with great care during the following year as it was believed to be 'a powerful charm against witchcraft', a custom also known in Scotland.⁸ It seems as if the well at Disserth shares a long heritage with these other places and the custom does have the air of a pagan ritual or belief.

GLASCWM – St. David
(SO 156 532)

There is written evidence for an early site, it is a known *clas* church and there are legends regarding a miraculous bell.

The church of St. David is about 9 miles east of Builth Wells in beautiful high rolling Radnorshire hills. It lies in the bottom of a steep valley just to the west of the village, a quiet setting described in *c.*1539 by Leland as 'Arow risith not far from Glascumbe, wher is a chirche but few houses.'[1] This description, as accurate now as it was then, gives no clue to the importance of the church which was the mother, or *clas*, church of the area. Glascwm's value in the 'Taxatio' of 1291 is £13 6s. 8d. — Cregrina was valued at £2 13s. 4d., and Llanbister, the highest value in the diocese, at over £30. Glascwm had therefore developed into a relatively wealthy foundation, which probably reflects its important origins although the high value of Llanbister is surprising.

When St. Illtud was in hiding from the king of the area around Llantwit Major in South Glamorgan, he disclosed his whereabouts to Gildas, who was travelling to visit St. David, carrying with him a bell. It was the sound of the bell that had attracted Illtud, who requested it. Gildas refused and delivered the bell to St. David, who on hearing of the request, had it returned to Illtud — portable bells were beloved by the early saints. The bell was said to have been brought to Glascwm by St. David's two legendary oxen.[2] A Welsh poet, Gwynfardd Brycheiniog, writing in *c.*1180, describes 'Two oxen of Dewi, exalted were they; two kinsmen who used to walk yolked together side by side to convey a gift running (swiftly) to Glasgwm' and refers to three objects 'the three dignified ones' being transported: 'sweet, beloved Bangu [the portable bell] was left and the two other large ones for (in) Brycheiniog.' Henken suggests the bell given to Glascwm may have been that reputedly given to St. David in Jerusalem, and the two other 'dignified ones' may also have been bells, but nothing more is known about them.[3]

A 'handbell which has most miraculous powers' called 'Bangu' was described by Giraldus Cambrensis in the late 12th century as being preserved at Glascwm. He recounts how a woman took the handbell in an attempt to free her husband who was chained up in Rhayader castle. The castle keepers refused to free the man but seized the bell. Divine vengeance was wrought when the whole town was burnt down 'except the wall on which the handbell hung.'[4] The bell is no longer present at Glascwm, nor, indeed, is its whereabouts known.

The church structure is dated to the 13th to 15th centuries and it is thought that the church 'almost certainly originated as a mother church in the early medieval period,' which is suggested by the Glas (*Clas*) part of the name. It is possible that the chapelries of Rhulen and Colva were annexed to Glascwm at an early period.[5]

The churchyard is of moderate size, not as large as might be expected of an important early site, and is situated on the north-facing slope above the Clas Brook. The enclosure is basically curvilinear, although the long sides of the northern and southern boundaries are straight.[6] It may have been enlarged to the north as the remains of an earlier inner bank appear on this side where there is a considerable drop down to the Clas Brook. The site is next to water like Cregrina and Rhulen, befitting of a St. David site as he was called 'the Waterman' because he would only drink water (never alcohol), and because it was he who blessed and purified the waters at Bath[7] and was responsible for the miraculous rising of a number of springs. On the north side of the church there is a dramatic and very steep scarp bank up to nearly 10 feet high, this starts to fade in the north-east area and 'a continuation on the east and south can be made out only with the eye of faith,' but on the flat western side it re-emerges as a scarp bank topped by yew trees. The one to the right is hollowing and thus likely to be of some age — the others are mature but not ancient-looking even though they have a fairly wide spread. It is suggested that the bank may have been an inner or an earlier enclosure, although it is also possible that it was a 'deliberately constructed platform for the building.'[8] Internal embanking is visible along the western and southern perimeters. On the latter the level of the churchyard is lower than the surrounding land and is quite waterlogged. The enclosure is on a south to north slope.

Glascwm is a fascinating site and the first view of it, nestling in the valley surrounded by the wild hills when approaching from the east, is second to none — it is easy to visualise this site as an important early Christian foundation.

LLANANNO – St. Anno
(SO 096 744)

Dedication and siting suggest an early foundation.

This pleasant little church is sandwiched between the A483 and the River Ithon. It is dedicated to St. Anno, a little known saint, to whom there is a second dedication at Newborough in Anglesey. Even the name of the saint is in question, being suggested as Amo or Wonno in the case of Llananno, the latter of whom Baring-Gould and Fisher describe as 'imaginary'. The festival date for St. Anno is listed as 20 May in some calendars, but the date of the saint is unknown, as is their sex.[1] The fact that the church has retained the dedication, when it could so easily have changed to St. Anne, is suggestive that this is an early foundation, as is its position close to the river.

The site is raised a little above the River Ithon on what is considered to be a possible relict river terrace. The churchyard is a roughly rectangular shape. The eastern boundary is said to be lightly curved, but this is difficult to see because of the heavy planting of conifers. In contrast to the usual lie of the land on early sites, the churchyard is actually a little lower than the external land in places on this and the north-eastern sides. However, the western and southern boundaries look relatively undisturbed and are noticeably higher than the surrounding land. Within the churchyard on the north, and to a lesser extent to the south, are 'traces of a low slightly curving bank'[2] providing some evidence of a former curvilinear churchyard. Although the church is next to the main road, which runs almost at the same level as the eaves, it is the peaceful meandering river and pasture that dominate the scene.

The church was completely rebuilt in 1876–7, only the font and screen are older. The 15th- to 16th-century screen is described by Haslam as 'the best example left reasonably intact of the work of the imaginative Newtown school of screen-carvers';[3] it is outstanding, and merits a visit in its own right.

LLANBADARN FAWR –
St. Padarn (SO 087 643)

One of the eastern group of Padarn dedications.

The church of St. Padarn is 2½ miles north-east of the centre of Llandrindod Wells and less than ¼ mile south of Crossgates. The site, like that of Llanbadarn y Garreg, Llanbadarn Fynydd and the easterly group of St. Padarn dedications, is probably early, and is also a riverside site. It lies immediately next to the main A483. The River Ithon flows against the western and southern churchyard boundaries. Other than a farm complex to the north-west, it is on its own and not obviously part of any settlement. Full details of St. Padarn's history are given in his biographical sketch on pp.65-68. Howse reports that Giraldus Cambrensis took refuge in the Norman precursor of the church in 1176 when 'engaged in an ecclesiastical dispute' and was released the next morning by Prince Cadwallon of Wales, his wife and son.[1] In 1291 the church was referred to as *ecclesia de Lampadern*, clearly containing St. Padarn's name, and was valued at £5 6s. 8d., a moderate amount.[2]

The church structure was completely rebuilt in 1878, but physical proof of an old church exists in the form of a Norman tympanum over the south doorway with an estimated date of 1100–1150 from the design of two lion-like animals, other creatures and a tree of life. It is 'one of only two Romanesque carved tympana in Wales', and is thus notable.[3] Clwyd-Powys Archaeological Trust also note the presence of a Roman inscribed stone on the inside of the west wall of the church, and two Romanesque carved stones set high up on the inside of the east wall and reputedly depicting 'a Janus-type head and a Sheila-na-gig'.[4] The latter is a pagan fertility symbol and Janus a pagan Roman god. These probably came from the earlier church on the site and were reset when the church was rebuilt in the late 19th century. Howse notes the existence in 1949 of 'a Roman centurial stone' in the wall of the porch which is probably the same as that noted above, and which he suggests originated from the Roman station or fort at Castell Collen, near Llandrindod Wells.[5]

The church enclosure is an irregular rectilinear shape, that reaches a rounded blunt area to the south-west. Early boundaries are not evident and some of the churchyard walling was only built in 1892.[6] Much of the site is raised by a couple of feet above the surrounding area. There is a yew with a sizeable girth in the churchyard suggestive of some age.

LLANBADARN FYNYDD –
St. Padarn (SO 098 777)

One of the eastern group of Padarn dedications.

The church of St. Padarn lies about 2¼ miles north of Llananno and 10½ miles north-north-east of the centre of Llandrindod Wells. It is sandwiched in a tight space between the River Ithon and a lane to the north and west, and the main A483 to the east which is at eaves' level. The church structure was heavily restored in 1894/5. The first mention of the church is in 1513 when it is called *Llanbadarn Vynith*. In 1818 this earlier church was described as 'rude and mean in its form and construction ... [bearing] a stronger resemblance to an antique barn than to a temple.'[1]

The site, like that of Llanbadarn y Garreg and Llanbadarn Fawr, is one of St. Padarn's easterly dedications (see pp.65-68), and is probably early.

The churchyard is fairly small, shaped roughly like a rectangle and occupies a low river terrace which has a slight west/east slope. However the land to the east (over the main road) rises dramatically into bracken-clad slopes and falls steeply to the river to the west. There are slight differences in levels within the churchyard which has been described as 'minor terracing ... and some irregular banks, but nothing of obvious significance.'[2] The original shape of the churchyard can therefore not be determined.

Howse reports the presence of St. David's wells 'some three miles west' which furnished 'an infallible cure for mangy dogs' bathed in its waters.[3] Jones reports that it was very much frequented and esteemed, and also refers to a Butter Well in the parish.[4]

LLANBADARN-Y-GARREG –
St. Padarn (SO 112 488)

One of the eastern group of Padarn dedications, and two yews in the churchyard give a 'feel' of age.

The church, south-east of Builth Wells in the beautiful valley of the River Edw, is one of a small grouping which lie to the east of the central Cambrian mountain range dedicated to St. Padarn (for whom see pp.65-68). The church is probably early and established under his jurisdiction, although this cannot be proved.

The single-celled church is a simple structure, probably of 13th- to 14th-century date.[1] It is set beside the river and there is a steep drop directly into the water. The churchyard is a long 'D' shape with no obvious changes or extensions and the river forms the south-eastern boundary. It is quite small and the church is set away from the Edw on the north side, It is possible that part of the enclosure has been lost to the river. The site is in a relatively flat valley surrounded by bare hills, with stone cliffs forming a northern backdrop.

There is a very ancient looking yew to the north-west corner of the enclosure. It has a twisted and slanting hollowed trunk and a very wide foliage spread. Standing beneath this tree it is easy to appreciate why yews were chosen as shelters by the early saints. Another mature yew stands in the south-east corner of the churchyard.

LLANBISTER – St. Cynllo
(SO 110 733)

The site of an early *clas* church, dedicated to a 6th-century saint.

This church is a most interesting site. Cynllo's history is sparse, although he may have been the elder brother of St. Teilo and possibly returned to Wales from Brittany with Saints Cadfan and Padarn. He would have been a contemporary of St. David, but have started his religious calling slightly earlier.

Llanbister was a *clas* church (mother church) for the cantref of Maelienydd and the churches of Llananno, Llanddewi Ystradenni, Llanfihangel Rhydithon and Llanbadarn Fynydd were dependent upon it, itself suggesting an early origin for Llanbister. Although a direct comparison cannot be drawn between the 13th century and the 6th, the 'Taxatio' return of 1291 recorded the income of Llanbister as in excess of £30, which was higher than any other church in the Archdeaconry of Brecon. Giraldus Cambrensis is said to have spent a night at this church in about 1176 during one of his religious expeditions.[1]

The position of the church is unusual. The village is set on a hillside above the valley of the River Ithon which is about 150 yards away. The site holds a commanding view of the valley which, prior to drainage works and land improvements, was susceptible to flooding and so fitted the remote, isolated sites initially sought by the early saints.

The steep topography of the site has meant that the church tower is unusually built at the east of the chancel, whilst the church itself is orientated north-west/south-east instead of the general east/west alignment.[2] The nave may date from the 13th century going on the design of windows, but tradition describes older blocked openings that are now covered over. Most of the structure, however, is of the 14th and 16th centuries. The entrance to the church is up a large flight of steps, at the top of the dog-leg of which is a large immersion bath. This is for full baptisms and is the only modern version that we have seen amongst the sites visited. The west end of the church has a slightly vernacular appearance and was used as a school room. There are the remains of 17th-century wall paintings, a late medieval screen, and re-used carving probably from nearby Abbeycwmhir, most notably the stoup by the south door.[3] The tower is substantial and could easily have been used for defensive purposes.

The churchyard is best described as an irregular elongated rectangle on a spur set between two valleys that drop down to the River Ithon. Both the churchyard and the land upon which the church is built is terraced because of the steepness of the slope, and the land slopes upward from the west gate to form a substantial mound which may be man-made — is this the vestige of a burial mound? On the south side of the church is a pronounced scarp, which has four yews upon it, also considered to be the early boundary prior to extension. From the south-eastern side a clear earthen bank is visible and this too is probably early; on the northern side there is a suggestion of a low bank beyond the present boundary. A scarp bank to the south-west of the church is likewise thought to be a continuation of the original boundary. Within the northern area of the churchyard, which is largely unused, is a large, vacant platform terraced into the land with several 'less well-defined scoops' — this could be significant in terms of the site's early history,[4] and may have held the early monastic buildings that would have been required for a site of this importance.

Jonathan Williams recorded the tradition that near Llanbister church is an area of land on which it was intended to build the church but that every night a supernatural being took away what had been constructed during the day — even as late as 1859 an annual rent of 2s. 6d. was still being charged for 'the vacant and unconsecrated church.'[5]

A spring close to the church called Pistyll Cynllo was recorded in 1811 as 'a noted spring'. There were also three 'black sulphurous mineral springs' used for the relief of skin conditions, as well as a Soldier's Well within the parish.[6]

Another saint, St. Cynon, is associated with an area two miles north-east of Llanbister where, in the early 20th century, was an ancient mansion called Croes Cynon; 'Here, it is said, was his Cross.' He also had a hermitage scooped out of a rock called Craig Cynon and drank from a nearby brook called Nant Cynon. St. Cynon travelled from Brittany with the saints Padarn and Cadfan, and attended the monasteries of Llantwit Major and Llancarfan. Later, when St. Cadfan founded a monastery on Bardsey island, Cynon accompanied him there and became his chancellor.[7] Quite why St. Cynon is linked so closely with an area near to Llanbister in Radnorshire is unclear.

LLANDDEWI FACH –
St. David (SO 146 454)

Legends of an early Celtic hermitage, and a partial ring of yews suggest an early site.

One of the remotest churches in the guide, St. David's lies 5 miles west-north-west of Hay-on-Wye. It is about 1½ miles down a narrow, no-through road off the Clyro to Painscastle road, where there is a small signpost to it. There is no vehicular access to the church itself which is reached by a footpath over fields. The site lies on the north slope of a wooded valley and has distant views of Painscastle and Llanbedr. The church of Llanbedr Painscastle is actually less than a mile distant, as the crow flies.

The church was completely rebuilt in 1860[1] and there are no early remains. The churchyard is small and described as rectilinear[2] but at ground level appears to be a rectangular oval shape. The only existing grave markers on the western side are simple sections of plain stone; in the past these were sometimes used to mark children's graves.[3] One yew to the south of the porch has been dated to 650 years old, and what appears to be a partial circle of yews extends from the porch to the west. However, close to the walled boundary to the west is a yew of some considerable age, possibly over 1,000 years old. It has a partially hollowed trunk with a new trunk growng up inside and is in the same regenerative state as the yews at Linton-by-Ross (Herefordshire) and at Bettws Newydd (Gwent), albeit probably much younger. Coupled with the remains of the yew ring, this is suggestive of an early site. There is also a fairly ancient-looking yew to the east of the church, opposite the east end of the chancel. Is this the remains of a Celtic east/west deliberate yew planting from the early medieval period?

The dedication to St. David possibly fits in with the Glascwm group of St. David churches, being in the same block of hills, although in the 19th century the church was still attached to Llowes as a chapel. There are no early historical records of the church, but the bench of ground occupied by the churchyard has been described as 'probably largely a function of centuries of use' and the church is terraced into the hill-slope to a depth of over 5 feet.[4] House platforms exist outside the churchyard demonstrating that the settlement, which now consists of a few scattered farmsteads, was once more populous.

The ancient yew by the western boundary wall

An information board inside the porch states that, although the origin of the church is not known, it was 'almost certainly built on the site where a Celtic hermit once lived, probably in the 7th century, and where later his shrine became venerated as a place of pilgrimage and worship ... could it be that the hermit associated with this place was a disciple of his namesake, St. David ...?'. The remoteness and wild natural beauty of the location is certainly in keeping with other putative early foundations.

LLANDEGLEY – St. Tecla
(SO 139 629)

The form of the site and its dedication suggest that it is probably early.

Llandegley lies six miles north-east of Llandrindod Wells. A small cluster of buildings is grouped around the church of St. Thecla, of which several border the churchyard. Of interest within the church is the late medieval screen and the south doorway which is said to have come from Abbeycwmhir. The nave was rebuilt in 1876 and the tower in 1953.[1]

The name originates from Thecla, the female virgin-martyr and companion of St. Paul, who gave rise to a popular cult across the eastern and western Church.[2] Pennant states that 'St. Thecla, virgin and martyr ... after her conversion by St. Paul, suffered under Nero at Iconium'.[3] However, such a dedication in Wales would have been unusual practice at the time, and the likelihood is that Thecla was a local Welsh saint with her own cult which became confounded with the Pauline Thecla. An Irish St. Thecla (or Etha) is documented who visited Cornwall and established a church at Breage, and there was a St. Thecla in Germany, probably sent from Dorset or Essex by St. Boniface in about 758,[4] but there is no positive connection with either of these saints to the two Welsh dedications, the second being at Llandegla in Denbighshire. It is of course conceivable that the Thecla of Llandegley is in fact the Pauline Thecla, and that the church was dedicated before the Roman withdrawal of power in Britain.

In a 13th-century manuscript containing the *Life* and the *Miracula S. Teclae Virginis*, details are given in which Llandegley's church is probably indicated and suggest that the tract originated from here. Miracles mentioned include the

145

punishment and repentance of three Radnor robbers; a man's sight being restored; a leader being cured of pain on condition that he set prisoners free, and a miracle involving two women from '*de uilla Peona*' (probably one of the Pyon villages in Herefordshire).[5]

Pre-Christian origins are faintly recorded at Llandegley in the form of a putative healing well. It would appear that the well and its dedication have been forgotten, for although a sulphurous spring close to the church was once well visited, there is no legend is attached to it.[6] There are no remains of a holy well at Llandegley, only an unpleasant-smelling ditch which perhaps are one and the same as the following indicate. In 1825 a 'very strong sulphurous spring [stood] opposite the inn.' In 1830 the waters were described as 'covered with a brown scum ... [having] an abominable stench ... but not an unpleasant taste.' The waters were said to cure 'St. Tegla's' (or 'falling') disease. Doughty records the presence of a chalybeate spring close by which has a very high iron content. In the Victorian era buildings were constructed for those seeking the cure from the waters and a bath was available at the spring, but by the 1930s they had become derelict — one of the problems was a lack of accommodation for visitors.[7]

The church itself is built on a slight platform which may represent rubble from an earlier building. Visible to the west of the tower is a scarp of about 3 feet high which is the original line of the churchyard enclosure. The churchyard has been extended to the west since the late 19th century,[8] is bordered at a distance by the Logyn Brook to the west and south and set on a terrace above the brook with fairly marshy ground below. The churchyard is small and sub-oval and most of its boundaries are raised, noticeably to the south nearest the brook and to the north where the height difference above the road is most clearly visible, typical of one of the forms of an early churchyard. There are two very old yews in the churchyard, one of which is little more than an overgrown stump.

LLANDEILO GRABAN –
St. Teilo (SO 093 447)

A number of minor place names referring to 'henllan' or 'old church' plus evidence of the potential churchyard shape suggest an early origin relating to St. Teilo.

The church is on a hilltop high above the Wye valley about 2½ miles north of Erwood. Llandeilo Graban is the only Radnorshire dedication to St. Teilo (for whom see pp.55-59). The dedication suggests the possibility of his presence in the area, either in person, or more likely represented by his disciples or a later cult. There was a building called St. Teilo's Barn less than half a mile north-north-east of the church which was shown on mid-20th century OS maps as an old building. It is no longer shown as such, for it has since been converted into a house. There is also St. Teilo's Pool about half a mile to the north of the church in the moorish hills — this small cluster of Teilo names is similar to the localised cluster found around Llanhamlach concerning St. Illtud.

The church appears to be mainly of 14th- to 15th-century date. The churchyard is described as having a 'curious shape, part angular but with a distinctive curve on the north-east' with no obvious alterations made to its form. Even so it is considered that this is not its original shape.[1] The church site is in the angle of a minor crossroads of lanes and tracks. The study of a large scale Ordnance Survey map shows that a lane marking the present western and south-western boundaries appears to cut through a circular-shaped enclosure that straddles each side of the lane — might this be a ghost of a much larger, near circular church enclosure? The present churchyard is fairly flat but there is a slight slope to the south and east beyond the churchyard to a small stream which discharges into the River Wye — this stream is called Nant Henllan, (the 'stream of the old church'). East of the source of the stream, about 2½ miles north-north-east of the church, is a pool named Henllyn ('old pool') and between this and the church is a small cluster of buildings called Blaenhenllan a short distance north-east of St. Teilo's Barn (SO 101 455), which again incorporates the 'henllan' or 'old church' element. This suggests that a much earlier church preceded the present one, albeit further north or north-east and, while all traces and memories have gone, the names given to natural features and buildings may recall it.

There is obvious embanking on the inside of the churchyard boundary walls on the western boundary as well as on the other sides — Clwyd-Powys Archaeological Trust remark that debris has been dumped against these boundaries which gives the impression of a raised interior to the churchyard and possibly disguises an earlier bank,[2] — a suggestion with which we strongly agree. There are three quite substantial yews in the southern area of the enclosure.

LLANFAREDD – St. Mary
(SO 069 508)

This is a small single-chambered church with one of the oldest yews in Britain on the churchyard boundary (visible beyond the church in the photograph).

The church of St. Mary lies about 2 miles due east of Builth Wells, at the back of a cluster of farm buildings through which there is access. The church was heavily restored during 1891, but retained the bell which is dated to about 1280 in a little bell turret, and the 14th-/15th-century font as the oldest identifiable architectural items.[1]

Clwyd-Powys Archaeological Trust state that the 'location and the shape of the churchyard hint at an early medieval origin, but there is nothing to confirm this supposition.'[2] However there is one massive, ancient yew tree opposite the west end of the church and on the boundary with modern farm buildings. It has a measured girth of 36 feet[3] and was recorded with the same circumference in 1811. It is estimated to be 3,000 years old and is female. It is a superb-looking specimen with a huge gnarled and split trunk — a grand dame of yews! Brueton and Chetan report that another massive yew was found on Alltmawr 'just across the river [Wye] on a hilltop' and note the presence of a spring or well to the east of the church. There are also tumuli on Aberedw Hill due east and south-east of Llanfaredd, which points to the great antiquity of the area which had some ritual significance in the prehistoric era. If the age of the churchyard yew is plausible,

148

and if the yew on Alltmawr is of similar age, it is just possible they were planted as part of a wider pre-Christian religious landscape and the Llanfaredd yew was then Christianised by being taken into the enclosure of an early British church. A visitor to Llanfaredd in 1944 learnt that around the third Sunday after Easter it was customary to place sprigs of yew in the church vases. He also discovered that the cross and candlesticks on the altar were made of yew. Chetan and Brueton remark that it may seem strange that yew, which so often symbolises death in churches, was being used at a time of resurrection and renewal, but suggest that this was perhaps 'the remnant of many ancient customs ... representing original rites and celebrations beneath the sacred yew.'[4] It is remarkable that such a small and modest site might have such a potentially ancient and pre-Christian past.

The ancient yew on the churchyard boundary

The churchyard is irregular in shape and is small, but partly curvilinear to the east and west. Its boundaries are walled with stone and it is slightly raised above the surrounding land,[5] being on a low river terrace just above the flood plain of the River Wye which runs about 200 yards away to the west. The dedication to St. Mary is probably a replacement of an earlier British saint.

LLANFIHANGEL-NANT-MELAN – St. Michael (SO 180 582)

A classic example of a probable Christianised pagan site.

The church was completely rebuilt in 1846 and the nave and semi-circular apse are said to have been 'consciously modelled on Kilpeck church.'[1] If the earlier structure had to be demolished, it is fortunate it was rebuilt in such a delightful manner. In the late 12th century the church was given to the Knights Hospitallers.[2]

    The churchyard is of great interest and has every indication of an early origin, very likely pre-dating the dedication to St. Michael. The present churchyard is roughly rectangular and is built on a south/north orientated slope that terminates in the Summergill Brook some 65 feet away. Howse records the tradition that the church is said to have been built 'within the ring of a stone circle; an ancient stone will be noticed embedded in the hollow trunk of one of the yews surrounding the church.'[3] Chetan and Brueton remark that a stone about 4 feet in length and 2 feet across was found by Allen Meredith 'half-buried at the base of one [yew] tree' but otherwise nothing else of the reputed stone circle survives. There are five yews of considerable age in the churchyard growing on a slightly raised embankment, two to the south, two to the west and one to the east — a sixth yew has been cut down. The girth of one yew to the south-west has been measured at 30 feet and has an estimated age of about 1,800 years.[4] However Bevan-Jones states that the

150

yews also include specimens with girths of about 33 feet and are suggestive of 'an early saint's presence'.[5] The yews' presence on raised banks indicate the very early age of an inner boundary which Clwyd-Powys Archaeological Trust refer to as 'the fossilised circuit of an earlier enclosure.'[6]

The church stands on a platform which is most obvious when viewed from the north and is over 6½ feet high where it takes in part of the edge of the natural river terrace. To the west it is not as high but still apparent and Clwyd-Powys Archaeological Trust suggest it may link with a lightly curved embankment in the south-east area of the churchyard[7] — the artificial nature of the platform is quite striking when first viewed.

The re-use of pagan burial mounds for Christian religious sites has been discussed (see pp.22-24), and Llanfihangel-Nant-Melan is one of the clearest possible examples. Chetan and Bruetan suggest that the yews in the churchyard may mark out the boundary of a burial mound, or that they are the descendants of an ancient, now vanished, parent tree that stood at the summit of the putative barrow — the existing yews resulting from layering and rooting of the branches of this parent yew.[8] The surrounding hills contain a number of mounds and barrows showing this was an area of prehistoric activity.

Howse notes the existence of two wells in the parish which may have been sacred, although nothing is known of their history: Penny Well, near the waterfall, Water-Break-its-Neck, and a well near Cwm Galley called Peter's Well in the 1850s.[9]

Part of the ring of yews around the churchyard

LLANSANTFFRAED

CWMDEUDDWR (SN 967 677)

Documentary and evidence on the ground and on maps indicate an early Christian site.

The church is in the centre of Llansantffraed Cwmdeuddwr, on the west bank of the River Wye opposite Rhayader; the two settlements are situated at each end of a ford.

The church was built between 1868–70 and replaced a church built in 1778 which stood a little closer to the road than the present church. However the early 19th century historian, Jonathan Williams, described a still earlier church 'built in the form of a barn — low, long and dark. Its roof was covered with shingles.' Thornley Jones suggests this was the ancient church of a *llan* which he argues was located on the hill out of Cwmdeuddwr village on the Elan valley road. He reports that in 1966, just beyond the crown of this hill on the left-hand side of the road, were two barns belonging to Neuadd Farm at a place named Clas on the Ordnance Survey Radnorshire sheet XV SW. He argues that the area was the centre of a monastic settlement called the 'llan of St. Ffraid' (Bridget) and that it was a *clas* church whose affairs were managed 'without outside interference by a chapter or council of monks'. Thornley Jones also notes the name of a large field sloping towards the church, which in 1966 was already partly built over, was Llawrllan — 'the lower part of the llan'. Two wells exist nearby, and with the ford over the river, it would have made an attractive settlement site.[1]

Thornley Jones considers that the llan was established by 'Irish refugees from the Northmen, who in the ninth century were gaining a strong foothold in Ireland'. He also notes the celebration of the Cwmdeuddwr Feast, which was observed on the Sunday after 14 February and the Wednesday following. The Feast was celebrated in farmhouses until fairly recent times on the Sunday. On the Wednesday a fair was held at Rhayader which was also a holiday for farm workers. If 11 days are subtracted from 14 February to account for changes in the Calendar, the date of the Feast is pushed back to 3 February. Thornley Jones suggests that in medieval times the ruling prince and his court visited the court of Deuddwr — which was part of an annual visitation to the commotes of which the parish of Cwmdeuddwr was one — on the first three days of February, which would then not only coincide with the Feast, but also St. Bridget's feast day on 1 February, and the festival day of the suggested *clas* church. The Cwmdeuddwr Feast would thus post-date 'the adoption of St. Bridget as patroness of the llan'. St. Bridget was an Irish saint and possibly supplanted a pagan female deity, a nature goddess. There are several Llansantffraed (Ffraed is the Welsh version of

Bridget) sites within our remit and they are usually found in fertile valley areas in which the Irish settlers preferred to live. However St. Bridget of Kildare did not found any churches in Wales and Thornley Jones considers that many of her dedications belong to the 11th century or later. Likewise, the fixing of the dates of the Cwmdeuddwr Feast on 1 to 3 February must have been dictated by the Llan of St. Ffraid once the dedication had changed.[2]

It is possible that in 1778 two churches existed in Llansantffraed Cwmdeuddwr: one on the hillside which was derelict, and the other on a new site in the present churchyard. Indeed Jonathan Williams makes a passing reference to a church of 'Clas, Noyadd, then along the Vale of the Elan'. On the Ordnance Survey Radnorshire Sheet XV SW the present parish church is referred to as being 'St. Winifred's Church on the site of St. Bridget's Church', demonstrating a re-dedication which Thornley Jones determines occurred in 1868–70 when the new church was built. However in 1966 he asserts that St. Bridget had 're-asserted herself, and the usurper Winifred is now hardly remembered there.'[3]

The early stoup in the porch showing the three crudely-carved heads

Of the former churches virtually nothing survives, although there is an early stoup within the porch of the current church which is described as 'crudely incised with three heads' and perhaps of early Norman date.[4] This may be the case, although we suspect it is earlier. The carving is so simple and basic in design, especially with respect to the three faces depicted on the sides, that the image of the stoup has stayed with us long after visiting the site.

LLANSANTFFRAED-IN-ELVEL – St. Bridget (SO 100 549)

Some evidence for an early enclosure and a near complete yew ring around the church.

The church of St. Bridget at Llansantffraed-in-Elvel lies about 4 miles north-east of Builth Wells. St. Bridget was an Irish saint and the original area of her cult in Wales belonged to those areas which were colonised by the Irish during the 5th and 6th centuries. It is possible that Bridget, like St. Anne, supplanted a pagan female deity, a nature goddess, and Bridget was sometimes identified with the Virgin Mary.[1] There are several Llansantffraed (Ffraed is the Welsh version of Bridget) sites within our remit and they are usually found in fertile valley areas in which the Irish settlers preferred to live.

The church was rebuilt in 1895 and only the font is definitely medieval, although it is possible that most of the north wall and parts of the eastern and southern walls may be from an earlier building, or might consist of re-used masonry.[2] The earlier church was of the simple Welsh vernacular type, appearing rather more like a barn in an early photograph, that has so often disappeared.

When viewed from a nearby hilltop the churchyard looks wholly circular (see the photograph above) but the tree-line partly obscures the boundary. On examining an aerial photograph it is clear the enclosure has an irregular D-shape or even the shape of a round-sided triangle. It has a pronounced curved boundary to the west, one flatter curve to the north, a lightly bulging curve to the east, and the southern end is like the rounded top of a triangle. It is proposed by Clywd-Powys Archaeological Trust that there was an earlier church enclosure which was originally small and curvilinear; they have detected the traces of an inner bank within the churchyard, clearer to the east and south-west of the church but faint to the west, which is no more than about 1½ feet high anywhere. The ground level within the present churchyard is fairly flat and a slight drop which runs north to south may be due to the putative earlier enclosure — around the current boundary there is 'evidence of a low wall or revetted bank usually with a hedge on top of it or enveloping it' and to the south-west and east the external land is up to about 3½ feet lower.[3]

Unusually there is a ring of yew trees around the church. Most of them are not ancient, but may have been planted to replace an earlier defined ring of yews, such as may be seen at a few other sites, for example Llanelly near Abergavenny. However Chetan and Brueton record a girth of 28 feet of a male yew in the south-west of the churchyard,[4] which would certainly make it old enough to have been planted in the time of the early saints.

A Cistercian nunnery was founded at Llansantffraed-in-Elvel by an abbot of Strata Marcella in mid-Wales before 1176 but it may have been dissolved before 1186 — its location has never been discovered.[5] One wonders if it was on the church site. Giraldus Cambrensis reports of the scandal that ensued when Enoch, the abbot of Strata Marcella who founded the nunnery, eloped with one of the nuns. Giraldus reports that Enoch 'soon came back, a much humbler man and so much chastened that he could hardly be said to have sinned at all.' Of the nun, there is only silence.[6]

LLANSTEPHAN –
St. Stephen/Ystyffan (SO 120 422)

Indications are that the site is early, and the dedication to the Welsh saint St.Ystyffan has been anglicised to Stephen, as in the case of Old Radnor.

The church of St. Stephen or Ystyffan is high up in the Radnorshire hills in a remote location about 7½ miles south-east of Builth Wells. (For details on the patron saint refer to the entry on Old Radnor p.163). The site has a substantial stone lychgate of unusual design with a double gateway for pedestrians and vehicles separated by a stone wall, and a stable at one end which was originally for the parson's horse. It is probably of the 18th century. The majority of this attractive church is of 13th- or 14th-century date onwards with some 19th-century reconstruction. The squat stone tower was probably rebuilt in the 16th century.[1] There is also a stone-lined well in the south of the churchyard which is still flowing but is overgrown and not recorded as having been a holy well.[2]

The churchyard is medium-sized, roughly oval-shaped and lightly raised in relation to the external ground, although this is accentuated on the north side as it is next to a hollow way. It is on the east side of the Wye valley and is high above the river. A stream runs past the eastern boundary, and there is a scarp running across the churchyard approximately in an east/west direction which has three old yew trees growing on it indicating this was an earlier boundary.[3] It is visible from the south side of the church, although it is at most about 2 feet high. The yew trees are clearly of considerable age and there are a couple of younger ones further south. This putative smaller churchyard would correlate more closely with the expected size of an enclosure of an early foundation.

LLANYRE – St. Llyr
(SO 044 623)

The presence of an original sub-circular enclosure that may have been a barrow, coupled with the dedication to an obscure early saint support the idea that this was an early Christian site.

Llanyre is two miles west of Llandrindod Wells. The dedication to St. Llyr the Virgin, or Llyr Forwyn, is only known through the Demetian Calendar (of saints' festivals) and is 'nowhere entered in the Welsh saintly genealogies.' The name Llyr was also used for males at that time, but St. Llyr of Llanyre, as a Virgin, is presumably female! There is no other historical reference to the saint. The church was referred to as *Llanllyr yn Rhos* in a document of *c*.1566, but the dedication was changed during Victorian times to All Saints.[1] The old dedication was re-adopted in more recent times.

The churchyard has been extended and, despite the replacement of the original 'humble structure ... with a low tower' with the present building in 1885–7, the original early churchyard banks have miraculously survived. On the south side they have been incorporated into the present boundary but otherwise they appear as an earthen bank on the northern and western sides, and on the eastern side as a scarp, reaching heights of more than 3 feet. They give the clear impression of the ghost of the early site. There are also four yews of some age growing on the earthen banks to the north and east, which indicates the great age of the banks. The external diameter of the early enclosure is about 150 feet. It is possible that the church is built on a burial mound, the remaining early boundaries marking the perimeter of the mound, and Clwyd-Powys Archaeological Trust state that it was formerly 'noted as a barrow'.[2] If this is the case then Llanyre would be a good example of the re-use and Christianisation of a pagan feature.

LLOWES – St. Meilig/Maelog
(SO 192 417)

Putative early monastic site, an 11th-century (or earlier) 'St. Meilig's Cross', and the foundation of an early British saint.

St. Meilig's church at Llowes is about 5 miles south-west of Hay-on-Wye and is mentioned in the Llandaff Charters. In 680 King Morgan gave *podum Liuhesi* — which Davies identifies with Llowes — to a bishop Euddogwy.[1] At a later time the church at Llowes was dedicated to the two saints Meilig and Llywes, the latter the eponymous saint of Llywel (about 12 miles west of Brecon). Nothing much is known of St. Llywes except that in the *Life* of Gildas he is said to have been joined by St. Meilig 'in the district of Elmail' (Elvel), probably at Llowes.[2]

The 6th-century St. Meilig was the son of Caw, a chieftain in Strathclyde in Scotland, and brother of St. Gildas in whose *Life* he is mentioned. The *Life* informs us that Meilig was placed under religious instruction by his father but afterwards abandoned his patrimony and set up a monastery at Llowes (spelt Lyuhes) where he spent a life renowned for its virtue and miracles. However, in truth it seems that Meilig took up the religious life as a last resort and, rather than choosing to give up his patrimony in Scotland, was forced out as a result of incursions by the Picts and Scots.[3]

Meilig also appears in the Welsh medieval epic, the *Mabinogion*, in the story of Culhwch and Olwen. Meilig was at King Arthur's court with his brothers Gildas and Hueil when he was asked by Culhwch to help woo Olwen, but the saint chose to leave the court and follow religious instruction under St. Cadoc at Llancarfan. He then followed St. Cybi to Cornwall and the two were involved in a political insurrection whereby Cybi (presumably before he became a saint) tried to seize the Cornish throne from its king, Constantine. The insurrection failed and the two were obliged to leave. They went to the Isle of Aran but fell out with the existing monks and so left for Anglesey where King Maelgwn of Gwynedd gave Cybi land. Meilig founded a monastery at Llanfaelog, after which he left for Llowes.[4] One might wonder why at Llowes, which is hundreds of miles away from Anglesey. Gill believes the tale in the *Mabinogion* of Culhwch and Olwen may provide the reason. This states that Meilig's brother, Hueil, was on bad terms with King Arthur. In the *Life* of Gildas, Hueil is described as provocative and insubordinate to Arthur, and states that he plundered land south of Scotland. Arthur eventually killed him and it is suggested that blood-money was demanded by Caw's family as a result of which Arthur ceded land to them, an area of which was at Llowes. Thus it was on land already belonging to his family that Meilig founded the monastery.[5] Given the aura of myth surrounding King Arthur, and therefore any 'facts' behind the tale, it still begs the question of why Caw's family should have been granted land in Radnorshire. The story continues: as a result of political pressure Meilig was eventually forced to leave Wales for Ireland and then moved on to Brittany where he died. There are traces of the saint in dedications in both regions, along with others in central Radnorshire, north of Brecon, in Glamorganshire and Cardiganshire.[6]

The most notable feature in Llowes church is a roughly rectangular cross-slab which stands over 6 feet 9 inches tall. Every surface on the stone has been worked and there is a wheel-cross on what is now the eastern face which is described as 'a decorated Latin cross of Celtic type in high relief ...'. On the reverse face is an 'undecorated Latin cross of Celtic type, without the connecting ring and with the

upper arm slightly tapering.' On the north side there is shield-shaped panel. In November 1956 the stone was moved from its site south of the main path in the churchyard, where it had stood for at least 300 years, to its present position so as to protect it from the elements. When the stone was extracted from the ground its full height was estimated at 12 feet and it weighed about 3 tons. The lower end was described as tapering 'to a point, rather like a chisel.' The antiquarian Edward Lhuyd drew the stone in the late 1690s and it was depicted as having a 'band of relief along the bottom on both sides' that formed shelves (podia) on which smaller crosses were probably put.[7] The way that the cross is now set, means that these bands of relief are no long visible.

The cross-slab has a number of legends attached to it including the story that it was hurled there by Moll Walbee, a giantess, from Hay castle (some accounts say Clifford castle). Apparently the stone had fallen into her shoe and was so irksome that she threw it out in anger and it fell into Llowes churchyard. Another version states that it fell from her apron as she passed the village. Moll Walbee has been identified with Maude/Matilda de St. Valerie, wife of William de Breos/Braose, who died in 1210. Another tradition records that the stone marked the burial site of an anchorite of Llowes called Wechlan, who was a contemporary of Maude and, like her, a friend of Giraldus Cambrensis.[8]

St. Meilig's Cross showing the 6th- or 7th-century carved face

Although the stone is now commonly referred to as 'St. Meilig's cross', the several 19th-century historians who investigated the stone did not make any connection between the 6th-century saint and the monument. The earliest association appears in the inventory of the Royal Commission of 1913 where it is suggested that the plainer carving might date to the 6th or 7th centuries,

with the more ornamental dating to the 11th century, so that the cross could indeed have once been 'the cross of St. Meilig, the patron saint of the parish.'[9] W.H. Howse follows this dating and adds that St. Meilig is believed to have been buried on the site.[10] Nash-Williams, the doyen of such monuments, believed that the Llowes cross-slab probably dated to the 11th century, and later scholars tend to agree with this. Gill adds that cross-slabs in other parts of Wales, which also have a disparity in ornamentation between the crosses on their two faces, are believed to date from the 10th to 12th centuries and considers the Llowes monument to have been carved towards the end of that span and the carving to be all of one date.[11]

Gill suggests that the local place-name Croesfeilliog (Meilig's Cross) at SO 181446, two miles north-west of Llowes, may represent a connection between the saint and a cross (or cross-roads) but that this putative cross is not the one in Llowes church, rather a wooden cross that would have stood by a track over the hills. Alternatively the cross referred to in the place-name may have been a standing

St. Meilig's Cross showing the 11th- or 12th-century carved face

stone which was revered by pagans that St. Meilig Christianised 'by the simple expediency of purification and the light incision of a cross on its surface.' And yet there is the persistent tradition that the Llowes cross-slab was brought down from Bryn Rhydd Common, an atmospheric area of ferny and scrubby common-land immediately west and above Llowes village, while other traditions suggest the stone was moved from Llowes Common, a mile to the north-east.[12] One wonders if the putative stone at Croesfeilliog was confused in memory with the one at Llowes and the story of the latter's removal was invented to explain its presence at the church.

It is not known whether St. Meilig's monastery was on the same site as the present church or whether it was on Llowes Common, Bryn Rhydd or at Croesfeilliog. There is no evidence on the ground, or from aerial photographs, of an enclosure or monastic settlement around the church or within the village of Llowes or, indeed, at Croesfeilliog. Such a settlement would probably have had a 'banked enclosure surrounding a group of small huts, a wooden preaching cross and a timber-framed church.' However on Bryn Rhydd Common an examination was made in 1913 of circular mounds. It was concluded that these were the remains of prehistoric huts and that a nearby large rectangular enclosure was used for sheep and cattle. Gill suggests that this site may have been re-used by the 6th-century monastic commune.[13] There is also the possibility that this site was a retreat for the main monastic settlement at Llowes village. We feel that St. Meilig's monastery was more likely to have been on the site of the church as religious buildings tend to be rebuilt on approximately the same site over succeeding years. In this case, when the church was rebuilt in Norman times, the foundations would have destroyed any earlier evidence.

Most of the church was rebuilt between 1853–5 and stands on a low river terrace of the River Wye, which flows a few hundred yards away to the south. The churchyard is sub-oval and of medium size, and there is small stream to the west. Also on the west side of the churchyard and running through to the south-east corner there is a drop of up to 6½ feet. Interestingly when viewed from the east and north-east the church can be seen to be on a platform which is about 3 feet high under the chancel; it is not known whether this is a deliberate platform or a demolition layer from an earlier church.[14] All of this is suggestive of an early, reused site.

There is holy well at Ffynnon Gynydd (SO 163 413) about 1½ miles west of Llowes on the northern edge of Ffynnon Gynydd Common, which was known locally as a wishing well. Between 1900–10 a small, open well-house was built over it and the earlier well-chamber was partly covered.[15] Howse refers to it as St. Cynidr's Well,[16] but it is tempting to associate this well with Meilig and his religious community. The well can be found easily under its rustic canopy which encloses a small area of water with a step on either side.

NANTMEL – St. Cynllo
(SO 034 664)

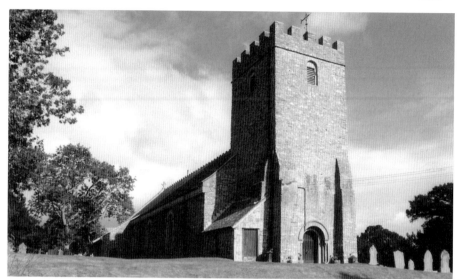

Evidence for a possible early site with ancient yews.

The church of St. Cynllo lies in the centre of the dispersed village 4 miles east of Rhayader on an elevated site. In some genealogies St. Cynllo, to whom the church is dedicated, is said to have been the brother of St. Teilo. If this is so, it is interesting that Cynllo is styled 'king' as well as confessor which suggests he was the oldest son. Other dedications to Cynllo in Radnorshire are at Llangunllo and Llanbister, and it is thought that the church at Rhayader was originally dedicated to him. He is also associated with Cardiganshire. It is possible that he crossed from Brittany with St. Padarn and St. Cadfan, although mis-spellings of his name makes this uncertain.[1]

Nantmel church was largely rebuilt at the end of the 18th century. It is set on a south-facing spur of land overlooking the Dulas brook. The churchyard was originally sub-circular, indicative of an early site. On the north side of the church an overgrown curving bank and external ditch probably represent the original boundary prior to enlargement. On the southern side, a short distance from the south door, is a well-defined scarp bank topped with several yews which may mark an earlier southern boundary. When approached from the main entrance one can appreciate that the church is on a raised site, and on the west there are drops of between 3 to 10 feet to the adjoining land.[2]

In 1818 the Radnorshire historian Jonathan Williams observed that very large ancient yews were growing in the churchyard.[3]

OLD RADNOR – St. Stephen
(SO 250 591)

Ancient hollowed boulder used as the font, evidence for a circular churchyard and other features, all suggestive of an early site.

The church of St. Stephen lies 3 miles east of Kington and dominates the centre of Old Radnor village. The present dedication probably superseded an earlier British saint, for the 46 ancient dedications to St. Stephen in England were introduced by the Normans. Whilst there is no record of an earlier dedication it is possible that it was to Ystyffan, which became anglicised to Stephen.[1] This 6th-century saint was the son of Mawan/Mawn, prince of Powys and traditionally is said to have had a close friendship with St. Teilo. In Ystyffan's two other dedications: Llanstephan in Radnorshire and Llanstephan in Carmarthenshire, there are churches in the adjoining parish dedicated to Teilo. Ystyffan is credited with having written the stanzas *Englynion Cain Cynnwyre* although this cannot be proven. He was possibly taught by St. Cadoc at Llancarfan, for he was apparently one of the seven wise men for whom Cadoc set the question 'What is the greatest folly in man?' His reply was 'To wish evil to another without the power of inflicting it.' The text of this dialogue is late but it does portray a level of vindictiveness apparent in Celtic society.[2] It also appears that St. Tysilio, one of the major saints of northern Powys, was his cousin and that both were descended from the family which ruled the kingdom of Powys between 600 and 850.[3]

Leland records in the mid-16th century that 'At Old Radenor (as sum say) was ons a market kepte. Ther is yet a veri fair chirch and welle servid.'[4] The church is on a raised site. Close to the church are the earthworks of a fortified manor house and a quarter of a mile down hill, almost at the valley bottom, is another small fortified site called Castle Nimble. Adjoining the churchyard is the Harp Inn (itself of historic interest) and is reminiscent of other old church sites which have an inn adjoining and almost abutting the churchyard. One wonders whether the monastic tradition of hospitality is echoed in this arrangement?

Howse states that the lands of Old Radnor church 'were given to the chapter of Worcester Cathedral in 887', but does not elaborate.[5] Interestingly, in a taxation record of 1291 the church is given a very high value of £26 13s. 4d. which no doubt reflects its past importance. Clwyd-Powys Archaeological Trust suggest the it may have been burnt down by Owain Glyndwr in 1401/2 as the present building dates mainly to the 15th century. The presence of five altars in the pre-Reformation church has been suggested 'indicating that it had a status greater than that of a simple parish church.'[6] Its high 13th-century value perhaps suggests a mother or *clas* status in the pre-Norman period.

The font at Old Radnor

There are exceptional late medieval features within the church, for instance the superb screen and the organ case dating to about 1500[7] and it is described as one of the finest medieval churches in Wales.[8] The font is most unusual being carved from a massive glacial erratic, with four stumpy legs. It is clearly of much older work than the church. The sheer weight and size of the font make it unlikely that it came from another church and in 1911 the Royal Commission for Ancient Monuments noted that the block from which it is carved 'bears considerable resemblance in size and form to the huge boulders called The Four Stones on the plain below, hardly a mile distant from the church.'[9] The Four Stones are a prehistoric stone 'circle'. Haslam suggests an 8th-century date for the carving of the font.[10] Built into the perimeter walls are several large unworked stones that may have had prehistoric use.

The church is set dramatically on Old Radnor Hill with extensive views over the Radnor basin. Such a commanding position suggests the church may have been built on an earlier — prehistoric? — defensive work.

There is strong evidence for an older and larger curving churchyard. Although now sub-oval and of medium size, the northern area of the original churchyard extends into the gardens of the Harp Inn where the boundary is visible as a scarp.[11] This area has been truncated by a straight wall.

RHULEN – St. David
(SO 138 499)

Pronounced raised, curvilinear churchyard and the dedication point to an early Christian site.

Rhulen lies 9 miles south-east of Builth Wells in a peaceful valley at the centre of a small community of scattered farmsteads. The church is small, and when large weddings and services are held here, the congregation spills outside of necessity. On these occasions the white church, within its curvilinear churchyard, can be viewed from the road that circles high over the head of the valley, and the singing carries uphill for over a mile and gives a timeless feel to the place. Haslam describes it as 'the most unassuming of all the Radnorshire rural churches' and we would add that it is one of the most charming and atmospheric. Haslam's further description of it being 'shaped like a hull — the walls lean out every which way' is also most apposite.[1]

The church structure is claimed to be the earliest in Radnorshire and has survived any Victorian reconstruction. In fact it was last restored in 1723, and, because of its individualistic nature, is difficult to date. The south door is irregular in shape and narrows on both sides with obtuse angles to the top. The nave has been divided in two with the west end now forming a store-room and bell chamber. In 1291 a taxation document refers to 'Ecclesia de Royl', thought to be Rhulen church, which is given a very high value of over £10 for such a small establishment[2] — is this an indication of an early and important status?

It has been suggested that Tillo may be the original dedication, pre-dating that of St. David.[3] Yet there is some evidence that the dedication to David may be an early one. Rhulen and Colva, 7 miles away, were both chapels to Glascwm, the early *clas* church for the area, Colva and Glascwm being two of a handful of sites that are described in David's 11th-century *Life* as being established by David. Their proximity with that of Cregrina, also dedicated to St. David, increases the likelihood that Rhulen is part of a tight, early cluster of dedications.

The churchyard is a prime example of a curvilinear, tree-lined raised enclosure. On the west it is raised by about 15 to 20 above a brook that flows along Cwm Tillo, and all other sides are impressively raised. The site is 'set on the edge of a valley just above [a] stream confluence'. Clwyd-Powys Archaeological Trust note that outside the east and north sides there 'is a scarp bank, its line continued as a more gentle slope across the south-east quadrant of the present churchyard' but its purpose and date is unclear.[4]

The presence of a massive and very old yews to the east and south within the churchyard are very suggestive of an early site. A girth of one of the yews is 27 feet[5] and has an estimated ago of over 1,600 years. In the 14th century it is said that a 'formidable yew curtailed the extension of the chancel ... Even so the east wall was pushed right up against the tree to enlarge the sanctuary as much as possible.'[6] It would thus appear that yews were present on this site in the days of the saints.

Part of the curvilinear churchyard enclosure

ST. HARMON – St. Garmon
(SN 989 729)

Evidence of a 5th- to 10th-century monastic site and a lost holy relic.

St. Harmon lies about 4 miles north-north-east of Rhayader. The church is actually dedicated to St. Germanus, but probably not the St. Germanus of Auxerre who arrived in Britain in 429 to counter the Pelagian Heresy. Fenn and Sinclair have made a good case for the St. Germanus of St. Harmon being 'the patron of Peel and the bishop of Man' and suggest that the dedication belongs to the 9th century rather than the 5th. It appears that St. Germanus of Auxerre has been conflated with St. Germanus of Man by the 9th-century historian Nennius, for Nennius has Germanus of Auxerre pursuing Vortigern — the much maligned king who 'invited' Saxon mercenaries into England to help protect the country — and also an unjust and tyrannical king called Benlli through Wales. However, no mention of this is made in the 5th-century *Life* of Germanus of Auxerre, in Gildas's 6th-century work, or in Bede's 8th-century history where we might expect to find such an account. Vortigern, in fact, was not a personal name but a title, rather like the Anglo-Saxon term '*bretwalda*' which means 'overlord'. A Vortigern is remembered in an inscription on the 9th-century Pillar of Eliseg near Llangollen. Traditionally it is this latter Vortigern who was based in Wales and was considered the founder of the kingdom of Powys. In the early 9th century, when Nennius was writing, traditions about the Isle of Man, which included the activities of St.

Germanus bishop of Man, were being circulated around Powys and Gwynedd, and Nennius simply conflated and exaggerated stories about Germanus, making him the 'legendary adversary of Vortigern'.[1]

Baring-Gould and Fisher suggest that St. Germanus of Man was born in Brittany in c.410 and went to St. Patrick in Ireland in c.440. Ten years later he left to take charge of the future saint Illtud, amongst others, and at some stage returned to Gaul and thence to Britain in 462. Four years later he went back to Ireland and was appointed the first bishop of Man where he died in c.474, aged about 64.[2]

St. Germanus of Man has several dedications in Denbighshire and Caernarvonshire. Llanfechain and Castle Caereinion in Montgomeryshire are dedicated to St. Garmon, together with St. Harmon in Radnorshire. There are several holy wells dedicated to him throughout the parishes. Baring Gould and Fisher report on the existence of the township of Clas Garmon at St. Harmon and remark that this points to 'the existence of some kind of monastic community at an early period.'[3] Clwyd-Powys Archaeological Trust state that a monastery was founded in c.6th century which was 'possibly dissolved after 1066,' and that it was a *clas* foundation which became the mother church of the area. The exact location of this monastery is not known but they suggest it may have been in the present churchyard. Interestingly the settlement was still called *Glascarmon* in 1500 in St. David's Episcopal Registers with the first element Glas presumably representing *clas*. Thus although the present church at St. Harmon is relatively modern, being completely rebuilt in 1821 with some further modifications in the early 20th century, the site appears to have had a venerable history.[4]

On his journey through Wales in 1188, Giraldus Cambrensis described a relic held at St. Harmon's:

> A staff which once belonged to Saint Curig, or so it is said, can be seen in the church ... It is completely encased in gold and silver, and the top part has the rough shape of a cross. Its miraculous power has been proved in all manner of cases, but it is particularly efficacious in smoothing away and pressing the pus from glandular swellings and gross tumours which grow so often on the human body. All those who suffer from such vexatious afflictions will be restored to health if they go to the staff in faith and offer an oblation of one penny. It happened in our time [late 12th century] that a person with a tumour handed a halfpenny to the crosier: the result was that only one half of his swelling went down. Soon afterwards he completed his oblation by offering the staff a second halfpenny, whereupon he was immediately cured. Another man came to the staff and promised faithfully that he would give a penny at some later date. He was cured, but on the appointed date he failed to pay. To his consternation his tumour swelled up again. His sin was pardoned, for he trebled the oblation ... with the happy result that he was completely restored to health.[5]

One of the many tumuli in the parish of St. Harmon

It seems odd that St. Curig's staff was at St. Harmon rather than Llangurig — perhaps it was moved from Llangurig after it was re-dedicated by the Normans to one of their own saints. The staff no longer exists at St. Harmon.

St. Harmon's churchyard is described as 'one of the most circular examples in Powys'. It is walled and to the south, inside the wall, is a wide bank that may be an original boundary,[6] being reminiscent of the boundary banks at Llanmerewig. In the south-west corner of the churchyard there was reputedly a mound, although there is no trace of it now, which was possibly a preaching mound. On all sides of the churchyard there is a drop in height to the surrounding land, on the east side it is at least 3½ feet and increases on the other sides, although the now disused railway line on the west is responsible for the steep drop. The site is large enough to have accommodated other buildings if it was a monastic site.

Looking towards the hillside on the near slopes of which a settlement once existed

The Radnorshire historian, Jonathan Williams, noted that 'there is on the bank of the River Marteg, at the eastern extremity of the parish, near to the confines of the parish of Llanbister, a remarkable and conspicuous tumulus, named Bedd Garmon, i.e. the Grave of Garmon' and adds that one of the townships or parishes of Rhayader manor was called *Tu Sant Harmon* or the House of St. Garmon.[7]

About half a mile north-east of the church, and on a hill-top, are the remains of village earthworks, marked on the Ordnance Survey at SN 995 735 which suggests that, in the Middle Ages, the area was more populated. There are several tumuli within a short distance of the church at various locations which also demonstrates it was of some importance in the prehistoric era. The possibility of the church site at St. Harmon dating back to the 6th century bridges the gap between these eras and indicates that it was an area suitable for the life of at least one early Welsh saint.

Breconshire

Llanwrthwl

Llanafan Fawr

Llanelwedd

Llanganten

Llanafan-fechan

Llanddewi'r cwm

Llanlleonfel • Llanynis

Llanwrtyd • Llangammarch Wells

Llangynog

Llanigon

Merthyr Cynog

Llyswen

Waun Chapel

Llandeilo'r-Fan

Llandefalle

Talgarth

Llanfilo

Llanelieu

Llandefaelog Fach

Capel-y-ffin

Llywel

Llanddew

Trallong

Llanfihangel Tal-y-llyn

BRECON

Llanspyddid

Slwch Tump

Llangors

Defynnog

Llanhamlach

Ty Illtud

Llanilltud

Llanfrynach

Llangasty-Tal-y-llyn

Cwmdu

Partrishow

Llanfeugan

Llandetty

Llangenny

Llangynidr

Llangattock

CAPEL-Y-FFIN – St. Mary
(SO 254 315)

The presence of the curved, raised bank with these yew trees in its setting shouts 'early site'.

The church of St. Mary is at the centre of the small village of Capel-y-Ffin ('the chapel on the boundary') set in the stunning Black Mountain landscape about 10 miles south of Hay-on-Wye.

The church was apparently rebuilt in 1762 and no remains of the previous structure rsurvive. The building is very small, whitewashed, with wooden-framed windows set high in its walls and a wooden bell-turret. It is of interest in its own right for its simplicity. There is a probable medieval font[1] and in the churchyard there is the remaining vertical pillar of a churchyard cross. The date of this is unknown, but the side is decorated with simple vertical moulding, and allowing for weathering in such an upland site, it does appear to be of some age.

The churchyard has two reasonably straight sides to the north and east, but more curving lines to the south and west. The enclosure is positioned on a spur of land between two watercourses and is on gently sloping ground. Within the boundary is a line of yew trees on a slightly raised bank that runs quite close to the wall and Bevan-Jones notes that several yews form the remnant of a circle and quotes Kilvert who describes the church as 'squatting like a stout grey owl among its seven black yews.' One of these to the south-west has a girth of 20 feet and an estimated age of 1,500 years and Bevan-Jones remarks that the oldest yews 'may have originated as shelter for a pre-tenth century [saint's] cell'.[2]

There was a Benedictine monastery at Capel-y-ffin, about a quarter of a mile from the church[3] up the byway from the village, with its own chapel, but only founded in the 1870s.

CWMDU – St. Michael
(SO 180 239)

One of the early incised stones at Cwmdu

The church contains early incised stones.

Cwmdu is about 5 miles north-west of Crickhowell. The church is attractive and substantial, but was largely reconstructed in the 1430s, and sections of it in the 1830s and in 1907. The only part of the structure which may date to the 11th century might be encased by the west tower.[1] In 1809 Theophilus Jones described the church as a white-washed sepulchre and because of its then ruinous condition added that 'We pray [to] God the living may not be buried in its ruins ... its ruinous state could not be helped by the pernicious custom of burying within the walls'.[2]

The churchyard is sub-rectangular, quite large and mainly walled. To the north and west it is raised by up to 6½ feet above the external levels, but to the east and south there is hardly any difference. No earthworks of any significance within the churchyard have been recorded.[3]

Two factors place foundation of the church in the 11th century or earlier. In *c*.1060 Bishop Herwald of Llandaff is recorded as consecrating the churches of Cwmdu, Partrishow and Llanbedr.[4] According to the *Book of Llandaff*, he also conducted ordinations at the time of the consecrations.[5] It sounds as if he was touring his diocese, blessing the churches, promoting new staff and his authority, and certainly lends credence to the thought that these churches were already established.

In the Llandaff charters, there is a charter for land granted by King Tewdwr who gave *Lann Mihacel Tref Ceriau* with its 'terra' to a bishop Gwrfan — Davies dates the charter to *c.*750 and identifies the church with Cwmdu.[6] This land was regranted in about 925 by the current king to the bishop in compensation for stealing his food rents and general bad behaviour (see under Llangors). Thus the evidence suggests strongly that a church existed at Cwmdu long before the consecration of the mid-11th century.

The early inscribed stones at the church are of great interest. The first stone is nearly 5 feet tall and 1 foot wide and is built into the outside of a south buttress of the church. It was moved in 1830 to the church from a field called Tir Gwenlli — Theophilus Jones remarked in 1809 that the stone was 'thrown down, in a field about half a mile from Tretower' and Bailey adds that Tir Gwenlli was about a mile south-south-west of the church. However the stone was reputedly found in *c.*1700 at Penygaer (the Gaer) nearer the church. It has the Latin inscription: CATACUS HIC JACIT FILIUS TEGERNACUS ('Here lies Cattoc the son of Teyrnoc'). Bailey suggests that it may celebrate St. Cadoc, and notes that the saint's father was Gwnynllyw, which conflicts with the carving on the stone, but that 'it is a curious coincidence that the stone ... was removed from a field called 'Tir Gwenlli ...'.[7] This stone is dated to the 7th century. The church also contains a 'pillar slab with incised cross' of the 7th to 9th centuries, with a 'Lombardic style inscription' dating to the 12th to 13th centuries on another side, as well as a further small stone with an incised Latin cross dating to the 7th to 9th centuries.[8]

There was also a chapel dedicated to St. Decumen (a late 7th-century saint), called Llandegeman Fawr Chapel, within the parish at SO 194 211 about 2½ miles south of Cwmdu church. The chapel no longer exists. Clwyd-Powys Archaeological Trust note that the site is 'now occupied by farm buildings showing no identifiable early features.'[9]

DEFYNNOG – St. Cynog
(SN 925 279)

A variety of pre-Norman remains and ancient yews indicate an early site.

The church of St. Cynog lies 8 miles west of Brecon overlooking the valley of the River Senni with spectacular views up the valley and over the surrounding country. The site is positioned on the lower reaches of a spur of land towards the centre of the village. It is generally accepted that Defynnog was a mother or *clas* church for the area; in 1254 it was valued at nearly £9 and in 1291 at over £17, both high values for the respective dates and perhaps reflecting the church's early importance and high status.[1]

The church has some early remains. Within the porch is an early pillar stone about 5 feet tall and 1 foot wide, having a circular Celtic ring-cross toward the top with vertical lines below, and a four double-beaded triangular panel above the cross. There is also an inscription in Latin running vertically up the lower half of the front below the cross, which reads '*Rugniatio [Fi]li Vendoni*', translated as '[The stone of] Rugniatis, son of Vendonius'. Haslam dates the inscription to the 5th or 6th centuries, and the crosses to the 7th to 9th centuries.[2] It would appear that the stone once marked a grave. There are also traces of Ogam script which suggest an Irish influence.

In the porch to the right is a stoup of possible pre-Norman date.[3] It is of square design with raised panels, particularly visible to the front where the carving resembles a square cup or beaker.

Within the church the font is tentatively dated to the early 11th century. There are two inscriptions on the rim of the bowl, one in Lombardic letters reading 'Siwurd + Gwlmer' and a second inscription in Runic letters. This is the only example of Runic writing in Wales and is an indication of Viking settlement in this area even though Defynnog is a long way from the sea.[4] However it is possible, of course, that the font came from elsewhere.

Part of the walling in the north side of the nave may be from an earlier pre-Norman church along with a squarish window which is now blocked. Clwyd-Powys Archaeological Trust, however, feel that a pre-Conquest date for the window and walling cannot be definitely ascribed.[5]

The church is of considerable size with a large battlemented tower, and a nave and arcade, making the church look as if it has a double nave, most of the main structure dating from about 1500. The River Senni runs about 100 yards to the west of the churchyard and the western edge of the latter is 'perched on the lip of its river terrace'. The churchyard has a gentle west/east slope (particularly noticeable by the tower) and is roughly the shape of a broad leaf, i.e. broadly rectangular at its northern end and tapering to the southern tip. It is orientated north/south with most space on these sides and much less to the eastern and western sides. A row of cottages abut onto the north-eastern and eastern boundary, as in the case of some early foundations, and the level of the churchyard is raised along this boundary so that some of the cottages' windows are level with the enclosure.[6] There are no clear indications of an early boundary within the churchyard, but there are two massive female yew trees to the north of the church which are estimated to be 3,500 years old.[7] Between the trees there are

The pillar stone now within the porch

177

table tombs. The trees may be positioned on the site of the original boundary, as in the case of Llanfihangel-nant-Melan. There is also a substantial yew on the southern side of the church towards the eastern end, opposite which is a conifer on a noticeable mound. Clwyd-Powys Archaeological Trust note the existence of a scarp bank over 3 feet high with quite pronounced curves along its length running from under the tower to a point opposite the chancel, and suggest that this may have been a boundary at some point. They also note that if the church enclosure was curvilinear in the past there are 'no convincing signs of it today'.[8] However, if the northern yews are the remains of an early northern boundary, then a smaller and sub-circular enclosure could be envisaged taking a line around to the southern yew and continuing the circuit along the scarp and beneath the tower. If the northern yews are 3,500 years old, then they would have been about 2,000 years old if the church was founded in the 6th or 7th century — a significant landscape feature which may have determined the siting of the building. The only documented change to the churchyard is a small extension to the southern tip in the 19th century.

The dedication is to St. Cynog, whose biographical details are given under Merthyr Cynog (see p.240). A peculiar tradition concerning the saint existed in Defynnog until the 19th century. Theophilus Jones writing in about 1809 noted that Cynog's memory used to be treated 'most scurvily at their annual wake, held in October (and not upon the 11th February, the Saint's day), when a poor boy was hired and called the Cynog, who was carried at night about the village in a chair, and thrown into every dirty puddle through which his bearers could stagger along. I believe this custom is very properly discontinued, and how it came to be adopted is very extraordinary.'[9] Baring-Gould and Fisher add that the wake was called Gwyl Mabsant. A fair was held on the second Thursday in October in preparation for the wake and produce was sold outside the The Bull Inn. The wake began the following Sunday and lasted for the week. It was on the Monday — called Dydd Llun Gwyl Gynog — that the custom of carrying the Cynog took place. A man was hired 'for the consideration of a suit of clothes or money', dressed in a suit of old clothes, carried once through the village, and then thrown into the river in front of a jeering crowd and had to scramble out under his own devices. The next day the tithe of cheese was laid out on the gravestones and sold.[10] This odd behaviour bears out legends told of Cynog's life which state that he was derided by the general population of the area because of his unusual appearance. St. Cynog may have appeared eccentric, and therefore have been abused by a population who were also quite willing to accept his help when they needed support from an individual who was not afraid to show force and more ability then those around him when required.

Defynnog is a fascinating site and is unusual in having a collection of pre-Norman artefacts, not to mention those awe-inspiring yews!

LLANAFAN FAWR – St. Afan
(SN 969 558)

Group of early cross-slabs, evidence for a circular churchyard, and the possible site of an early episcopal see.

Llanafan Fawr lies six miles north-west of Builth (Buellt) Wells. The dedication is to the early 6th-century St. Afan who was the son of Ceredig ab Cunedda Wledig. Afan's mother was St. Tegfedd, or Tegwedd. Afan would have been an approximate contemporary of St. David. A second dedication to Afan is about 3½ miles south at Llanafan Fecan, or Llanfechan, and he has a further dedication at Llanafan-y-Trawsgoed in Cardiganshire.[1]

It has been suggested that Llanafan Fawr was an episcopal see at one time, an idea that originates from an inscription on a stone known as St. Afan's tomb. It is positioned in the churchyard to the south-west of the nave and the top slab bears the inscription '*Hic Iacet Sanctus Avanus Episcopus*' in Lombardic script dating to the late 13th or 14th centuries,[2] during the era when pilgrimages were popular. At the beginning of the 20th century the slab was recorded as standing 7 feet high and surrounded by a drystone wall,[3] whilst Baring-Gould and Fisher at much the same date describe it as it is now, suggesting that the existing altar-like structure was made sometime in the early 1900s. The tomb allegedly marks the site where St. Afan was murdered by Irish pirates (or Danes according to one account).[4]

If an episcopal see did exist at Llanafan Fawr, which Baring-Gould and Fisher think unlikely, then it was very short-lived for there is no other evidence to support its existence. However it has been suggested that St. Afan may have been the third bishop of Llanbadarn Fawr, near Aberystwyth, and that his churches were in the area assigned to the diocese of Llanbadarn; other 19th-century scholars acknowledge that a see of Llanafan may even have existed for a short time 'either coincident with Llanbadarn (the seat of the episcopate being transferred for the time from Llanbadarn to Llanafan Fawr), or taken out of it.' If such a see existed at Llanafan, Baring-Gould and Fisher suggest it was merged with that of Llanbadarn and they were both subsequently merged with St. David's shortly after 720. They think it more likely, however, that Afan was a bishop 'without other diocese than his own Llan.'[5] Bishops could be so titled and have no territorial jurisdiction.

St. Afan's festival is given as 16 or 17 November in different sources. In the vicinity of the church in the 1900s Baring-Gould and Fisher record the presence of a smallholding called Derwen Afan ('Afan's Oak'), whilst the rectory was curiously called Perth y Sant ('the Saint's Bush').[6]

The site has much to recommend it as being of early British Christian origin. The church stands in a large churchyard which was previously even larger and

The stone carved with an 'equal-armed' cross near the altar

more circular. The shape of the enclosure, the position of the site on the approximate line of a Roman road between the Roman forts of Beulah and Castell Collen near Llandrindod Wells, and the presence of early medieval stones of a design that has its origins in Ireland suggest a major monastic centre here, within the Cantref of Buellt (Builth).[7]

Inside the church next to the altar is an 'equal-armed' cross with a circular surround carved on a vertical stone 2½ feet high, 1 foot wide and 9 inches thick. It is dated to between the 7th and 9th centuries.[8] Of equal interest are the three stone fragments now set in the east wall of the porch, but discovered in the walls of the church during restoration in 1887. They are considered to be fragments of cross-slabs. One (A) has a ringed cross design with a herringbone style infill between the arms of the cross. It has been cut down at some stage for re-use as a building stone and now measures 7½ inches by 12 inches — although the original width is thought to have been about 14 to 16 inches. The second stone (B), measuring about 8¼ inches by 19¼ inches on the exposed face, is thought to have been broadly its original size and shape, and was intended to rest horizontally over a grave rather than being part of a larger slab intended to be set upright. The design is described as a 'pecked linear cross whose horizontal arms are much shorter than the vertical arms. From each of the vertical arms spring three pairs of pecked diagonal lines giving a herringbone effect.' The third stone (C) measures 6¾ inches by 14¾ inches at its maximum and

The stones set in the east wall of the porch

has a pecked spiral but is incomplete on its longer edge. It is considered that this was once part of a larger slab which had a cross on the upper part with the spiral and perhaps other decoration set below. Interestingly the only other known Welsh cross-slab which has a similar spiral is at Llangammarch Wells church, about 6 miles south-west of Llanafan Fawr (see p.206). Knight considers that the Llangammarch stone is closely related to those at Llanafan and both may represent a single tradition and even be by the same hand. The ringed cross in the churchyard at Llanspyddid (see p.227) may also be from the same group. There are also 'Llanafan type ringed cross' carvings from Tregaron in Cardiganshire and Moylgrove in Pembrokeshire. They are also closely paralleled by a distinctive group of cross-slabs found in southern County Dublin and in the north of County Wicklow in Ireland. As Knight observes, the first two Llanafan stones (A and B) are so similar that they may have been fashioned by a sculptor who 'had worked in the school of monumental masons which produced the Dublin slabs.' Seven of the Dublin slabs have 'groups of multiple concentric circles' which are the equivalent to the spirals found at Llanafan and Llangammarch. A broad date range between the 7th and 9th centuries is suggested, with the caveat that simple designs of crosses very alike those found on early cross-slabs have been found cut over much later medieval stonework — indeed there is no reason why simple cross designs should not have been used as humble grave markers over many centuries. Knight prefers a date no earlier than the 9th century for the Llanafan group on the basis of the sculptural elements, and this accords with the suggestion of Viking influence on the parallel cross-slabs in Ireland. Indeed several cross-slabs in Breconshire show Viking influence in their decoration, for example at Llandefaelog-Fach (north of Brecon) and Llangors (pp.189 and 213). Knight suggests that the Llanafan fragments may have been the work of an 'itinerant Irish craftsman, possibly a cleric … who practised his craft somewhere near Llanafan Fawr' and warns against pinning too an exact date on them as Irish émigrés were present in Breconshire 'at widely differing dates.'[9] What is surprising, perhaps, is that a such small group of stone fragments in a remote Breconshire church can have such important historical and cultural ramifications.

Within the churchyard to the east of the chancel is an ancient female yew with a girth of 32 feet and approximately 2,000 years old.[10] The east end planting is, if we agree with Allen Meredith's theory (see p.26), of Celtic influence and may suggest a deliberate pre-Christian planting. The fact that the chancel (and its predecessor) faces the tree may be significant — is this an example of the Christianisation of a previously pagan totem? The yew now dominates the eastern end of the church and is much higher than the church itself. There are also several younger yews around the southern side of the churchyard. The church itself stands 'eccentrically on a raised oval platform some 50m [c.164 feet] in diameter which may be the remains of an earlier smaller churchyard or even a contemporary inner enclosure.' One might also suggest that this is the platform for an earlier church which respected the presence of the yew. The platform is much clearer when viewed from the north and west sides and the position of an earlier chancel is shown by the presence of a further raised rectangular area.[11]

The large churchyard is suggestive of an early and important Christian site. Although now truncated by the main road and a lane to the west and south it was originally sub-circular and over 425 feet across. (The present B4358 Beulah to Llandrindod Wells road has cut into the churchyard and meant the original boundary has been lost on this side.) The former boundary may be reflected in the alignment of the Red Lion Inn just over the road. To the south a lane has further truncated the churchyard, but the original bank and ditch which enclosed the site is visible as an earthwork in a field to the south. The only obvious drop between the churchyard and surrounding land is to the west above the B road, but this is the result of the road cutting through in much more recent times. It is a timely reminder that not all early Christian sites are on raised, embanked enclosures. In the outer area of the churchyard there are 'faint traces of what appear to be radial ridging' but their origin and purpose in not known.[12]

The Red Lion Inn across the road is worthy of inspection as it is a 'cruck-framed former hall-house'[13] which dates to medieval times — a sign outside describes it as being the earliest inn in Wales, accompanied by a date of 1186. Its position next to, or within, the old boundary continues a tradition, often swept away in later years, of church and inn being linked closely in the community. A ring motte lies 200 yards to the west of the church and is about 45 yards in diameter, again indicating a possible link between manor house or defended site, inn and church.

The raised plaform upon which the church sits can be seen

LLANAFAN FECHAN /
LLANFECHAN – St. Afan

(SN 972 337)

The original shape of the churchyard, the possible *podum*, the early dedication and proximity to Llanafan Fawr all suggest that this is an early British Christian site.

The church of St. Afan at Llanafan Fechan is about 3½ miles south of Llanafan Fawr and about 4 miles west of Builth Wells. It is the second dedication to St. Afan in the Builth area and would probably have been a dependency to Llanafan Fawr as it is a small site. (For Afan's known history see Llanafan Fawr, p.179). The likelihood is that Llanfechan was established by the saint or, more likely, by his followers during the 6th or 7th centuries.

The church was rebuilt in 1866. The churchyard is not officially described as circular, but from the air can be seen to be essentially curvilinear with one or two straighter sections to the walls, and is raised above the surrounding land by between 2½ to 5 feet. It is stated, however, that the enclosure was 'originally sub-circular and the church itself occupies an artificial mound'. This mound is about 3½ feet high on the west and is traceable to the north and eastern sides, although it merges with the general slope of the land to the south; it measures about 82 feet across. This clearly pre-dates the foundation of the present church and one is reminded of the idea of a *podum* where land was levelled and raised for the construction of a church. Interestingly traces of an earlier *llan* (enclosure) have been found just beyond the present northern boundary, although there is no sign of it in what was a former garden to the west and it is suggested that this 'truncated the original line'. If this enclosure is indeed part of the original church site, then it suggests a larger site of some importance that has since contracted. There is a middle-aged

yew to the east of the chancel and another near by to the south, close to the path.[1]

The church's only immediate neighbours are a substantial farmhouse to the east and farm buildings to the south-east, echoing the tradition of adjoining manor house and church in the Middle Ages.

LLANDDETTY – St. Tetta
(also Dedyw/Dedyu) (SO 128 202)

Indications that the site is early are suggested by the dedication to an obscure British saint, the carved pillar stone within the church and the churchyard shape.

The church of St. Tetta lies about 10 miles north-west of Abergavenny in a remote and leafy setting on the southern bank of the River Usk, and is sandwiched between the river and the Brecon and Monmouth canal.

Rees and Theophilus Jones identify St. Tetta as the abbess of Wimbourne in Wessex and of Anglo-Saxon origin, which Baring-Gould and Fisher describe as 'mere guesswork'. Instead they draw the conclusion from sources concerning Brychan, that Tetta was his grandson and that his name was actually Dedyu or Dettu/Detia — the name Detiu appears as one of St. Cadoc's three clerics who witnessed a grant of a church to his Irish disciple Macmoil.[1] If this is correct then he was roughly contemporary with St. David and under Cadoc would have had the best religious tuition available at the time.

That there was early activity in the locality is suggested by Theophilus Jones when he notes that during the construction of the Brecon canal close by in 1806 a workman 'found a small instrument of base metal called a Secespita or knife used by the Romans in sacrifice'. He also points out that the Roman road from Caerphilly to Brecon ran north to south through the parish.

The carved pillar stone within the church

Within the church, the shell of which may be 13th century, is a pillar stone dated to the 9th century that has been broken in half but repaired. It is about 4 feet 3 inches tall, is unusually narrow (about 5 inches square) with Latin inscriptions to three of the surfaces.[2] Bailey notes that in the early 1900s 'two very ancient stones' were built into the wall of the left-hand window in the chancel and that they originally stood outside. The one stone is described as being '20 inches long and 5½ inches wide … ornamented with straight lines bent at right angles, forming a slight kind of Greek fret.' The other stone 'is very rudely inscribed +GURDON +SACERDOS with the letters S set horizontally and the G and R of the genuine Anglo-Saxon form'.[3] Haslam states that the inscription reads: 'GAUDON SACERDOS / FECCIT CRUX P(RO) AN(IMA) NI(N) ID ET ANI(MA) GURHI/GUADAN'.[4] It appears that Bailey was referring to the two stones that have since been reunited. The origin of the stone is unknown. There is incised decoration on all faces of the stone including a ring-cross.[5]

The churchyard is relatively flat and of a sub-oval shape. To the south it has been extended towards the road and the line of the old boundary wall is visible as a 'scarp bank disguising the foundations.'[6] In 1864 the church was described as being white-washed and the churchyard as 'quite lonely, close to the Usk, and amidst the most lovely scenery of wood and dale. In it was a fine growth of wild hyacinths',[7] a description that fits the rural idyll of today.

LLANDDEW – St. David
(SO 054 307)

Early stone inside the church, a *clas* foundation and site of a bishop's palace.

Llanddew lies about 1 mile north-west of Brecon. The church is not early, the tower was rebuilt in 1620, and the nave has been largely restored, but it is a fine example of a cruciform church. It is delight to walk around, with re-worked Norman arches under the central crossing tower. The structure is very large for the size of village, but is explained by both the presence of the bishop's palace across the road and that Llanddew was a *clas* or mother church earlier in its history. The palace belonged to the bishop of St. David's as well as being used by Brecon priory. The ruins of the palace are still present within the grounds of a private house, and in 1800 these were described as having the appearance of a ruined castle. There was a chapel on the site of the palace, parts of which are still visible.

There is also the impressive Bishop Gower's Well, described in 1800 as having 'most excellent water' reached by steps from the palace side and emerging through a low arch in the wall to the roadside. Theophilus Jones presumed it was originally built to serve a court on each side of the wall.[1] In the later 12th

The church seen across the ruins of the bishop's palace

century Giraldus Cambrensis was resident at Llanddew in his role as archdeacon of Brecon and had a house which he loved greatly; he translates the meaning of Llanddew as 'the Church of God'.[2] Leland visited between 1536–9, by which time the palace was 'now no thing but an onsemelie ruine'. It would appear that the palace and Archdeacon's house were separate buildings for at least some of the period as Leland related that the 'Archidiacon of Brekenok hath a house even there, and that is also fallen doune for the more part.'[3]

There is an early stone now housed in the chancel of the church which is inscribed and has a ring-cross carved on it.[4] Its date is uncertain, and original site unknown, but it may be an 8th-century monument that was subsequently reworked in the 12th century. The RCAHMW also make reference to two fragments of 'sculptured sandstone, possibly of a pillar-cross' of the 11th–12th centuries.[5] In 1800 Theophilus Jones described the church as 'dark and dirty, the floor of earth, and uneven, in consequence of the vile and pernicious habit of burying within the walls'![6]

The churchyard has been described as 'a polygonal D shape'. What is particularly striking is the way cottages and stone outbuildings abut directly onto the churchyard on the southern side, the walls of the buildings in effect denoting the boundary. There is some curving to the boundary on the eastern side which hints at an earlier oval enclosure and, when taken with a low scarp just inside the eastern entrance, could mean that the churchyard was once curvilinear.[7]

Bishop Gower's Well

LLANDDEWI'R CWM –
St. David (SO 034 626)

Raised curvilinear churchyard suggests that this is an early site.

The church of St. David lies two miles south of Builth Wells, on a fairly elevated site in a peaceful setting. The hilly location fits in well with the pattern of St. David dedications to the north-east of Builth Wells.

The present church was built in the early 1200s with Early English (13th-century) lancet windows in the chancel. Extensive repairs were carried out in 1847. It was first mentioned in a taxation record of 1183.[1]

The churchyard is sub-rectangular, and its south and western sides are curvilinear with some angularity to the churchyard wall. There is a drop of about 7 to 8 feet to the adjoining field that falls away gently to the south with a platform extending from the wall. There is also a suggestion of a platform on the western side. The former appears to be formed from rubble, perhaps arising from recent activity on the neighbouring farm.

Within the churchyard on the south is a low platform which extends from the church but finishes before the wall — is this perhaps the original extent of the *llan*? Clywd-Powys Archaeological Trust report the presence of a scarp bank of up to 3 feet on this side which extends to the west and east and a 'possible relict ditch beyond the scarp on the north-west side of the church'.[2] These indicate that the original churchyard was smaller and possibly circular. It would seem that this is a raised site with a fossilised earlier church enclosure within the present churchyard.

There is an aged yew on the outer edge of the scarp bank on the south-eastern side of the churchyard. It has a measured girth of 25 feet[3] and may suggest an early Christian planting on the site.

LLANDEFAELOG FACH –
St. Meilig (Maelog) (SO 033 323)

Pre-Norman cross slab and indications of an early churchyard enclosure.

The pre-Norman cross-slab

The church of St. Meilig/Maelog lies 2 miles north of Brecon on the B road to Upper Chapel. The dedication is to St. Meilig (for whom see Llowes, p.158). Theophilus Jones considered that as his father was a prince of Brecknock in the early 6th century, the tract of land upon which Llandefaelog and Llandefalle (which church is also dedicated to him) were built probably made up part of his patrimony. Jones also remarks that the suffix of 'Fach' to the place-name signifies that it was a lesser establishment, Llandefalle therefore being the senior foundation, mentioning 'a very old MS' confirming that Llandefalle was the greater Maelog foundation. He also describes the state of the church in the early 1800s as a 'barn roofed and unceiled; it seems formerly to have been of greater height than it is at present … indifferently paved, the stones being broken and loose in several places, the pews are decayed …'.[1] The church was rebuilt in 1831 and 1856.[2]

There is a pre-Norman cross-slab in the church which stands about 8 feet tall and 15 inches wide and tapers downwards. It has been broken in the past and repaired, but is a complex design with a double-lined cross to the top with forked ends, around which there is ornamental rope-work. In the centre of the pillar is the figure of a man clutching weapons or ecclesiastical symbols in each hand who is surrounded by scroll-work. The bottom section has an inscription with lattice-work carved beneath it, the inscription reading '+Briamail Flou', which is thought to commemorate a warrior. The stone has been described as being 'one of the most interesting of the early sepulchral incised slabs in Wales'.[3] In the early 1800s Theophilus Jones reported the tradition that it was the grave marker of Brochwel Ysgythrog (ruler of Powys) but Jones thought it more likely it marked the interment of Rhain or Drem Dremrhudd, one of the sons of Brychan.[4] In a document called *De Situ Brecheniauc*, 'About the Circumstances of Brycheiniog' (see also under

Llanspyddid, p.227), there is the following statement: 'The grave of Rein, son of Brachan, in Landeuailac [Llandefaelog Fach]', one of four royal burials listed in the document. Thomas notes that this points to a later 6th-century cemetery at this site, as well as at Llanspyddid and Merthyr Cynog.[5]

Theophilus Jones also refers to a second stone 'which forms the threshold entering this church, [which has] the following letters rudely sculptured C A T V C; from whence it was brought or when it was placed in its present situation is uncertain … though how Cadocus or Cattwyg [St. Cadoc] was connected with the parish does not appear.'[6] In the early 1900s Bailey refers to it as the Cattuc stone and relates that in *Archaeologia Cambrensis* for 1862 there were anonymous statements claiming that 'the stone had been inadvertently built with the letters inwards into the arch between the nave and tower of the church.'[7] The stone has thus in effect been lost.

The significance of these stones in relation to the site is uncertain as their provenance is unknown[8] but Jones' theory that the remaining stone was a grave-marker to a son of Brychan is not tenable as it has been dated to the late 10th century by Haslam.[9]

The churchyard is roughly oblong in shape with a curvilinear northern boundary and a straighter southern edge, but the latter is due to an extension. A probable earlier southern boundary is marked by a 3 foot scarp bank that runs to the south of the church, although to the south of this, and between it and the new boundary, is a curving line of yews on a different alignment. These could mark an even earlier boundary but they are not on a bank. To the north of the church is evidence of an earlier embanked boundary immediately inside the present wall. The churchyard is raised above the surrounding land by about 1½ feet to the north and over 3 feet to the south; however on the western side the road surface is higher than the church enclosure. The church itself occupies a partly natural shelf.[10] There is a yew in the western part of the churchyard with a girth of about 20 feet and an estimated age of 1,200 years[11] which is further evidence for an early medieval date for the site.

LLANDEFALLE – St. Matthew
(or St. Maelog) (SO 107355)

Evidence for an early site from the dedication and the shape of the churchyard with the possible remnants of an early boundary.

The church lies 3 miles north-west of Talgarth. The church is on a terrace, positioned on a steep slope with expansive views over to the Black Mountains. The church is large for its setting and apart from an 18th-century rectory, it is on its own. The previous structure dated from the 13th century, some portions of which remain, but the present structure is mainly of the 14th and 15th centuries. Attractive features of note within the church are the *c.*1500 delicately carved screen, the wall-paintings, rood loft staircase and the squat, rotund font dated to the 13th century.[1]

The churchyard is medium-sized and has some curving boundaries. Along the southern boundary there is a steep drop to a stream about 100 yards below, but there does appear to be the remains of a slope within the present boundary nearer to the church, possibly indicating that the southern side has since been extended as far as it was possible. To the east there is a bank up to about 1½ feet inside the churchyard wall. On the west the surrounding land is about 5 feet below the churchyard by the gate. The north side of the churchyard is noticeably devoid

Remnants of the possible early boundary

of graves, as is usually the case unless space has become at a premium. Walking over a small stone clapper bridge to the north of the church from the maintained area to that which is now overgrown, one enters an area of scrub in which there is a spring; there is no legend attached to it and it is no longer even photogenic for a manhole has been placed very near to it — practical, but with no aesthetic sensitivity. Clwyd-Powys Archaeological Trust refer to it as a well, but it is so overgrown no man-made features in or around it are readily visible. Between the maintained area and the scrub is what appears to be an old boundary, raised up to 4 feet high and up to 13 feet wide — it is quite definite on the left-hand side and curves around the north and north-western sides. A ditch about 9 feet wide and 1½ feet deep has been identified on the other side of this bank and this carries the brooklet/stream coming from the well. The stream forms part of the western boundary too. Clwyd-Powys Archaeological Trust believe that the bank is most likely a feature related solely to the well, notwithstanding two old yews growing upon it, yet concede it may be associated with an earlier enclosure.[2] We tend to think it is an old churchyard boundary, although the location of the well does seem a little odd as one would expect it to be within the churchyard itself. On the north-west is a hollowed yew next to another fairly old-looking specimen. There are also two yews south-east of the chancel near the lychgate, one looks mature, the other is middle-aged, and there is a yew, which is hollowing, facing the south wall of the chancel.

There is some confusion concerning the dedication. Baring-Gould and Fisher consider that the received information that is was to St. Matthew, Tyfealog or Maethlu is based on mere guesswork from the place-name. They name St. Tyfalle, of whom they state that nothing is known.[3] Elsewhere is it stated that it was originally dedicated to St. Maelog, but has since changed to Matthew.[4] Theophilus Jones tells us that Llandefalle 'is dedicated, according to Ecton, to Saint Teilaw [Teilo], but according to Willis's MS in the Bodleian ... to St. Matthew ... we have no doubt but the above author is wrong ... [and] therefore put in a claim for Saint Maelog.' He also tells us of his 1809 visit that 'The font is of stone, but the pewter bason, used at christenings, is disgraceful, and looks like part of the furniture of a barber's shop'![5] It is safer to hold with St. Tyfalle, the unknown saint, as Baring-Gould & Fisher are the most reliable source, and they suggest that the patron of the extinct *Lann Tipallai*, which is mentioned several times in the Llandaff Charters and which they tentatively identify with Parsonage Farm, a little west of St. Maughan's in Monmouthshire, as being the same patron as that of Llandefalle.[6]

LLANDEILO'R FAN – St. Teilo
(SN 896 347)

Indications of an early churchyard, backed up by charter evidence.

The church of St. Teilo is set in very remote countryside on the edge of the desolate Mynydd Eppynt but in a leafy, secluded valley and reached by several miles of high-hedged, twisting lanes.

In a charter of *c*.720 'King Awst and his sons Eiludd and Rhiwallon returned *Lannguruaet*, with its *territorium*, which previously belonged to Dyfrig and Teilo, to bishop Euddogwy.' Davies observes that the charter has a very high proportion of editorial formulae, and also 'a witness list appropriated from some other record, of *c*.685 … It is unlikely that any original charter lies behind this record', although she concedes that 'it may of course reflect some tradition of the grant of this estate by Awst.'[1] The boundaries of the estate ran to about 3,500 acres. Even if the grant is suspect, the boundary of the estate can still be traced. The church is named as *Lann Guruaet* in the charter and its boundary began at the source of the Ethrim, which Evans and Rhys suggest is an alternative name for the Mawen, although it is interesting to note that the stream bounding the south of the churchyard is called Nant Eithrin. The boundary then goes uphill to Bryn y Garn and the 'old road' (one wonders if this is a Roman road?). Going on it passes the 'foot of *Croes Guerion*' which suggests a cross named after the saint. The boundary then goes 'downwards as far as the moor of the three boundaries' and eventually descends to a brook called the *Cleudach*. In the late 19th century, it was reported that people living on its banks still pronounced it as 'Cleudach' even though the Ordnance Survey spelled it as Clydach, which shows an astonishing preservation of the verbal language. From the source of the brook the boundary went 'across the mountain, along it as far as the Shepherds' Hill' and so along the mountain back to the beginning.[2] It is remarkable that such an old document, perhaps even dating back 1,300 years, can paint such a vivid picture of the landscape around the church — with its cross to the founder saint reached by the old road across a place of mountains and moors, brooks and stream valleys.

The dedication to Teilo is clearly not the original one, for the patron of the church was Gurmaet who had been a disciple of Dyfrig, and then of St. Teilo.[3]

The church structure was almost entirely rebuilt in 1875, with the exception of a blocked priest's doorway, which may be as early as the 12th century, and perhaps a few other features.[4]

The churchyard may once have been sub-circular, but some of the boundaries have been straightened; there is a rectangular extension to the north which was added early in the 20th century, and some encroachment by road and houses has occurred. The boundary is curved to the southern side where it adjoins the stream called Nant Eithrin and the sides are straighter to the north and east. There is a low scarp bank to the north of the church which indicates the earlier boundary prior to extension; there is also a low scarp to the south at the edge of the river terrace which could denote an early perimeter. An earthen bank behind a short stone wall to the west, east and part of the southern boundaries rising to nearly 3 feet may also indicate an earlier earthwork boundary.[5] The churchyard is raised above the external ground level in these places and to the north-east the internal level is banked upwards against the perimeter. Indications are of an early enclosure.

To the north of the church on the boundary is a yew which has the appearance of being about 1,500 years old. This was potentially planted

The yew in the churchyard that is c.*1,500 years old*

as a commemoration of the church's foundation. In 1901 the churchyard was described as having 'several fine yews'.[6]

LLANELIEU – St. Ellyw
(SO 185 342)

The dedication and churchyard design indicate an early medieval origin, and there are two pillar stones of early medieval date.

The church of St. Ellyw lies 2 miles east of Talgarth. The hamlet, situated on the lower slopes of the Black Mountains and just below some of the highest sections of the range, lies in a striking landscape. The site is in a meander of a stream and because of the slope of the enclosure, the church has been 'terraced into the slope on its south side'.[1] The church is a single-chambered structure constructed from coursed rubble stone with a bell turret, probably dating to the 13th century and with later modifications. Internally it has the fragmentary remains of medieval wall-paintings and part of a simple and rather lovely screen that may be as early as the 14th century.[2] This retains the red background paint on which are painted small white roses, in the centre of which is a large white painted cross. Squint holes are also visible.

It has been suggested that Llanelieu and the two Llanelly churches, one in Breconshire and one in Carmarthenshire, share the same saint, but Baring-Gould and Fisher disagree with this theory as they point out the names Ellyw and Elli are not derivatives of each other. Theophilus Jones states Ellyw was a grand-daughter of Brychan but others point out that there is no evidence that he had a grand-daughter of this name.[3] However, Brychan is reputed to have had a rather astonishing number of children and the area is appropriate for Brychan's family.

The churchyard is large, indeed very large in relation to the size of church and the small settlement. The entrance into the yard is up a flight of sandstone steps from the lane. There are some gravestones on the southern side of the churchyard but the rest of the graveyard is grassed over and looks empty, although there are visible undulations especially to the west which may indicate earlier structures/burials. The church is tucked into one area, with the east wall of the chancel very close to the boundary, which drops sharply to the stream. The stream borders the north and east of the churchyard and there is a steep drop on the northern side to the stream. There is also a significant drop, upwards of 10 feet in places, to the lane on the western side of the churchyard, although hollowing of the lane through use will have undoubtedly accentuated the drop. However there is no appreciable height difference between the lane and the churchyard on the south, but here there is some internal embanking against the stone wall. There is a noticeable platform running out from the north side of the church and a suggestion of a low mound or a continuation of the platform on the western end. There is no indication that the churchyard has been extended, therefore the present area is probably original.

On the outside of the left-hand wall of the porch are two early pillar stones,

one quite tall and narrow, the other shorter and squatter. One has an incised ring-cross with four small rings in the angles; the other has a cross 'ringed with three circles' They are dated to between the 7th and 9th centuries.[4] They are weathered and have heavy growths of lichen which makes the incised decoration almost impossible to see. Their provenance is unknown, but they are of the same approximate date as the putative foundation of the church and it is possible that they originated from the site.

The two early pillar stones outside the porch

LLANELWEDD – St. Eluned/
Eilwedd (SO 043 522)

A mound at the back of the Royal Welsh Agricultural Society Showground, reputedly the site of a Dark Age church.

The present stone church at Llanelwedd is dedicated to St. Matthew and was rebuilt in Victorian times, but this site is not the historic site of the church. The old church site at Cae Henllan was probably dedicated to St. Eluned/Eilwedd, different spellings of the same name.[1] This is half a mile north-north-east on the A483 just inside the back entrance of the Royal Welsh Showground and is accessible at times when that area of the showground is officially open. It can, however, be seen from the large gateway next to the road where it appears as a grassy mound that overlooks the gravel car parks and modern showground buildings. It is ringed intermittently by fairly young deciduous trees. There are no visible remains above ground today, but the site of *Cae Henllan* is believed to be the site of the Dark Age church that was partly excavated in 1910 when wall foundations and flooring were found. Three sides of a possible pentagonal enclosure have been found which are now marked out by a bank which is about 6½ feet wide by about 1½ feet high; there is an inner ditch at the south-west side.[2] The date of its abandonment is not known.

The legend of the saint is to be found under St. Eluned's Chapel, Slwch Tump (see p.247).

LLANFEUGAN or
LLANFIGAN – St. Meugan
(SO 087 245)

Remarkable ancient yews and some possible charter evidence for an early monastic site.

The church of St. Meugan lies about 3 miles south-east of Brecon in a dell by the River Usk. The size and substantial structure of the church is unusual and there is no settlement around it. The name Llanfeugan is believed to be derived from Llanmeugan.

St. Meugan was an early saint and reputedly trained and served at Llantwit under St. Illtud, and at Caerleon under St. Dyfrig and therefore slightly pre-dates St. David. He was a grandson of Meurig ab Tewdrig, king of Morganwg and his brother was St. Henwyn/Hywyn. Meugan's father, Gwyndaf, was his superior at Caerleon and had his own dedication at Llanwnda in Pembrokeshire and another in Carnarvonshire. Meugan may have been the holy man, Moucan/Maucan, who appears in the *Life* of Cadoc to act as peacemaker between Cadoc and Maelgwn. If this is correct, to have acted in such a roll for Cadoc, who was very learned and formidable, suggests that Meugan was a substantial character with some influence. He appears to have travelled the country to quite a degree as there are dedications to him in Anglesey, Denbighshire and many in Pembrokeshire. He was buried at Bardsey.[1]

There are fragments of poems supposedly attributed to St. Meugan in the *Black Book of Carmarthen* and the *Myvyrian Archaiology*. One is an elegy on Cynddylan, prince of Powys, another 'an historical, prophetical, rhapsodical composition in uncouth rhyme'![2]

St. Meugan appears to have attracted a cult following as, for example, one chapel in Llanfair Nant Gwyn in north-east Pembrokeshire was pulled down in 1592 as it attracted 'superstitious pilgrimages to its shrine.' This was on order of the Privy Council who did not approve of such goings-on! In the same deanery there was a Capel Meugan which was referred to as a pilgrimage chapel. Meugan is said to have had a college, *Cor Meugant*, on the banks of the River Wye, one of a number of colleges that together trained 2,000 'saints' presided over by St. Dyfrig as principal. In the 'Taxatio' of 1291, Llanfeugan is referred to as '*Eccl'ia de S'c'o Mengano*',[3] perhaps indicating that the college had been at Llanfeugan if *S'c'o* refers to scholars or school.

The dating of the present church is complex, but the north aisle is probably the earliest part, with Norman style arches; the present nave dating from the 14th century.[4] The floor of the north aisle has been raised by at least 20 inches as a result of sand being brought in. Bailey observes that it is uncertain why this was done, but it might have been to help dry out the building as a result of its use for burial. In some parts of the church he noted there were traces of two layers of bodies, one buried above the other.[5]

The churchyard is quite long and narrow and is described as 'an irregular quadrilateral' shape which is determined by the steepness of one side of the valley to the north (explained by quarrying) and its position on a spur. The churchyard is raised some 1 to 5 feet above the surrounding land. There is a barely discernible hollow to the north-west of the church which is purportedly the remains of a cockpit.[6]

The most striking features of the churchyard are the 12 superb yews which curve around part of the boundary; 13 were recorded in the 19th century. In the late 1990s a male yew to the north was measured and found to have a girth of 37 feet, 3 inches. This clearly predates the church and Bevan-Jones remarks it 'must be associated with an earlier sphere of influence, perhaps an early saint,'[7] the saint in question probably being Meugan. Most of the yews are ancient, venerable specimens, some with huge hollowed and split trunks. The fact that two at least probably predate the introduction of Christianity into Britain (another female yew to the east has a girth of 32 feet and an estimated age of 2,000 years)[8] and that they form part of line, perhaps a boundary, suggests they have a pre-Christian origin and it is possible that here we have an example of a pagan site that was Christianised. Walking beneath the yews engenders an understanding of how these trees were seen as symbols of immortality — they are astonishing.

Some of the yews on the churchyard boundary

LLANFIHANGEL TAL-Y-LLYN
– St. Michael and All Angels
(SO 114283)

There is a suggestion that the site may be early due to the location and the possibility that the churchyard was once curvilinear;[1] the presence of the early stone increases this possibility.

The church of St. Michael is at the centre of the village, about 4 miles west of Brecon.

Theophilus Jones derives the meaning of the place-name as 'Saint Michael's at the head of the lake,' which nicely describes the position of the village in relation to Llangors Lake. However he gives a vociferous account against the disgraceful state of the church in the early 1800s: '… on the east or rather north east, for the church is not due east and west, is a compartment called the chancel, the pine-end wall of which bulges out considerably, the floor is of earth and uneven … Within this place were two boards nailed together, with four posts to support them, worth about sixpence for fire-wood and for no other purpose; these are covered by a dark woollen cloth, so incrusted with dirt and dust, since the year 1755, when it was bought or given to the church, that it is nearly as hard as the wood it covers and of about equal value. On this the Holy Communion is administered!'[2] The church was 'thoroughly restored' in about 1870 and is today a rather lovely medieval building. The fabric of the nave is either 14th or 15th century, possibly earlier, and the tower and porch appear to be 15th century.[3] There is an attractive Norman font with cable moulding near the rim.[4]

The dedication gives no clue as to the date of the foundation of the site, although some St. Michael dedications are as early as the 8th century. The churchyard is roughly rectangular with curving corners and some curving along its length and it is thought that it has been encroached along it western and southern sides. The village inn is positioned at the south-west corner, continuing a fast disappearing tradition of the association of church and tavern. The straight boundary and shape of the churchyard to this side, together with the approach to the second churchyard entrance leading through the inn's back yard, invite speculation as to whether the inn was historically included within the church precinct. The churchyard slopes east to west and on the eastern side the Tawel Brook runs past the boundary. There are cottages and gardens abutting and forming the churchyard boundary for about half of its length; a characteristic of religious sites which are early and which, over time, have attracted building next to their enclosure. The northern boundary is irregular, and the western is again curved, although it appears to have been cut through to obtain access to adjacent property in times long past. The internal churchyard levels are raised by 4-5 feet along these boundaries, and by about 3 feet on the southern side; a stream terrace running north-west to south-east across the churchyard east of the church may have formed an earlier boundary. There is noticeable internal banking on the inside of the western boundary which Clwyd-Powys Archaeological Trust suggest may 'indicate a former perimeter.'[5]

A charter of *c.*925 in the *Book of Llandaff* mentions the church of *Lann Mihachgel meibion Gratlaun* and records a grant of land from King Tewdwr to a bishop (see under Llangors). In this charter Llanfihangel Tal-y-Llyn is named as the place granted but the accompanying bounds fit those for Llanfihangel Cwm Ddu (Cwmdu). Indeed Davies notes that the 'title identifies … Llanfihangel Tal y Llyn, for no apparent reason', but the fact that a mention was made in the 10th century may support a case for an early foundation.[6]

Within the porch and to the left is what Haslam refers to as a 'pagan columnar pillar stone'.[7] It is about 4½ feet tall, of sandstone and cylindrical in shape, being slightly wider at the top which has a squarish but quite shallow hole. It looks remarkably like a phallic/pagan fertility symbol. Information within the porch states that its origin and use are unknown and that it was placed in its present position in 1920. No date is ventured in any written sources available. There has been no attempt to Christianise this stone and it is likely to be pre-Christian. An unsubstantiated note in the church porch states that the church replaced a pagan temple. Whether or not this is the case, there is enough to this church site to suggest an early Christian foundation, even if it is circumstantial.

LLANFILO – St. Bilo
(SO 119 332)

The dedication to an early Welsh saint (and formerly to an Anglo-Saxon saint and princess), coupled with details of the churchyard indicate an early site.

The church of St. Bilo is about 2 miles west of Talgarth at the centre of the village. The church itself is of several periods, the nave being partly Norman according to Haslam, although Clwyd-Powys Archaeological Trust question this, saying there is nothing *in situ* to suggest it being this early although remark that 'ornamental lintels do reveal a Norman predecessor.' Inside the church is an oval, boulder-shaped font which Haslam suggests is 'probably Norman'.[1] It has two bevels cut as decoration around the top but has inexplicably been painted cream, as has the outside of the church which covers the detail of both. The screen has been carefully restored, in particular the statues of the apostles have been replaced, the originals of which were probably destroyed during the Reformation and are described as missing by Theophilus Jones in 1809.[2] Jones describes twelve niches, and there are now only five. The carved detail and design of both the front and the back of the screen are breathtaking.

Inside the porch, on the internal right-hand wall, is a rectangular slab with geometric diamond and circle patterns, for which we have no date. On the left hand jamb of the porch door is incised graffiti of a dissected circle. There is also a blocked Norman doorway on the north wall of the nave with an interesting lintel which has a carved geometric design. The appearance of the church and yard with its substantial lychgate is delightful and deserves a long visit for its architectural merits alone.

The shape of the churchyard is most suggestive of an early site. It is roughly oval, measuring about 165 feet by 245 feet, and has probably been altered to

The probable pre-Norman font

the north-east near the lychgate, but is likely to be original along most of the perimeter. It slopes and the church is set about half way down on a slightly flatter area. The northern boundary is curved with a significant drop to the surrounding land. The same is true of the eastern boundary and there is internal embanking up to the boundary walls on both sides. The south side is also curved with a steep drop to the lane; the south-western boundary is similarly shaped and is embanked internally. Clwyd-Powys Archaeological Trust record that on the south and west side there is 'evidence of an earlier bank to which the wall was added'.[3] It is obvious that the churchyard has been in use for a long time as the tips of old gravestones can be seen peeping out of the grass. That the enclosure is raised above the adjoining land, has curved boundaries and is on a naturally elevated site is also suggestive of a defensive site. The presence of a mature yew opposite the west end of the tower also add some support to this being an early medieval foundation; there are also mature yews in the churchyard to the south-east and south-west.

There has been confusion for some centuries about the patron saint. In the 1800s Theophilus Jones states it was dedicated to St. Mildburgh, abbess of Much Wenlock[4] who was the daughter of King Merewald of the Magonsaete, a kingdom based in Herefordshire and a sub-kingdom of Mercia. The dedication to an Anglo-Saxon saint in Breconshire seems rather strange, although Much Wenlock Priory was recently found to have had burials from an earlier foundation dating to Romano-British times, thus it probably had a British Christian origin. In Anglo-Saxon times the abbey had a long-distance link to Iken on the coastline of Suffolk. However, Baring-Gould and Fisher state that the church at Llanfilo is in fact dedicated to St. Belyau who was one of the daughters of King Brychan of Brycheiniog,[5] the ruler of the Breconshire area. This complies more sensibly with the geographical dedication pattern, as Brychan's son is the patron saint of Boughrood, and a putative grand-daughter is the patron of Llanelieu a few miles from Llanfilo. Baring-Gould and Fisher also remark that the place-name clearly takes its name from St. Belyau as the personal name has mutated into Beilio and then to Bilo. At Llanfilo there was a spring or well called Ffynnon Filo and a hill to the south-west of the church is called Allt Filo/Fillo.[6] The dedication to St. Beilo is clearly documented in 13th and 14th century documents[7] and in ancient charters the church is referred to as Lanbilio and Lanbiliou,[8] thus the dedication to St. Milburgh is of later origin although it was used until quite recently.[9] Everything about this site indicates an early medieval origin.

LLANFRYNACH – St. Brynach
(SO 075 258)

The dedication, the existence of a pre-Norman carved stone and the unusually large size of the churchyard all suggest an early and important foundation.

The church of St. Brynach lies three miles east of Brecon at the centre of Llanfrynach village. The large churchyard and the age and clustering of the village buildings in the fertile Usk valley is indicative of a major site. The church was largely rebuilt in 1885 when the nave and chancel were replaced; the tower is of 14th to 15th century date,[1] so none of the structure is early.

An early Christian stone was found in the church foundations during rebuilding in 1885[2] along with two others which have since been lost. The former, now inside the church, is about 6 to 7 inches wide, tapering to the top, and over 5½ feet tall with an asymmetrical rope coil pattern down the centre, with a small Maltese-style cross to the top and a large one to the bottom. Towards the top is a small figure of a man one foot tall. It has been questioned whether this symbolizes a crucifixion, but the figure looks more as if he is preaching, and the similarity to other figures portrayed in saintly teachings is called to mind. The stone is dated to between the 10th and 11th centuries by Nash-Willaims.[3]

The titular saint is the Irish St. Brynach who was described as the 'soul-friend' or chaplain and confessor to King Brychan, as well as being his father-in-law. Brynach apparently travelled abroad early in his career and visited Rome, where he is said to have slain 'a pestiferous monster', and then visited Brittany on his return home. He travelled back floating 'over the sea on a stone' which Baring-Gould and Fisher remark probably meant no more than he carried his 'lech' or tombstone about with him wherever he travelled 'as was a common custom among the Celtic saints …'. Upon his return to Milford Haven he found himself in the middle of an uprising, as Cunneda's sons and Urien Rheged had joined forces with the Welsh to expel the Irish rulers and settlers. The Brychan family was split between its Welsh and Irish members but endeavoured to side with the Welsh, and Brynach was caught in the in-fighting and injured, probably at his wife's instigation.[4] He recovered from his wound but was badly received in Carmarthenshire where he was offered only a cowshed for lodging and is remembered in the place-name Llanboidy/Llanbeudy 'the Church of the Cow-house'. He was accepted in Pembrokeshire at Llanfrynach, where he built an oratory and cell by a spring, the rectangular remains of which existed in the 1900s. While encamped near Nevern he met, and was accepted by, his wife's kinsman, Clechre/Clether, who requested that he instruct his twenty sons. Clechre was the lord of that area, so Brychan settled at Nevern. Over time he was able to set up churches in Glamorganshire, Carmarthenshire, as well as others in

Pembrokeshire. A legend relates that he owned a cow which supplied him with abundant milk, and also a wolf-dog which accompanied the cow and was used to guard it. The king, Maelgwn of Gwynedd, travelling south, sent word to order Brynach to act as host to himself and his followers, an order which Brynach refused as he did not want to set a precedent for the king to claim lodging with him as a right. Maelgwn therefore seized the cow, despite the presence of the dog. The two men managed to overcome their bad start, and agreed that Brynach would provide the king's party with sustenance providing it was not claimed as a right. The upshot was that Maelgwn exempted him from royal dues and granted him land. However Brynach appears to have been driven out of Wales and travelled to Devon where he was reputedly buried at his church at Braunton.[5]

Llanfrynach church in Breconshire is near to the centre of Brychan's kingdom. From the details gleaned from the accounts of St. Brynach, it is likely that this foundation pre-dates those in west Wales, and it is the only Brynach foundation in central Wales. The churchyard is described as 'exceptionally large and flat' and its present shape as 'sub-square', i.e. roughly square. The only earthworks visible are about 6½ feet outside the present eastern boundary wall indicating that this side of the enclosure has shrunk. It may therefore have been more circular than it is now although Clywd-Powys Archaeological Trust state there is 'no evidence to indicate an earlier fossilised boundary'.[6]

On the Ordnance Survey map, less than a third of a mile due west of the church, is marked the site of a Roman bath house, making early post-Roman activity in the locality all the more likely.

The early Christian stone found in the foundations of the church during a rebuild of 1885

205

LLANGAMMARCH WELLS
– St. Cadmarch (SN 935 474)

The dedication to an early Welsh saint, the topography of the site and the presence of an early medieval stone suggest the church is an early foundation.

The church of St. Cadmarch is set on a somewhat vertiginous spur between the rivers Ithon and Cammarch, close to the centre of the small town, which, despite attempts to promote health spa facilities during the Victorian era, failed to grow, unlike its distant neighbour Llandrindod Wells. The steep hill on which the church stands is the most obvious feature of this church on first sight. At the base of the boundary wall adjoining the road are large rough hewn boulders which adds to the

rugged, impressive character. It is a naturally defensible site and one wonders what preceded its Christian use.

The church was completely rebuilt in 1913–16 and is both striking in design and unusual in that not many churches were constructed during the First World War. The tower was added in 1927. The design is simple and refreshing in its detail. Its predecessor was only built in about 1850 and was described as 'a mean church situated on an abrupt eminence'. The church before that had been described as being in a ruinous state in 1840 with only the nave surviving.[1]

The dedication to St. Cadmarch is confused. He is described as the son of Gwynllyw Filwr and so the brother of St. Cadoc, but his name has been mis-translated from the early manuscripts as Cammab and Cannen. It is considered that these names are in fact mis-readings of Kenmeu/Kemmeu, a very old form of the name Cynfyw[2] who was Gwynllyw's son and Cadoc's registrar at Llancarfan.[3] However it is claimed that the nickname of St. Cynog, son of Brychan was 'cammarch', which word means literally 'crooked horse' and in modern Welsh means camel! Cynog's reputed burial place is at Merthyr Cynog about 8 miles to the south-east. He also shares the same festival date of 8 October with the St. Cammarch who is listed in the Iolo Manuscripts and other sources. We feel that the date of the festival could have been superimposed in medieval times because of the confusion in names and nicknames and that, as his correct name Cynog is used in his other foundations, it would be strange to use a nickname for so serious a business as a church dedication. The River Cammarch runs directly against the western boundary of the churchyard, and the church may have even taken its name from this natural feature, or vice versa. Another point of contention is that a 12th-century bard, Cynddelw, states that Llangammarch is amongst St. Tysilio's foundations. In the *Lives* of St. Tysilio, preserved in Brittany, it is said that Tysilio spent some time in the Builth (Buellt) area.[4] There is no other church dedicated to St. Cynfyw or Cadmarch, presuming they are the same man, in the area, but Cynfyw has dedications in Montgomeryshire and Monmouthshire.[5] We consider this saint to be most likely candidate in the absence of clearer historical evidence.

In 1291 the church at Llangammarch was given a relatively high value of £13 6s. 8d. which indicates its importance in earlier times,[6] and increases the likelihood of it being an early foundation.

The churchyard's shape is determined by the spur of land on which it sits and is 'elongated following the natural contours'[7] with a roughly curvilinear/rectilinear shape. The southern boundary bank slopes steeply down to the road. The earlier churches lay close to the tip of the spur and would have overlooked a steep drop. The present church is set close to the northern boundary, which has a considerable drop down to the River Cammarch; the chancel nearly abuts the boundary on the eastern side where it adjoins a garden with no difference in height.

There is a section of 'pillar' stone carved with a ringed-cross and a spiral set into the gable-end of the porch. The spiral is similar to one of the early medieval stones at Llanafan Fawr and is the only other example on a Welsh cross-slab. The Llangammarch stone also has a series of annulets (mouldings in the form of a

The carved stone now set into the porch

ring), recessed squares below the ring-cross and what Knight refers to as a 'frontal outline figure (best described as resembling a ginger-bread man)' to the bottom left of the cross.[8] The annulets are similar in design to those on the Bryngwyn stone some 20 miles to the east. The ringed-crosses and spirals at Llanafan and Llangammarch seem to form a distinct group and may have been carved by the same mason (see entry on Llanafan Fawr p.179). The example at Llangammarch has been dated to between the 7th and 9th centuries[9] but its provenance is unknown.

LLANGANTEN or CILMERY – St. Cannen (SO 009 517)

A riverside church with some topographical evidence of an early site.

The church of St. Cannen is about 2 miles west of Builth Wells just off the A483. The site is hidden away down a track to the River Chwefru.

St. Cannen or Canten appears to have been related to St. Cadoc, but in some early manuscripts the two men are confused. In one manuscript he is even described as a female. He also appears as Kemmeu, and is variously described as the brother or nephew of St. Cadoc (see under Llangammarch Wells, above). In a taxation record of 1291 the church is called Langanten which suggests the saint is Canten rather than Cannen.[1]

The church was partially rebuilt in 1882 but some medieval masonry survives within its walls. Upon his visit to the church in the very early 1800s, Theophilus Jones noted that the church resembled 'an ill swept barn' and added that 'one or two human skulls were thrown upon the ground with apparent inattention, but perhaps designedly to remind the thoughtless stranger that he was near a place of interment …'![2]

The churchyard shape is rather like a fat triangle with rounded edges, two sides of which are dictated by watercourses (the river and a small tributary). Clwyd-Powys Archaeological Trust feel it is unlikely that this is the original shape of the church enclosure for immediately to the south of the church there is 'a low, broad scarp … [with] a slightly curving course', and there is another 'faint bank' to the south-west and much closer to the modern boundary.[3] Both of these need an eye of faith to see them. From the eastern end it can be seen that the church is built on a faintly raised platform.

In the south-west of the churchyard there is an old gnarled yew with a hollow trunk on top of a low mound. It has a wide spread and, although the existing girth is not huge, the tree has a look of some age.

LLANGASTY TAL-Y-LLYN
– St. Gastayn (SO 133 261)

Archaeological evidence for an early use of the site which appears to have had an enclosure and where legends record St. Gastayn built a hermitage or monastery.

The church of St. Gastayn lies on the south side of Llangors lake, 3 miles from Talgarth.

This is the only dedication to St. Gastayn, who appears to have been responsible for baptising St. Cynog, the eldest son of Brychan, and to have provided him some of his training, Certainly Brychan's court at Talgarth was close by. There is a legend which names Gastayn as the son of Myfig, the last of the princes of Syfaddon, the town which legend records was swallowed up by water because of the 'wickedness of its principal inhabitants.' Gastayn, then a child, was apparently found floating in his cradle on the edge of the newly-formed lake, called Llyn Syfaddon, or what is now Llangors Lake, under which the town had disappeared. He was baptised and took up an aesthetic life, establishing a hermitage where he was subsequently buried.[1]

The unique dedication, the location, and recent archaeological work in the churchyard suggest that 'an early medieval origin is likely.' The enclosure is quite small and of polygonal shape, with one slightly curved section to the north-west corner. Clywd-Powys Archaeological Trust state that a 'recent geophysical survey hints at a curvilinear ditch just outside [the] east side.'[2] A trench was cut by the churchyard wall and evidence of an earlier enclosure ditch was found, possibly part of the churchyard, that had several phases of silting and recutting. A second trench identified another ditch, and finds included a sherd of possible Bronze Age pottery.[3] None of this of course proves the existence of an early monastery or church.

Two yews of some age are found against the north wall of the churchyard and there is another along the southern side, suggesting a possible deliberate north-south planting.

Llangors Lake reputedly covered the town of Syfaddon of which St. Gastayn's father was one of the last princes

LLANGATTOCK – St. Cattwg or Catwg (SO 210 178)

An early medieval date seems probable due to the shape of churchyard, location and dedication.

The church of St. Cattwg, which is an alternative spelling of Cadoc, is on the edge of the picturesque village of Llangattock, less than a mile from Crickhowell on the opposite bank of the River Usk. There are several dedications to Cadoc in the area, for whose history see pp.59-65.

The church structure is mainly of 13th- to 14th-century date with a 16th-century tower.[1] Clywd Powys Archaeological Trust describe the churchyard as an 'irregular D-shape', with 'a straight-sided northern perimeter ... suggestive of a truncated boundary'. There is noticeable embanking of up to 3½ feet on the western boundary which is considered to be an earlier boundary bank. The Trust note that this is an inner bank which curves around the north-west corner and suggest it is a 'relic of the former enclosure'. A similar bank exists on the northern side but, in this case, it includes ash and cinder and is thought to be the waste from the church boiler. They also remark on the wall to the south-east which sits astride a bank with an external gully. As with many riverside sites, the internal and external ground levels are very similar. A few feet from the east end of the church the ground drops by about a foot; no explanation has been offered for this.[2] Two fairly old yews are to the east of the church. The churchyard is divided into two by a footpath.

The church is first mentioned as *Ecclesia de Lancadok* in a taxation report of 1291 when it had the value of about £20, which indicates it was a wealthy establishment and was probably a mother, or *clas*, church, in the pre-Norman period.[3] Bailey suggests that Llangattock was one of the original parishes in the county, its boundaries stretching from Llangynidr in the west to the eastern and southern boundaries of the county, with the parish of Crickhowell being carved out of it in 1303.

LLANGENNY – St. Cenau
(SO 240 181)

The dedication and shape of the original site, together with the existence of an earlier oratory nearby indicate a pre-Norman foundation.

Llangenny is 2 miles east of Crickhowell and the church is 1 mile off the main road up a winding lane. The patron saint is St. Ceneu, who is termed a confessor, a son of Coel Godebog and grandfather of St. Cynllo. Very little else is known about him. Theophilus Jones identifies Cenau with a daughter of King Brychan of Brycheiniog and also suggests that the present church was probably not built until the oratory of St. Cenau (see below) was in ruins and the saint's name almost forgotten, as the annual wake or feast in the 1800s was held annually on St. Curig's day.[1] However St. Cenau's festival is on 15 June, only a day earlier than St. Curig's day.[2]

The church is of 14th- to early 16th-century date and the churchyard is described as an 'irregular polygonal' although it is thought to have been a smaller curvilinear enclosure originally.[3]

A partial line of largely middle-aged yews on an embankment of up to about 1 foot high faces the western end of the church and it is possible that they mark an original boundary. On the eastern side a low bank runs inside the later perimeter drystone wall and this is also suggested to be the remains of an earlier boundary. The original enclosure thus appears to have been quite flat and

211

very small, Clywd-Powys Archaeological Trust therefore remarking that 'an early medieval origin for this church site seems assured.'[4] The eastern boundary drops about 20 feet to the sizeable stream, the Grwyne Fawr. Even when visited in a heat wave in July the sound of the stream rushing by was one of the first things noticed. The churchyard has been extended to the west and the north.

There was once an oratory, or separate chapel, of St. Cenau within the parish on top of a small rocky knoll east of the church at a farm formerly called Pen y Daren, now labelled Pendarren House on modern maps. Towards the end of the 18th century, the farmer was clearing building rubble from a site reputed to be that of the oratory, when he found a chapel or oratory bell with four sides or faces. Theophilus Jones stated in the early 1800s that the bell weighed less than 20lbs., but 'the iron, which was formerly cased with bell metal or brass, is much corroded, and the tongue or clapper is gone.'[5] The bell was weighed more accurately at 7lbs. at the end of the 19th century when it was described as made from 'two iron plates hammered and riveted together, [which] was once covered with bell-metal'. In the early 20th century it was kept in the library of University College, Cardiff.[6] Of the oratory or chapel Jones observes 'No vestige of the walls appears, but there was a considerable heap of rubbish where the bell was found, which was cleared away by the farmer.'[7]

There was also a holy well to St. Cenau, Ffynon Genau, near the oratory,[8] which had a great reputation for its medicinal properties. Theophilus Jones quotes the belief that whichever of a newly married couple should first reach the well and drink the water would rule the roost.[9]

The well and oratory site are on the opposite bank of the river from the church on private land.

LLANGORS – St. Paulinus
(SO 135 276)

A collection of pre-Norman memorial slabs, and site of an early monastery.

Llangors lies 4 miles south of Talgarth and 1 mile north of the lake named after it. Theophilus Jones records the alternative name of Llan Yn Y Gorse means 'the church in the Fen or Marsh'.[1]

The church is dedicated to Paulinus, who was one of the leading religious figures of his day. He appears to have come from a noble family who lived near Llandovery and may have trained initially in Ireland but later taught St. David. He took over the running of the monastic school of Ty Gwyn in Pembrokeshire and was hailed as a great religious teacher in the *Life* of St. Teilo, who was one of his disciples. Paulinus appears to have set up a monastery at Llanddeusant which is on the western edge of the Brecon Beacons, and, as the patron saint of Llangors church, probably founded this too. Llangors is referred to as the Church of S. Paulinus de Lancors and S. Peulinus de Mara in the Cartulary of Brecon Priory. He is referred to as an aged bishop at the Synod of Brefi in *c*.545 and it is possible he was buried south of Llanddewi Brefi. Baring-Gould and Fisher refer to a stone found a long time ago in a field called Pant-y-polion near Maes Llanwrthwl in the parish of Caio, south of Llanddewi, on which there was a Latin inscription which, in translation, reads:

> Guard of the Faith, and Lover of his Land,
> Liegeman of Justice, here Paulinus lies.[2]

Llangors in mentioned twice in the Llandaff Charters. In *c*.720 'King Awst and his sons Eiludd and Rhiwallon gave *Lann Cors*, with its *territorium*, to bishop Euddogwy.' The boundaries given enclose about 1,000 acres. Davies considers that it is unlikely to be a genuine record but 'may have been constructed to substantiate the tradition of a gift from Awst.'[3] In *c*.925 Llangors appears again. There had been a major dispute between the king of Brycheiniog, Tewdwr, and the bishop Llandaff whose food rent he had stolen. The two men eventually met at Llangors monastery where the king was ordered to compensate the bishop with gold and other goods. Tewdwr could not meet such high a demand, whereupon the bishop of St. David's interceded with the result that the king was pardoned on the gift of land at Llanfihangel Cwm Ddu to the wronged bishop. Davies believes that this record was written down shortly after the transaction.[4] Theophilus Jones adds further detail. He relates that Awst and his sons also gave the whole territory of Llangors to the see of Llandaff in compensation for a serious crime. In another document 'preserved in the Monasticon' Jones records that Tewdwr and his sons were forced to compensate the Church for the affront to the bishop of Llandaff which comprised 'leaving the prelate alone, in his monastery at Llangors; having first deprived him of his dinner by force of arms. The angry bishop and his family next day left the place, having first hurled a curse and perpetual anathema at the head of the royal freebooter, for his impious robbery and the rudeness of his conduct, and afterwards he excommunicated him in a full synod of his clergy.' After the intercession of the bishop of St. David's, Tewdwr was brought back into the fold of the church upon granting land as compensation which Jones supposed was at Llanfihangel Cwm Du or Llanfihangel Crucorney.[5]

One should not assume that the monastery of Llangors was on the site of the present church. Indeed local historians favour a site at Cwrt-y-Prior (SO 151 282) off a minor road out of the village which was used as an occasional residence for the priors of Brecon.[6] There are no monastic remains left.

One of the three early stones stones now housed in Llangors church

Llangors church does, however, house three early medieval stones. The first has a Latin style ring-cross with a Latin inscription '+GURCIBLEDRUS'[7] and is dated to between the 7th and 9th centuries; its original site is unknown.[8] The second stone, described as a sandstone pillar, is about 3 feet long and nearly one foot square with a Latin burial inscription reading 'HIC IACET (S)I(U)LERD (F)ILIUS/VULMER' which is dated to the 11th or 12th century; interestingly it was found in the churchyard.[9] Bailey in Theophilus Jones remarks on the similarity of this inscription to the one on the font at Defynnog which reads 'S.I.W.V.R.D. + G.W.L.M. E.R.' and suggests this may have been 'the maker or donor of this font, the Llangorse stone being his memorial. The name of his father, in the form WULMERE, is to be seen in the inscription at Llanddew.'[10] The third stone is a narrow section of grave-slab with a section of incised design,

214

probably showing a mythical beast in a double border and a foliate cross, and is dated to the 10th or 11th centuries; its original position is unknown.[11] It is unusual to find more than one early fragment at any site.

The churchyard is medium-sized, relatively flat and roughly rectilinear, although the eastern boundary shows some curving. It is suggested that the churchyard was once larger and more rounded, and that the road to the west together with the Castle Inn and old school to the south, have encroached upon it. A stream, the Nant Cwy, runs along the northern side of the churchyard. On the eastern side there are the remains of an internal bank within the enclosure which probably predates the wall, and to this side the churchyard is somewhat raised above the external ground level.[12]

Half a mile south of the village is Llangors Lake with its Dark Age crannog. In the Abingdon Manuscript, (C) of the *Anglo-Saxon Chronicle* under the year 916, it states that on 19 June Aethelflaed (King Alfred the Great's daughter, who was known as the 'Lady of the Mercians') 'sent an army into Wales and broke down Brecon Mere, and there took the wife of the king as one of thirty-four.' Swanton identifies Brecon Mere, which was written as *Brecenan mere*, as 'presumably a structure at or near what is now Llangorse Lake, where there was a cross-ridge dyke controlling traffic'.[13] An identification with the crannog is quite possible, even probable. Brecon Museum has a superb display on the crannog and other aspects of Dark Age Wales, including a striking collection of early medieval stones

LLANGYNIDR – St. Cynidr and St. Mary (SO 155 194)

The site is considered to be of early medieval origin because of the dedication, the shape of churchyard and its position.

The church lies at the centre of Llangynidr which is about 3¼ miles west of Crickhowell. The church was damaged by fire and as a result was completely rebuilt in 1928, only retaining a stoup and a damaged 13th-century font from the earlier church.[1] Theophilus Jones referred to this church as of a 'miserable fabric, barn roofed, very indifferently flagged, the seats irregular and decayed ...'. This was itself rebuilt in 1873.[2]

The church was recorded in the 'Taxatio' of 1291 as being valued at £5 6s. 8d.,[3] a moderate sum. The enclosure is a good example of a curvilinear raised churchyard, albeit that the western walled boundary is fairly straight, whilst the churchyard to the north seems to have been encroached upon and now has a fairly straight boundary. At the eastern side of the churchyard the boundary is ill-defined and there is a row of middle-aged looking yews set forward which may mark an earlier boundary. It is suggested that the church enclosure may originally have been circular.[4] On the side by the road the exterior ground level is about 3 feet lower than the church enclosure. There is a yew near to the porch on the western side which, although not of obvious antiquity, is strapped with iron. There is another old gnarled yew on the southern side of the churchyard in line with the western porch which has a stone wall around its base. The churchyard is full of graves and this obvious heavy use would probably have destroyed any earlier boundary earthworks.

The dedication to two saints, Cynidr and Mary, is probably a late variation and it is likely that Cynidr was the earliest of the two dedications. He is described as bishop and confessor and appears to have lived in the 6th century. He was reputedly a grandson of Brychan and possibly brother to Cadoc. It was probably Cadoc who trained him as his name seems to appear (in altered form) as one of Cadoc's disciples in a deputation sent to King Arthur at the River Usk, where the subject of the length of sanctuary was decided upon (see p.62). Cynidr also had a hermitage on an island in the River Wye at Winforton in Herefordshire, and was probably the titular saint of Winforton church; he was certainly the patron of Glasbury church in Radnorshire and of Kenderchurch in Herefordshire. He also appears to have travelled to Cornwall with Cadoc.[5]

Llangynidr was also known as 'Eglwys Iail' and 'Eglwys Fair a Chynidr',[6] Iail also being the name of the nearby brook according to Theophilus Jones. who also refers to the saint as Cynedr or Kenneth.[7]

LLANGYNOG – St. Cynog
(SO 024 460)

The dedication, the shape of the churchyard and enclosure strongly suggest that this is an early Chrisian site.

Llangynog lies about 4 miles south of Builth Wells, some 400 yards south-east from the B road to Upper Chapel, and can be reached along a footpath which is signposted from the lay-by on the road.

The dedication of this site is to St. Cynog, for information on whom see pp.241-242. The church site is on a small plateau of fairly level ground with a marshy area to the east and high hills in the distance. The enclosure is nearly circular with defined low boundary banks of crumbling stone walls and earth, with an average height of about 3 feet, although the embanking on the northern side rises up to 6 feet. There is an old yew within the enclosure which is ringed by coniferous and deciduous trees. The ground falls away to a small stream on the north.

Within the enclosure, which slopes gently upwards towards the centre, can be seen (at least in a dry summer) the parch-marks of the walls of the church that was demolished in recent years. Theophilus Jones reports in *c.*1809 that although the church had been rebuilt 'a few years back, from its exposed situation, is again nearly dilapidated and ruinous'.[1] Bailey observes that this is the only Cynog church which lies north of the Eppynt Hills and that it appears to have been rebuilt in the late 18th century and was again rebuilt in 1882.[2] There is now just a modern altar built from stone blocks and a few scattered gravestones, along with a wooden structure holding a small church bell which is used for the occasional services which are still held at the site. It is easy to appreciate here how once a building has been demolished the enclosure can melt back into the landscape, leaving no trace. The fragility of this site is apparent and it is only a matter of time before it becomes difficult to discern through a process of natural erosion and damage by livestock. This must have been the fate of many small church sites for which there is historical record in the Llandaff Charters, for example, but no clue on the ground.

There is something quite special about Llangynog, not only in its remote spot on the edge of the wild Welsh moors, but in the fact that it reminds us of the many early Christian sites that are now lost by the very fact that it still remains. But, one wonders, for how long?

LLANHAMLACH – St. Peter and St. Illtyd (SO 089 264)

The early pillar stone, coupled with the dedication and the partial curvilinearity of the churchyard suggest an early medieval site.

The church of St. Peter and St. Illtyd lies 4 miles east of Brecon at the centre of the small, dispersed settlement and about ½ mile from the Neolithic burial mound which bears St. Illtud's name. The cluster of dedications to Illtud in this area is discussed on page 35.

Jones remarks that Llanhamlach, 'universally pronounced Llanhamwlch

The pillar stone inside the church

in common conversation; ... is derived and indeed sometimes written in old documents Llan-aml-llech, the churchyard situated upon or abounding with flat stones or slates, of which kind of stone the rock on which it is built is thought to be composed.'[1] However we would agree with Baring-Gould and Fisher's suggestion that Llanhamlach may contain the name of Brychan's father Anlach,[2] the church being located at the centre of Brychan's kingdom.

Within the church is a pillar stone which is over 3½ feet tall, roughly 1½ feet wide and ½ foot thick, known as the Moridic Stone. Its original position is unknown as it was found in the demolished medieval rectory being used as a lintel.[3] It has been dated to the 10th or 11th century, and bears the inscription 'IOHANNIS MOREDIC SUREXIT HUNC LAPIDEM'.[4] Several inches of the top of the stone are missing, but it bears a Latin cross with forked ends, and male and female figures with their arms raised to the sides of their heads which Haslam states 'are, naturally, identified as St. John and the Virgin Mary'.[5] Below and around there are geometric and rope-type decorations cut into the stone. The striking feature is the informality of the decoration being fluid, even exuberant, and is rather like early folk art; it is quite common for memorial stones, even early ones, to have a rather inexpressive, formal design, and that to an extent exists on the reverse which is not readily visible in the stone's present position. In the external western wall of the tower, about 3 feet above ground level, is another small section of carved stone showing about 6 inches of rope-work decoration. It is obviously early and reused.

The churchyard is D-shaped with curving sides to the south and east, but with straight sides to the north and west. On the north-eastern, north and eastern sides the boundary is embanked internally and this is thought to 'define the earlier boundary of the churchyard', but there is little difference in the external ground levels at these points. However, on the south-west corner and continuing around to the south-east, the churchyard is raised to up to 6 feet above external levels.[6]

The 16th-century antiquarian, Leland, recorded that St. Illtud 'prayed for and was granted the privilege that no adder might live within his parish.'[7]

The dedication to St. Peter is a later addition, possibly early Norman.

The small section of re-used carved stone in the external western wall of the tower

LLANIGON – St. Eigen
(SO 213 399)

There are enough clues in the dedication of Llanigon and place-names in the vicinity to suggest a very early origin to this site — the connection with semi-mythical saints suggests the possibility that a long forgotten cult was introduced in the very early medieval period.

The church is in the old, southern part of the village about 1¾ miles south-west of Hay-on-Wye and stands in a medium-sized churchyard with a definite south to north oriented slope. The patron saint is St. Eigen (also Eigion), for whom there are three shadowy contenders. The first, Eigion, is styled bishop and confessor. Very little is known about him and he does not figure in any genealogy of the Welsh saints. Llanigon is the only church dedicated to him, although the dedication has sometimes been to St. Nicholas. St. Eigion's mother may have been one of the daughters of Brychan and is named as Kehingayr or Ceingair, but Eigion's father is not named. St. Eigion's feast day of 10 September is only recorded in the Iolo Manuscripts Calendar, although it was observed on the first Sunday after 20 September until the late 19th century. Baring-Gould and Fisher record Eigion's Well, Ffynnon Eigion, as 'not far distant from the church.'[1] Francis Jones suggests it may be the same as the Boiling Well and relates how a farmer's wife used to pass the Boiling Well on her way to Hay-on-Wye and 'on one occasion a "spirit in white" jumped behind her on the horse as she passed this well, and rode with her until she reached home,' after which it vanished.[2] The well is on private property.

Alternatively, Theophilus Jones suggests the church is dedicated to either the 1st-century St. Eigen, daughter of Caradog, or to the 6th century Eigion son of Caw and brother to St. Gildas. St. Eigen was allegedly the first female saint amongst the Britons, and is only mentioned in the Iolo Manuscripts, which are notoriously unreliable in parts. Here she is said to have been the daughter of Caradog ab Bran and to have been married to Sarllog, who was either the lord of Old Sarum in Wiltshire; the lord of Garth Mathrin; or a Roman chieftain

Old font now in the porch

depending on which document is read! Sarlogg was also said to have been the principal of a monastery of *Côr Sarlogg* of thirty saints at Llandaff. Elsewhere in the Iolo Manuscripts, St. Eigen is said to have been converted to Christianity with her father in Rome by St. Ilid who is elsewhere identified with Joseph of Arimathea. The legend then relates that Joseph came to Britain with Caradog and Eigen and converted the country to Christianity. Eigen founded a monastery for twelve saints and it expanded to become 'the most eminent *côr* in the world.' Baring-Gould and Fisher remark that 'all this story is pure fiction.'[3]

However, Eigion/Eigron, son of Caw, is also an unlikely candidate for the founder or patron of Llanigon as he is not recorded as having a church dedicated to him in Wales, 'nor does his festival occur in any calendar.'[4]

In the very early 1800s Theophilus Jones described how the walls of the nave were 'bedaubed with caricatures of death and time, a wretched imitation of the King's arms, and "many a holy text strewed around", instead of which a little white lime would be more ornamental.' Jones also records that the ruins of an old chapel stood in a hamlet called Cilonw, a short distance south-west of the village. He considered that Cilonw was a corruption of Celin whom he describes as a 6th-century saint, a son of Caw, who was driven out of the north of England by the Picts. The only Cilonw close to Llanigon on the large scale modern OS map is to the south-east at SO 233 389 which has Cilonw Brook running close by, and very close to the south-east of Llanigon is Bryn Celyn and Plas Celyn. Jones mentions a will dated 1576 of a Robert Vaughan who describes himself as being 'of the parish of St. Kellines' but asks to be buried at Llanelieu, which suggests that the church or chapel of St. Celin's 'was either fallen or in ruins at his time.'[5]

It is interesting that the shadowy 1st-century St. Eigen supposedly had a brother called St. Cyllin[6] and it makes one wonder if Llanigon also had some

Old font now in the porch

connection to this other early, albeit rather mythical saint. Baring-Gould and Fisher question St. Cyllin's existence and state that his name 'occurs as a genealogical link in a pedigree that is purely apocryphal.' The Iolo Manuscripts state that 'he was the first among the Welsh to give proper names to infants; for, previously, persons were not named before maturity, when the faculties were developed.'[7]

The RCAHMW quote an account of *c*.1690 of the finding of a cross 'rudely shaped' which was found 'Pitch'd in a hedge by ye way side call'd hewl y groes within 3 qrs of a mile of Llaneigon Church — or of a yard broad, 5 inches thick, an ell high above ground. As the centre is not placed.'[8] Unfortunately this stone is now lost.

The earliest fabric of Llanigon church is in the nave and possibly dates to the 13th century; the chancel and porch are 14th century. The church was restored in 1857 and again in 1941 following bomb damage after an air raid. There is unusually a bell chamber over the porch. Clwyd-Powys Archaeological Trust remark that the churchyard is 'partially circular and is likely to have an early medieval origin' and note that before 1135 Llanigon was claimed to be the principal church in the Hay-on-Wye region, which suggests a pre-Norman importance. The churchyard is now D-shaped, being noticeably curved to the north-west, north and north eastern sides. The site is on a small spur of land with a steep drop to the Cilonw Brook to the north-east.[9] The enclosure is partly raised, with a significant drop to the farm adjoining the churchyard to the eastern and northern sides. It is possible that the level of the modern farmyard has been dug away in more recent times to create a flat working area. There is also a noticeable difference in height between the lane and the present churchyard at the south-east corner, which is deeply curved.

There is a mature yew in the south-west of the enclosure with four yews to the south and south-east forming an approximate arc. They stand some feet in from the boundary wall and perhaps delineate an earlier southern boundary. However, they do not look ancient.

LLANILLTUD – St. Illtud
(SO 971 261)

The church is no longer in existence, but the churchyard is almost circular and close by is said to the burial place of St. Illtud. The immediate area may be an example of a Christianised pagan religious site.

The site of Llanilltud church is about 4½ miles south-west of Brecon, near the Brecon Beacons Mountain Visitor's Centre above Libanus.

The church was demolished in 1995, having been rebuilt in 1858 on the site of an older building,[1] only the floor and plinth remain. A description of the church in 1911 stated that it 'occupies a lonely position on the hill [of St.Illtud] ... and is an ancient building of stone in the Early English style. It has a turret with one bell, and a nave with north porch; some repairs were carried out in 1888.' As it was used to serve Libanus, which is 1½ miles away, a mission church was built there to serve the villagers.[2] This probably explains why Llanilltud church was eventually decommissioned.

Although the building has gone, the site is still consecrated ground because of the burials within the churchyard. It is on a flat area on Mynydd Illtud Common — to the west are the Traeth Mawr and Treath Bach moors, and it is possible to imagine oneself back in the early period of wandering saints, seeking out solitude.

Llanilltud's churchyard is curvilinear, almost circular, with an indentation into the boundary to the north-west. There are many immature and rather spindly conifer trees around the perimeter which is embanked internally for much of its length to a height of 1½ to 2½ feet. The shape and embanking is similar to that of Llangynog, which has also lost its church, and is what one would expect to see at a small early medieval site.

A quarter of a mile east on the common is the Bedd Gwyl Illtyd or Illtud (SO 974 263), which Baring-Gould and Fisher describe as 'a small tumulus within a much-destroyed rectangular enclosure, near a pool on the mountain.'[3] Bailey adds that St. Illtud brought the Christian faith to Breconshire

> where undoubtedly he resided, and where, if the tradition of the country be believed, he died, *circa* A.D. 480, and was buried near the chapel ... His grave is now shewn near a pool on that mountain, where there are two large stones placed at the distance of about six feet, with a small tumulus between them, called Bêdd Gwyl Illtid, or the grave of St. Illtid's eve, from its having been a custom in ancient days to watch there during the night previous to that Saint's day.'[4]

The cult of Illtud was strong in the area, and surprising as it is unlikely that he was buried there. The site is difficult to see during summer as bracken has invaded the monument, which consists of faint banks and a couple of fairly large horizontal stones. It is interesting that an obviously prehistoric monument has been vested with the legend of an early Christian burial — at Ty Illtud (SO 098 263) a few miles south-east of Brecon, a Neolithic long barrow is supposed to have been St. Illtud's hermitage (see p.253). Indeed, in the immediate vicinity of Llanilltud churchyard and the supposed grave, there is a prehistoric standing stone to the south-west and one to the south-east of the church site, which are about 2 to 3 feet high. The Bedd Gwyl Illtyd lies offset, nearer the eastern of the two standing stones, and the church site is between them, but not equidistant. National Park information states that a straight line passes between them and through the circle of the churchyard. It is suggested these stones may be of Bronze Age date 'possibly marker stones of a route or boundary and even "pointers" to sunrise on summer solstice', although an alignment with the church site might suggest a later, perhaps early medieval origin. A Roman road or causeway also runs north-west and north of the church site and its presence might well have had some influence on the siting of the church. This stretch of road was built to link the Roman fort at Y Gaer, which is about 2½ miles from Brecon and was built in about A.D. 80, with the Roman fort at Neath which is about 30 miles to the south-west. On Mynydd Illtud its course can be seen quite clearly, as there has been little subsequent interference, and it is visible as 'an overgrown, cambered ridge; just south of the pond at the extreme western end of the common, and again at the southern end of the part of the Common known as Allt Lom.'[5]

Llanilltud appears to be a good example of how a previously pagan landscape was Christianised.

LLANLLEONFEL –
dedication unknown (SN 938 499)

The site contains an early memorial stone, the putative burial site of a 7th-century king and prince of Brycheiniog, and evidence for a circular churchyard.

Llanlleonfel lies 7 miles west of Builth Wells, some 300 yards up a track on a knoll. Theophilus Jones theorises that the name relates to a Roman road system, deriving from 'Llan lleon voel, the church upon the bare tract, through which a ... branch of the Sarn Lleon or Chester road passed ...' and does not commemorate 'any guardian saint or protecting angel.'[1] However Baring-Gould and Fisher state that a saint's name Llywen (or Llewen) is the first element of the place-name.[2]

The church appears to have no dedication, but Baring-Gould and Fisher suggest that the patron saint was Gwenfael, who may have been the esteemed daughter of Brychan also called Gwenfyl or Gwenful.[3] There is an early inscribed stone measuring some 3½ feet high, 20 inches wide, and 5 inches thick that now stands in the nave. It is of natural shape and tapers diagonally to the bottom left, which would have been set in the ground. The metrical inscription in Latin in 3 inch tall lettering reads 'I(N) (S)IN(D)ONE MUTI IORUERT RUALLAUNQ SEPULCRIS + IUDICII ADV(E)NTUM SPECTA(N)T I(N) PACE TREM(EN)DUM'.[4] Translated it reads 'In the shroud, silent — Ioruert and Ruallaun, in the graves, await in peace the dreadful coming of the Judgement.' Thomas suggests the inscription was completed between 640 and 660.[5]

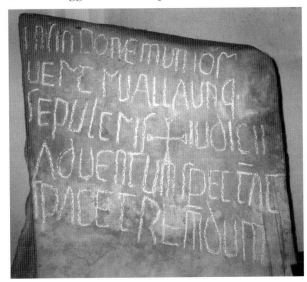

The early inscribed stone

In the 1690s the antiquarian Edward Lhuyd was told that a 'massive inscribed slab' stood upright in the churchyard, just east of the church, and 'had another stone 8 feet off opposite to it.' Thomas notes that on the reverse face of the slab, which is now in the church (it was brought inside in 1939), there are 'traces of three (pocked) ring crosses' which suggest it originally stood the other way up and 'may mark

Llanllywenfel [Llanlleonfel] as the site of a Christian burial-ground a century or so earlier than the inscription.' The five line inscription shows letters that combine 'a few capitals and a tall stilted bookhand' which was reproduced by a skilled hand. Thomas considers that this slab used to mark an 'open-air double tomb, a large slab construction above ground and above a double burial, of Riuallaun or Riuallon, a king of *Brecheniauc* (Brycheiniog) in the seventh century, and his son Ioruerth.' He further suggests that father and son fell in some battle and were buried and commemorated *in situ* and that the inscription may have been composed by a priest or court bishop of the same royal line, even of the same family. Ioruerth does not show in any later genealogies but his father does, and indeed the latter's daughter, Keindrech 'Fair-of-face' was married to the prince of Demetia (Dyfed) to which Brycheiniog was later and permanently subordinated.[6]

The church was completely rebuilt in the 1870s and no early part of the fabric remains. The previous building was recorded as being ruinous — 'a most deplorable object' — and Francis Kilvert remarked in 1873 that 'the only occupants [were] several white owls'.[7] If viewed from the east and western sides the church appears to be set on a low mound, but whether this is a natural platform or man made is unknown.

The churchyard is medium-sized and polygonal in shape. However it is difficult to determine exact boundaries in places because of the thick vegetative cover. Clywd-Powys Archaeological Trust suggest that, although the enclosure gives an impression of once being sub-circular, 'there are no obvious earthworks to signal expansion or contraction'. There is an interesting, rather striking mound to the south of the porch, which previously had a large and ancient yew growing on it; this has been felled since 1999, although a young sapling is growing from the stump. Tradition has it that this mound covered the grave of a Cistercian monk but, looking at the size of the stump, it suggests the mound is much older — perhaps even the grave of the founder, although the soil build-up around the tree may have been accentuated by other activity in the churchyard. One wonders if this is anything to do with the putative double grave of Riuallaun and Iorwerth. There is light embanking around the boundaries of the enclosure. To the north there is the impression of a shallow internal ditch, and to the east and south the internal ground level is somewhat higher than the exterior.[8]

The site has an unusual, atmospheric feel and has the air of an early Christian site. Its elevated hilltop position is also suggestive of a defended, secular enclosure.

LLANSPYDDID – St. Cadog
(Cadoc) (SO 011 281)

Reputed burial place of Brychan's father whose gravestone remains, there is also an early association with St. Cadoc and vestiges of an ancient site.

Llanspyddid lies about 2 miles west of Brecon along the A40. St. Cadoc, to whom the church is dedicated, was one of the most learned and influential churchmen of his time (see pp.59-65). On arriving at Llanspyddid to study under the Italian scholar, Bachan, he was warned that their food supplies were insufficient as the area was gripped by famine. Cadoc's *Life* states that

> in the course of that day, it happened that a certain mouse went out if its hole carrying in its mouth a grain of corn to the blessed Cadoc, and in a playful manner placed it on a table before his eyes. The same mouse came and returned seven times, and hid as many grains in its heap, shewing by a sign that the divine mercy was present with him. At length he caught the same little mouse, and tied it by the foot, that he might diligently search into the mystery of the affair; afterwards he sent for [Bachan], drew out the grain, and related to him minutely what had been done ... and Cadoc asked and received from a certain widow, a long and fine thread, which he tied to a foot of the mouse, and letting it proceed with the loosened thread, he followed it, until the said little animal came to a certain mound, under which was a very beautiful subterranean house, built of old, and full of clean wheat. And there it presently went in, through a dark hole, and soon returned bringing in its mouth one grain of corn as before. But who had built that house, or who had placed there such a large quantity of corn, is hitherto unknown.'[1]

The storyteller's affection for the mouse is obvious and rather touching. It is most likely that the building was an underground Roman corn store probably associated with Y Gaer fort not far away. Needless to say the famine was averted as food supplies were replenished.

St. Cadoc appears closely associated with this parish, and it is likely that when he retired that he returned to Llanspyddid.

There is every indication that the site is of early medieval origin. The present church is an attractive, single-storeyed structure with a bell-turret and may be of the early 14th century. It has a late Norman dog-toothed rimmed piscina or stoup, and 16th-century carved bargeboards over the porch.[2]

The churchyard is said to be the burial place of Anlach, Brychan's father, and an early medieval pillar stone in the churchyard is reputed to be his grave marker. Charles Thomas suggests a date of the late 7th or 8th century for the stone and describes it as 'a Christian afterthought for a man whose burial-record in the narrative is the oddly specific *ante ostium*, "before the doorway", i.e. outside the church.' This detail is found in a document called *De Situ Brecheniauc*, 'About the Circumstances of Brycheiniog', which may have been composed at or near Brecon, and the last version, which is the only one that now exists, was written up probably in the earlier part of the 12th century.[3] The stone is to the back, or south side, of the church, and not to the north side as stated in some guides. It is about half way down the churchyard within a row of gravestones and between

a salmon-coloured 1970s gravestone and a black marble modern gravestone. Without careful inspection it can be missed — it took us three visits to find it! The broadly rectangular stone is about 3 feet tall and 1½ feet wide and is heavily weathered. There is a ring-cross toward the top, with four circles around it, and below this is a large ring-cross of simple design with arms of about equal length with a circle in the middle where the four arms meet. The details on the stone are more visible when viewed on photographs with a long exposure than on site where they are very faint. There was an inscription on the stone recorded in 1698 that is now invisible: HIC JACOB JA, suggesting the stone was reused at a more recent date. Its original site is not known but Theophilus Jones reports that it was on the south side in 1809 and suggests that the entrance to the church may have once been on this side of the church.[4]

The reputed grave marker of Anlach, father of Brychan

228

As an aside, Jones also describes the headstone of an unfortunate man at the extreme edge of the churchyard; he died in 1791 after being 'bitten by a mad dog, and died of the hydrophobia; a disorder which the surviving inhabitants seem to have considered as epidemical, and likely to be communicated to his sleeping neighbours, as all other graves are at a considerable distance from his.'[5]

The churchyard has been truncated on the western side, where an 'earlier boundary was detected during an evaluation of the adjacent plot in 1994.' It was originally probably twice the size and D-shaped. The enclosure is stone-walled and the boundaries have internal embanking to the southern and eastern sides. The churchyard is raised above the outer ground level. The large size of the earlier church enclosure is appropriate to the past importance of the site. About eight yews have been reported around the perimeter but interestingly there are none to the north.[6] These include an obviously old yew with a very large girth along the southern boundary facing the modern housing estate, and the remains of a possible ancient yew to its left. To the east end, facing the chancel, there is another old yew by the boundary wall, and a particularly ancient specimen in the north-west corner of the churchyard with a considerable girth. Chetan and Brueton record a girth of 27 feet for a female yew to the west with an estimated age of 1,880 years[7] which appears to be this ancient tree.

This site is unusually rich in written evidence for an early medieval origin. It would be easy to pass this church when motoring along the A40, but it is well-worth the stop.

The south side of the church and churchyard.
Anlach's stone is approximately near where the figure is standing

LLANWRTHWL – St. Gwrthwl
(SN 976 637)

Indications from the dedication, location and shape of churchyard are that the site is early.

Nothing is known of the saint to whom the church is dedicated. It has been suggested by Theophilus Jones that he was Morddal Gwr Gweilgi, mentioned in the Welsh Triads as teaching the population to build in stone during classical times, but Baring-Gould and Fisher disagree with this spelling of his name. They suggest that Gwrthwl may have been Gwrthmwl Wledig, a chief elder of Penrhyn Rhionedd in north Wales, who supposedly acknowledged King Arthur as 'supreme king'. The only other place name that matches Llanwrthwl is Maes Llanwrthwl, the name of an old mansion, at Caio in Carmarthenshire, and indications are that Gwrthwl was slain in neighbouring Ceredigion.[1]

The church was rebuilt in 1875, and, other than the attractive 11th- to 12th-century font, no earlier features remain.[2] In the early 1800s Theophilus Jones described the previous church as 'a dark low fabric, indifferently seated, and not ceiled.' He also mentioned a large stone 'about two yards in height' in the churchyard which is still there and stands to the right of the south porch. It is a roughly-hewn upright stone about 5½ feet high and was considered to weigh 'upwards of six tons.'[3] It looks unworked and is reminiscent of prehistoric standing

The possible prehistoric standing stone in the churchyard

stones. Haslam considers that the site may be pre-Christian due to its presence within the raised churchyard.[4] It is unusual to find a stone of this type in a church enclosure and is suggestive of a pagan totem — but we cannot discover if this is its original site or whether it has been brought in from elsewhere. However the stone seems to have been part of a wider prehistoric landscape. Jones observes that in the early 1800s

> On the road from Llandovery and Llangamarch to Rhayader, are seen stones placed irregularly in the ground, which have given a common, partly in this parish and partly in Llanafan, the name of Rhôs saith maen, or Seven-stone common; whether they are sepulchral, military or druidical remains, is not known, but from the name of Rhos y beddau, the common of the graves, not far from hence, nearer to the river Wye, it should seem they commemorate a battle, most likely that of Llechryd and the slaughter in the flight of Riryd and Cadwgan.[5]

The church is about 150 yards from the River Wye and is in a flat, village centre location. The churchyard was originally circular, and is raised by up to 4 to 5 feet above the external road level along the northern and eastern sides. It is now a rectangular shape, of small to medium size but still with curving boundaries on the northern and eastern sides. There is a gentle slope on the southern side of the churchyard and this boundary is delineated by iron railings. On the northern side the churchyard is bounded by a stone wall with no appreciable difference in levels with the adjoining field. These areas have been extended. Clwyd-Powys Archaeological Trust note the presence of a low scarp bank about a foot high running round the interior of the western and southern sides of the churchyard which is probably an earlier boundary, and two mature yews on what they presume is on an old boundary to the west of the church.[6]

LLANWRTYD – St. David
(SN 864 478)

The church contains an early Christian carved stone found a few miles away and there are rumours of more.

The church of St. David lies in a striking hilly location which feels quite wild and remote, 1½ miles west of its community of Llanwrtyd Wells. The site nestles at the foot of a hill which rises to the north-west and overlooks a wooded, hedge-lined valley to the south-east. There are very few buildings near the church which is generally of 14th- to 16th-century date,[1] and is an interesting squat, solid structure having a rood stair remaining in the thickness of the south wall. Some of the structure may be earlier as one blocked window has distinctly Norman characteristics, as have two on the south side along with a probable blocked doorway. There is also a blocked door on the west — its short height inidcating how much the ground level has risen.

The dedication to St. David may be an early dedication and is quite near to the Glascwm group of four hill-country St. David churches. The shape of the churchyard and location make an early dedication likely.[2] The quiet location near a river, in this case the River Ithon, also fits the pattern of David's dedications.

The churchyard boundary is partly curvilinear, particularly on the western and south-western sides. To the north of the church a scarp bank of about 3½ feet marks the earlier boundary and swings round to the south — it encompasses what would have been a very small enclosure. Because of the steep slope of the land, the churchyard is partly terraced.[3] The surrounding land is about 2 to 4 feet lower than the churchyard and the church itself appears to be set on a noticeable mound, most obvious on its eastern side.

The church now houses an early pillar stone to the left of the main door with a ring-cross design dated to between the 7th and 9th centuries. It was discovered at Llawdre Farm,[4] about 2 miles to the south, but demonstrates early Christian activity in the area. The details upon it are quite different to the decorated stones examined at Llanafar Fawr and Llangammarch Wells, which are much more sophisticated in design with quite advanced carving techniques. Here the pillar stone is carved with a cross-like pattern within a circle, which is not easy to see due to weathering and the simple techniques of carving used. The stone measures about 3 feet at its greatest height, and just under 1 foot wide at its broadest.

An interesting story attaches to the finding of this stone, which is not dissimilar to the finding of many of these early inscribed stones. In 1897 Breconshire County Council needed stone for highway repairs and other uses, and Daniel Jones was charged with obtaining stone from a derelict cottage called Ystafell-fach on a farm called Llawdre. On 27 March the stone was taken to the main road for collection. Whilst in conversation with Jones, Ernest Davies, the local postman, noticed that one stone had 'strange incisions upon it' and he asked Jones to 'place it on the side of the road for preservation,' which Jones did — near the end of the Berthddu Bridge. There it remained largely ignored until a solicitor from London saw it and wrote to Llanwrtyd Parish Council in 1902, telling them of the stone's importance, but no further action was taken until an historian, Granville Lewis, called on the vicar of Llanwrtyd, who then accompanied him to the site of the original find with Daniel Jones as their guide. They asked some

The pillar stone housed in the church

questions of the local people and found that there was a tradition that a town existed in Roman times, and that at Llawdr Farm 'large stones weighing from three to five tons have been unearthed' from an area covering 3 to 4 acres. Granville Lewis supposed that they 'formed the foundation of what was probably an ancient ecclesiastical edifice,' and added that it is strange to think how many such remains might have been used 'in the laying of the London and North-Western Railway which [in 1903] runs hard by.' He also remarks that on Llawdre Farm there is a field known as Cae'r-groes — 'field of the cross' and observes there are several fields in the neighbourhood which contain the word Croes/Groes including Bon-y-Groes, 'the base of the cross', near the parish church. Another of Granville Lewis' informants, a Mr. Jones of Ty'nypant Farm, Llanwrytd, showed him an incised cross-stone at his house 'rather similar to the one found at Ystafell-fach' and told him that two or three similar stones could be found in the vicinity.[5] All of which suggests the presence of an early Christian site in the locality of Llanwrytd church, which may support an early dedication of St. David.

LLANYNIS – St. David
(SN 998 508)

The location, former dedication to St. Llyr and the original shape of the churchyard point to an early medieval origin but there is no documentary evidence to support this.[1]

The church of St. David lies about 2 miles west of Builth Wells. Approach to the church should be made from the south taking the lane out of Builth on its south-west side and travelling to SO 002 501 and taking a footpath for about ½ mile down to the church and the River Ithon (Irfon). Do not use the footpath from the main road west of Cilmery, as this necessitates wading through the river — there is no bridge!

In the early 1800s Theophilus Jones suggests the name may have derived from Lan yn yr Ynis, or Islechurch, and he reported that the church had no dedication. However Bailey states that it was dedicated to St. Llyr,[2] but this barely helps for was it to Llyr the Virgin, as at Llanyre, or one of the several male St. Llyrs such as St. Llyr Merini who, according to the Iolo Manuscripts was a member of Cunedda's family, while others suggest he was Brychan's son-in-law, married to Gwen or even the Earl of Hereford![3] Perhaps to save the confusion the church is now dedicated to St. David.

The present churchyard is relatively quite large and sub-rectangular in shape. However it is thought that the original enclosure was much smaller and curvi-linear, and the church would have been more centrally placed; as it is, it stands close to the eastern end of the churchyard. On the north side there is drop of about 13 feet to the river. On the southern side and east of the main gate the boundary hedge is on a bank which is curved and this can be traced around the eastern perimeter to the north-east corner where the bank is more than 1½ feet high. To the west of the church there is also a slight scarp about 1 foot high that fades out to the north and south, and this, together with the fact that the eastern area of the churchyard appears somewhat raised, and that there is a bank beneath the modern boundaries to the south and east, delineates a curvilinear enclosure considered to be about 148 to 165 feet across.[4]

Set close to the River Ithon, the nave is constructed from small coursed rubble and the chancel from larger coursed stones. It is said to have been rebuilt in 1887[5] although subtle differences in areas of the outer north wall make us question whether this was a complete rebuild or a refurbishment leaving some medieval sections of masonry. Clywd-Powys Archaeological Trust state that the whitewashed exterior hinders the assessment of the building phasing but the 'uneven appearance of the chancel walls might suggest that they could be original medieval and that the nave has been rebuilt ...'.[6]

There is a modern concrete replica of a pre-Norman carved stone to the right of the porch. The original stood near to a house named Porth y crwys, or Portal of the cross, which belonged to a squire of Elizabeth I. By 1809 this had been demolished, the cross being moved and built into the wall of a cottage called Neuadd Siarmam, where it was present in 1900. The stone was retrieved, a replica made and the original taken to the British Museum. It is 57 inches tall and 8 to 12 inches wide and was described in 1900 as 'being one of the most elegant in Wales'.[7]

Local tradition states that the Welsh leader, Llewelyn, attended the church for mass in 1282 before he was killed at nearby Cilmery.[8]

The concrete replica of a pre-Norman carved stone that used to stand in the vicinity

LLYSWEN – St. Gwendoline
(SO 133 380) & LLANGOED (SO 113 394)

Some charter evidence suggests an early church at one of these sites, that at Llyswen having a churchyard that is suggestive of an early foundation.

Details of a grant of *c.*560 in Theophilus Jones' *A History of the County of Brecknock* states that in the park of Llangoed Castle there was once a church of *Lann Coit* and that the latter was given by King Iddon, son of Inyr 'with 3 *uncias* of land, and with all its liberty in woods and in waters, in fields and pastures.'[1] Davies substitutes hawking rights for the latter phrase with a suggested date of *c.*595, the beneficiary being Bishop Arwystyl. The charter has no surviving boundaries mentioned and Davies makes a tentative identification with Llangoed, spelled as *Lanncoit* in the charter (SO 113 394), about 1½ miles from Llyswen village church.[2] Llangoed was also granted to the see of Llandaff in the first quarter of the 11th century and again in 1119.[3] This is now Upper Llangoed which, on modern Ordnance Survey maps, is shown as a building but not a church. Interestingly, a short distance to the north of Upper Llangoed is a tiny cluster of buildings called Llanfawr which could be translated as the 'great/large church', but again there is no sign of a church today.

The church of St. Gwendoline at Llyswen lies 3 miles north-west of Talgarth near the centre of a small riverside village and about 300 feet from the River Wye.

The curving churchyard boundary at Llyswen

The churchyard shape is very suggestive of an early Christian site for it is almost circular and noticeably raised, especially in the south and south-eastern sides. The ground is fairly level within the churchyard and the boundaries appear to be original. We wonder whether this is an alternative site for the church mentioned in the 6th-century charter. In 1840 it was noted 'that in the garden of an ornamental cottage near the church is a tumulus, opposite to the remarkable horse-shoe bend in the Wye river.' A tumulus is shown on the Ordnance Survey map at SO 139 375, but the one described in 1840 appears to be no longer visible. A small hillfort (SO 127 379) lies west of the church on a steep hillside, not far distant from which Bailey notes 'may be seen the ruins of a Roman Camp with pavement, bath, &c.'[4] The presence of these pre-Christian monuments and activity may be one reason why Llyswen church was founded — to Christianise an area with a pagan presence.

The church at Llyswen was largely rebuilt in 1863[5] and the original was described as a small and narrow structure.[6] The present church has an attractive tower and general appearance, a circular Norman font, but no early medieval remains.

The church is dedicated to Gwendoline, whose main dedication at Talgarth is only three miles away, both churches being in the heartlands of her father's, Brychan, territory. However Theophilus Jones states that the dedication in the early 1800s was uncertain.[7] As the festival day of the church was held on 13 November, a day before that of Meilig at Llowes, it is considered that the church may have been dedicated to him 'under one or other of his three names, probably Meilig or Tyfaeolog.'[8]

LLYWEL – St. David
(SN 869 300)

The site was probably founded by a 6th-century saint and once held two early Christian stones (now just one).

Llywel is about 14 miles west of Brecon on the main Llandovery road. The site is in the valley bottom and quite close to the A40.

The dedication of Llywel church is a moot point, as the titular saint is not the saint whose name the church and settlement bear. St. Llywel's name has changed throughout time and is given as Iouguil, Iouhil or Iuhil in the *Book of Llandaff*. He is named as a disciple firstly of St. Dyfrig, then of St. Teilo. It is considered that the I was mistakenly swapped for an L, and that Louguil was the original patron of Llywel, and that a fellow disciple Gurmaet set up Llandeilo'r Fan in the next parish. By the end of the 19th century the church at Llywel had three patrons: David, Teilo and Llywel.[1] Llanhowell, south of the town of Usk, may also be dedicated to Llywel.

Iouguil (Llywel) and Fidelis were two disciples sent by St. Teilo to Aircol Lawhir, king of Dyfed, to restore peace as his household had dissolved into violent and drunken rowdiness over which the king had lost control. Iouguil and Fidelis calmed the situation and restored order, for which St. Teilo was given a grant of land near Tenby in a charter dated to *c*.500. However, Davies notes there is nothing in the record to suggest it derives from a 'contemporary or near-contemporary record of any early sixth-century transaction.'[2] As a little known saint, Iouguil seems to have been displaced by the famous names of Teilo, and latterly by St. David.

The church has two early stones associated with it, although neither originated on the site. The first, and most notable, is the Llywel Stone found in a cairn at Pentre Poeth Farm near Trecastle, two miles to the east, in *c*.1878[3] and thus is also called the Trecastell Stone. However it is said to have once been in the graveyard of the former Capel Ilud at Cwm Crai in the neighbouring parish. A plaster cast can be seen at Brecon Museum; the original is now in the British Museum. It is about 6 feet tall, tapers downward and has carvings that could come from three periods. On one side is a burial inscription of *c*.500 which reads (M)ACCUTRENI + SALICIDUNI (the name of a person) — the cross between the two words was possibly added in the 7th century; the name is repeated in Ogam script. The inscription is of 5th to 6th century date. On the other side are pictographs 'or linear symbols in four panels, including a saltire, two figures, and a bishop with a staff', decoration that most resembles pre-Christian art in Brittany. Brecon Museum give a broader date range for these pictographs of between the 7th and 10th centuries, and add that the stone was turned upside down and the pictographs were then incised on the back. They are thought to have some biblical significance, although their precise meaning is unclear. Redknap however states the pictographs have been interpreted 'as Christian doctrines and scenes, with a figure holding a crozier or shepherd's crook at the bottom.'[4]

The second stone, a pillar stone, is still within the church and was found in a hedge-bank at Traeanglas at Aberhydfer, less than 2 miles south-west of Llywel, in 1954 and moved into the church for safe keeping; it has a Latin inscription reading 'Taricoro' scored across by Ogam. It is about 5 feet 7 inches tall and is dated to the 5th century.[5]

The plaster cast of the Llywel stone held in Brecon Museum showing the pictographs

As neither stone was found at Llywel church, they only demonstrate early Christian activity in the area but indicate Roman and Irish influence in this fertile valley. However within the church is a possible pre-Norman font, and this is suggestive of an early date for the site.[6]

The churchyard is medium-sized and the shape is irregular, with curving to the south and south-western boundaries and straighter boundaries to the north and east. It is possible that the churchyard may have been encroached upon, straightening these boundaries, or that it has been expanded to the north, or even that an earlier enclosure was 'truncated on the east'. The enclosure is walled with internal embanking along the southern boundary. There is a height difference of up to 6 feet and more in places on the southern and eastern boundaries between the church enclosure and the road surface below. There is also a gentle scarp on the northern side of the churchyard running from east to west, the origin of which is uncertain.[7]

There is a sizeable stream close to the eastern boundary and a mature yew to the north of the church and two mature specimens to the south. One of these southern yews is male and has a measured girth of 20 feet, giving an estimated age of 1,200 years[8] — one wonders if this tree, and its counterparts, were the deliberate plantings of an early British saint.

MERTHYR CYNOG –
St. Cynog (SN 985 374)

Purported burial site of St. Cynog, and evidence for an early foundation of a mother or *clas* church.

The church of St. Cynog is about 6 to 7 miles north-west of Brecon in a remote, hilly position at over 1,000 feet above sea level.

The site is dedicated to Cynog, reputedly the eldest and illegitimate son of Brychan. Early manuscripts relate that Brychan was handed over by his father, Anlach, to the king of Powys as a hostage, but that, in time, Brychan 'violated' Banadlinet, the king's daughter who bore him Cynog. In one document it states that Cynog was baptised by St. Gastayn of Llangasty Tal-y-llyn,[1] fairly close to Talgarth where Brychan was said to have had a palace. St. Gastayn later became Cynog's preceptor. After the baptism Brychan gave the infant a torque taken from his own arm. This torque was allegedly still revered in Breconshire centuries later — in the late 12th century Giraldus Cambrensis describes it thus:

> From its weight, texture and colour one would think that it was gold. It is made in four sections, as you can see from the joins, wrought together artificially by a series of weldings and divided in the middle by a dog's head, which stands erect with its teeth bared. The local inhabitants consider this to be a most potent relic, and no one would dare to break a promise which he had made when it was held in front of him.[2]

240

Giraldus also records how there was a 'mark of a mighty blow, as if someone had hit it with an iron hammer' and recounts how a man had tried to break the torque for its gold and was rendered blind for the rest of his life. He also adds that in his own day Rhys ap Gruffyd was disgraced and imprisoned with his own sons 'and this is well worth bearing in mind, he had stolen the torque of Saint Cynog of Brecknockshire and had hidden it in Dinevor. For this alone he deserved to be captured and locked up, as an example of the judgement of God.'[3] The torque was subsequently lost.

In about 1702 the legend of St. Cynog was written down by the Breconshire herald, Hugh Thomas who had gained the information from 'the poor ignorant Country People' of Merthyr Cynog. From this it appears that Cynog became a hermit in his youth, dressed in a very poor habit and wore a ring or wreath of twisted iron upon his head. He was insulted and abused by the local inhabitants because of his appearance. Outlaws, called Ormests, who were said to 'eaven eate up mens flesh', were ravaging the country, and a widow with several small children begged help from the poor, quiet Cynog, who resolved to remain outside her door overnight in prayer to protect her, as many of her neighbours had been killed by the bandits the previous night. The Ormests arrived at midnight and duly surrounded the cottage with a view to killing him. Cynog (instructed by a voice from heaven), threw his torque at the leader with such force that it killed him outright and his 'Bowells ... burst in sunder and fell to the ground which so terified the rest of the Crew that they presently Flead' and were never heard of in the area again. This gained Cynog respect from some members of the community, but angered others. In passing a smith's forge, around which were loitering a 'parcell of Idle fellows', Cynog was derided and the smith called him into the workshop to make sport. Seizing the torque, the smith said it had never killed an Ormest, and banged it on the anvil. A splinter broke off, pierced his brain and killed him. Attitudes quickly changed.[4]

There is a tradition that Cynog worked in Ireland for a time assisting St. Patrick. It is also likely that he lived in Cornwall for a time as the county has a few dedications to Cynog. According to a 15th-century poem, *Cywydd Cynog Sant*, in the Iolo Manuscripts, on returning to Britain from Ireland, he encountered a cannibalistic giant living in a cave in Cardiganshire. To save another victim, Cynog allowed the giant to cut a large piece of flesh off his leg, over which grew a protective layer of wool. The giant relished the meat and came back for some more, but Cynog slew him with his trusty torc.[5] The picture emerges of the saint as a retiring and humble man who could be raised to action when needed.

The manner of his death is confused. The *c*.1702 account records that Cynog joined 'a society of Sertaine Religious men that led a hermiticall life under the government of a superior in little cells upon the hill call'd the Vann about four miles from Brecknock and about 2 miles from Carevong the place of his birth which is now destroyed and called the Gare where he built him a hermitage under a steepe Rock neare the top of the Mountain.' However the other monks were frustrated and wearied by the constant task of having to bring water from the river up the steep slope of the hill to their hermitage. Cynog undertook this labour cheerfully and 'Reprehended them for their Murmerings and Slouth against a Labour which in it selfe was holy and worked an exceeding reward ... This raised their whole spleen against himselfe.' Further spleen was raised when the monks had found that God had provided water for Cynog on the rock over his cell which was barred from all others, 'this so enveterated their Rage thinking themselves mock'd by him that they Resolved to murther him.' Two of the monks climbed up to his rock on Sunday and, seeing him in prayer with a 'Christiall spring at his feet, they furiously ran at him and cut off his head with a sword which dropt into the Well where the Water immediately gave way to his head and dried up ...'. Cynog then proceeded to pick up his head and carried it down the hill, 'from thence he walked on to a rising ground about a field's bread[t]h beyond the Church and layed it downe under a Bush of Brambles.' Over this a church was raised.[6]

Another Welsh tradition records that Cynog was murdered by pagan Saxons on the mountain called Y Fan Oleu or the Van, but it is unlikely that the Anglo-Saxons had any part in his death as they were only making headway in the east of Britain in the late 5th or early 6th century. It is, however, possible that Cynog was killed during the expulsion of the Irish Brychan family from Breconshire. As Baring-Gould and Fisher note, if he did in fact die in Breconshire, it may be that 'he headed his clan pouring curses on the enemy, which failed in their effect, and he was slaughtered, and the rest of his kinsmen either fell with him or fled to Cornwall or Ireland.'[7]

Cynog has dedications at Defynnog, Llangynog, Merthyr Cynog, Ystradgynlais, Penderin and Battle in Breconshire, Boughrood in Radnorshire, and Llangynog in Montgomeryshire. Cynog was probably the patron saint of the *Lann Cinauc* mentioned in the Llandaff Charters which has been identified with Llangunnock (SO 510 233) but at which there is no church now, and the saint of *Lann Guern Cinuc* or *Henlenic Cinauc* which is identified with another Llangunnock, on the Pill in Monmouthshire. The latter was said to be in ruins in the 1900s and close to a farmhouse called Llys Brychan — 'the hall or palace of Brychan'. However, it is the church at Mertyhr Cynog that is traditionally believed to be the resting place of the saint, as indicated in the name. A 'merthyr', or *martyrium*, does not necessarily denote a place of martyrdom but where the person so killed was buried. There were formerly two churches dedicated to Cynog in the parish of Merthyr Cynog and, in *c.*1702, Hugh Thomas observed that the oldest one was pulled down in the reign of Charles I. He noted 'simple country people ... showed me the ruins of the church then remaining, with the yew trees then growing about it, and the church dore then to be seene.'[8] It is not clear where this church stood.

The earliest sections of the present church probably date to the 12th and 13th centuries in the case of the nave; the chancel is probably 14th century, and there is an attractive screen of that date.[9] The tower has a Norman appearance. Theophilus Jones observed that, although the church did not appear earlier than the Norman period, some material, including crosses, may have been re-used from an earlier building. He records a cross of about 5 feet in length and 1 foot in breadth lying flat 'in the middle of the eastern pine end wall' and of another cross in the church porch of the same height. Jones provides a disturbing description of the state of the church in the early 1800s: 'This church, like most of the other country churches in Breconshire, and we fear in Wales, resembles a large barn, into which something like pens for sheep have been thrown in disorderly regularity to rot ... the floor is partly of earth and partly flagged, the seats and benches are decayed and broken, the pulpit is old and crazy, what is called the communion table nearly rotten, and the windows are frequently broken.'[10] Bailey notes that the church stayed in this miserable state until 1862 after which, thankfully, it was restored.[11]

Clwyd-Powys Archaeological Trust observe that the 'churchyard is large and sub-circular, [and] a fine example of a medieval "llan"'. It is likely that Merthyr Cynog was the *clas* or mother church in the early medieval period. The churchyard is raised to all sides except the north which can be fully appreciated when walking around the boundary on the lane outside — to the east there is over 6 feet in height difference, whereas to the south-west the churchyard is about 16 feet higher than the surrounding land. Internal banking on the inside of the boundary also rises to about 2 feet for most of the perimeter and could be an early feature. In 1992 a section was dug through the churchyard wall which 'revealed underlying features and layers of charcoal and burnt bone', unfortunately no dating evidence was given. There is a suggestion of a scarp bank within the churchyard on the south-west and western sides which is closer to the churchyard wall than to the church.[12] Although its purpose and age is not known, it may be an early feature. The site has many mature trees along the boundary with mature yew trees to the south.

Merthyr Cynog is one of the four royal burial sites mentioned in an early document called the *De Situ Brecheniauc* (see also Llanspyddid, p.227) The other named places are Llandspyddid and Llandefaelog Fach (also in Breconshire) and probably Lundy Island. Charles Thomas observes that this note of royal burials 'points to later sixth-century cemeteries' at Merthyr Cynog and the other two Breconshire churches. However he suggests that the merthyr element in this place-name may not be 6th century (and therefore particularly early) but that the site with its 'large curvilinear enclosure suggests a monastic settlement, one where Cynog's corporeal remains would be enshrined.'[13]

PARTRISHOW – St. Issui
(SO 278 224)

The church contains an Eglwys y Bedd, a structure which purportedly houses a saint's grave, nearby is a holy well, there is a dedication to a little known saint and references in early documents which, together with its isolated position, all indicate an early site.

The church of St. Issui is succinctly described by Haslam as 'little and lonely, in a remote site with far views'.[1] It lies about 6 miles north of Abergavenny in a secluded wooded valley on a minor road within the lower reaches of the Black Mountains.

The statuette of St. Issui contained within the church

St. Issui (also spelt Isho or Ishow) was an early saint, but little is known of his life. His parentage is unknown, although there is some slight evidence that his name corresponds to a son of Brychan.[2] The only record of his life is from local tradition. In the early 1800s Theophilus Jones wrote the following vivid account: 'he was a holy man, who led a religious life in this retired spot, and his little oratory upon the bank of a small rivulet called Nant Mair or Mary's brook (a name probably given it by himself in honour of the Blessed Virgin), which runs at the bottom of the hill on which the church is built; that having long lived in high estimation among the natives, whom he instructed in the principles of Christianity, he was at length murdered by an ungrateful traveller, who had been hospitably received and entertained by him in his humble cell. A small cavity scooped out in the side of a bank and walled with stone, but open in front, is still pointed out as the chapel, or as others say, the well of Saint Ishaw; if either, it was the latter, as the space is by no means calculated for the offices of a chapel, and besides, in the back, close to the ground, is an aperture evidently intended for the admission of water; in the walls are several small niches formed apparently for the reception of oblations from pious votaries.'[3]

The earliest documentary evidence for the church is in the *Book of Llandaff* in the 12th century, where it is referred to as *Merthir/Merthur Issiu* when it was consecrated by Bishop Herwald (1056–1103), however this church probably replaced an earlier one. The spelling of Partrishow varies from Pertrissw, Partrisw and Llanysho throughout various medieval documents. It is considered that the first part of the name in the first two could represent the word merthyr, with the later change of the M to a P, although this would be unusual in Welsh,[4] signifying either the place of death or the burial place of a murdered saint.

The church is an outstanding structure with a wonderful restored rood loft and screen which Theophilus Jones described in 1805 as 'an excellent specimen of carved work in Irish oak' and suggests it may have been a gift from the abbots of Llanthony.[5] The intricate carved latticework panels date to about 1500. There are also notable wall-paintings, including a mid-16th-century doom figure of a large skeleton with a shovel hanging from its arm, an early parish chest, and a font the inscription on which is dated to *c.*1055, pre-dating the present church structure. Unusually there are two altar slabs in addition to the one already in use. Bailey describes them as 'plain, wholly of stone, and some marks of the original crosses may be discerned on the slabs.'[6]

At the west end of the church is the Eglwys y Bedd, the only example that we have seen at the sites in this book, except for Pennant Melangell. The only communication between it and the nave is a square grille about three feet from the floor, and it has a separate entrance in the south wall. An altar is placed over the saint's grave to the right and there is a statue of St. Issui alongside it. The structure is 13th century, but the nave is basically Norman and does not have any windows to the north whilst there are Tudor windows to the south.[7]

The churchyard was extended in the 19th century and was once a very small enclosure with a curvilinear western boundary. An original western boundary is visible as a scarp-bank and an early north-western boundary is marked as an internal scarp. To the north of the church is a derelict stone wall which marks another earlier perimeter.[8]

In a leafy, secret hollow before the lane climbs steeply to the church is Ffynon Isho or St. Isho's Well, mentioned above. A small tunnel has been dug near to the stream and built around on three sides with drystone walling, arched over and open to the front. Within this are several niches presumably for religious items or offerings, and toward the back is a stone basin into which water flows. The tunnel appears to go partly under the present road surface. A stone near the lane has a Maltese-style cross carved on it, perhaps by an early pilgrim. Francis

The holy well (right) and incised cross on a stone by the lane

Jones quotes Richard Fenton's diary entry of his visit in 1804 when he: 'saw the Sainted Well of (Isho), being a very scanty oozing of water, to which, however, was formerly attributed great Virtue, as within the build[i]ng that encloses it are little Niches to hold the Vessels drank out of and the offerings they left behind.' Jones adds that by 1903 the well appears to 'have lost its ancient esteem.'[9]

The well and the church site have a very special feeling, an atmosphere of a remote and important early place that certainly merits more than one visit.

ST. ELUNED'S/EILWEDD'S CHAPEL, SLWCH TUMP, BRECON (SO 057 285)

The site of an early medieval chapel and a holy well dedicated to a female martyred saint on the hills above Brecon.

Slwch (pronounced Sloop) Tump is just east of Brecon. The chapel is now ruined with no standing remains visible. The site is reached by a steep holloway through a tunnel of trees from the outskirts of the town, the traditional pilgrimage route for those visiting the saint's chapel. Her name is spelt in a variety of ways, and we have opted for that of Eluned which is the popular spelling of her name locally.

St. Eluned was Brychan's 23rd daughter,[1] and a legend applies to her that has also been adopted for several other virtuous female saints. This legend is found amongst the Harley Manuscripts and was written up in the late 17th century. We are told that she had decided to follow a religious life at an early age, but was being pressed by her family and a prince to marry. She ran away and disguised herself, and attempted to live in several villages in Breconshire. She first visited Llanddew, but was so ill-treated that she moved on to Llanfilo, but because of her poverty and ragged clothing, she was treated as a thief. Leaving there, she headed toward Brecon and tried living at Llechfaen, a mile from Brecon, but nobody would help her, and she ended up sleeping in the village street where the high road 'ever since is called of her name in Welsh, Heol S. Alud.' She gave up trying to live amongst humans and retired to Slwch Tump, which was then wooded, to live in solitude. She asked permission of the lord of the manor to remain there and he also granted her other charity as well. She begged her bread of the occupants of the Castle of the Slwch who treated her hospitably, and she was able to construct a cell or oratory at the tump.[2]

Having settled there she prophesied that God would chastise the inhabitants of Llanddew for the injuries done to her there; that Lanfilo would be plagued by thieves 'as they are to this day above all others', and that the village of Llechfaen would be consumed by envy 'as indeed they are almost continually in contention and law with one another.'[3]

Unfortunately her abandoned suitor discovered her location, and surprised her one day. Frightened, she attempted to run downhill to the lord of the manor's house, which is thought to have been on the site of the present Slwch Farm, but he followed on horseback and decapitated her. Her head rolled downhill, and where it landed a 'clear spring of water issued out of the rock where it rested,' which became St. Eluned's holy well. She was buried at her own cell. Her oratory was converted into a chapel, which by Norman times was of some importance. The chapel continued in use until the Reformation and Dissolution of the Monasteries, when it fell into disuse and was converted into a barn. In the late 17th century 'the top was quite fallen to the ground, and the walls would shortly follow it.' By the time Theophilus Jones wrote at the turn of the 19th century the chapel was 'completely ruinated and can only be traced by tradition to a spot where a heap of stones and an aged yew tree, with a well at its root, mark its site.' At the turn of the 20th century Baring-Gould and Fisher noted that the well was 'almost choked by mud and weeds' but that a 'fine old yew tree' spread its branches over it. By 1906 the yew had disappeared and only the well or spring marked the site.[4] Today the remnants of the fallen building debris are grass-covered, but the raised areas left by the building are still just visible. A structural feature at ground level in a hollow below the site may cause short-lived excitement, but, alas, it is the remains of a disused agricultural borehole! However about 100 yards down the field by the nearest hedgerow to the chapel site, is an ancient tree-stump next to a shallow damp hollow which flows with water in wet seasons. Thanks to work done by the Wellsprings Fellowship the tree-stump has been identified as a dead yew, which would correlate with Jones' description.

It is recorded that the chapel lay at the centre of a large, nearly circular enclosure about 295 feet in diameter which was still visible in the late 19th century.

The site of the holy well by the tree stump on Slwch Tump

The Sites and Monuments Record notes that 'Traces of [the] structure [were] visible in [the] early 19th century but worked ashlar in Slwch Farm, noted in 1949, may have come from the chapel.' There are four rectangular terraced platforms and the easternmost of these is about 79 feet long and is thought to be the site of the chapel — the three other platforms are smaller and it is suggested that they may be 'outbuildings or domestic buildings associated with the chapel and shrine.'[5] These platforms take some finding.

Giraldus Cambrensis visited the chapel in the late 12th century on St. Eluned's festival, the first day of August where her 'feast-day is celebrated with great solemnity in this same place. On that day great crowds of ordinary folk assemble there from far and wide.' Giraldus records how

> You can see young men and maidens, some in the church itself, some in the churchyard and others in the dance which threads its way round the graves. They sing traditional songs, all of a sudden they collapse on the ground, and then those who, until now, have followed their leader peacefully as if in a trance, leap in the air as if seized by frenzy. In full view of the crowds they mime with their hands and feet whatever work they have done contrary to the commandments on sabbath days.'

Some mimicked their work of ploughing or goading oxen with a stick 'all as they go singing country airs, to lighten the tedium of their labour', another man imitates the cobbler at work at his bench, another miming a tanner, while a girl, distaff in hand, mimics the weaving of cloth. 'When all is over, they enter the church. They are led up to the altar and there, as they make their oblation, you will be surprised to see them awaken from their trance and recover their normal composure.'[6] It must have been a sight indeed.

TALGARTH – St. Gwendoline
(SO 157 338)

The dedication to St. Gwen and certain aspects of the site suggest an early origin.

The church of St. Gwendoline is set in a densely populated part of Talgarth, uphill from the centre and at the highest point in the town. It thus has an impressive, elevated position although is somewhat hemmed-in by buildings. The dedication to Gwendoline should be more correctly expressed as Gwen, who, according to all available records, was a daughter of Brychan who supposedly had a court at Talgarth.[1] We would question whether this was actually in the town, or 3½ miles uphill at the striking and more recently re-fortified Castell Dinas, 1,476 feet above sea level and a very sound defensive position. Indeed in c.1539 Leland states that the 'people about Dinas did burne Dinas Castel that Oene Glindour shuld not kepe it for his forteres',[2] which shows its immense defensive potential.

Gwen is said to have been Brychan's eleventh daughter.[3] She is said to have shared the dedication with another of Brychan's daughters, Clodfaith, and in the Iolo Manuscripts it states Gwen was killed by pagan Anglo-Saxons at Talgarth.[4] However, as in the case of her elder brother St. Cynog, she may have been killed during fighting which occurred when the Irish Brychan family were expelled from the area. She was, according to tradition, buried at Talgarth church.[5]

The church is a surprisingly large and attractive sandstone structure, mainly of 14th-century date with some re-used 13th-century windows, and a 15th-century tower. It appears that the church was of cruciform shape in the 13th century, and that the vestry may be the surviving north transept of the earlier church. Squints to the chancel arch substantiate this theory. It is possible that Talgarth was a 'clas' or mother church as a cruciform plan is often associated with this grade of church.[6]

The churchyard is quite large, of an irregular rectangular shape and is relatively flat. The ground slopes away on the south and eastern sides, thus the church is built on a spur of land. The churchyard is partly raised above the surrounding land by up to 3 to 4 feet, but the significance of the banking underneath some yews on the southern side has not yet been ascertained.[7]

It appears that Talgarth once stood in a small kingdom which was called *Garth Matrun* in the 5th century — a name which Thomas suggests 'harks back to its pre-Christian, late-fourth-century roots.' The garth in question is Mynydd Troed, a western spur of the Black Mountain range, below which is Talgarth 'place at the brow of the garth'. In Thomas's words 'This district was spread out below the Garth of the Matrona, "The Great Mother", a goddess probably personified by the lake of Llan-gors, a fish-rich and life-supporting water whose other title (Llyn Syfaddan) appears to conceal an alternative "divine" name.'[8]

TRALLONG – St. David
(SN 966 295)

A good example of a raised church site with an early inscribed stone.

St. David's church lies 5 miles west of Brecon high above the Usk Valley in an exceptionally lovely location. The church was partly rebuilt in 1861, although a priest's doorway and a few other features survive along, with an attractive 13th-century font.[1]

Clwyd-Powys Archaeological Trust state that the churchyard is 'strongly curvilinear on the north but rectilinear on the remaining sides. Its appearance is indicative of an early circular 'llan', but there are no relict earthworks to confirm this hypothesis.'[2] The churchyard is also certainly raised. There is a definite slope down to the church from the north side and the building appears to sit on a ghost of a platform on a break in the slope, seen best from the southern side. The slope continues down to the southern boundary and then there is a steep descent of about 25-30 feet to the pasture below. There is also a significant drop on the western side to the adjoining land, and a drop of between 7 to 9 feet to the adjoining lane on the north where the boundary is embanked. The tips of gravestones can be seen in places and shows how much the level of the ground within the churchyard has built up within the last few centuries.

There is an early inscribed stone to the back of the nave inside the church. Haslam records the stone as being 5 feet 3 inches tall and that the broad end was originally bedded about 16 inches into the ground.[3] However in the early 20th century Bailey recorded the measurements as being out 6 feet long, 1½ feet wide at the upper point and tapering to a point at the bottom and being uniformly 6 inches thick — which suggests the stone has shrunk or he gave an approximation! He records that it was discovered when the church was rebuilt in about 1856 'at the side of one of the windows of the old church' and that the inscription had been facing inwards 'and consequently its existence was unknown until thus suddenly brought to light.' It has a Latin ring-cross at the top and both Latin and Ogam script, the Latin being carved to the front surface running vertically upwards and reading 'CVNOCENNI FILIVS CVNOCENI HIC JACIT'. Bailey states that the identical names of the father and son do not appear in the Welsh records but repeats a theory that it was connected with St. Cynog who reputedly died at Merthyr Cynog a few miles away.[4] The Ogam script carved to the sides gives a similar meaning. The inscriptions have been dated to the 5th or early 6th century by Dr. Nash-Williams, and Haslam suggests that the Latin ring-cross was 'cut on the previously buried [and wider] end' in the 7th to 9th centuries.[5]

There is, of course, no proof that the stone originated on the site, although the fact that it was built into the old church fabric, probably in the later medieval period, suggests that it probably did. It is a gem of a find, and continues a pattern of discovery of carved stones, particularly bilingual ones with Ogam, or Irish influenced scripts, found in association with the fertile Breconshire valleys of the Wye and the Usk.

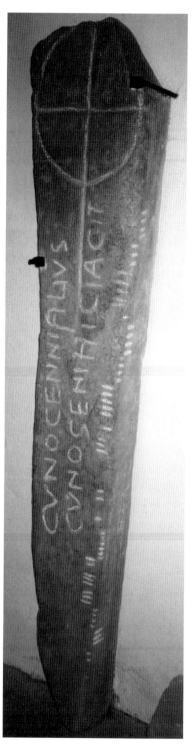

The early incised stone in Trallong church

TY ILLTUD
(SO 098 263)

A prehistoric chambered tomb with various Christian carvings subsequently carved on it, and the reputed site of St. Illtud's hermitage.

Ty Illtud is a Neolithic long barrow, also described as a chambered long cairn, about 4½ miles south-east of the centre of Brecon on private land. Opposite Manest Court Farm and over ½ a mile up the hill. Permission from the farm is required to visit the site. The stones have lost their original covering of soil.

The tradition has developed that St. Illtud used the cairn as a hermitage, hence the name Ty Illtud, Illtud's House[1] although Theophilus Jones is scathing about this idea. 'How is it possible' he asks 'after all that has been said about this house or hermitage, to convince the reader that it is more like a hen coop or a small pig-stie than a temple or the habitation of man ... As to its having been the dwelling place of Illtid, it must be treated as an idle fable; for with all his love of austerity he would hardly have resided in a hole where it was impossible he could stand upright, and where he could not even lie down with ease.'[2]

The first impression on visiting the site is how small the chamber is — it is just possible for a small adult to get inside. However, the height of the chamber has reduced over the years due to soil build-up. It was recorded as being 3 feet high in 1809 and 4 feet high in 1695. Grinsell suggests the original floor level may have been 5 to 6 feet below the ceiling, making its use as a hermitage possible, albeit a very small, cramped, space. Part of the adjoining forecourt may have been roofed over, and thus the chamber may have been more habitable centuries ago. Chambered long cairns elsewhere were very occasionally used by saints, for instance the early 8th-century Anglo-Saxon St. Guthlac reputedly used a prehistoric cist or chambered barrow at Crowland in Lincolnshire, whilst St. Marnoch allegedly retired on occasion to a Neolithic chambered tomb in Strathclyde.[3]

The north-east forecourt slab of the monument has a date of 1311 or 1312 carved in Roman numerals; the north-west forecourt slab has the date of 1510. The south-west slab, which forms the west wall of the chamber, has the most markings including 40 simple incised crosses, 16 small crosses in lozenges or diamonds, 3 crosses 'with barred or crossleted ends' in the style of the 7th to early 10th century, 'two eight-rayed star symbols' with other worn or weathered markings probably crosses. The south slab, which forms the south wall of the chamber, has a simple depiction of what appears to be a lyre measuring about 2½ inches by 1½ inches carved onto it, and the south-east slab, forming the east wall has about 8 crosses with a partly weathered inscription. The markings are difficult to see because of lichen growth and weathering. Unfortunately the slabs are poor quality laminated Old Red Sandstone which flakes — prior to 1925 there was an obvious cross-in-diamond carving on the south-west slab which Grinsell reports had gone by 1975 'presumably by flaking resulting from winter frosts and perhaps also from sheep rubbing themselves against the wall'.[4] No doubt other carvings have disappeared for similar reasons.

The carvings are a puzzle and various suggestions have been put forward. The 'lyre' drawing is particularly interesting and Grinsell makes a comparison with examples originally from part of an altar east of the Temple of Sulis-Minerva in Bath (now forming part of the north-east buttress of Compton Dando church),

One of the stones of the chamber with carved crosses

and the depiction on a mosaic floor, the Orpheus mosaic, originally from Barton Farm, Cirencester but now in the Corinium Museum. In considering a Roman date for this carving, Grinsell points out the proximity of Ty Illtud to the Roman road running between Brecon Gaer to Abergavenny. However it is not possible to date the carving firmly, only draw a comparison with dated examples. Thus a variety of dates have been ascribed to the other carvings ranging from prehistoric to early modern. However Grinsell states that the large number of crosses and their variants 'must surely leave no reasonable doubt that they were the work of pilgrims and other devotees of the cult of St. Illtud to whom the site was ascribed at a date unknown but well before 1695 when the monument with its carvings receives first mention in the literature'.[5] There are many other prehistoric stone monuments that do not have such Christian markings and it is, surely, no coincidence that Ty Illtud was believed to have been the saint's hermitage.

Ty Illtud is very close to the boundary between the parishes of Llanhamlach and Llansantffraed and it is just possible that some of the carvings were made during 'periodical perambulations of the bounds of these parishes',[6] probably in medieval times. Children and Nash note that the carvings have also been interpreted as the work of 'shepherd boys'; that some marks were regarded as being of prehistoric origin, if not contemporary with the monument's use as a tomb, while the Royal Commission for Ancient and Historical Monuments (Wales) observed in 1997 that an early date for the markings, or graffiti, is 'unlikely as the graffiti has close associations with masons' marks contemporary with the robbing of the monument for building stone.' Children and Nash add that they do not consider that the carvings are prehistoric for they have no direct parallels with other prehistoric art.[7] Theophilus Jones adds, rather refreshingly, that 'the crosses and other figures of caprice are irregularly placed … and may have been made with a tenpenny or a twopenny nail'![8] Whatever the date and meaning of these carvings, a link with St. Illtud, whether real or imagined, is of long-standing. Sitting by the cairn and gazing down the valley to Llanhamlach church it is no surprise that the church is dedicated to Illtud; the two sites feel oddly connected.

Grinsell notes that ,with the possible exception of two cairns in Pembroke-shire — Carreg Samson at Mathry and Ffust Samson at St. Nicholas, Ty Illtud is the only chambered cairn in Wales that is named after a saint; it is also the only known British megalithic tomb that has been decorated with crosses 'and related carvings including the unique "lyre"' and suggests the place must have been used as cult centre for Illtud.[9]

As for the hermitage, it may have been a building close to the tomb, for Theophilus Jones notes that close by were 'great heaps of stones, and the appearance either of a ditch or intrenchment, among which grows an old yew tree.'[10]

WAUN CHAPEL
(SO 238 388)

Scant remains of a putative early chapel on a windswept moor, with crosses carved in to a few stones.

This building is now a ruin, but one of the most exciting visited because of its setting. Positioned on the level upland 'allt' below Hay Bluff and Gospel Pass, this site, more than any other, brings home the isolation and difficult locations that were sought by some of the early saints. It is a ¼ of a mile off the road on a rise of ground that has, in times long past, been quarried.

The few remaining upright stones, which take accurate map-reading and a little pacing around to find, form three sides of a very small rectangle about 5 feet wide and 20 feet long, at the 'south end of a small quarry ... not obviously related to it'.[1] The stones protrude several feet above the turf at crooked angles, and on one stone incised crosses are carved which closely resemble those found within the chambered long cairn at Ty Illtud which is traditionally believed to

have become a hermit's cell (see previous entry) The crosses at Waun Chapel have to be sought for as they are faint and partly obscured by lichen. They are about 3 to 4 inches tall. The old quarry, which is now completely grassed over, actually cuts into what would have been the floor level of the structure.

The name of the site may mean 'Monk's Chapel', but it has no recorded history. Was the putative chapel positioned in a prominent location to attract converts, or was the reverse true in that it was in the wildest situation to keep people away?

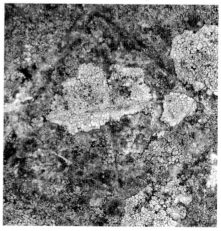

Carved lozenge containg a cross on one of the stones

Herefordshire

KINGTON

LEOMINSTER

Winforton

Bredwardine

Moccas

Cusop

Dorstone

Peterchurch

HEREFORD

LEDBURY

Woolhope

Little
Dewchurch

St. Devereux

Ballingham

Kilpeck

Much Dewchurch

Llanveynoe

Llandinabo

Foy

Clodock

Kenderchurch

Llanwarne

Sellack Upton Bishop

Llancillo

Pencoyd

Peterstow

Linton

St. Weonards

Hentland

ROSS

Garway

Michaelchurch

Llangarron

Whitchurch/Huntsham/
Welsh Bicknor

BALLINGHAM – St. Dubricius
(SO 576 317)

Early charter evidence for a site at Ballingham or at nearby Carey.

The church of St. Dyfrig is about 5½ miles south-east of Hereford, on a spur of land above a tight loop in the River Wye. It is considered that the place-name relates to the position of the site — 'Badelingahamm' would translate as 'land in a river-bend belonging to the followers of Badela'.[1]

In a charter of c.620 'King Gwrgan gave *podum sancti Budgualan* with two and a half *unciae* around it to bishop Inabwy.'[2] This was regranted in c.860 with five other churches to bishop Grecielis — here Ballingham is referred to as '*ecclesia Lannbudgualan*',[3] and is listed as '*Lann budgual*' in the churches in Erging listings.[4] The implication, therefore, is that this early site was not established by St. Dyfrig to whom the church is dedicated under the Latinized version of his name, but either that one of his disciples founded it, or that it was founded after his death and attributed to Dyfrig. However Baring-Gould and Fisher consider that the original founder, St. Buddwal or Buddwalan, was a very early saint of pre-6th century date of whom no record survives.[5] Coplestone-Crow suggests that a chapel at Carey, called *capella de Cari* in 1162, may have in fact been the site of *Lann Budgualan* (amongst its other appellations). The bounds mentioned in the charter suggest a site at Carey, now a small hamlet less than a mile south-west of Ballingham church. The ecclesiastical centre of this land unit may have subsequently been moved to Ballingham.[6] One only has to look at a map to see how many putative early church foundations existed in this area, often only a few miles apart. Whether they all were established at about the same time is another matter.

The structure of Ballingham church was restored in 1884–5, but the tower and sections of the nave have indications of 13th-century origins, with a 14th-century doorway and porch.[7] The surviving lancet windows speak of the age of the building and, in the late afternoon sun, the warm sandstone of the church glows a beautiful golden-pink.

The churchyard is small to medium-sized, curvilinear along some boundaries and raised quite noticeably above exterior levels. The site has the circumstantial evidence for an early medieval church site.

BREDWARDINE – St. Andrew
(SO 335 445)

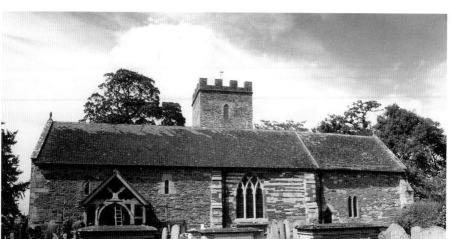

A possible monastic site with some interesting structural evidence in the church.

Bredwardine may be the site of *Lann Iunabui* (*podum Junabui*) mentioned in the Llandaff Charters for *c*.585 although Davies prefers an identification with Llandinabo (see p.281). The land was regranted in about *c*.625 and *c*.745 with the grants being made to Dyfrig's church rather than to him in person.[1] Coplestone-Crow prefers an identification with Bredwardine as the charter boundaries attached to the grant fit much more easily. 'From the ford above Ilan [probably llan, the church], downwards above the honeysuckle to the breast of the Allt, straight over the Cecg till it descends above the old ford that is on the stream in the great wood, through the wood straight on to Guartha Cambwll. From the Cambwll straight on to the Wye.'[2] A ford is recorded by Bredwardine Castle in *c*.1200 and the castle stood close to the church. After this ford over the Wye, Coplestone-Crow suggests the boundary would have gone through Finestreet Dingle at SO 323 440 to Bredwardine Hill (SO 318 446) (the *Allt*) and thus to Merbach Hill (SO 303 447) (the *Cecg*). The great wood appears to be remembered in the place-name Middlewood (SO 289 447) which is west of Merbach Hill where the Bach Brook runs. Coplestone-Crow suggests the second ford, 'the old ford', stood on this brook in the great wood. At Clock Mills (SO 290 455), where the Bach Brook empties into the River Wye, there was also a ford 'which gave access to an island in the Wye (on which there was a hermitage dedicated to the Welsh saint Cynidr), and beyond that to Winforton'. The hermitage was on an island of land cut off by the northern arm of the Wye, this latter began at about SO 292 462 and went by a very crooked course (which is today visible by a series of small lakes) past Court Barn at SO 302 463 (just over the Wye to the north) and north-north-east to a point on the Wye at SO 322 468 which would then lead back to Bredwardine, thus completing the circuit of the charter boundary. Coplestone-Crow suggests that this 'crooked creek', the northern arm of the Wye, could be the Cambwll of the charter.[3] With the aid of an Ordnance Survey map the reader can follow this course and it is surprising that something that was written possibly as early as the 7th century can still be followed today in the modern landscape. With the evidence of the charter one is minded to agree with Coplestone-Crow that Bredwardine rather than Llandinabo is the place meant in the charter.

Herefordshire Archaeology Unit have identified an 'earthwork enclosure ... comprising an earthen bank surrounding the crest of the ridge on which Bredwardine church is located. The enclosure extends northwards from the church for approximately 150m [about 494 feet] and is approximately 50m [about 165 feet] wide.' The enclosure appears to take in the present church and churchyard at its southern end 'suggesting some form of early monastic enclosure.'[4]

Bredwardine church has some early structural evidence. The misalignment of the present chancel with the nave has long been commented upon but generally it was thought that the original chancel had been incorporated into an enlarged nave and a replacement chancel built in about 1300 on a different orientation. However, as Ray points out, this does not explain why such a procedure should have produced the present odd alignments as the 'three distinct 'cells' of the church here each have different orientations, the most eccentric of which is the eastern-most'. He suggests that the odd orientation of the present chancel is explicable as the result of the linking up of two formerly separate buildings and considers that the present chancel is actually the earliest part of the surviving structure and stands within the southern area enclosed by the earthworks noted above. Ray observes that the western end of the nave, which once had a monumental west front, actually stands on the western bank of the enclosure and suggests that 'what is represented here is a complex succession starting with an early (presumably British) church enclosure, and then followed by a succession or grouping of church structures built within its bounds.' The present chancel and nave indeed have evidence of pre-Norman, albeit probably very late Saxon, elements within their structure.[5]

Bredwardine is a delightful site and generously repays a detailed visit. The churchyard is the resting place for Francis Kilvert, the famous diarist of the Welsh Borders.

CLODOCK – St. Clydog
(also spelt Clitauc/Clydawg) (SO 327 275)

Reputedly founded by St. Clydog in the 5th century and home to a probable 9th-century funerary tablet.

This lovely site stands beside the River Monnow just south of Longtown in the Black Mountains. The church, which according to the church notice board was founded in about 485, stands in the centre of a dispersed village in a flat area but to the west of the long, bracken-topped ridge of the Black Mountains. The churchyard is walled, of medium size and has some curving boundaries. There is a drop in levels between the churchyard and adjoining road to the north-west and western sides of about 3 to 4 feet, with an increasing drop towards the south-west corner. The Cornewall Arms abuts directly onto the south-west corner of the churchyard with the building actually forming part of the boundary.

The River Monnow rushes by along the eastern boundary and there is a ford leading directly to the back of the churchyard. It is an interesting feature with slabs of bedrock forming a crossing point (see the legend below). A modern concrete weir is on the left-hand side but there are remains of older stone workings running out from the river bank on the churchyard side.

The interior of the church is very interesting with the remains of wall paintings on the north and south walls and a wooden gallery. The present church

The ford just below Clodock church

The stone slab with 9th-century funerary inscription in the church

is of Norman origin and is constructed from coursed-rubble sandstone which has a grey-brown hue with a crenellated tower. Projecting out from the east wall of the chancel is a low-walled platform with three evergreen trees on the outer edge. Could this represent an earlier chancel platform?

The earliest feature in the church is a small stone slab set on a small stone shelf (originally used to hold statues) to the east of the pulpit. It has a funerary inscription in Latin which translated reads 'This tomb holds the remains of the faithful and dear wife of Guinndas, who was herself a native of this place'. The stone was found under the nave in 1917 and is thought to date from the 9th century.[1] The inscription is reckoned to be one of the earliest in Latin found in Herefordshire. That the stone was found under the nave suggests it may have originated from the site and, if so, proves the use of the church in the pre-Norman period and that the person commemorated was local to Clodock. Built into the outer face of the porch over the door are what appear to be thin pottery tiles, suggestive of re-used Roman tiles.

The legend of Clodock's titular saint, Clydog, is mentioned in the *Book of Llandaff*. Brychan, king of Brycheiniog, is variously listed as his father or grandfather, although there may have been two different saints, as Clydog was not an unusual name. However, according to the *Life*, the saint remembered at Clodock was a king of Ewyas (an area which incorporated parts of western Herefordshire and eastern Monmouthshire) who ruled his land peacefully and justly. Subsequent representations of Clydog show him wearing a prince's crown and holding a sword in one hand and a lily in the other, indicating these attributes. The daughter of a nobleman fell madly in love with Clydog and swore she would marry no-one else which enraged the girl's admirer, a comrade of the king, who determined the girl should be his. This man therefore killed Clydog when they were out hunting. Clydog's body was placed on a cart pulled by two yoked oxen towards the ford across the Monnow by the present church, but on reaching the riverbank the yoke snapped and the oxen refused to go further. It was therefore determined that Clydog's body should be buried at this site and a church built, the only church to be dedicated to him. In the Llandaff Charters the place was sometimes referred to as Merthyr Clydog, 'Clydog's *martyrium*' or burial place and, as merthyr place-names are among the earliest Christian place-names, the site has much to recommend it as being of 6th or even 5th century foundation. As one antiquarian records, Clydog's 'strayte and perfyte lyfe yt was cruelly slayne by a fals traytour at whose deth were shewed many myracles and at his tombe after many moo [more].' Against this legend the Iolo Manuscripts suggest that Clydog was killed by pagan Anglo-Saxons rather than a jealous comrade. Clydog's *Life* in the *Book of Llandaff* records that the 'hermits Llibio, Gwrfan and Cynfwr were the first inhabitants and cultivators of the place after the martyrdom of Clydog' and that it was they who built an improved church.[2]

The saint's festival is recorded as being on 3 November in most sources, although a few others record it as 19 August. The church guide records that the saint's day is 3 November while the 'Feast of the Martyr Clydawg' was celebrated on either the 16 or 19 of November.

Clodock is mentioned in three Llandaff Charters dating to the 8th century. In the first land is given to the above-named hermits (Llibio, also called Libiau, and Gwrfan are referred to as brothers while Cynfwr is 'their sororius') near Clodock by the king. Davies is suspicious of this charter describing it as 'essentially a reference to the known or supposed holy men of Merthyr Clodock, eked out with a few spurious charter formulae'. However she does note that two of the hermits' names are the same as two bishops of Brycheiniog who were associated with grants of Llanfihangel Cwm Du (Cwmdu, 4 miles north-west of Crickhowell).[3] Two other charters refer to Clodock, one dating to about 740 in which King Ithel gave the '*territorium Merthirclitauc* to the martyr Clydog and to bishop Berthwyn, with the guarantee of his sons' and in another undated charter which appears to represent 'some notion of the origin of lands in the possession of the church at Clodock'.[4]

CUSOP – St. Mary
(SO 241 415)

Yews give a hint of an early site.

Just in Herefordshire, Cusop church is less than a mile south-east of Hay-on-Wye, in a rural location outside the centre of the village. Baring-Gould and Fisher suggest that the name Cewydd (see entry under Aberedw, p.121) in its shortened form Cewi may be involved in the place-name Cusop which was 'anciently Ceushope'[1] — it is certainly in the area of other St. Cewydd dedications. However Coplestone-Crow lists the first spelling of Cusop in the Domesday Book of 1086 as Cheweshope and states that the second element is 'hop' which means 'secluded valley'. As for the first element he quotes Ekwall's *The Concise Oxford Dictionary of English Place-Names* which suggests a Welsh stream name Cyw meaning 'chickens',[2] which alas is certainly nothing to do with St. Cewydd, the Welsh rain saint. The dedication to St. Mary may of course be a later dedication.

There are some Norman remains in the church: a blocked north doorway with its 'enormous red-sandstone lintel', the remains of a south window, the chancel arch, and the font.[3] However the survival of several very old yews in the churchyard suggest a much earlier date to the site. One of the yews, a male tree to the south-west, has a measured girth of 30 feet and an estimated age of 1,800 years.[4] Indeed, there are ancient-looking yews at each corner of the church. The church itself is set in a relatively large, D-shaped enclosure and does appear to sit on a low mound within the churchyard. Is this the remains of a very eroded barrow? The yews may delineate an earlier churchyard boundary which would have been very small. However it is possible these yews are the descendants of an original yew that stood on top of a barrow (see, for example, Llanfihangel-nant-Melan, p.150).The jury is out on whether this is an early site but the great age of the yews hint at an early British saint's foundation.

DORSTONE – St. Faith
(SO 314 418)

Charter evidence for an early site, probably of a monastery founded by Dyfrig or his followers.

There is some rather compelling charter evidence that suggests the site originated in the 6th century. In the Llandaff Charters it is noted that Cinuin and Gwyddgi granted 'three *unciae* of land (at) *Cum Barruc* (to Dyfrig)' in about 595. Davies does not suggest an identification with Dorstone but an area in Valley Dore (presumably in the Golden Valley), although others have suggested *Cum Barruc* is Dorstone. In a second version of the above charter, Cinuin is styled king and Gwyddgi his brother and here they returned 'three *unciae* of land (at) *Cumbarruc*, formerly given to Dyfrig by Peibio [his father], to bishop Elgistus [Arwystl]'. The land was regranted in about 745 when it, and ten other churches, were returned by King Ithel to Bishop Berthwyn when he recaptured the land after Anglo-Saxon devastation of the area.[1] Coplestone-Crow identifies *Cum Barruc* with Dorstone because in the *Book of Llandaff* the former is said to be in the Ystrad Dour or Golden Valley, and elsewhere it is mentioned in association with *Tir Conloc*, identified with Preston-on-Wye (about 3½ miles due east), whose lands are said to stretch as far as *Cum Barruc*. For the latter to have bordered 'onto lands whose centre lay on the banks of the river, it must have been sited at a point where the Valley goes nearest to the Wye', which occurs in Dorstone parish. If this is the case, then the most likely site within the parish is the present site of the village. The *Cum* element may refer to the side-valley of the Golden Valley (at the mouth of which Dorstone lies), '*Barruc*' perhaps remembers a St. Barrog or Barrwg. In addition the bounds of *Cum Barruc* also make reference to a prominent stone, '*ad lech*', which rather suggests Arthur's Stone (SO 319431), still an impressive prehistoric monument on the border of Dorstone parish.[2]

As to the site itself, there is a large area of churchyard to the south-west of the church with a wide tongue leading to the main door. Close inspection of a middle-aged yew to the south-west suggests it may sit on an old boundary as it is growing on a low mound — does this, and a middle-aged yew to the north-west, mark the original boundary of the churchyard, with the area to the west a later extension? If one took a line between the two yews the area enclosed around the church would be of a small but balanced proportion and of a curvilinear shape. An old yew faces the south wall of the chancel near to the south-east corner and, as with so many churches we have visited, the end wall of the chancel is quite close to the eastern boundary. The present church is quite large in relation to the present enclosure and, if our suggestion of the small, curvilinear boundary is right, then it would have dwarfed the churchyard. The presence of the old yew and the possible earlier layout of the churchyard is suggestive of an early Christian site.

The proximity of Dorstone with other known 6th- and 7th-century foundations suggests that this part of Herefordshire was sought after by the early saint/monks. The church guide suggests that the dedication to St. Faith comes from an original Celtic saint Moy, which was mutated in Welsh to Foy or Foi and then taken by the Normans to mean St. Faith (see also the entry for Foy.).[3] However Annett warns that the situation with the dedication at Dorstone is confused as different 19th-century sources give Peter, Thomas or Mary as well as Faith.[4]

Part of the churchyard at Dorstone

FOY – St. Mary
(originally probably St. Moi or Moe) (SO 598 283)

A known early site, with evidence on the ground in the raised churchyard and the presence of ancient yews.

From a cursory look at the map one would expect the church to be in an open, flat site, but in reality the site is quite enclosed within a fairly wooded churchyard and is set on a river terrace and is thus raised above the River Wye and its flood plain. Foy is a small isolated hamlet in a peninsula of land formed by a loop in the river.

The church is built from Old Red Sandstone of a pale pink hue and the chancel and north nave wall are constructed from slabby stones, while the south nave wall and tower are chiefly constructed from dressed blocks. The building dates to the late 12th or early 13th century.

The churchyard is of small to medium size. It is raised on the southern side because of the river terrace and is of an approximate wide rectangular shape with generally straight boundaries but curved to the south-west. There is an older middle-aged yew to the south-east corner of the chancel and the churchyard drops quite dramatically to the southern side affording expansive views over the river. On the outside of the churchyard the sandstone bedrock can be seen upon which is a reinforcing wall of stone. On closer inspection it appears that there is an inner southern boundary, varying from 8 to 9 feet inside the retaining wall with the gap narrowing as one heads south-east towards the yew. The eastern boundary is walled with a drop of approximately 4 to 5 feet and there is a line of young to middle-aged yews. The northern boundary is straight with no drop. However on the left-hand side of this boundary youngish-looking yews appear to be growing on top of the remains of a low bank and, at the one end, the boundary can be seen in section. This bank peters out and the stone walls of adjoining properties abut the churchyard, whilst to the right-hand side of the northern boundary there is a straight wall dividing it from a car park, demonstrating this part of the perimeter has probably been changed within recent times. The churchyard is larger on the northern side suggesting enlargement.

Foy is thought to be mentioned in the Llandaff Charters *c.*866 where it is referred to as *Lann Timoi*. The original dedication to a Welsh saint Moi or Moe was changed over time to Foi or Foe which today survives as the village name of Foy.[1] In the 12th century the church was also known as St. Faith, probably 'because of confusion between the saint's name and the French *foi*, Latin *fides*,' while today's dedication is to St. Mary.[2] Annett states that, according to the *Book of Llandaff,* the 11th-century Bishop Herwald dedicated a church at *Lanntivoi* and that Tyvoi or Foy (the titular saint) was a disciple of St. Dubricius,[3] which dates him to the late 5th or early 6th century.

The sense of isolation formed by the looping of the River Wye and the site's elevated position above the floodplain fit with the criteria sought by the early saints emulating the 'deserts' of the early founding saints.

GARWAY – St. Michael
(SO 455 225)

A remarkable Knights Templar church with a holy well and possible charter evidence of an early 7th-century foundation.

The church of St. Michael is about 7 miles north-north-west of Monmouth. The site is of great interest as the present group of buildings were established by the Knights Templar; there is a square early 13th-century tower connected to a late 13th-century nave by a 17th-century corridor, all of which are out of alignment. The whole is architecturally very unusual, but even more so when it is discovered that the forerunner comprised a round nave and chancel which were separate from the tower. Parts of this nave survive, such as the beautiful dog-toothed chancel arch, along with excavated foundations to the north. Garway was a preceptory of the Knights Templar who preferred round churches as these reminded them of the Holy Sepulchre in Jerusalem; they founded the church at Garway in the late 1180s.[1] There is also a superb medieval round dovecot south of the church. The medieval church demands a visit in its own right. However there is probable documentary evidence of a much earlier foundation.

In a charter of *c*.615 'King Gwrfoddw gave an *ager* of one *uncia* to bishop Ufelfyw, and he ... founded a church and put his *sacerdos*, Guoruoe [or Guorboe], there to serve it.' The site is attributed to Garway.[2] There is another charter of *c*.625 in which Garway is given by King Athrwys, with a number of other churches, to Bishop Comereg, who was named as abbot of Moccas in *c*.620.[3] In about 745 Garway was amongst eleven churches returned to Bishop Berthwyn by King Ithel after the Saxons had devastated the Hereford area.[4] The church is called *Lann Guorboe* or *Lann Guoruoe* and is identified with Garway, both by Davies and by Evans and Rhys.[5] However Baring-Gould and Fisher disagree with the attribution as the site is described as being '*in campo Malochu*'[6] which denoted country 'between the Dore Valley and the Wye from Moccas down to about Hereford, and the [river] Worm'[7] and incorporates the Madley area.[8] For the same reason Coplestone-Crow does not identify *Lann Guorboe* with Garway.[9] This does rather leave one at a loss, but the presence of a well on the church site might just tip the balance in favour of Garway. Sant suggests this holy well, located just beyond the south-east corner of the churchyard, was the reason why the Knights Templar chose the site. To the left of the stone spout, and set into the stone wall which backs the well, is a niche. Sant describes this as a 'true spring, a tributary to the nearby stream rather than a branch of it' and was once the only source of drinking water for the villagers and notes that it never failed.[10]

Little is known of St. Guorboe, styled confessor, to whom the church was probably originally dedicated. In the *c*.615 charter we are told the king of Erging

The well at Garway

gave the bishop the land "'in the midst of which he erected a building in honour of the Holy Trinity, and there placed his priest Guoruoe" to perform the offices of the church, which was named *Lann Guorboe* from its first priest-in-charge.' As Baring-Gould and Fisher remark this is a good example of the form of Welsh church 'dedication' from the earliest times.[11] Davies names Garway as an example of how a first incumbent was remembered in the place-name and dedication of the church and thereby achieved a sort of sanctity.[12] This charter is also one of a very few which actually refer to the foundation of the church on the site — most of the charters refer to churches already in existence. There are two later grants, but still in the 7th century, which were witnessed by 'Elhearn Abbas Lann Guorboe', Elhearn (St. Aelhaiarn, not to be confused with the saint of the same name who was patron of Guilsfield) being a disciple of St. Dyfrig who was also witness to the charters concerning Dorstone, Pencoyd and Llandinabo.[13] This of course all depends on whether the *Lann Guorboe* of the Llandaff Charters refers to Garway, but on balance we believe it does.

HENTLAND – St. Dubricius
(SO 543 264)

Site of an ancient monastery.

The church is reached by a deeply-incised, no-through lane which descends past cottages built from the warm red sandstone of the area. The church site still retains a hidden, secretive feel. The very name Hentland is indicative of an early site as it is derived from the Welsh *hen* and *llan* meaning 'old church'. It is alleged that Dyfrig's great-grandfather, Brychan, King of Brycheiniog, founded the church and this may explain why Hentland and neighbouring Llanfrother do not have any founding charters attached to them as they were Dyfrig's by hereditary right and therefore did not need to be granted to him.[1] However this does suggest a family connection with Brychan which cannot be proven. Herefordshire Archaeology Unit identified well-defined earthworks north of the church on the land of the Pengethly Estate on the 'edge of a terrace overlooking a steep valley to the east'. These consist of platforms with interspersing banks and ditches and a possible hollow way, indicating the site of a deserted settlement close to the church.[2] The date of this settlement is not known but it is almost certainly medieval than pre-Norman. However excavations some 35 years ago to the south side of the churchyard revealed sherds of Romano-British pottery[3] which approximates to the time of Dyfrig's monastery.

The present church is a substantial 13th- to 14th-century building, rather large for such a relatively isolated place, and retains its putative early dedication. It is set in a medium-sized churchyard which has an irregular but roughly rectilinear shape and has a gentle slope from the main entrance to the church. The churchyard is much smaller at the back, and in the north-east area is a middle-aged yew with younger mature yews flanking the main entrance. The church appears to be slightly raised within the churchyard. There is a slope away from the chancel end of the church and when viewed from this point the building appears to be slightly elevated.

The church is a joy for its late medieval interior. There are remnants of wall-paintings in the chancel and with the roof timbers similarly painted. In the north wall of the nave is an early 20th-century stained glass window depicting St. Dubricius (Dyfrig) and a hedgehog; the hedgehog, an 'erchin' in local dialect, is said to be the symbol for Erchinfield or Archenfield.

A charter dated to between 1045–1104 in the Llandaff Charters includes a reference to Hentland as '*Hennlann dibric et lann teliau in uno cimiterio*', which translates as 'the old church of Dyfrig and the church of Teilo in one cemetery' and suggests there were two churches on the same site or perhaps that one church was re-dedicated. Coplestone-Crow remarks that the first church on the Hentland site appears to have been dedicated to St. Teilo with 'the dedication to St. Dyfrig (dibric) being a later addition.' A first dedication to Teilo might seem odd when Hentland is so closely associated with Dyfrig, but his monastery may well have been at Llanfrother Farm which is on top of the nearby hill towards the Wye. Local tradition has it that it was here rather than at Hentland that Dyfrig established his famous monastery. In 1334 Llanfrother was spelt as *Hendresroudre* and then as *Henfrowther* in 1546. The former probably means the 'old place of the brethren'. The latter spelling appears to remember brethren as 'frowther' and Llanfrother appears to mean 'the sacred enclosure/church of the monks' — surely an unusual name for a farm. As Coplestone-Crow remarks, Llanfrother certainly fits the description given in the Llandaff Charters — '*super ripam Gui*' ('above the River Wye') — much better than the site at Hentland. Llanfrother is on top of a hill overlooking the Wye whereas Hentland is at the bottom of a hill and over a mile from the river. He further suggests that if Llanfrother was the site of Dyfrig's important monastery, then his church here would have been combined with Teilo's foundation at Hentland in or before the 11th century.[4] There is nothing above ground at Llanfrother of the putative monastery but ruins survived here as late as 1633 and, within living memory, small mounds and hillocks were said to have existed in the fields but with no traces of the ruins or stone.[5] Whether these remains were anything to do with Dyfrig's monastery is questionable as early monasteries were usually made from perishable materials, and it is unlikely anything would survive save for postholes which on their own would not prove the identity or date of a structure. Both Hentland and Llanfrother have a certain magic about them however. Their remoteness would have been one of the reasons why these places were chosen by the early saints: they were searching for the wilderness of the early Desert Father and this was their *desertum*.

KENDERCHURCH – St. Mary
(SO 403 284)

Early dedication to St. Cynidir and possible base of an early episcopal see.

The church of St. Mary at Kenderchurch is 11 miles south-west of Hereford at Pontrilas, on a hill immediately next to Pontrilas Timber and Builders Merchants. The entrance to the church is to the left of the saw mill complex, up a pedestrian track by a wooden bungalow and through a steep field.

The church used to be known as *Lanncinitir* or *Lannicruc*,[1] also written as *Lann i Cruc*, in the 'Churches in Erging' list of the *Book of Llandaff* which refers to a document written between 1066–87. A few decades earlier it was simply referred to as *Lann Cruc*.[2] The church was thus originally dedicated to St. Cynidr, as evidenced in the name *Lanncinitir*, who in some documents is referred to as the son of Gwynllyw and Gwladys, thus a grandson of Brychan, and brother to St. Cadoc.[3] Cynidr had several dedications (see under Llangynidr, p.216). The dedication to St. Mary is clearly later. The 'cruc' element of the name probably derives from the hill upon which the church stands — the old Welsh word 'cruc' means 'hill shaped like a tumulus'. Interestingly the approximate land unit in the Domesday Book appears to have been called Stane — 'stone' — and Coplestone-Crow suggests it was named after a prominent standing stone. Thus it may be that this hill had some pre-Christian relevance. He also considers that the episcopal manors of Kenderchurch/Stane, along with Didley/Wormbridge, may have been part of the 12 hides of land that Merewalh, the 7th-century king of the Magonsaete, a sub-kingdom of Mercia, gave to Wenlock Abbey.[4] In a 1291 taxation record the church is referred to as '*Eccl'ia Sci. Kenedr*',[5] thus still retaining Cynidr's name. Davies has raised the possibility of a bishopric existing from the late 6th to the early 10th century in the part of south-east Wales that now borders England and suggested a base somewhere near Kenderchurch (or at Welsh Bicknor or Glasbury).[6] It comes as something of a surprise that this modest, rather unassuming site has potentially such an early and important Christian history.

The eastern view of the church belies its age, for the structure is basically late medieval. There is a Norman decorated font, a screen with some late-medieval carving and a wagon-roof to the chancel with bosses.[7] Near the external east wall of the chancel is a sharply leaning vertical slab about 2½ feet tall with a carving of a large but barely visible Maltese-type cross. It is not mentioned in any texts we have found. It looks medieval, but is it pre-Conquest?

The churchyard is medium-sized and partly curvilinear, with irregular sections to the boundary. The churchyard is hedged with several yews to the south. There is also a yew of some age on the west side. The churchyard is mildly embanked on the southern boundary, with clearer embanking on the south-eastern side. This part was possibly ditched on the outer side at some stage but is now filled in. On the northern side there is gentle embanking, again with the suggestion of a filled-in, external ditch. The enclosure is raised by about 3 feet above the external ground level, particularly to the western boundary, which is noticeably embanked.[8]

The stone slab outside the east wall of the chancel with its carved cross

KILPECK –
St. Michael & St. Mary (SO 445 305)

One of the most remarkable churches in Britain which has a mid-9th century charter.

Kilpeck lies about 7½ miles south-west of Hereford. The church of St. Michael and St. Mary is a classic example of work of the Herefordshire School of Sculpture carried out in *c*.1135. The church is a Norman structure with nave, chancel and eastern apse. The chancel arch, the south door, the figures on the decorative corbel around the church and exterior of the west window are truly fabulous. Next to the church is the motte and bailey of the castle. There was also a Benedictine Priory nearby, founded in 1134. Beside these features, which command a lengthy and appreciative visit, the site is almost certainly a pre-Norman foundation.

A charter in the *Book of Llandaff* dated *c*.850 tells us that 'Fauu gave *ecclesia Cilpedec* with its *ager* around it to bishop Grecielis, and he and Gideon proclaimed it free, with the guarantee of king Meurig who had ordered everyone to release all the churches in his land from obligations.'[1] The site is referred to as 'CilPedec in Ercicg' at the heading of the charter and 'Lann degui cilpedec' in the list of Churches in Erging.[2] The 'cil' element of the name has been discussed under the entry for Kilgwrrwg (see p.333); the 'degui' element is another form of Dewi

The font at Kilpeck

(David). However the part 'pedec' has led to the suggestion that this was the name Pedic or Pedoric, and the name *Cilpedec* means the Cell of St. Pedic.[3] Although there is no saint listed under that name in Baring-Gould and Fisher's *Lives of the British Saints*, it is possible that there was an earlier dedication to a now forgotten British saint who was superseded as dedicatee by St. David. The phrase '*ecclesia Cilpedec* with its ager around it' is interpreted by Davies as meaning 'the church of Kilpeck with its estate around it' and is an example of how a church and its associated dwelling houses were surrounded by land which supported the religious community.[4] The charters signify an early Christian site, but whether it is a pre-David foundation is open to speculation.

LINTON-BY-ROSS – St. Mary
(SO 660 254)

The churchyard is home to a yew with an estimated age of 4,000 years.

The church of St. Mary stands at the centre of the medium-sized village at the top of the sloping village street, 2½ miles east of Ross-on-Wye. This is an enchanting church with a striking 14th- to 15th-century tower with spire. Parts date back to the Norman period, for example the exposed fragment of a south doorway, the north arcade with its two arches, and a solid piece of walling to the west of the arcade which once belonged to a Norman tower.[1] We wonder if there are late Anglo-Saxon elements.

A famous yew tree stands opposite the porch. The tree is hollowed and has suffered fire blackening on the inside. Another yew appears to be growing from within the hollowed out trunk, but this is in fact an example of an aerial root from the original tree which has regenerated and so gives the impression of a tree growing within a tree. Chetan and Brueton note that this internal stem is about 7 feet in circumference and that this offspring could be 300 years old. The main yew has a measured circumference of about 33 feet and is estimated at 4,000 years old.[2] Bevan-Jones, however, is rather more conservative and suggests a dating estimate of 1,500 to 1,600 years for yews with girths of 26 to 33 feet, although

The famous yew at Linton

277

there are a plethora of variables so the dates are only a rough guide. However he does remark that the Linton yew is almost identical in size to other ancient yews at Discoed and Llanfaredd in Radnorshire and Clun in Shropshire and suggests there is a 'serious historic possibility of a Celtic saint presence' at these sites, and possibly at Peterchurch too.[3] Chetan and Brueton observe there are several other old yews in the churchyard at Linton,[4] and there is certainly another venerable old yew facing the south wall of the chancel.

The churchyard is interesting and suggestive of an early foundation. It is raised, with partly curving boundaries and slopes steeply to the east but levels out from the chancel to the road on the west. There are undulations to the south of the church which may indicate an early boundary which perhaps continued in a circular arc, but a pathway and more recent landscaping disguise any potential evidence. The church appears to be on a raised area when viewed from the north and east. The western and southern areas of the enclosure are flatter and have straight boundaries.

Against the external east wall of the chancel there is a stone propped against the wall with carved equal-armed crosses of Maltese style. It is not mentioned in any literature but has a medieval appearance.

Although the earliest fabric of the church is Norman and the dedication is to St. Mary, the presence of the ancient yew and the topography of part of the churchyard give the impression of a site with early medieval origins. Its proximity to Upton Bishop (see p.305), Eccleswall Court (the place-name of which means 'Spring at a Celtic Christian centre',[5] and the site of the important Roman town of *Ariconium* adds weight to the possibility that this was an early Christian site which the Normans re-dedicated.

LITTLE DEWCHURCH –
St. David (SO 529 318)

Site morphology argues for an early Christian site, for which there is 9th-century charter evidence.

In *c.*850 there was a grant which records 'Guinncum freed *ecclesia Cum Mouric* with king Meurig's guarantee, and returned it with its *tellus* to bishop Grecielis, and Morien gave an additional piece from his villa across the road.' Davies tentatively identifies *Cum Mouric* with Little Dewchurch,[1] while Evans and Rhys add 'Morraston, Little Dewchurch'.[2] Morraston (SO 533 314) is a small collection of buildings just south-east of the church and one wonders if that is the additional piece of land from the villa mentioned in the charter. Notably, the church is not mentioned as a David (Dewi) dedication in this 9th-century charter. The first place-name evidence is in 1397 when it is called *Lytel Deuchurche* (*et Combe*).[3]

 The site, however, is suggestive of early Christian use. It stands on the edge of the small village and next to open land to the west and north. The church stands on a raised area or low tump within the churchyard. This is most noticeable when the church is viewed from the south-east and north-east corners. On the east the churchyard is raised and has a curving boundaries to the eastern and north-eastern sides with a gentle east/west slope. The western and southern boundaries are also curved. There are two middle-aged yews to the south-east. Although the church is a later 19th-century rebuild (except for the tower which is 14th century), evidence from the charter and the morphology of the churchyard suggests a much earlier church site, but whether it was an original St. David dedication is not clear.

LLANCILLO – St. Peter
(SO 366 255)

A fascinating site with a charter dating back to *c.*620 and once dedicated to an early British saint.

St. Peter's church is about 8 miles north-east of Abergavenney. We suggest using a good OS map as it is difficult to find. The church is disused and in the custody of the farmer of Llancillo Court, of whom you need to ask permission to visit.

The interior of the church is refreshingly simple with window designs from different periods, but in the north wall of the chancel is one of Norman origin.[1] Outside there is a medieval cross base with a more modern cross.

The churchyard is fairly small, of rectilinear shape and on a slope. It is bounded by drystone walling on the southern, eastern and north-eastern sides which contains re-used dressed stone, probably from the castle which stood on the adjacent motte. In the south-eastern corner of the churchyard there is a very old yew on an embanked mound against the boundary wall. It has a considerable circumference, suggesting a very great age — a pre-Norman origin perhaps? On the northern side the boundary is not embanked and has only mild embanking to the west. The churchyard is embanked on the north-eastern and eastern sides where the land drops down to a track.

It has been suggested that the original patron was St. Tysilio because of the similarity in spelling with Herefordshire's Sellack (*Lann Suluc*) in the *Book of Llandaff* and where Tysilio was the patron. Baring-Gould and Fisher consider this very unlikely and suggest the patron was St. Sulbiu as the church is actually called '*Ecclesiam Sancti Sulbiu*' in the *Book of Llandaff.*[2] Nothing else is known about St. Sulbiu. Alternatively they suggest the foundation could be attributed to St. Ufelwy, a grandson of Gildas, and a hermit in the Gower. A pupil of St. Dyfrig, who consecrated him a bishop, Ufelwy chose a district for himself in Erging and was given a grant of land at Bolgros, near Madley by the king of Erging 'as a thank-offering for victory over the Saxons.' Ufelwy was probably one of the church leaders who met Augustine in 603 at what became known as Augustine's Oak.[3]

Davies notes the existence of a charter dated to *c.*620 in which 'King Meurig gave *podum Lann Suluiu* with its *tellus* to bishop Ufelfyw'; the area of land granted was about 200 acres. The receiving bishop appears to be the same person as St. Ufelwy. The King Meurig referred to was probably King Meurig ap Tewdrig (see under Mathern, p.373).[4] Charter bounds exist for this grant and mention is made of 'Ishmael's dyke' and 'the spring of the Gwvalon'.[5]

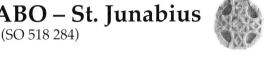

LLANDINABO – St. Junabius
(SO 518 284)

Evidence for an early site from charters and on the ground.

Llandinabo is about 8 miles south of Hereford. The church is set in a very small curvilinear churchyard in which there is a massive yew opposite the porch to the south and close to the church. This yew is female and, having a girth of about 28 feet, is estimated to be about 1,600 years old.[1] It is a tall tree with a healthy, wide spread and dominates the churchyard and the church. The age and size of the yew may suggest a planting by an early saint (see p.69), and thus an early foundation. There is another old yew in the north-east corner of the enclosure and this is growing on a slightly raised area.

Davies identifies the '*podum Junabui*' of the Llandaff Charters with Llandinabo.[2] In about 585 King Peibio of Erging 'gave *podum Junabui* with an *uncia* of land to (Dyfrig).' The land was regranted in *c*.625 and *c*.745. As Davies notes, Dyfrig does not appear in the witness list (and he would probably have been dead by 585) thus the grant was presumably made to Dyfrig's church than to him personally.[3] It was allegedly regranted as '*Lann Iunabui*' in *c*.625 by King Athrwys with several other foundations to a bishop Comereg who in *c*.620 was named as the abbot of Mochros (Moccas) — however this record is somewhat suspect.[4] In *c*.745 King Ithel returned Llandinabo — '*Lann Iunabui*' — with ten other churches to a bishop Berthwyn after the Anglo-Saxons had devastated

281

the area around Hereford. Davies considers that, although there is 'nothing to suggest the framework of an original charter', the mention of the Mercian king Aethelbald indicates 'an approximate date for the transaction', whilst the *Anglo-Saxon Chronicle* records the fighting between Britons and Mercians in about 743 which makes the circumstances of the record 'at least credible'.[5]

The identity of the titular saint, Junabius, has occasioned debate. Annett observes that the name, spelt variously as Iunabui, Iunapius and Iunapeius, occurs twelve times in the *Book of Llandaff*, mostly in charters dated to between 575 and 620, which suggests the saint's period of activity. It is possible that Junabius was St. Dyfrig's cousin. Annett and Coplestone-Crow remark that the identification of *podum Junabui* with Llandinabo has problems, as the bounds in the charter refer to the River Wye and the river is about two miles away from Llandinabo, but is close to Bredwardine, another early site and one which the charter bounds fit well (see p.260).[6] However there is a mid-11th century reference to '*Lann hunapui*'[7] which is listed between Llanwarne and Peterstow and Annett observes that this is obviously Llandinabo. He suggests that Hunapui is not the same person as Iunapui (Junabius) because, although the latter's name is spelt in a variety of ways, it is never spelt as Hunapui. It is possible then that Llandinabo was dedicated to Hunapui, who is otherwise unknown, and that his name was later confounded with the better known Iunabui/Inabwy (Junabius) who is described as priest and bishop in the Llandaff Charters.[8] This example highlights the complexities involved in using these early sources and the problems with interpretation. Interestingly Llandinabo is close to several other churches which are mentioned in the Llandaff Charters: Llanwarne, Foy, Sellack, Peterstow(?), Garway, Llangarron and Whitchurch.

Whichever the actual saint, the topography of Llandinabo suggests an early Christian site, if not a particularly important one if the small size of the churchyard is original. The church is a Victorian rebuild, partly hidden by a screen of trees, and is set back from the main A49 which rushes past, a field away to the west. It is a single-storey church with a timber-framed bell turret.

There is a drop of about 4-5 feet on the eastern boundary to the surrounding land. A small farm out-building abuts the north-eastern area of the churchyard and an old stone building of coursed rubble construction adjoins the northern boundary, which has meant some straightening of the boundaries. The churchyard is also higher than the surrounding land on the north-west and western sides and the latter boundary is curved. The south-east and south-west corners of the churchyard are curved and there is a height difference on the southern side. All the boundaries have stone retaining walls and, while the boundaries are curved, the enclosure is not obviously circular. Seen from the road this is a little island of a site in the midst of pasture, which turns out to have a surprisingly long history.

LLANGARRON – St. Deinst
(SO 530 212)

The church contains an early carving recently suggested to be of possible 5th- or 6th-century date. Charter evidence indicates an early site, borne out by the dedication.

The church of St. Deinst is 6 miles north-north-east of Monmouth, at the centre of the village and set in a raised, curvilinear churchyard. The church is a medium-sized structure built from warm Old Red Sandstone with an interesting mixture of styles and a chancel that is very inspiring architecturally. The tower is 14th century as is the chancel; other sections are later.[1]

Within the church and mounted on the south wall of the nave, by the door, is an early sculptured grave slab about 2¾ feet tall and 1 foot wide. Pevsner questioned whether it was of 13th-century date[2] and the RCHME interpreted it as the cover of a 15th-century child's coffin, but recently a 5th- or 6th-century date has been suggested. As Dr. Keith Ray notes 'it comes as something of a shock to be brought literally face-to-face with a sculpture ... that may represent a member of [the British] Church in the fifth or sixth century' — and so it does. The sculpture looks like a male figure wearing a robe, with hands folded left over right at the waist. Indications are that it was cut from a larger stone. The type of figure 'fits well within known traditions of Iron Age and Romano-British figure sculpture' with its 'half-round figure sculpting, the tapering proportions of the body (with a disproportionately-sized head reducing to tiny legs and feet), the triangular-cut jaw, and the protruding lentoid-shaped eyes'. The hair is treated in a late Roman fashion 'depicted as a covering of raised dots.' The gown that the figure is

The sculptured grave slab

283

wearing is considered to be another indicator of the antiquity of the figure — it is a 'simple clerical gown tied at the waist with a cord' and quite unlike the vestments usually shown on medieval grave slabs. Ray thus suggests that the figure 'appears to be a representation, whether from an altar frieze or a memorial stone, of a priest of the early British church.'[3] If this is the case, then this sculpture would represent a 'remarkable survival' and a rather breath-taking rarity, certainly along the Welsh Border. We would also raise the unanswerable question: is this sculpture meant to be a representation of the founder?

The place-name Llangarron is interesting. As Ray notes there are about 20 churches/llans in the valley of the Garren brook (a tributary of the River Wye) and its 'northern branch the Gamber (in Welsh Amyr)' but only Llangarron is afforded the name 'the church-enclosure or settlement on the Garren'. The question is whether it was given this name because it was the largest settlement, or is it possible it once housed a 'monastic community, wealthy and important enough to have sponsored figure carvings of its priests' or its founder which afforded it special status.[4] The site would certainly have had room for a monastery. However one might also ask why it was that the founder was not remembered in the place-name as usually occurs. St. Deinst, the titular saint, is identified with St. Deiniol, a 6th-century abbot-bishop. He only has one other dedication and that is at Itton, 3 miles west of Chepstow (see p.331). It is possible that the actual founder was some other, now forgotten, British cleric.

The church appears in the Llandaff Charters under a record of c.745 where King Ithel returned eleven churches to one Bishop Berthwyn 'which had previously belonged to Dyfrig ... after Saxon devastation in the Hereford area' and is referred to as Lann Garan.[5] There is also a reference in the 'Churches of Erging' in the *Book of Llandaff* which may link the consecration of the church to the ordination of a bishop. If so, this would further support the idea of an important monastic establishment. Information within the church states that during Edward the Confessor's reign a wooden church was consecrated at Llangarron and, during William the Conqueror's rule, Bishop Herwald of Llandaff re-consecrated 'lan garan'.

It is stated that not long ago the church was set within a circular churchyard[6] which today is quite large, raised and curvilinear, especially to the front. There is a slope away from the church on this side to the edge of a steep drop down to road level; to the south-east the height above the exterior level is about 3 to 4 feet, and there is a similar drop to the east where it adjoins a paddock. There is a middle-aged yew on the north-eastern boundary. A lane adjoins the northern boundary and there is evidence of internal embanking, especially noticeable to the north-west. To the north-west and west the churchyard is 12 to 15 feet above the external road level — it is possible this is a natural promontory and the drop has been enhanced by the hollowing of the lane.

LLANVEYNOE – St. Peter
(SO 303 314)

There are two early medieval crosses set within the church and a short-armed cross with potentially important links with the early saint, Beuno.

Pevsner's view that the church is 'beautifully situated in the hills, with views across the Olchon valley towards the noble range of mountains beyond which lies Llanthony'[1] perfectly describes the dramatic location of St. Peter's which is about 2½ miles north-west of Longtown.

It was at Llanveynoe that St. Beuno is said to have set up his first establishment after finishing his tuition at the ecclesiastical school set up by Ynyr Gwent at Caerwent in the early part of the 7th century. He lived here with his followers for some time, but left three of them in charge on being called away to his father who was gravely ill (see p.68).

The church is a rebuild dating mainly from the 19th and 20th centuries and was once dedicated to St. Beuno. However there are early incised stones and a cross at this site which are of great interest. Dr. Keith Ray notes that, although no memorial altars, *leachta* (an Irish term meaning a memorial cairn allegedly built over a saint's grave) or early crosses have been recorded from the county of Herefordshire, the three stones at Llanveynoe suggest that 'an ecclesiastical centre of some significance once existed here.' Two of the stones are set into the internal walls of the church and are described as cross-incised slabs. One depicts a figure of a crucifixion and is over 4 feet tall with the simple carving of Christ on the cross occupying much of the slab. The other stone is smaller and a broad lozenge shape and contains the bottom half of a deeply incised cross. There is some lettering on the arms of the cross with an inscription

The stone showing the crucifixion

along the right-hand edge of the stone. They have been described as being of 11th-century date and thus later commemorative works, but Ray notes that the crucifixion is very similar to representations as at Phillack in south-west Cornwall which have been interpreted as 'frontal panels of stone altars.' The smaller stone has alpha and omega signs and the lettering along the right-hand edge is a dedicatory inscription which, Ray notes, is almost identical in name formula and script 'to one on another cross-incised slab from the early monastic site at Ardwall Isle in south-west Scotland'. He suggests this may also be 'a frontal stone, or one of the quadrangular stones set in the top of a *leacht*-type altar', or, alternatively, it could be a fragment from a larger stone cross. Ray notes that the Latin form of the crosses could support at least a late first

The stone with part of an incised cross

millennia date, with the earliest dated examples of the 7th century.[2] The stones are striking in their design because of their simplicity. The crucifixion stone has a number of circular indentations to the surface which interrupts the design — the marks may have some significance but look more accidental.

In the churchyard is the third stone. It is a short-armed cross and, as Ray observes, it has largely escaped notice but 'comprises the best evidence presently observable on the site, for its former importance.' The short-armed cross is a form recorded from all over western Britain, but is 'especially associated with sites like Ardwall Isle in Galloway, and those on the Isle of Man.' That at Kilgwrrwg looks remarkably similar to the Llanveynoe example, (see p.285). Ray observes that the Llanveynoe cross is about 5¼ feet tall and this type of short-arm design is thought to have been made to support the superstructure of a wooden cross, one possible explanation for the 'stone step or "saddle"' visible on the back of the cross. The cross also tapers downwards from about 1¼ feet above the present ground level. It is thought that this taper, with the unusual groove down the front face and the apparent deliberate lean backwards of the upper part of the cross, have 'important implications for its original setting and use' — Ray suggests that the lower tapered end was 'inserted into a *leacht* or similar structure' and the cross itself can be identified as a memorial stone cross, possibly even commemorating St. Beuno's burial place. In the *Life* of St. Samson there is a description of how Samson was buried 'in the midst of quadrangular stones standing upright in the cemetery, a stone cross being placed above and the insignia of a bishop inscribed below.' Ray suggests that the cross at Llanveynoe is just such an example and that the tapering would have allowed it to be hafted within a cairn of stones over the

grave. However St. Beuno is most well-known for his foundation at Clynnog near the coast in north-west Wales where he died (see p.70) although Ray notes that it would have been quite usual practice at the time for relics from the saint's body to have been sent to Llanveynoe for immediate burial, or at some time after, when his cult had developed. The unusual groove on the front of the cross is thought to be original and imay have been cut to take 'the pouring of libations downwards into the tomb' and may explain why the groove runs from the very top to the bottom, even along the tapering part of the stone. If this is the case it suggests a fascinating continuation of religious practice from Romano-British times. A late Roman cist grave at Caerleon, for example, was found to have a 'libation conduit consisting of a lead pipe leading from above ground down into a lead tank containing a cremation ...'.[3]

The three stones are recorded as coming from a field next to the churchyard and an archaeological survey of the site in 2000 located the presence of an earthwork complex into which the churchyard has been placed at a later date. Ray notes that the link with St. Beuno's cult 'puts this site squarely within the wider tradition of early Christian monastic centres throughout the western seaboard of Britain.'[4]

The short-armed cross in the churchyard

LLANWARNE –
St. John the Baptist (SO 505 282)

A ruined church in an atmospheric location and with 8th-century documentation.

The ruined church of St. John the Baptist is about 7 miles south of Hereford
at the centre of the small village and close to the Gamber Brook. It is a short
distance from its successor, Christ Church, which was consecrated in 1864 when
the roof of the old church was taken off and it was left as a ruin.[1]

The old church looks somewhat forlorn, with no plaster remaining to any
walls, just the bare bones of the structure — it may be described as a picturesque
ruin. It is of 13th-century to late medieval date.

The enclosure is irregular in shape and very low lying. Indeed there is little
difference between the level of the stream, which flows along the northern edge,
and the church enclosure; even in recent times there was often standing water
in the south entrance of the chancel and in the south porch and it was this very
damp situation that led to the abandonment of the church and building of a new
one further up the hill.[2] The meaning of Llanwarne is indeed 'church by the alder
swamp',[3] and to the north-west and west of the church is a marshy, overgrown
area just beyond the enclosure evocative of a much earlier time. The stream curves
around to the east and south-east beyond the churchyard to a small lane.

There is documentary evidence to support an early medieval foundation. In
a charter in the *Book of Llandaff* dated *c*.758[4] — although a date in the early 7th
century is also suggested[5] — 'It is to be understood that Catvuth, son of Coffro,
offered to God a piece of land of three *modii*, that is, a fourth part of an *uncia* of
land; that is, the church of Henlennic on the bank of the Amyr; that is, Lannguern,
... Its boundaries between the Aymr and the hyacinthe road are its width, and its
length is as far as the old ditch.'[6] The hyacinthe road must have been lovely sight!
Lannguern means 'the church by the alder trees' (probably Llanwarne church).
The *Amyr* is identified with the Gamber Brook and *Henlennic* is translated as 'the
little old church', and has been identified with Lenniston which is a homestead
about a mile south of the ruined church and just outside the parish boundary.[7]
It is interesting that in the 8th century a church was referred to as 'old' — was it
superseded by Llanwarne, the *Lannguern* of the charter?

In a charter of *c*.855, although an early 8th century date is also suggested:[8]
'Mainerch son of Milfrit and Guiner son of Iacuan gave an *ager* of three *modii*,
super ripam amhyr fluminis, to bishop Grecielis', which is interpreted as being in
an area around the River Gamber;[9] this is the same amount of land given in the
previous charter and we suggest it too refers to Llanwarne church. The bounds

for the second charter run from 'The ford of Pallan to the ditch, the ditch leading to the green tump, and from the tump from the district as far as the Amyr river, with part of the wood of Mamilet.' It was concluded in 1924 that these boundaries were similar to the present parish boundary and the green tump was the mound at Wormelow which was destroyed in modern times. However, it is reckoned that an *uncia* was about 500 acres, thus the quarter of an *uncia* given in the grant is about 100 to 150 acres which Shoesmith remarks is considerably less than the 2,500 or so acres which comprise Llanwarne's present parish. He concludes that the area indicated by the bounds is likely 'to be much closer to the original church site than the present parish boundary.'[10]

Llanwarne church appears again in the records in the time of William the Conqueror when Bishop Herwald 'consecrated Llannguern, and in it ordained Gulcet ap Asser priest, and after him Simeon'. Confusingly, at around the same time, there is also reference to Bishop Herwald consecrating 'Llan Geunn Aperhumur (the church in the alders at the confluence of the Gamber) ... and in it ordained Jacob and after him Elgar.' Although both sites have been identified as Llanwarne, there is no confluence of the Gamber Brook in the immediate vicinity.[11] Are we therefore talking of two separate churches in close proximity? It seems unlikely, although the reference to the 'little old church' may hold the clue.

A reference in the *Book of Llandaff*, dated to between 1045–1104, refers to the church as '*Lann Guern Teliau ha Dibric*' which Coplestone-Crow suggests may be an example of two churches — one dedicated to St. Teilo and another to St. Dyfrig — being combined on one site, which perhaps occurred in the 11th century following the devastation of Archenfield (Erging) by the Welsh.[12] This also happened at Hentland/Llanfrother and probably at Ballingham/Carey which are both quite close to Llanwarne. This strengthens the case of there being two separate churches at the latter — we may suggest one was on the site of the ruined later medieval church and the other perhaps at Lenniston to the south.

This is an atmospheric place which still retains a somewhat marshy, hidden topography and it is not difficult to imagine the scene 1,500 years ago.

MICHAELCHURCH –
St. Michael (SO 522 255)

The church houses a re-used Roman altar.

This beautiful little church is approximately 7½ miles north of Monmouth. Parking is difficult, however this church is a must for the visitor as it seems to have escaped later restoration and rebuilding and is home to some rather remarkable medieval features. It is said to have been founded by Bishop Herwald of Llandaff in 1056 and there are a few Norman windows remaining, the partial remains of a Norman north doorway and a fragment of a tympanum. There is also a tub-shaped Norman font with knot frieze, zig-zag, cross and interlaced arch decoration. There is also much 13th-century wall decoration with 'feigned ashlaring, with a flower in the centre of each block, also chequerwork and two encircled crosses'; it is unusual to see such a complete example.[1]

The re-used Roman altar in the church

The main point of interest for this guide is the re-used Roman altar, inscribed with the words '*Deo Tri-(vii) Beccicus donavit ara(m)*' — it has been partly cut back to form a capital and can be found in the nave along the north wall.[2] Anderson refers to it as a stoup and suggests it originally stood at a road junction.[3] Its origin is unknown as is the age of the alteration and date when it was brought into the church, although it is one of a very few obviously pagan items which was Christianised that we have encountered in the area under study.

MOCCAS –
St. Michael & All Angels (SO 357 433)

Early monastic site reputedly founded by St. Dyfrig, with other possible early connections.

Pevsner observes that if it were not for the bellcote and the tall windows, Moccas church 'would be the perfect example of a Norman village church.'[1] It is a delight to behold, set away from Moccas village and standing in the grounds of Moccas Court. Set in pasture on slightly higher land than the surrounding area, it gives an impression of standing on a little island close to the River Wye, which flows a short distance to the north. That the site was originally marshy is suggested by the place-name which means 'swine-moor' or 'pig-marsh'.

Although founded by Dyfrig (see pp.37-45), the present dedication of St. Michael has early associations. St. Michael the Archangel appeared on the Welsh borders as a dedication in the 8th century — indeed Herefordshire has the highest density of ancient St. Michael dedications in Britain. St. Michael 'was honoured as the guardian and escort of the dying and many of his early dedications in the west are associated with cemeteries'. There are 67 Llanfihangel ('Church of St. Michael') place-names in Wales and 84 ancient dedications to St. Michael the Archangel and they are most numerous in the counties adjoining England, with Radnorshire and Monmouthshire heading the list. Fenn and Sinclair suggest that, as the cult of St. Michael was popular on both sides of the Welsh Border, there must have been some 'involvement rather than isolation' between the peoples at a time when there was traditionally hostility between the Welsh and the English.[2] He also notes that the origin of St. Michael dedications probably dates back to the second half of the 7th century when St. Chad built his refuge in honour of St. Michael at Lichfield. The saint's popularity, however, began on the Continent when he came to attention in a series of visions, the first being at Mount Gargano in Southern Italy in the 490s, and thence over a series of buildings or mountains. These visions and St. Michael's 'activities in the heavens' help to explain why many churches with St. Michael dedications are found in (comparatively) high places in Britain.[3]

In Gaul the cult of St. Michael is thought to have replaced the worship of the pagan god Mercury. The similarities in their roles make this quite possible: both were active in the heavens and both were regarded partly as the protectors of souls. Mercury was also regarded as the guardian of flocks and herds, with the hunt and chase in wooded areas 'so that a correspondence with Michael in the uplands and some other areas of Britain where a pastoral economy was practised could help to explain the uneven distribution of Michael dedications.' However Mercury can be identified with other deities, for example a pagan god called Moccus — 'pig' — occurred at Langres in Gaul and 'was equated with Mercury.'[4] Moccas in Herefordshire, originally Mochros, has a rather uncanny resemblance in spelling to Moccus. As has been noted, Moccas means a pig or swine moor, and there is the tradition that St. Dyfrig was directed by an angel to build a church where he found a white sow suckling (see p.42). Could it be that a pre-Christian deity was worshipped at Moccas which had links to Mercury/Moccus and which was Christianised through St. Dyfrig founding a monastery.

Moccas appears in the Llandaff Charters when in charters dated *c.*620 an abbot of 'Mochros' called Comereg is mentioned in relation to grants of land at Llanlowdy (Llancloudy) and Ballingham.[5] In about 625 Athrwys, King of Gwent, granted seven churches (mostly in Herefordshire) to Bishop Comereg(ius) suggesting the abbot of Moccas was now a bishop. In a procession around the land we are told 'Bishop Comeregius, with his clergy, was present, and the king carried the gospel-book on his back.'[6] Davies suggests that this may indicate that Moccas was then a bishop's house (an episcopal monastery) but suggests that no conclusion is possible and adds that the charter is a 'doubtful early record'.[7] In the *Book of Llandaff* a list of bishops is given in which Comereg(ius) is the eighth, and Doble adds that he probably continued to live in Herefordshire[8] — possibly at Moccas itself. In about 745 when King Ithel returned eleven churches to Bishop Berthwyn following the Anglo-Saxon devastation in the area, Moccas is one of those listed.[9] Bishop Comereg(ius) appears to have been the last known abbot of Moccas and in later Llandaff charters, Moccas appears simply as a church. However the following appears in the *Book of Llandaff*: 'the *locus* of Mochros on the bank of the Wye, which in the former time the blessed man Dubricius had first inhabited, was given by King Mouric to the church of Llandaff and its pastors for ever, decreed that the former *locus* should always be in subjection to the latter'. It seems then that Moccas' early significance gradually dwindled from the important monastery established by Dyfrig in the late 5th century to that of a relatively unimportant church in the post-Conquest period.

MUCH DEWCHURCH –
St. David (SO 482 311)

Charter evidence along with some faint evidence on the ground for an early site.

An abbot of Dewchurch (Guordoce/Guordocui/Gurdocoe) was mentioned in relation to two grants to different churches of *c.*620 in the Llandaff Charters under the name *Lanndeui*.[1] In *c.*625 *Lann Deui* is mentioned in a grant of churches by King Athrwys to Bishop Comereg (abbot of Moccas).[2] *Lann Deui* was also one of the eleven churches King Ithel gave back to Bishop Berthwyn in *c.*745 after the Anglo-Saxons had devastated the area.[3] Davies make the identification of *Lann Deui* with Dewchurch and gives the OS coordinates for Much Dewchurch. This was also called *Podii Deui* in the early 8th century in the *Book of Llandaff*.[4] The fact that an abbot of Dewchurch was mentioned in about 620 suggests it was a well-established monastery in the early 7th century.

The church contains some Norman architecture and the font is considered to be Norman.[5] The churchyard is shaped roughly like an irregular wide rectangle on a gentle north-south slope. There is a middle-aged yew to the north-west corner of the churchyard with wide spreading branches, and a younger-looking yew close to the porch and towards the south-east. There is a mildly raised area in front of the porch and to the left of the latter yew and a suggestion of a faint scarp running in a line east/west across the middle of the churchyard on the south side about half way down — is this part of an original boundary?

Interestingly the settlement of Dewsall (SO 486 335) lies about 1½ miles to the north. It too has a church but it is dedicated to St. Michael. In *c.*1148 Dewsall was referred to as *Fonte Dauid* ('St. David's Spring')[6] and it is believed that a well hereabouts was named after St. David, but it is no longer visible.[7]

PENCOYD – St. Dennis
(SO 517 266)

Possible early site mentioned in a charter purporting to date to *c*.555.

The church sits in the centre of the small settlement of Pencoyd in a pastoral location and is set in a squarish, small to medium-sized churchyard with some curving to the boundary's corners. On the southern, western and eastern sides the site is bounded by buildings and a lane runs in front of the northern boundary. There is a drop of between 4 to 5 feet between the level of the churchyard and the adjoining land on the north-west and northern sides. Although the churchyard is somewhat raised, it lies in a mildly undulating wider landscape. There is a middle-aged yew to the south-west corner of the tower. The church is built of slabby, rubble-coursed Old Red Sandstone which now has a greyish-pink hue.

Although on first sight the church does not have a particularly early feel, it does have a very long history. In *c*.555 the Llandaff Charters record that 'a *tellus* called Cil Hal was granted to Dyfrig by King Erb' which Davies suggests is Pencoyd. She notes that it is 'just conceivable that a genuine record lies behind this charter since the lay witness list is credible'.[1] The statement that it was given to Dyfrig does present problems, however, in that he appears to have been dead for about 10 years before the charter was given! However it is likely that it was given to his church and followers. Pencoyd's proximity to other Dyfrig churches, for example to Hentland which is about a mile due west, does support the identification of Cil Hal with Pencoyd and an early date for its establishment. The one sentence bounds given in the *Book of Llandaff* to the *c*.555 charter also supports this identification as they can fit the topography of the parish. Coplestone-Crow suggests the following translation of the bounds: 'From the great marsh as far as Arganhell' and identifies a group of houses in the north of Pencoyd parish at SO 516 274 called The Marsh. These lie close to a dried-up meander of the River Gamber which could have been the great marsh in the 6th century. He also observes that the feature called Arganhell lay south of the present church and notes that 'on the southern boundary of the parish a spring gives rise to a small brook that runs west by south into the Gamber'. As this brooks forms part of the current parish boundary for some its length he remarks that it may be the Arganhell mentioned in the charter bounds.[2]

The present dedication to St. Dennis (or Denys) is a later dedication.

PETERCHURCH – St. Peter
(SO 345 385)

Various early church sites and wells in the vicinity, with references in the Llandaff Charters.

The earliest feature of the church site is the ancient female yew estimated to be about 1,700 years old.[1] It stands almost opposite the porch and is surrounded by a low stone wall, and could have been planted by the earliest founder of the church or already have been a young tree when the church was founded.

The churchyard is quite large and irregularly shaped. It is flat and is bounded on the west by the River Dore. This latter boundary is open to the river although partly demarcated by a stone wall and there is a drop and a suggestion of embanking on the un-walled section. The churchyard is very large to the north with a much smaller area to the south and east. There is evidence of embanking along the inner northern boundary and this, and the north-western boundary, are raised by several feet above the adjoining road, reducing in height towards the church.

Pevsner describes the church as a 'very well preserved, large Norman church.'[2]

The apse and altar

Its interior is magnificent with much Norman architecture. The ceiling of the apse is night-blue on which stars are painted — quite breathtaking! On the front of the porch can be seen three carved heads, the top one depicting St. Peter, the one to the left reputedly Bishop Theophylact (the late 8th-century bishop of Todi in Italy) and that on the right King Offa of Mercia. The altar is claimed to be of Saxon date and parts of the walls and undercroft are said to have Saxon stonework. There is a legend that St. Peter (the titular saint) landed in Gwent and left his companions on the Gospel Pass near Hay-on-Wye while he came through the Golden Valley to Peterchurch where he blessed the spring (see below for St. Peter's Wells).[3] There is a coloured carving of a trout above the south door which has a gold chain around its neck, to which St. Peter is also attached by legend. He is believed to have baptised converts to Christianity in the Golden Well and 'threw into it a trout with a golden hair round its neck, which was to live there forever.' By others it is said such a trout was caught by a local fisherman in the Golden Well at Dorstone or that 'some poor monks caught it in the River Dore when they were almost starving.' Kilvert relates another version which he heard in 1876 from an old man at Peterchurch:

> They do say the Fish was first seen at Dorstone and speared there, but he got away, and they hunted him down to Peterchurch and killed him close by the church. He was so big as a salmon, and had a gold chain round his neck. They do say you can see the blood now upon the stones at Dorstone where the Fish was speared first.[4]

The above-mentioned folklore has been confused with the Golden Well at Dorstone and St. Peter's Wells at Peterchurch. The former is a small pool north-west of Dorstone at SO 308 423 which Sant believes was almost certainly considered to be a holy well as it was traditional source of the River Dore and legendary original home of the sacred trout. It is not known for certain whether the spring at the Golden Well still flows because ditches and land-drains now run into the pool, but it is about 250 yards east of a Bronze-Age standing-stone which Sant records is being used as a gate-post.[5] St. Peter's Wells (where there were formerly three springs) at Peterchurch are about ½ mile north-north-east from the church at SO 353 388 up a small lane and on higher ground. They are

St. Peter's Well, with the carved face in the recess now invisible below the mouth

to be found tucked away beside a track to the aptly named Wells Cottage. The main spring flows from a carved stone head which is supposed to depict St. Peter, but which is now scandalously concreted up to his mouth. Water that used to issue from the mouth supplied a shallow bathing pool that was used to alleviate rheumatism. There are also two eye-like holes in the stone wall above the carved head where two more springs once flowed and were used to cure eye complaints — pins used to be thrown into the holes but they have been closed up.[6] Pins were often used as offerings to wells — for example there is Crooked Well at Kington so called because a crooked pin was deemed to be a necessary offering.[7] Sant reports that an iron cross was found in the wood above St. Peter's Wells and suggests it may have come from the site of the springs 'where it would have lent a less pagan air to the place'.[8] The presence of the stone head (the head was a symbol prized in pagan Celtic religion), the reputation of the springs for healing, and the presence of an ancient yew in Peterchurch churchyard which may pre-date the earliest Christian foundation, suggests the presence of an ancient pagan cult in the vicinity which the early church would have been keen to Christianise.

The site of the church may have been mentioned in the Llandaff Charters under the name of *Mafurn*. In *c*.605 there is a record that King Cinuin gave *Mafurn* to Bishop Aidan. Although Davies makes a general identification with Valley Dore,[9] Coplestone-Crow suggests *Mafurn* may be Peterchurch. A one sentence boundary record of the 6th century exists: 'from alt rudlan [as far as] the dour'   and he suggests that 'alt rudlan' may be the hills east of Peterchurch, while the Dour could be the River Dore which runs immediately to the west of the church.[10] The land, '*podum Mafurn*', was regranted in *c*.625 by King Athrwys to Bishop Comereg

The ancient yew opposite the church porch at Peterchurch

(of Moccas) with several other sites which were described as the *territorium* of *'ecclesia Cynmarchi'* (identified with Chepstow).[11] *Mafurn* is also mentioned in grants in the 8th and 9th centuries. Although a clear association cannot be made with Peterchurch, it is likely as it is in a line of early foundations within the Golden Valley, and the above-mentioned springs and yew add circumstantial evidence for an early Christian site. The early British saint who may have founded it is lost to history.

Two other sites are listed in the Llandaff Charters which are east and north-east of Peterchurch. They are *Tir Conloc* and *Bolgros*. Both places have occasioned debate over their identity. Davies favours Madley for *Tir Conloc*. In a charter dated *c.*575 King Peibio is recorded as giving 'four *unciae* of land (at) *Conloc* to (archbishop Dyfrig).'[12] However Coplestone-Crow favours an identification with Preston on Wye as the charter boundaries locate land associated with *Tir Conloc* stretching as far as *Cum Barruc* (Dorstone), and Madley is too far east from the Golden Valley, as is the alternative suggestion of Eaton Bishop which is just east of Madley.[13] Moreover in 1086 Preston-on-Wye was referred to as *Prestretune* which means 'estate of the priests' and could recall a pre-Norman monastic settlement which may well be the 6th century *Tir Conloc* foundation.

As for *Bolgros*, the Llandaff Charters record the foundation of a church here. In about 610 'King Gwrfoddwr gave an *ager* called *Bolgros*, measuring three *unciae* to bishop Ufelfyw, who founded a church there …'.[14] The monastery of *Bolgros* must have been quite sizeable as it is recorded as having its own abbot, Iudnou (Iudon) who witnessed charters to Llanlowdy (Llancloudy), Ballingham and Chepstow between *c.*620 and 625.[15] *Bolgros* was among the eleven churches returned by King Ithel to Bishop Berthwyn in about 745 after the Anglo-Saxons had devastated this part of Herefordshire.[16] The site was perhaps at Preston-on-Wye or at Byecross (SO 375 424) immediately to the west, for *Bolgros*'s position in the Llandaff Charters is given as '… *super ripam Guy eminus Mochros*',[17] 'above the banks of the River Wye at some distance from Moccas', and the 8th-century spelling of *Bolcros* does echo today's Byecross. There is no evidence of an early Christian site in this flat arable area, though Byecross is next to the Wye in a rather exposed landscape of the type favoured for some early foundations. The other suggested site is Bellamore (SO 394 406) about a mile due west of the Wye which now comprises Upper and Lower Bellamore farms set in a fairly remote mixed farming landscape. If this is indeed the site of an early 7th-century monastery it now lies forgotten beneath the open Herefordshire fields. Evans and Rhys, without explanation, identify Bellamore with Belly-moor in Madley.[18] *Bolgros* is one of the few sites for which there is firm evidence of its foundation but for which nothing remains in the landscape — it has disappeared.

PETERSTOW – St. Peter's
(SO 563 249)

Megalithic boulders in the nave wall indicate possible early origins.

Peterstow church lies just out of the village along a narrow lane and has quite an isolated feel. The church is built from Old Red Sandstone and has a small spire. Of particular interest are the large, irregular boulders which are built into the lowest courses of the north side of the nave wall. Two are quite sizeable. It is possible that their presence indicates an early, possibly British, origin for the church. Other features that may indicate an early date are the dedication to St. Peter — and to Martin at nearby Martinstow — which may 'indicate the active presence of the cult of these two saints from early on.'[1] The dedication to apostolic saints does not always mean that an earlier British saint was superseded through the re-dedications of the Normans.

Peterstow is possibly mentioned in the Llandaff Charters. In *c.*738 there is a record that 'Mabsu gave *Uilla Iuduiu* to bishop Berthwyn; and he made over the food rent ... to him in an assembly of the better men of Erging and commended that villa to him free from all tribute'. Davies suggests that *Uilla Iuduiu* may be

The north wall of the nave showing the large irregular boulders used in the lower courses

Peterstow.[2] It is interesting that the term villa is mentioned and not the church, but it shows there was some early, important activity in this village.

The medium to large church-yard is of an approximately square shape, and has an old yew in the north-west corner which is showing the beginnings of hollowing and thus appears to be of some age. The churchyard is not raised but there is some mounding near to the church on the north side. There is a gentle east-west slope. There is also a younger middle-aged yew opposite the west end of the spire by the boundary wall. On the west the churchyard is bounded by a straight wall and adjoins pasture with no drop, whilst on the east there is a drop to the adjoining land.

ST. DEVEREUX – St. Dubricius
(SO 441 312)

Evidence from the dedication, place-name and churchyard suggest an early site.

St. Devereux is a tiny settlement less than half a mile north-west of the superb church at Kilpeck. Devereux is a Norman-French rendering of the Latin form Dubricius, and which in Welsh is Dyfrig. The church is of late 13th-century and subsequent date but, as one stands at the back of the churchyard looking towards the tower, it is clear that the present church stands on a rise within the churchyard and there is a ring of yews bordering this mound. Is this the remains of an earlier church enclosure? There is no record of the site in the Llandaff Charters and the earliest place-name evidence is from 1279 when it was called (*Ecclesie*) *Sancti Dubricii*. However Coplestone-Crow suggests the modern form of the place-name was 'probably due to [the] influence from the name of the Devereux family, who were widespread in Herefs. in medieval times'.[1] Doble remarks that, in a Kalendar of the 12th-century breviary belonging to the chapter library of Hereford, the words *Dubricii episcopi et confessoris* has 'S. deuerecke added in a later hand, on November 14', the day on which Dyfrig supposedly died. Doble considers deuerecke to be a vernacular form of Dyfrig/Dubricius and 'proves that the place in Herefordshire called St. Devereux [is] undoubtedly dedicated to Dubricius (which hitherto has been only an assumption).' The dedication of the church and the suggestion of earthworks within the churchyard do, therefore, suggest an early origin for this site. Doble even suggests that St. Devereux may be the identity of the *Lann Guruoe* (Guorboe) but this is usually identified with Garway.[2]

ST. WEONARDS – St. Weonard
(SO 496 244)

A slightly raised site mentioned in early records and with the only definite dedication to St. Weonard.

St. Weonards is about 10 miles south of Hereford and is visible for some miles away due to its hill-top location. The site is mentioned in the *Book of Llandaff* as *Lann Santguainerth*,[1] the only dedication to Gwainerth or St. Weonard, about whom information is limited. Baring-Gould and Fisher state he is 'said to have been a hermit, who sought retirement here, and was formerly represented as an old man sustaining a book and with an ox in the painted glass that adorned the north chancel window of the church.'[2] In the *Oxford Dictionary of Saints*, St. Weonard is said to have possibly been connected with St. Dyfrig but, as Annett observes, no evidence is given for this statement; local tradition has it that he was a hermit and a woodcutter. This is the only dedication to this saint in England although Annett suggests Llanwenarth near Abregavenny in Gwent might also preserve his name.[3]

 The present church is on a slightly raised site within the hill-top village and is a large medieval building. Most of the structure dates to the 14th to 15th centuries. There are later medieval features inside the church worthy of inspection: namely a cusped niche with a carved stone angel above in the north wall; a most unusual 13th century 'dug-out' chest with metal banding and iron nails hammered over the front for strength; an excellent parclose screen, and an unusual stoup in the south porch with a large carved face upon it for which no date is suggested.[4]

 The churchyard is medium-sized, of irregular but fairly curvilinear shape, and appears to have been extended more than once. To the east of the church there are several yews in a line on a low scarp of about 1½ feet in height, half way between the church and the present boundary. This may represent an earlier boundary. The churchyard is embanked with a significant drop to a farmyard on the north and western sides, and with a gentle rise up from the eastern edge to the church itself. If one stands in the field adjoining the southern side and look back towards the church, the raised nature of the enclosure is apparent.

Seventy yards south-south-west of the church, behind the telephone kiosk, is a Bronze-Age round barrow which is about 130 feet in diameter. It is very overgrown with trees and vegetation. Although not directly associated with the church, it would have been a focal point when approaching the hill, as the church is today, and was perhaps what drew the putative Gwainerth and others to establish a Christian site. The mound was excavated in 1855 and two cremation burials without grave goods were found within it, 'covered with a primary mound of earth upon which stones were heaped.' There are traces of a surrounding ditch on the eastern side.[5] The mid-19th century excavator was a Thomas Wright who described the top of the mound as being 'a rough oval' and about 76 feet across; he also describes how a 'decayed yew, of considerable age, together with other trees, adorned the hillock.' Bevan-Jones observes that yews do not appear much decayed before they reach about 20 feet in girth, and suggests an age of 700 years and 'probably more' for such a specimen. Decayed yews are reported from other burial mounds and suggests 'a deliberate planting, perhaps marking the site of an early saint cell.' It may be that this was an attempt to Christianise a prehistoric and, thus, a pagan monument. Wright recorded in 1855 that the barrow was 'until recently the scene of village fetes, especially chosen for Morris dancing', — an activity which in itself has strong pagan overtones.[6]

An illustration in The Illustrated London News *of the excavation of the barrow at St. Weonards in 1855*

SELLACK – St. Tysilio
(SO 566 277)

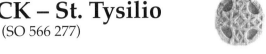

Both charter and churchyard evidence for an early site. The church has an 'out of place' dedication.

The church is set in a most attractive, tranquil rural setting with a few cottages close by and near to the River Wye. It is a handsome sandstone building with an impressive spire and an interior which, in part, dates back to the Norman period. Although St. Tysilio has several dedications in Wales, the church at Sellack in Herefordshire is a unique dedication within England.

The churchyard is a squarish-oval shape with straight and curving boundaries, all walled with sandstone. On the eastern side there is a noticeable rise in ground level running up to the chancel and the church, when viewed from this angle, does appear to be on a low platform/mound, perhaps marking the extent of the early churchyard. The present churchyard has fairly straight northern and eastern boundaries; on the western boundary a track, house and garden border it, whilst the southern boundary is adjoined by the lane. There is light curving on the churchyard's corners and the south-west boundary is curved. The northern boundary of the churchyard appears to be defined by the lower river terrace. When viewed from the river meadows between the river and the church, it can be appreciated that the churchyard is actually a few feet higher than the surrounding land.

There are middle-aged yews to the south-east and south-west of the church and a weathered, stepped cross-base with a niche to one side of the main entrance porch to the south.

Sellack in mentioned in the *Book of Llandaff* in the late 9th century under the name *Lann Suluc*.[1] Tysilio lived during the 7th century and was brother to Cynon, the King of Powys. As Annett notes the 'Ty' element of his name is a 'detachable "familiar" prefix' and the saint is also recorded as Suliau and Siloc.[2] Tysilio was primarily a saint of northern Powys and it is not clear why there is a dedication to him in southern Herefordshire, although Llancillo (north-north-east of Abergavenny) has the same dedication.[3] Doble refers to Sellack as 'evidently one of the most important monasteries in Archenfield' and that in 1742 it had three chapels: King's Caple, Pencoyd and Marstow. The *Book of Llandaff* records that in the time of Edward the Confessor (1042–66) 'Bishop Herwald consecrated *Lann Tiuoi* [Foy] and ordained in it Joseph son of Brein as priest *sub titulo Lann Suluc*', which Doble points out shows that Foy was must also have belonged to Sellack before it was given to Gloucester Abbey, this abbey inheriting 'much ancient Celtic monastic property' over time.[4]

UPTON BISHOP –
St. John the Baptist (SO 650 272)

The church houses a carved stone which may be of a very early Christian origin.

Upton Bishop is a delightful place about 3 miles north-east of Ross-on-Wye. The church of St. John the Baptist is on an elevated site slightly out of the village in a hilly, pastoral location. The church is an imposing structure with a large tower of the 14th to 15th centuries. It has an attractive interior and interesting stained glass windows. The nave is basically Norman, as is the south arcade, and the chancel was rebuilt in the early 13th century.[1]

Inside the church to the left of the south door and in a security cabinet, is a sculpture of the head and shoulders of a man in a round-headed recess with his right hand raised. There is a fragment to the left of another recess with a fragment of a raised left hand. These were once thought to have been part of a Roman tombstone.[2] It is finely carved from red sandstone and was recently moved from the external south chancel wall. Unfortunately it is difficult to see the carving with any ease because of the glare off the cabinet's glass and the somewhat excessive warnings about getting too close. An early medieval date has recently been suggested by Dr. Keith Ray for this sculpture, which has important ramifications for the presence of an early British church in the area. The way in which the right hand is raised, the formal banding of the hair, the way in

The carved figure

which toga folds are represented, and the presence of the other figure suggests it may have been part of a frieze or panel which could date from the 4th century. The manner in which the right hand and forearm are raised are considered by Ray to be very similar to figures represented in the late Roman wall paintings at Lullingstone villa in Kent. Moreover he notes the 'treatment of the palm and the thumb is identical, as is the form of the elaborate cuffs or wrist-bands.' The Lullingstone figures stand in the open-handed position — 'orans' — used by early Christians in prayer and the implication is that the Upton Bishop figure is in the same posture. Because of the fragmentary nature of the left-hand piece of the sculpture, it is impossible to say if the figure on the left is in the same posture but it is possible it may have had both hands raised, in which case it may have been at the centre of a group of three. As Ray remarks a 'high density of tripartite niched stone friezes exists in the Gloucestershire Cotswolds, and as such they are typical votive sculpture addressed to or invoking local deities. While a non-Christian votive function cannot be ruled out, a Christian frieze of this kind might after all have been a piece of funerary sculpture, or even part of a sarcophagus.'[3] He also observes that, although the classical treatment of the figure is unusual in a late Roman sculpture in such a remote country area, it is likely that the sculpture is local because of the type of stone used; indeed it is not thought that the fragment has travelled far from its original place of deposition. The proximity of Upton Bishop to the Roman and post-Roman iron-working centre of *Ariconium*, close to Weston-Under-Penyard, in an area with a strong local church community with St. Dyfrig at its head in the 5th century, would mean it was quite possible that a Christian community flourished in the vicinity of Upton Bishop, perhaps even on the site of the church itself. However, the origin and age of the sculpture is still under debate, and a date as late as the 12th century has also been suggested by another leading authority.[4]

The churchyard is walled on all sides and of moderate size, and appears to be of rectilinear/oval shape. It has a north-south sloping aspect. The northern half is probably a modern extension and this is the most rectangular part of the churchyard. There is a scarp half way up on this side with trees along it, which may indicate an earlier boundary. The churchyard adjoins arable land on the eastern and northern sides with no discernable height difference with the surrounding land; it is bounded by a lane on the western side where there is a height difference and a long but shallow curve to the boundary wall. There is about a 4 to 5 foot drop on the southern boundary with the garden orchard that adjoins it. Considering the slope, the enclosure appears to have been made as curvilinear as the topography of the site would allow.

WELSH BICKNOR –
St. Margaret (SO 592 177) &
WHITCHURCH –
St. Dubricius (SO 556 175)

Charter evidence of an early important church.

These two churches have been grouped together as there is some disagreement about whether an entry in the Llandaff Charters refers to Welsh Bicknor, Whitchurch or even the Hentland opposite Symond's Yat Rock. There are two charters referring to *Mainaur Garthbenni*, one of which probably refers to the foundation of a church in *c.*575:

> … King Peipiau son of Erb gave Mainaur Garthbenni as far as the Black Marsh between the wood and field and the water and the ferry of King Constantine his father-in-law across the River Wye unto God and Dubricius the Archbishop of the See of Llandaff, and to Iunapeius his cousin for his soul and for the writing of his name in the book of life with all its liberty, without any earthly payment and subjection small and moderate, except to God and to Saint Dubricius his servants and to the Church of Llandaff for ever.
>
> And Peipiau held the Charter upon the hand of Saint Dubricius that it might be a house of prayer and penitence and an episcopal place for ever for the Bishops of Llandaff. And in witness he consecrated the Church and left there three of his Disciples.[1]

It is unlikely that the grant was to St. Dubricius (Dyfrig) in person for he would have been long dead by 575, so it was more probably to Iunapeius, and the Dubricius element was meant in terms of his church/territory.[2] But there are doubts about aspects of the charter (see below).

Other Llandaff Charters make reference to an abbot of *Lanngarthbenni* in *c.*620 and to the church in *c.*700 and *c.*743. It is thought that the *c.*575 charter has a 'ring of unreality' about certain aspects and it likely the charter has suffered from bogus amendments when it was written into the *Book of Llandaff* in the 12th century. Certainly the insistence on the church belonging to Llandaff for ever, and the erroneous statement about Dyfrig being its archbishop (he never was) must date from this time. However Davies remarks that the substance of this charter may belong to a compilation that was possibly made at Welsh Bicknor between *c.*860 and 1000, and that an 'original brief record of Peibio's gift of *Garthbenni* to Inabwy [Iunapeius] lies behind the ninth/tenth century elaboration…'.[3]

The grant of the land was sizeable: the 'mainaur' is equivalent to a later medieval manor or estate. Several historians have tried to locate the bounds of the charter and it is generally agreed that it includes the area of land within a tight loop of the River Wye containing Huntsham Hill and Huntsham Court (SO 563 172). Although this area is liable to flooding, it has produced evidence of activity since prehistoric times, as well as a Romano-British villa which was used up until the 4th century. Huntsham Pool has been tentatively identified with the 'Black Marsh' of the charter bounds; the partly wooded slopes of Huntsham Hill may have been the 'wood', whereas the 'field' could refer to the flat lands intermittently covered by flood waters in the western half which provides fertile alluvial soils. In the early 1960s Watkins observed that when the river was in flood, the apparently flat land of the peninsula clearly appeared as two levels, with the western half under water while the eastern half was above the flood level. When the waters receded a 'series of shallow pools are left along the boundary between these two portions' which Watkins suggested may indicate the site of a former channel or artificial boundary ditch running for over 1,000 yards from Huntsham Pool to Huntsham Bridge. The 'water' of the charter bounds probably referred to the River Wye, whilst 'King Constantine's Ferry' may have referred to the ferry which probably existed since Roman times before Huntsham Bridge was built. However a ford at Whitchurch (west of the Huntsham peninsula) has also been identified. It is notoriously difficult to locate lands given in charters but, as can be seen, the Huntsham peninsula does contain most of the features mentioned in the estate of *Garthbenni*, but no church.[4]

However the church in question — known as *Lann Custenhann Garthbenni* or the Church of King Constantine at Garth Benni — might have been at Whitchurch.

The church at Whitchurch (SO 556 175) is dedicated to St. Dubricius (Dyfrig) and stands immediately next to the River Wye and out of the village centre. It is an attractive single-storey church built of Old Red Sandstone and is set in a small to medium-sized churchyard which is roughly rectangular. The church is mentioned in 1291 as '*Ecclesia de albo monasterio*' suggesting it was 'something more than a simple Parish Church'[5] and perhaps recalls

The remnant of an early pillar at Whitchurch

*The possible late pre-Norman font
at Whitchurch*

an early monastic status. However Coplestone-Crow states that the church was called *Lann Tiuinauc* in the late 11th century in the Llandaff Charters, with *Albi Monasterii* recorded in the mid-12th century. The name *Lann Tiuinauc* appears to celebrate a St. Gwynog who is also remembered at Llanwonog near Clodock; at some time before 1325 the dedication was changed to Dubricius (Dyfrig).[6] The *albi/albo* element of the later names perhaps makes reference to the whitewashing/limewashing of the medieval building which can be seen in a remnant of a pillar in the internal south wall of the chancel. The estimated date is 13th century but one wonders if it is indeed older, possibly pre-Norman? Ray suggests that the possible late pre-Norman font is indicative of a former high-status structure and believes the church may have had a multiple dedication[7] presumably to saints Gwynnog and Dyfrig. A stream bounds the northern and western sides of the churchyard, whilst there is a pronounced drop at the east end from the chancel to the Wye. The site does have a 'watery' feel, most apt for a dedication to Dyfrig whose name appears to mean 'waterling'.[8] The east wall of the chancel is very close to the Wye. Indeed the church's situation looks rather precarious and has probably worsened over the centuries as the river has cut into the bank. Any early putative remains east of the present church will have been washed away.

Hentland (SO 567 163) is another contender for St. Constantine's church of the 6th century charter. It is opposite Symond's Yat Rock, which looms on the other side of the River Wye, and, like its name-sake near Ross, means 'old church'. Although 12th-century sources refer to the church at Welsh Bicknor being St. Constantine's church, Coplestone-Crow suggests that prior to the 11th century this church was actually at Hentland in Goodrich with the 'church at Welsh Bicknor … known as 'the church of the Twelve Saints' (*Lann i doudec sent*)'.[9] When the two were combined, the site at Hentland was subsequently forgotten. Hentland sits on a peninsula of land formed by a tight loop of the Wye and on a narrow strip of land sandwiched between the Wye to the west and Coppett Hill to

Hentland, opposite Symond's Yat Rock

the east, which runs as a steep ridge northwards. Today there are farm buildings, some of which are ruined, but there is no sign of a church.

Davies and Doble identify the church of the 6th-century charter with Welsh Bicknor.[10] Welsh Bicknor is situated on the neck of another peninsula of land. Again it is sandwiched between the Wye running immediately south, and steep, wooded slopes rising at its back to the north. It is an ornate Victorian rebuild but has a rather sad, neglected feel. There is a gentle but noticeable slope rising from the river to the church. The churchyard is roughly rectangular and fairly small and is about three feet higher than the surrounding land on its southern and eastern sides. There are derelict, post-medieval looking buildings to the east of the churchyard with a disused cider press and these are most evocative. The remoteness of Welsh Bicknor and perhaps its riverside location are indications of an early site, but the present structure and shape of the churchyard are not.

Wherever the actual site of King Constantine's church, it is considered that it was a place of importance. Doble notes that the phrase *episcopalis locus* used in the 6th century charter may be a Latinzation of the Welsh *escop-ty* or 'bishop's house' which, in the 10th-century Laws of Hywel Dda, appears to mean 'an episcopal monastery with special privileges'.[11]

WINFORTON –
St. Cynidr's Hermitage (SO 295 460)

Remnants of an early hermitage dedicated to an early British saint.

St. Cynidr appears to have been remembered at the holy well west of Llowes called Fynnnon Gynydd (see under Llowes, p.158). In 1675 it is recorded by Thomas Blount that a Canon of Wormesley Priory had built a chapel on an island near the River Wye at Winforton 'called by the Inhabitants "Hermit Island"' and dedicated it to Mary and Kenedro, but that it was afterwards called St. Kendred's Chapel. Blount records that the feast of dedication was kept shortly before Christmas and the 'place where St. Kendred's Chapel stood is yet called the Chapel Close, where the foundation stones have been lately digged up, and where yet stands an Yew tree, and the place is only surrounded by the River Wey [Wye] in the Tyme of a flood.'[1] Blount appears to assume the hermitage was established by a canon from Wormesley and thus is post-Norman, but Cynidr was an early saint. Ray suggests this may have originally been a monastic site.[2] In 1898 the hermitage was described as being half a mile from the River Wye but that its site 'may still almost claim the name of island, for a deep moat, crossed by a stone bridge, protects it on the north, and in time of flood it is altogether surrounded by water. The actual remains consist of an oblong mound, artificially raised some ten feet above the level of the soil, and approached by raised causeways on the south-west and north-west. Stone crops out here and there, and from the appearance of the ground it would seem as if the building had terminated in an apse at the east end.'[3] Baring-Gould and Fisher remark that Winforton church, which is a short distance north of the hermitage and beside the A438, may have originally been dedicated to St. Cynidr although St. Michael the Archangel is the present dedication. Blount's spelling of St. Kenedro/Kendred is more easily understood when we read that St. Cynidr is probably Keneder, St. Cadoc's disciple who was part of the deputation with King Arthur at the Usk near Tredunnock (see p.62). A Cheneder is also recorded as a clerical witness 'in the Cartularly appended to the [Cadoc's] Life.'[4] (For more on St. Cynidr, see under Kenderchurch, p.274). The hermitage in the Wye would have been a most suitable spot for an early saint seeking isolation, especially in autumn and winter when the Wye can flood.

WOOLHOPE –
Lower Buckenhill
(SO 365 336)

Evidence from written records only.

Lower Buckenhill lies about 2 miles south-south-west of Woolhope. In 1535 a *capella S'c'i Dubricii* is recorded and this 'chapel of St. Dyfrig' had been referred to as 'the priour' in 1526. However Coplestone-Crow remarks that 'as far as is known the chapel did not at any time since the coming of the English in the 7th century mark the site of a religious community.'[1] However Doble suggests that it shows the 'territory of the saint formerly included both banks of the Wye'. In 1514 Bishop Mayhew 'granted an indulgence for the support of the chapel … of the Trinity at Hope Wolwith (Woolhope), commonly called Saint Dubricius' which Doble considered of great interest as it proves the continuing popular cult of Dyfrig even as late as the 16th century in Herefordshire.[2] Alas, nothing remains of an ecclesiastical structure on the site today.

Gwent

Llangua

Llanfihangel Crucorney

Llangattock Lingoed

St. Maughan's

Llanvetherine

Rockfield

ABERGAVENNY

Llantilio Crossenny

Llanelly

Llantilio Pertholey

MONMOUTH

Dixton

Llanfoist

Llanvapley

Penrhos

Wonastow

Llanarth

Dingestow

Penallt

RAGLAN

Bettws Newydd

Llandenny

Trelleck

Llangovan

Llanhilleth

Llansoy

Llandogo

USK

Llanishen

Gwernesney

Trelleck Grange

Mamhilad

Llangeview

Llangwm

Llanllowell

Kilgwrrwg

Llangibby

St. Arvans

Llandegfedd

Tredunnock

CHEPSTOW

Llanhennock

Caerleon

Caerwent

NEWPORT

Llanvaches

Caldicot

Mathern

Llanwerne

Itton

Bishton

BETTWS NEWYDD –
dedication unknown (SO 363 058)

One of the oldest yews in Britain is in the churchyard.

Bettws Newydd is a most attractive small village about 6 miles south-east of Abergavenny. Diane Brook lists Aeddan as a possible dedication,[1] a name also mentioned on the main church board against 'dedication unknown'. Baring-Gould and Fisher list Aeddan as Aidan, of which there are two saints of the same name: St. Aidan of Ferns, son of Gildas or of Caw, and St. Aidan of *Mavurn* who is styled bishop and confessor. The latter was a disciple of St. Dyfrig, was with him at Hentland and was later consecrated bishop. He was granted *Mavurn* (also spelled *Mafurn*) in the Dore Valley in Herefordshire by a King Cinuin, the son of Peipiau (Dyfrig's reputed grandfather). Of the two Aidans, it seems more likely that the patron of Bettws Newydd was Aidan of *Mavurn* who was broadly based in the area. It may have been he, under the name Maidoc, who was amongst the deputation that intervened in the dispute over Cadoc providing sanctuary for seven years to a man who had murdered three of King Arthur's followers (see p.62).[2] Very little else is known of Aidan of *Mavurn*, and there is no reference, alas, for his involvement with the church at Bettws Newydd.

Early documentary evidence for the site is also scant, the first reference being in 1188. However the churchyard boundaries are largely curved and partly earth-banked, suggestive of an early origin. Brook notes that a feature of curvilinear churchyards in Gwent is an 'earth-banked, hedge-topped boundary, or one with a stone wall on one or more sides and an earth bank on the remaining sides.' She also notes the early status of some churchyards with earthen banks and suggests that these may be an early feature in Gwent and possibly connected with the construction of curvilinear enclosures.[3] The churchyard at Bettws Newydd has a low earthen bank visible on the southern boundary which is topped by a grown-out deciduous hedge, while the northern and eastern sides have stone walls. There is a small drop in height to the adjoining field on the southern side and a noticeable ridge running across the field in a curve — it is possible that this is a natural feature but it may well be a man-made earthwork, perhaps related to the church. The enclosure is large in relation to the present church and would have been of sufficient size to accommodate further buildings.

The church is a delight, quite small but, as Newman remarks, 'There is no preparation for the spectacular survival inside of rood screen, loft and tympanum, perhaps the most complete rood arrangement remaining in any church in England and Wales.' The carving to the front is detailed and spectacular. There is also an 'unusually fine' Norman font which is a simple basin design sitting on a 15th-

The ancient yew in the churchyard

century shaft and base. In 1952 the foundations of an earlier eastern wall were found about 20 feet east of the present wall; and, in the inner face of the west wall, there are 'traces of an earlier, steeper roof'.[4] These could be the outline remains of an early Norman, or pre-Norman church.

Probably the most remarkable survival at Bettws Newydd is the spectacularly old female yew to the north-west of the church. It had a measured girth of 30 feet 6 inches in 1876. Bevan-Jones gives a girth of 31 feet while Chetan and Brueton give a measurement of 33 feet and an estimated age of 4,000 years. Even if this age was halved to be conservative, it suggests the tree predates the advent of Christianity. What is truly extraordinary about this yew is that there is another yew growing up within the remains of the ancient trunk; in 1998 its girth was measured at 7½ feet with the measurement taken 3 feet from the ground. This 'second' tree is the result of an internal root sent down by the ancient tree inside its old rotting trunk. As Bevan-Jones notes, this transition of growth to the root can slow the growth rate of the girth down, and gradually return a hollowed yew to solidity by reducing the need for it to increase its girth.[5] Such regeneration ensures the continuation of what may appear an impossibly old tree. On the eastern side of the churchyard, and just away from the south-east end of the chancel, is another ancient-looking yew with a considerable girth. It has some evidence of hollowing, although not as dramatic as its north-western counterpart. However it still looks of great age and has a hefty bulk. The presence of north-west and south-east orientated yews of such antiquity raises the question of whether these were deliberate east/west Celtic plantings with, perhaps, pre-Christian overtones of the observance of sunrise and sunset.

BISHTON – St. Cadwaladr
(ST 386 874)

The church site dates back to about 710 and retains its dedication to an early 7th-century British king.

The church of St. Cadwaladr is about 2½ miles east of the outskirts of Newport. To the immediate south lies the main Cardiff to Bristol railway line and the enormous Newport steel works which extend for over 3 miles east to west. With the steel works only 100 yards away and the railway line even closer it is something of a miracle that this church, first mentioned in *c.*710, survives.

The present church has fabric dating back to the 14th century, with 15th-century remodelling and later repairs — one of which was necessary in 1760 when part of the tower fell through the nave![1] The tower is tall and slender with a gothic appearance and seems rather large for the remaining structure.

The church enclosure is curvilinear to the south and south-western boundaries but the other sides are straighter. They are partly embanked. The churchyard may have been extended on the northern side, but nothing obviously indicates any earlier boundaries. There is no significant difference in height between the churchyard and the surrounding land.

The patron saint is St. Cadwaladr, son of Cadwallon, who was the last of the Welsh princes to assume the title of chief sovereign of Britain. His father had been defeated by King Edwin of Northumbria and had fled to Ireland but returned and, allied with King Penda of Mercia, defeated Edwin at Heathfield in 633. Edwin's successor, Oswald of Northumbria, killed Cadwallon at Heaven's Field near Hexham in 634 or 635, and the British forces withdrew west of the River Severn, never to regain control to the east. Cadwaladr was not as successful a soldier as his father and it is said he 'was of an amiable and peaceable disposition, more disposed to frequent churches than camps'. He fought a substantial battle against the West Saxons at Peonne in Somerset in 658, but was badly defeated.[2]

However, in the *Welsh Triads* it is said that Cadwaladr hit Golyddan the Bard on the head with an axe because the bard had boxed his ears — the famous Celtic temper again! The *Triads* also state that Cadwaladr was one of the three sovereigns of Britain who wore gold bands, an insignia of supreme power, and that he was one of Britain's 'three Blessed Sovereigns', on account of the protection that he afforded to 'the faithful who fled from the faithless Saxons and the foreigners.' He is sometimes confused with his grandson, Ceadwalla, who murdered the population of the Isle of Wight and is described by Baring-Gould and Fisher as 'an atrocious ruffian'; but Cadwaladr had died 24 years before Ceadwalla in 664 of the plague which had swept through Britain. Apart from his dedication at Bishton, he was originally patron of Magor (8 miles south-west of Chepstow) and of Michaelston-y-Vedw, 5 miles south-west of Newport. There is a Llangadwaladr church in Denbighshire/Clywd near Llansilin and another in Anglesey 2 miles east of Aberffraw where the kings of Gwynedd lived. Among the 'Sayings of the Wise' the following is attributed to Cadwaladr: 'The best crooked thing is the crooked handle of a plough.' Rather like King Arthur, Cadwaladr was long expected to lead the 'Brythons to victory, to asset the ancient rights of his family … and to restore to them their rightful 'crown and sovereignty" which is somewhat surprising considering his supposed ineffectiveness as a war leader.[3]

There is an early charter, dated c.710, in which 'Gwyddnerth gave *Lann Catgualatyr* with all its *tellus* [property/land] and woodland and shore rights to bishop Berthwyn.' This was apparently given as penance for Gwyddnerth murdering his own brother. The record of the grant is thought to be correct, but the identity of the recipient of the original grant is uncertain. It has a long narrative of the murder of Gwyddnerth's brother and the former's 'subsequent pilgrimage to Brittany and eventual return and pardon,' and Davies suggests it may represent a genuine tradition.[4] The bounds for the charter survive and begin with 'From Aber Nant Alun into the marsh as the brook leads upwards to its source.' It subsequently makes mention of a wood on 'the ridge of the Allt near Cestill Dinan' on which Evans and Rhys suggest may be Bishton Castle, the remains of which are to the north-north-east of the church at ST 392 882. As castles were a 11th-century phenomena, perhaps Cestill Dinan referred to an earlier fortification, or is this an anachronism which suggests the bounds were transcribed in the 12th century? The 'spring of the Glyblè' is also mentioned, as are the macabre 'Dead Pools' which probably referred to stagnant, brackish water.[5] Several references are made to marshland which demonstrates the low-lying nature of the land which is close to the mouth of the River Severn.

There is a charter of c.862 for the grant of *Uilla Guliple Minor,* which was near Bishton, by Eli to Bishop Cerennyr which contains a suspicious and verbose narrative of Eli's enmity and murder of one Camog and his subsequent penance.[6] There is also grant of c.900 in which 'March ap Peibio gave and returned *Uilla Cyuiu*, an *ager* of three *modii*, and part of the *territorium* of *Merthir Teudiric*, to bishop Cyfeilliog, having been pardoned for killing his cousin Beorhtwulf' — the land granted was near Bishton. It is interesting how all three grants relating to Bishton were a result of the donor killing a close relative and undergoing penance for it. Were people more badly behaved in this area, or more likely is it that this is an unusual survival of the records?

It may then come as a surprise that this church, so close to the disturbance and visual intrusion of modern industry has such a long and secure history — it is a case of look one way and you can sense the early history, look the other and your senses are overwhelmed by the modern era.

CAERLEON – St. Cadoc
(ST 339 906)

The site of the early martyrdom of Julius and Aaron, and evidence for a very early Christian community.

The church of St. Cadoc lies in the centre of the small Roman town of Caerleon. It is close to the famous Roman remains and the well-known amphitheatre, which command a visit in their own right.

The church lies within a medium-sized churchyard, which being a town centre site, has undoubtedly been subject to many changes throughout the centuries, and therefore has few signs of an early origin. However, as the site lies within the area of the Roman fort, it is probably of Roman or immediate post-Roman date. Brook proposes two scenarios: either town life had 'decayed completely' and there were areas in the former town which were free for new buildings and for burying the dead, or that a population, which was now Christian, remained and built churches even if the size of the town had reduced.[1]

The current church has a Norman nave with remnants of Romanesque arches in tufa visible at the back of the nave from the north aisle, and a 13th-century south-west tower.[2] Roman tile appears to have been reused in the lower stages of the tower, visible on the outside. There are stained glass windows behind the altar which depict St. Cadoc, to whom the church is dedicated, and his father, amongst other saints. However, one of Gwent's rare early Christian monuments was dug up in the churchyard in the mid-19th century.

The dedication to St. Cadoc falls within the expected area of his dedications, and, in a town with such an ancient background, it is likely that it is an early foundation. However it is considered by some that the early patron of the church was St. Cadfrawd who is styled bishop and who, it is surmised, is the same person as Adelfius, who was present at the Council of Arles in 314. Baring-Gould and Fisher warn however there is no evidence that St. Cadfrawd came from Caerleon; indeed they think it more likely that he was bishop of Lincoln.[3] But if Cadfrawd was bishop of the area of Caerleon and if the present parish church was once dedicated to him, it would make the site a very early foundation indeed. The town does have a late Roman connection with Christianity as two of the earliest Christian martyrs were executed here, the saints Julius and Aaron. They are believed to have been near contemporaries of St. Alban and probably lived in the early 4th century (see pp.2-4).

There is a charter in the *Book of Llandaff* dated to *c.*864 in which the '... sons of Beli, gave the whole *territorium* of the martyrs Julius and Aaron, with its weirs and shore rights, which had previously belonged to Dyfrig, to bishop Nudd'.[4] The bounds include a reference to a dyke, Nant Merthyr and the River Usk, but nothing to help with a ready identification of the area. Although Evans and Rhys state that the 'Merthir Julii & Aaron' refers to St. Julien's near Chepstow, Baring-Gould and Fisher and Davies consider — and we can only agree — that it refers to the neighbourhood of Caerleon.[5] The sites of the earliest dedications to these Romano-British martyrs was known in folk memory as late as the 16th century to have consisted of two chapels, one on the east and one to the west of Caerleon; they were dedicated to each saint and were about two miles apart. One of these was St. Julian's which by the early 20th century was a farmhouse but had been a mansion which is said to have occupied the site of St. Julian's Church. However we are also told that 'soon after the Norman Conquest there was a church in Caerleon itself dedicated to Julius and Aaron, which was granted by Robert de Chandos to the Priory of Goldcliff, founded by him in 1113.'[6]

On his visit to Caerleon, the late 12th-century writer Giraldus Cambrensis tells us that Julius and Aaron were buried in the city and 'next to Albanus and Amphibalus, they were the most famous protomartyrs of Great Britain'. He also says that 'in former times there were three fine churches in Caerleon. The first was named after Julius the martyr: this was graced by a choir of nuns … The second was founded in the name of Saint Aaron, his comrade: this was noted for its distinguished chapter of canons. The third was famed far and wide as the metropolitan church for the whole of Wales.' This was written between 1136–9. If there is any element of accuracy in the statement (and we must discount that the church was metropolitan), it shows there was another church in Caerleon prior to that founded in 1113. Giraldus also states that Amphibalus, who taught St. Alban (the earliest British martyr), was born at Caerleon which he describes as 'beautifully situated on the bank of the River Usk. When the tide comes in, ships sail right up to the city. It is surrounded by woods and meadows.'[7] In the earlier 16th century Leland adds that there was only one parish church 'and that is of St. Cadocus.'[8]

Caerleon is quite a remarkable place with its rich Roman past much in evidence. The smell of the sea can be caught on the river reached by narrow medieval-looking streets.

The remains of the Roman amphitheatre

CAERWENT – St. Stephen and St. Tathan (ST 468 905)

Caerwent was the site of a monastery reputedly founded by St. Tathan in the 6th century of which there is some documentary and archaeological evidence.

Lying in the centre of the small Roman town of Caerwent is the medieval church of St. Stephen and St. Tathan. St. Tathan trained St. Cadoc at the monastic college at Caerwent of which he was principal. Tathan's *Life* states that he was the son of an Irish king, but later Welsh saintly pedigrees in the Iolo Manuscripts make him the grandson of Meurig ab Tewdrig, king of Morganwg, which would make him the nephew of St. Illtud and brother of St. Samson. However Baring-Gould and Fisher observe that if Tathan was St. Cadoc's teacher he would have had to have been a generation older than Samson, thus an Irish origin seems more likely. Tathan's *Life* states that he was given up by his parents to be educated in the religious profession but Baring-Gould and Fisher think this is unlikely as his *Life* also describes him as an only son. Nevertheless the story goes that Tathan was directed by an angel to leave Ireland and cross to Britain, a command he obeyed, taking with him eight disciples in 'a sorry boat without tacking' and sailed without oar or sail, directed only by the wind until they landed on the coast of Gwent, probably at Portskewett. King Caradog of Gwent heard of Tathan's arrival and invited him to a meeting which Tathan refused. Undeterred Caradog, with 24 of his knights, went to see him and invited Tathan and his monks to found a monastic school at Caerwent, an offer that Tathan accepted. Caradog gave him a piece of land near to the town, extending from the Via Julia (high road) to the Neddern Brook. Here Tathan founded a 'collegiate church in honour of the Holy and Undivided Trinity and placed therein twelve canons.' It was at this church that Tathan buried the body of the virgin martyr Machuta in the floor of the church (see Llanvaches, p.366).[1]

Tathan was given a cow to supply milk for himself and his monks by a nobleman who wanted one of his ten sons to have a religious training. This cow was famed for its milk production and some of King Caradog's men turned 47 horses into Tathan's meadow in order to spoil the hay crop for the cow. The horses were struck dead as a punishment, but when Caradog apologised for his men's 'wicked act' in person to the saint, all the horses were restored to life. The cow was subsequently stolen by Gwynllyw's men on the night of St. Cadoc's birth (Gwynllyw was St. Cadoc's father and had a stronghold nearby). Sometime later King Caradog left Caerwent and 'built a palace on the banks of the Severn' possibly at Caldicot, a couple of miles to the south, and 'bestowed the city of Caerwent and the adjoining territory upon Tathan "for a perpetual inheritance".' It was here that Tathan established a monastic school amongst whose illustrious pupils were St. Cadoc and probably St. Beuno. We are told that when Tathan died he was laid to rest in the floor of Caerwent church and that 'his seven disciples that were with him clave [clung] unto their master's tomb.'[2] Tathan's college was still running in the 11th century.

A somewhat different account of Tathan is given in late documents in the Iolo Manuscripts. In this it states that Tathan was a saint of Bangor Illtyd and that he founded the church of Llandathan in Glamorgan and then visited King Ynyr Gwent to 'promote a Bangor at Caerwent, where he became principal' and Ynyr Gwent's confessor. The documents record that the monastic school at Caerwent had 500 saints, as did his establishment at Llandathan. Elsewhere they note that 'S. Tathan, of Ewyasland [largely south-west Herefordshire], founded Llandathan; and he had there a small Côr [monastery] of forty learned saints.' Baring-Gould and Fisher identify Llandathan with St. Athan's, 3 miles east of Llantwit Major, but remark that it is not dedicated to St. Tathan but to an otherwise unknown female saint Tathana.[3]

It is considered that St. Tathan was the original patron of Caerwent church, a dedication he now shares with St. Stephen. However he does not appear to have had a wide cult — his only other dedication is the now extinct Llanfeithin in Llancarfan parish, near to St. Cadoc's monastery. St. Tathan's festival is on 26 December, the same day as St. Stephen's, but occurs in a very few calendars.[4]

There are several charters in the *Book of Llandaff* which mention Caerwent. The earliest appears to be in 955 when it was the site of a meeting to settle a dispute concerning the murder of a peasant by a deacon and of the latter's sanctuary at St. Arvans (see p.383).[5] Caerwent is mentioned under its names of

Guentonia urbs/urbis and *Guenti urbis*, and an abbot is noted[6] as well as a 'lector *urbis Guenti*'[7] (a lector is a member of a monastery appointed to read aloud during meals). Given the tradition of Caerwent as a monastic school, it would have needed no introduction.

Caerwent Vicarage, with its 28-acre glebe, corresponds to the area given by Caradog in Tathan's *Life*. In 1911 the Vicarage orchard, just outside the eastern gateway of the Roman town, was investigated archaeologically as it was thought to cover the site of Tathan's college. The excavation revealed mainly Roman masonry but over 12 skeletons were uncovered lying in an east/west orientation. One was enclosed in a 'somewhat rude coffin of stone slabs, or cist' and was thought to be the remains of St. Tathan. With this possibility it was transferred to the church and re-interred in the floor of the south aisle in April 1912, on which a slab with a Latin inscription was placed.[8] The Vicarage orchard is now under modern housing.

Five samples were taken for radio-carbon dating from post-Roman graves outside the east gate and these gave dates which ranged from the 5th to the 8th centuries. Two skeletons from burials around the church and within the town were also radio-carbon dated and produced dates in the 6th and 7th centuries. Another burial was also dated to the 8th century from an area north of the churchyard. As Brook remarks, from this limited evidence it appears that burial within a churchyard was 'not the only acceptable rite in early pre-Norman Gwent'.[9] It also suggests a flourishing population in Caerwent in the early medieval period for such burials are usually quite elusive.

In August 1992 a pre-Norman disc cross-head was discovered in the up-cast of a newly dug grave to the south-east of the church which probably dates to the 10th or 11th centuries. Made from Sudbrook stone, the fragment appears to come from a free-standing cross indicating 'that the earlier *clas* or *monasterium* lay in the

*A fragment of a pre-Norman free-standing cross found when a grave was dug,
now housed in the church*

323

vicinity of the present church.' The oldest part of the present church, however, is the chancel which is 13th century. The church also houses Roman carved and inscribed stones and these include an inscribed statue base in the porch which dates to shortly before A.D. 220 and records a commander-in-chief of the Second Augustan Legion based at Caerleon. It was found near to the modern war memorial in the town centre. Within the porch, and in an alcove, is a Roman altar a few feet tall and made of yellow limestone. It is wider at the top and base with carved horizontal mouldings, and a translation of the Latin inscription in the middle reads 'To the God Mars Ocelus Aelius Augustinus Optio [a junior officer] Paid his vow willingly and duly'. In the south aisle is a section of mosaic flooring,

and also the supposed grave of St. Tathan. Built into the walls of the south aisle are pieces of carved Roman masonry and an ancient consecration cross. There is also a Roman cinerary urn behind a glass front in a niche in the west wall which contains cremated human remains.[10]

The churchyard at St. Tathan's does not strike one as being of obvious early medieval origin. It is quite flat and of a quadrangular shape and is raised by only a small amount above the surrounding area. The enclosure is, however, quite large and could have accommodated other buildings. There are undulations within the churchyard, but none which may be easily interpreted; interestingly the church stands on a slight rise when viewed from the south — could this be formed from the remains of an earlier church? The existence of a pre-Norman monastery, possibly dating back to the post-Roman era, is fairly certain and shows that not all early Christian sites accord with the popular image of a raised and circular enclosure. Of all the sites covered in this guide, Caerwent is amongst the few that can be positively identified as belonging to the early medieval period through documents and archaeological investigation.

The Roman altar
now housed in the porch

CALDICOT – St. Mary
(ST 484 887)

A *c*.895 charter refers to two churches, one associated with a castle, and presents a glimpse of everyday life in Caldicot in the late 9th century.

The church of St. Mary is at the centre of the recently expanded village, 2 miles south-east of Caerwent, and 5 miles south-west of Chepstow. The churchyard and church are large in comparison with many rural churches. The church has a Norman central tower, a 14th-century chancel and nave, and a 15th- or 16th-century porch, north aisle and upper tower stage.[1]

The churchyard is irregular in shape, and ascertaining the original boundaries is difficult, if not impossible. The enclosure is certainly raised above ground level to the sides adjoining roadways and there is a perceptible rise of ground — a faint platform even — on which the church stands. There is some noticeable embanking on the inside of the eastern boundary, but it is too crisp for an old boundary. There is less crisp embanking on the western side, so perhaps that on the east has simply been reworked.

A *c*.895 charter refers to Caldicot in which 'King Brochfael ap Meurig gave two churches, *ecclesia Castell Conscuit* and *ecclesia Brigidae*, both with six *modii* of land, together with free landing rights for ships at the mouth of the [River] Troggy, and with their weirs, to bishop Cyfeilliog' — Davies remarks that the bounds include the rights of shipwreck.[2] Evans and Rhys state that '*Castell Conscuit*' and

'*Ecclesia Sant Breit (Brigidae)*' are translated as 'Caldicott Castle' and 'Church of St. Breit',[3] perhaps the original church patron but who is otherwise unknown. Brook observes that the early status of the present St. Mary's was as a church[4] and does not appear to have had monastic use. The church and castle seem to be linked in this late 9th-century charter, possibly in the same way that chapel and castle were linked in the later medieval period. It is also interesting that mention is made of two churches, which adds some weight to the theory that one was connected solely with the castle. Newman considers that the earliest phase for the present, important castle at Caldicot was an earthen example built in the late 11th to early 12th century;[5] therefore the one in the late 9th century was possibly on a different site and unconnected. One wonders if the mention of the castle means that the charter was actually concocted after the Norman invasion — or more likely that there some fortification present in the late 800s? The charter bounds regarding Caldicot are worth quoting in part, for their evocation of the 9th-century scene around the town:

> From the Crug to the boundary cairns of Trev Peren. From cairn to cairn downwards to the sea. Along the Severn Sea with its wears and windings with a free mooring for ships at the mouth of the Troggy where the boundary began.[6]

DINGESTOW – St. Dingad
(SO 457 104)

A late 9th-century charter applies to this site and it is dedicated to an early British saint. The churchyard is also slightly raised and curvilinear.

Dingestow church is about 4½ miles south-west of Monmouth, at the northern end of the village, and just south of the site of Dingestow castle. It is on the banks of the River Trothy and adjoins a large caravan park.

The saint of the dedication is unclear, for there are two St. Dingads. St. Dingad ab Brychan, son of Brychan, is described as father of Pasgen and Cyblider in one manuscript, but then Cyblider is listed as son of Brychan in another, and Pasgen as Brychan's son elsewhere! What can be said is that this Dingad was related to Brychan. In one document he is said to be the patron of Llandovery, known as Llandingat, and later sources describe him as lord of the area of Dingestow, and Bryn Buga (the town of Usk). The Breconshire herald, Hugh Thomas (d.1714), states that Dingad was probably buried at Llandovery and that his feast day is 1 November.[1]

St. Dingad ab Nudd Hael is said in some medieval sources to be of the race of Maxen Wledig, an ancient Welsh line, and to be the father of five children, two of whom were the saints Tegwy and Tyfriog.[2] In another manuscript he is said to have been king of Bryn Buga (Usk) and to have had 12 children, who all served God. In the Iolo Manuscripts however the children are said to be those of

Nudd, not of Dingad to which are added three more; they are said to have been saints of Llancarfan and to have subsequently accompanied St. Dyfrig to Bardsey. However Dingad is still said to be king of Bryn Buga and patron of Llanddingad or Llaningad, otherwise known as Dingestow. Either of the two could be the patron of Dingestow, although Baring-Gould and Fisher suggest it is more likely Dingad ab Nudd Hael is the patron.[3]

Dingestow is referred to as *merthir dincat/dingad* in 1119, although its earliest reference is in a charter for *c.*872 where it is called '*ecclesia Dingad*'[4] which works against this being an early merthyr, or martyr, church. Indeed there is no reference to either St. Dingad suffering martyrdom.[5]

The *c.*872 charter in the *Book of Llandaff* records that 'Tudfab gave *ecclesia Dincat*, with three *modii* of land, to bishop Nudd, for the soul of his father Paul, with king Hywel's guarantee.'[6] The bounds to this charter make an interesting reference to Ffynnon y Clevjon — 'the well of the sick' — which is perhaps an early reference to a healing well.[7]

The tower is of 1846 and the church structure was restored in 1887–8. The south wall looks older but the restoration replicated the late medieval arrangements for lighting the rood loft.[8]

The churchyard boundaries are largely curved and the enclosure is quite small. The boundaries are embanked in places and the enclosure is partly raised, suggestive of an early site.

DIXTON – St. Peter
(SO 519 136)

The possible site of an early monastery.

This most attractive church is about two-thirds of a mile north-east of Monmouth town centre, on the very edge of the west bank of the Wye. The tower and chancel are of late 13th-century date, the nave is probably earlier and is described as being disproportionately long. There is an exposed section of herringbone masonry low down in the north wall of the nave, which is given a probable date of the late 11th century although it could be earlier. In 1397 the church was described as being 'intolerably dark', and subsequently more windows were added.[1]

The medium-sized churchyard is of quadrangular shape[2] and there is a very faint hint of a scarp to the south of the church, which may indicate an earlier, curvilinear boundary.

Of the dedication, the Welsh name for the church is Llandidwg and in the 730s Dixton was called *Henlann Titiuc* or *Lann Tidiuc*[3] which identifies the original saint as St. Tydiwg. In one source he is mentioned as a descendent of Cunedda but little else is known about him. His name was Latinized to Tadeocus in a grant of Tadinton to Monmouth Priory after 1134, where one of the lay witnesses was a Johannes de Sancto Tadeoco, Sancto Tadeoco being identified with Dixton.[4]

In the *Book of Llandaff* there are two grants relating to the site. In a charter of *c.*735 'Ithel gave *podium Hennlann*, glossed i. eccl'a Tituuc sc'i, with land of four *modii* around it and its weirs, to bishop Berthwyn, for the soul of his son Athrwys.'[5] The site is also referred to as '*dehennlann titiuc*'[6] under a charter of *c.*866, where 'Abraham gave *Uilla Branuc*, with two *modii* of land, to bishop Nudd, and with it he gave the monks' field beside the arable, at the influx of the Gamber ... and his ploughs/ploughlands ... there,'[7] which appears to deal with land above Llangarron and the reference to Dixton appears to be part of the witness list.

Brook notes that the early status of the site was as a monastery.[8] Davies mentions Dixton as one of the few examples where fishing rights were mentioned in charters in the early 8th century.[9] It is a site that merits further investigation, especially as the church was described as 'old' (*Hennlann*) in the 730s!

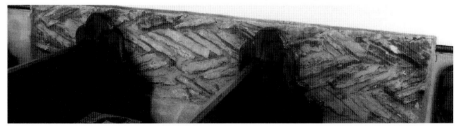

The exposed section of herringbone masonry in the nave

GWERNESNEY – St. Michael and All Angels (SO 415 018)

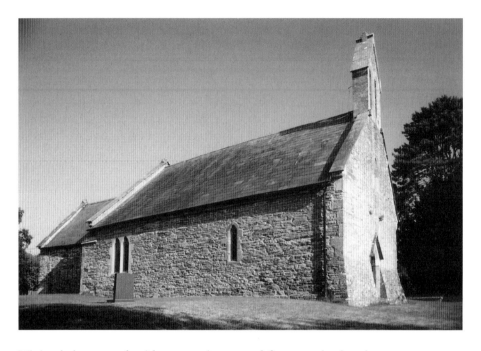

Minimal charter and evidence on the ground for an early church.

This 13th- and 14th-century Old Red Sandstone coursed-rubble church is built on a slightly elevated site. It has an interesting medieval interior with an imposing chancel arch and a wooden screen in the western end. The northern boundary of the roughly rectangular churchyard is slightly raised and embanked. Some of the other boundaries are also embanked and, in places, partly curved, such features being signs of early foundations in Gwent (see under Bettws Newydd, p.315). It has been suggested that Gwernesney may be the *Lanngverntivauc* (also spelt *Lann Guern Tiuauc/Timauc*) in a charter of about 970, although Davies appears to make the identification with Llanwern.[1] An examination of the bounds of *Lann Guern Timauc* by Evans and Rhys has favoured an identification with Llanwern, whilst not ruling out Gwernesney[2] which only proves how difficult an identification can be when there is so little to go on. If the document does refer to Gwernesney, then the site must be significantly older than the mid-10th century as the church was being returned to the bishop. As for the church's foundation date and the saint to whom it was originally dedicated, these are unknown. The present dedication to St. Michael may be original but the name in the charter suggests otherwise.

ITTON – St. Deiniol
(ST 493 953)

Mentioned in the mid-9th century and purportedly founded by the 6th-century St. Deiniol.

Itton is about 3 miles north-west of Chepstow. St. Deiniol was the son of an abbot, had two brothers who were also saints and was the father of St. Deiniolen. The paternal family lands were lost in North Britain, and they moved to Wales where they were given land by King Cyngen of Powys. Deiniol's father set up the monastery at Bangor Iscoed (Bangor-on-Dee). Deiniol and his brothers are said in the Iolo Manuscripts to have trained under St. Cadoc at Llancarfan, and were then sent to run their father's establishment and did so very effectively. Deiniol then went on to found Bangor in Caernarvonshire with the help of the king, Maelgwn Gwynedd, who is said to have raised it to an episcopal see coterminous with the kingdom of Gwynedd. Deiniol spent the rest of his life there as abbot and bishop, and was succeeded by his son. He was reportedly buried at Bardsey after his death in about 584.[1]

St. Deiniol must also have travelled about, because he was present at the Synod of Llanddewi Brefi in approximately 545, and it was he and St. Dyfrig who went to St. David's to persuade David to attend the synod. Deiniol had a great cult following in North Wales, which has most the churches dedicated to him, with other surviving or subsequently replaced dedications in Herefordshire, Cardiganshire, here at Itton in Monmouthshire, as well as several churches in Brittany.

There is a charter relating to Itton in the *Book of Llandaff* where it was granted, along with six other churches and their lands, to Bishop Grecielis. The charter is reasonably early, as Grecielis' dates as bishop were *c*.850–860, and it has 'no suspicious elements'.[2] In the charter the church is referred to as *Lanndiniul*[3] and as '*ecclesia Diniul*'.[4] As the church was being given to the bishop in about 860 it implies an earlier foundation. Bounds exist for this church and its land which amount to about 900 acres.[5]

The present church was heavily restored in 1869. Parts of the fabric, namely the tower and chancel arches, are of early 14th-century date and the porch has a probable Tudor arch, otherwise the structure is of later date.[6] Information at the church states that this is the third church on the site and that in 1133 it was listed as belonging to the see of Llandaff.

The churchyard's shape is polygonal and the enclosure moderately elevated above the road. From the proportions of the enclosure, it appears to have been extended to the north. Minor undulations exist within the churchyard, but not so clearly as to suggest earlier boundaries.

There is part of a cross-shaft to the south of the church about four feet tall and of an unusual quatrefoil design. No date is suggested in sources, but it appears to be medieval.

KILGWRRWG – Holy Cross
(ST 463 985)

Possible early 8th-century site, with a probable early cross and carved head.

Kilgwrrwg is the most perfect example of an early Christian site. It is a difficult place to find if unfamiliar with the area — but what a gem when discovered! Using OS Explorer OL14, take the right-hand no-through lane off the B4293 just south of Devauden which is shown leading to Kilgwrrwg Common. Follow this lane until it reaches a private metalled road. From there walk down this road which descends steeply. After about ½ mile the road runs out opposite a private driveway. Bear right through the bottom of a garden and follow the mown, grassy track and look for a gated, wooden footbridge over a stream on your left. Cross this and to your right look for the circular cluster of trees on top of the hill crest. The church is in the midst of this.

The church is built from rubble-coursed Old Red Sandstone. In the early 19th century the building was used for housing sheep during inclement winter weather; they were shooed out and the church swept in readiness for the Sunday service. The church is small and utterly charming, as is the churchyard which has a ring of deciduous trees around the boundary. There is some embanking on the inner side of the walls and most of the space in this small enclosure is on the northern and southern sides. Brook describes the churchyard as partly curved and notes the presence of possible earthworks to the south which are visible from aerial photographs.[1]

On the southern side, offset and opposite the porch, is a short-armed plain monolithic cross on a relatively tall shaft. Its plainness militates against precise

The crudely-carved head on the west wall

The short-armed cross in the churchyard

dating, but it is possibly pre-Norman. On the west wall is a blocked-up, round-headed doorway of Norman appearance, over which is set a rather crudely carved head. The amount of weathering and the early style of carving indicates it may also belong to the pre-Norman period. We have seen two carved heads of similar style at Hope Bagot church in southern Shropshire which have been deemed to be of Iron-Age pagan date — might the example at Kilgwrrwg be of the same era?

Davies observes that Kilgwrrwg may be the place named in the Llandaff Charters in a grant dated to *c.*722 in which 'King Ithel and his sons Ffernfael and Meurig gave three *unciae*' to Bishop Berthwyn.[2] Brook notes that the prefix Kil- is first mentioned with regard to Kilgwrrwg in 1254 and is derived from the Welsh '*cil*' which means 'retreat' or 'corner'. In fact the use of 'cil' place-names in the Llandaff Charters imply that they originated in the pre-Norman period and also during the Norman period as secular place-names. On occasion this element was applied to religious sites, for example at Kilpeck in Herefordshire which was earlier called *Lann degui cilpedec.*[3]

LLANARTH – St. Teilo
(SO 375 108)

An ancient yew, and charter evidence for a church or monastery dating back to
A.D. 600

Llanarth is about 5 miles south-east of Abergavenny and the church is at the
southern end of the village. It was at Llanarth that King Iddon found St. Teilo
in prayer when he needed him to pray for his success against the Anglo-Saxons
(see entry Llantilio Crossenny, p.363). The church's early status is considered to
have been monastic.[1] There is a charter in the *Book of Llandaff* dated to *c*.600 in
which 'King Iddon gave *Lanngarth* and its *territorium*, previously owned by Dyfrig,
to (Archbishop) Teilo.'[2] This is one of the earliest charters listed and is strong
evidence for the similarly early establishment of Llanarth church. Charter bounds
exist for this early grant and they are worth quoting in full as they evoke the
landscape at the turn of the 7th century:

> The Clawr along the high road as far as the mound of Ffrwd Mur. From the
> mound of Ffrwd Mur straight to the ditch, as far as the stone at the four
> boundaries. From the stone as far as to the end of the Cecyn, as far as the
> head of the ditch. From the head of the ditch right on to the black well,
> (cp. Black House, and Llaca Du). From the well through the wood to the
> Clawr, near the head of the ditch, as far as the Clouric, (the Little Clawr),
> to the Clawr.'[3]

Brook describes the shape of the churchyard at Llanarth as being partly curved. Aerial photographs have indicated a ploughed-out field boundary south of the churchyard. There appear to be ditches marking 'a large rectangular area' which may represent a bigger monastic enclosure. However, these may relate to a farm south of the church and have no ecclesiastical origin.[4]

In a charter of *c.*864 concerning Caerleon, there is a brief narrative of a conflict between the donors and 'bishop Nudd's *familia*, residing at Llanarth.'[5] which certainly suggests that Llanarth was a monastery and had a continuing importance in the early medieval period. Llanarth is also mentioned in connection to a grant of Llantilio Crossenny in *c.*600 and in relation to a *c.*720 grant of Monmouth[6] which again show the continuity of a church/monastery at Llanarth throughout the early 7th to late 9th centuries.

There is a female yew in the southern side of the churchyard with a measured girth of 26 feet and an estimated age of 2,000 years.[7] The tree has an aerial root now growing as an internal stem within the hollowed trunk — a sign of a very old tree. Was the tree here before the Christian faith arrived, or is it a few centuries younger and the deliberate planting of an early saint?

LLANDEGFEDD or
LLANDEGVETH – St. Tegfeth
(ST 338 957)

An early merthyr (or martyr) church of a 5th- or early 6th-century female saint whose possible remains were found in a side wall in the 19th century.

Llandegfedd or Llandegveth is 4 miles south-west of Usk. The church is dedicated to St. Tegfeth or Tegfedd, a rare female saint. She was the daughter of Tegid Foel, lord of Penllyn in Merionethshire and the mother of St. Afan Buellt, patron of Llanafan Fawr and Llanfechan, also covered in this book. She was murdered by Saxons,[1] perhaps at the site of the church as it was originally called *Merthir Tecmed*, which indicates the burial place of the saint.

In the *Life* of St. Cadoc we are told that St. Teilo was given the 'villa of *Merthir Tecmed*' for helping Cadoc settle a dispute with King Arthur (see p.62)[2] and demonstrates that she was already dead at the time of Cadoc and Teilo's period of activity. This means that she must have been alive in the late 5th or early 6th century.

In a charter of *c.*750 it states 'Brii ap Idfyw gave *podum Merthir Tecmed*, with half an *uncia* of land around it, to bishop Tyrchan, with the consent of the two sons of Rhydderch, Ceredig and Iddig, and their kindred.'[3] In *c.*1072, there is another grant in which King Caradog gave land near '*merthirtecmed*' to Bishop Herwald in penance 'for his *familia*'s consumption of the bishop's food rent ... at

St. Maughan's',[4] and it is interesting that the merthyr name is still used. Brook notes that the site's early status was as a monastery and that it survived as a free chapel in the late medieval period.[5] She observes that the present church stands in 'a circular, earth-banked churchyard, raised about two metres [about 6½ feet] above the surrounding land.'[6] In fact, along the curved southern boundary, the height difference is up to 8 feet. There is also a very old yew opposite the eastern wall of the chancel and two middle-aged looking yews to the south-east.

A burial was found within the side wall of the church when it was rebuilt in the 19th century. In 1548 there is a record of the 'site as having land for a priest and to pay for "light before the Sepulchre"', Brook remarks that this may have been 'for an image of Christ's sepulchre, but may have been for the relics of Tegfedd, if that is what the burial found represents.'[7]

LLANDENNY – St. John the Apostle and Evangelist (SO 415 039)

The partly curving boundaries of the churchyard and the low rise on which the church is built are indicative of an early site, which documents imply existed in the 7th century.

This is a large and attractive church in the village centre. The churchyard boundary is walled with curving boundaries and a small new extension to the north. The church is set on a small eminence within the enclosure and there is a drop in height on the southern side between the churchyard and adjoining garden.

Llandenny is mentioned in the Llandaff Charters in a grant dated to *c*.760 when it was called '*Mathenni*' : 'King Ffernfael gave his wife ... all its (animal) stock, and *Mathenni* with three *modii* of land; then, with the king's guarantee, she gave them with their inhabitants and offspring to bishop Cadwared'.[1] Baring-Gould and Fisher therefore suggest that the original dedication of Llandenny church was to St. Tenni, but nothing is known about him. They point out that the church is referred to as '*Ecclesia Mathenni Mustuir Mur*' — 'The Church of Tenni's Field belonging to the Great Monastery' i.e. Llandaff,[2] implying that Llandenny was a church and not a monastery. Llandenny was then returned by someone called Morcimbris in about 785 in what Davies considers is a regrant of the land mentioned in the *c*.760 charter.[3]

LLANDOGO – St. Oudoceus

(SO 527 042)

Early monastic site evidenced by charters but with no signs left on the ground. The current church is a Victorian rebuild.

The church of St. Oudoceus lies 6 miles south of Monmouth, and is only slightly elevated above the flood plain of the nearby River Wye.

St. Oudoceus was bishop of Llandaff after Teilo, and probably its first consecrated bishop. The *Life* of Oudeoceus records that he was the son of Budic, a prince in Brittany, and nephew to St. Teilo. Budic had made a promise to Teilo that he would give his next born child to the Church and this turned out to be Oudoceus. Born in Brittany, Oudoceus was brought up in south Wales from the age of about 8, being elected abbot and bishop in *c.*580, after Teilo's death. He does not appear to have visited Brittany again. There are several legends referring to him. One relates that while Oudoceus was wrapt in devotion in his establishment on the Wye (probably Llandogo) a monk informed him that someone was stealing timber beams to be used in his building. Oudoceus seized a hatchet, and ran to the banks of the Wye to find that the thief was none other than the historian and saint, Gildas, who was then spending some time in retreat on the Isle of Echni (Flat Holm) in the Bristol Channel, and who wanted timber for his own building. Oudoceus shouted after Gildas as he rowed away with his gains, but the latter ignored him. In rage he drove the hatchet down onto a stone which split. However the story is chronologically impossible as Gildas died in 570 and Oudoceus was not a bishop until 580, thus a folk memory of Gildas's strong and unscrupulous character appears to have become attached to Oudoceus, rather than to St. Teilo to whom it probably belonged.[1]

Oudoceus also appears to have been a strong leader. Meurig and Morgan, kings of Morganwg at different times, each committed murder, having previously approached the saint to make peace between them and their victims. On both occasions Oudoceus called a synod of the abbots of Llancarfan, Llantwit and Llandough to sit in judgment, judgments that increased the authority of Llandaff. In the first instance, besides doing penance, Meurig had to give four villas to Llandaff; in the second, Morgan was obliged to release the monasteries of Llancarfan, Llantwit and Llandough from all royal services. This was at a time when parts of Herefordshire and Gloucestershire were seized by the Anglo-Saxons and became part of the sub-kingdom of Mercia under the Hwicce, and when Ewyas was wasted.[2]

When Einion, king of Glywysing (approximately Glamorganshire) was out stag hunting, a stag ran to Oudoceus who sheltered him. The saint used the opportunity to ask for a donation of the land that the stag had encompassed that day. This was granted and is now represented by the parish of Llandogo, which is his only dedication, besides that at Llandaff, which latter is shared with St. Teilo and St. Dyfrig. He used Llandogo as a retreat and died there, probably in about 615. His shrine was at Llandaff where he was interred.[3]

The site does not have the appearance of an early establishment even though it was a pre-Norman, probably late 6th-century monastery. As Davies notes, an abbot of *Lannenniaun* is mentioned in c.625, which shows the site's monastic status in the early 7th century at least, possible even in the late 6th century. The main interest is the historical background of the foundation and the importance of the saint in the religious and political life of his times. There is a charter dated to *c.*698 in which 'King Morgan returned *Lannenniaun* [as in 'church of (King) Einnion]', and, through a note added later, '*Lannoudocui*, with its four weirs, to bishop Euddogwy [Oudoceus]' which encompassed an area of about 2,100 acres.[4] As the charter is dated c.698, the grant is made to Oudoceus's church and not to him in person as he had died in about 615. The bounds are recorded as 'From the Civilchi to the Stone of Oudocui, to the ridge of the Allt on the upper side, along it to the ford, as far as the Cledon. Along the ridge as far as the bottom of the Weun, to the middle of the mountain, to the Red Pool, right to the Olway. Thence from Trilech Vechan [just south of Trelleck] right to the White brook.'[5] Even though it is not clear where the landmarks are, the passage paints the scene. In a charter *c.*942 there is reference to a synod being called at Llandogo[6] which indicates the importance of the monastery at least until the mid-10th century.

LLANELLY – St. Elli
(SO 232 148)

A superb near complete ring of yews surround the church, which was in Breconshire until the county boundary changes of 1974.

'This chapel (for such it is reputed to be) is situated about a mile south of the Usk, upon a steep eminence and is much exposed to the fury of the north and east winds.'[1] Jones' description is most apt for this church which is 3 miles south-east of Crickhowell high above the Wye Valley.

Its patron saint is the 6th-century St. Elli, a disciple St. Cadoc. Elli's mother was queen of the 'Islands of Grimbul' (thought to be in the Mediterranean) and she was barren. She asked St. Cadoc to intercede on her behalf with God, promising to devote any child she had to God's service. Her prayers were answered and Elli was born. Cadoc took the child to Llancarfan for his education and, in time, Elli became 'the dearest to him of all his disciples.' Cadoc gave him one of the three 'remarkable stone altars' which had come from Jerusalem and which he prized. Elli was one of the three disciples whom Cadoc sent to convert his wayward father to Christianity and it was Elli who was left in charge of Llancarfan when Cadoc retired (see p.63).[2]

The church was restored in 1867–8 and contains a 12th-century font and an exceptional Jacobean altar table.[3] There is also the remains of a medieval preaching cross to the south of the church.

Part of the ring of yews that all but surround the church

The churchyard has been extended three times in recent centuries, with the latest addition in 1868 on the other side of the road from the church.[4] It is considered that the original church enclosure was circular. The most striking feature is the prominent, near complete circle of yews on a low embankment within the present churchyard. Some of the yews within the circle are clearly of great age and are hollowed. Thirteen yews remain but Chetan and Brueton suggest that the gaps in the circle indicate that there were originally 18.[5] Whether the yews demarcated the boundary of a burial mound or were planted there in the early medieval period we will never know, but as an example of a yew ring, it is among the country's best examples.

The church spire peeps out from the ring of yews which stands within the present churchyard and probably marks the extent of the original enclosure

LLANFIHANGEL CRUCORNEY – St. Michael
(SO 325 206)

An early St. Michael dedication of *c*.800, and home to an ancient yew.

Llanfihangel Crucorney is 4 miles north of Abergavenny. The first documentary reference to the church is in a charter in the *Book of Llandaff* dated *c*.970. In this, a group of churches, with their territories, were returned by King Morgan to Bishop Gwgon of Llandaff. The church is called '*Lann Mihacgel cruc Cornou*'[1] — 'the church of St. Michael at the corner of the Rock (or mount)'.[2] The rock in question is the odd-shaped but very striking eminence of the Skirrid to the south which would have always been a prominent landscape feature. Not surprisingly it was invested with religious importance — one old tradition has it that Noah's Ark rested on the Skirrid during the great flood, another that an earthquake on the day of the crucifixion caused the mountain to split and so form its prominent outline. In early Christian times a chapel dedicated to St. Michael was built near the top of the Skirrid, an apt location as St. Michael was connected with high places and was seen as the leader of the angelic hosts (see under Moccas, p.291). In about A.D. 800 a second church was built on the lower ground where the present church now stands, but nothing of this early 9th-century church remains.[3] The fact the church was being returned to the bishop in *c*.970 shows it was established earlier, and a foundation date of *c*.800 sounds right as St. Michael's cult was taking off in the Welsh Borders at about this time. Thus Llanfihangel Crucorney is likely to be an early and an original St. Michael dedication.

The present church is large and built from Old Red Sandstone, with a nave and chancel of the late 13th or 14th centuries and an imposing tower of the 15th century — all of which was restored in the 19th century.[4]

The church appears to stand on a low platform within the churchyard which is sizeable and, although Brook describes the shape as quadrangular,[5] from ground level it appears to have a somewhat irregular configuration with a tendency towards curvilinearity. The churchyard is 15 feet or more above the road surface on the southern side, but may have been altered in the recent past as the area behind the revetment wall is acutely inclined. At the top of this bank and to the left of the steps is a section of clear embanking which peters out further west — is this an original boundary bank or more recent work? On the eastern side it is bounded by a straight stone wall with some gentle embanking. There is a sizeable yew in the south-east corner of the churchyard with a measured girth of 25 feet,[6] that is clearly of considerable age. It may date to the early medieval period — perhaps even to the original foundation of the church.

An old print showing the Skirrid (right) with the Sugar Loaf in the background

LLANFOIST –
St. Faith / St. Ffwyst (SO 287 133)

The early dedication, a yew, and raised enclosure indicate, although do not prove, an early medieval foundation.

The church is on the north-western edge of Llanfoist, one mile south-west of Abergavenny and below the wooded slope of the Blorenge. The otherwise unknown St. Ffwyst is entered in the Iolo Manuscripts as a saint of Gwent, the implication being that he was the patron saint of Llanffwyst, now spelt Llanfoist. The church is now dedicated to St. Faith, perhaps as a corruption of Ffwyst.[1]

The church is a medieval structure built of local sandstone and there is an unusually complete medieval cross in the churchyard with the base, four steps and most of the shaft.[2]

The churchyard is a medium-sized enclosure and is of a wide, rectangular shape and is raised above the exterior levels. Because of the large number of burials, it is difficult to see any potential earlier earthworks/boundaries within the enclosure. There is an ancient female yew to the south of the church with a girth of 25 feet and estimated to be 1,500 years old,[3] that has sustained lightning blast damage. There is also a fairly old looking yew near to the boundary wall on the north-east side.

LLANGATTOCK LINGOED
– St. Cadoc (SO 362 201)

A superb church in an idyllic location with the remains of earthen banks perhaps delineating the original boundary of the *llan*.

Llangattock Lingoed is about 5 miles north-east of Abergavenny, in an area of St. Cadoc foundations (see biographical section on Cadoc pp.59-65).

The church is very striking as it has been plastered and white-washed, with the edgings and copings left in the original Old Red Sandstone. It dates mainly to the 13th to 14th centuries with more recent alterations. Inside are the remains of wall-paintings, one of which shows a soldier on a horse with sword raised. There is an exquisitely carved bressumer — all that remains of the rood loft — and a rare survival of high backed pews with one set dated to 1634.[1]

The churchyard is quite large and is shaped rather like a broad, rounded triangle. Brook describes it as being largely curved.[2] Below the hedged boundaries on the southern and south-eastern sides and by the wall on the northern side are the remains of embanking — the original perimeter of the *llan*? Earthen banks are indicative of early church enclosures in Gwent (see under Bettws Newydd, p.315). There is large yew next to the tower. The church itself is built on a flat area within the enclosure which slopes gently from north to west, and a level area immediately north of the church is large enough to have held further buildings.

The church is not mentioned in the *Book of Llandaff* — indeed the earliest reference is in 1254 in the Valuation of Norwich.[3] However the shape of the churchyard and the fact it appears to have kept some of its original earthen boundaries, along with the dedication to St. Cadoc suggest the possibility of an early medieval origin.

LLANGEVIEW – St. David
(SO 397 007)

An enchanting site with evidence of an early enclosure and a previous dedication to an obscure British saint.

Llangeview is 1½ miles east of Usk, on the east side of the A449 which thunders close by but thankfully out of sight. The dedication is to St. David but the original patron was St. Cynfyw who is styled as a confessor. Cynfyw was the son of Gwynllyw and brother to St. Cadoc. Cynfyw's name, which is sometimes reduced to Cyfyw and Cynyw, is also misspelt in medieval documents as Cennen, Cannan and Kemmeu with other variations (see also p.206), thus the village is sometimes spelt as Llangyfyw and Llangifiw. Cynfyw is said to have been a saint or monk at Llancarfan where he acted as Cadoc's registrar. It is likely Cynfyw was also the patron of Llangynyw in Montgomeryshire. In the *Book of Llandaff* there is also mention of an *Ecclesia S. Ciuiu (Cyuiu)* which was once at, or near, to Bishton, near Newport in southern Monmouthshire.[1]

The church is a simple 14th-century structure with a few later alterations. It is built from coursed Old Red Sandstone rubble and, unusually, has a porch to the west — they are normally to the south. It is a pity that the church is locked as, peering through the windows, a gloriously unmodernised interior with white-washed walls comes into view. There is the rare survival of box pews which are probably early 18th century, and a rood loft which Newman describes as an important medieval survival.[2] The bressumer (the large horizontal beam that supports the loft) is substantial and has simple, deep mouldings.

Brook describes the enclosure form as largely curved, although from ground level it looks almost circular. The perimeter is demarcated by earthen banks, but these are rather difficult to see as most of the boundary is hedged. However on the northern side the embanking is fairly clear. The bank is quite low, undoubtedly degraded through centuries of weathering and neglect. Earthen banks which define a curvilinear enclosure are an indication of an early site (see entry for Bettws Newydd, p.315). The churchyard is raised to differing heights on all sides and there is a rise within the enclosure, making it appear that the church sits upon a low mound. Perhaps the church is one of those built on an old burial mound or barrow. There are no obviously ancient yews, although there is a middle-aged yew on the southern side. The earliest mention of Llangeview appears to be in 1254 when it is called *ecclesia de Langiwen* and in *c*.1566 the church still retained a dedication to Cyfiw (no doubt another variation on Cynfyw).[3]

LLANGIBBY or LLANGYBI
– St. Cybi (SO 374 967)

The church has an early dedication and a related holy well.

The church of St. Cybi is about 3 miles south-south-west of the town of Usk. (For details on St. Cybi see the entry under Tredunnock, p.388).

The church structure is substantial and is basically of 14th- and 15th-century date with signs of alterations. The church fabric is very interesting and has 'remarkable 17th-century fittings', late medieval wall paintings and 17th-century inscriptions.[1]

It is a fairly small churchyard in relation to the size of church. The south side of the churchyard is walled and about 4 feet higher than the external road level. There are no suggestions of earthworks to indicate any earlier boundaries, so it is possible the present churchyard denotes the original church enclosure.

The holy well, Ffynon Gybi, is tucked away into the hedge on the other side of the lane to the south-east of the church, directly opposite the new extension to the churchyard. Visitors will have to be determined to find the well and in summer will be stung by nettles in the process, but there is a square, stone-topped chamber with clear water coming in at ground level into a stone basin.

There is a standing stone in the floodplain of the Usk at SO 381 964, south-west of the church, which Newman reports is 'traditionally associated with the arrival of St. Cybi from Cornwall,' although he suggests it might in fact be of Bronze Age date as there was a barrow, known as the Tredunnock Barrow, which used to stand close by.[2] Certainly standing stones are now more usually ascribed to the Bronze Age.

The holy well near the churchyard

LLANGOVAN – St. Govan
(SO 457 055)

Documentary evidence for the existence a church in the 8th century.

The church of St. Govan is in an elevated position in a remote setting about 6 miles south-west of Monmouth.

A charter exists dated *c.*755 which details a grant of land, the boundaries of which are considered to relate to Llangovan by Davies and by Evans and Rhys.[1] The grant mentions a church of *'Lann Uvien* and St. Nuvien', of whom little is known. However, Baring-Gould and Fisher believe *Lann Uvien* to be a chapel at Crick, about 9 miles south of Llangovan which, at the turn of the 20th century, was a barn in the yard at the manor house at Crick.[2] The church is also called *ecclesia Mamouric* in the same grant.[3] Instead they consider that the dedication of Llangovan is to a shadowy St. Cwyfen as a result of information in the Calendars in the Iolo Manuscripts and a *Prymer* of 1546, where his name is given as Cofen. They record that the church-name appears as *Lancomen* in the Norwich Taxatio of 1254, *Lanchouian* in the *Book of Llandaff* in a later appendix and as *Llangofien* elsewhere. St. Cwyfen's mother hailed from Denbighshire and his other three dedications are in north Wales and Anglesey. In one document he is styled as St. Cwyfyn ab Arthalun of Glyn Achlach, which latter is identified with Glendalough in Ireland and the saint with St. Coemgen or Kevin, who was the abbot.[4]

350

St. Govan is now the patron, perhaps as a result of a transliteration of the final part of the settlement's name over the years, rather than for any likely connection with the church, for neither of the two St. Govans would seem to have any claim to a connection with the site. Both Govans were Irish where the name was known as Gobhan, said to mean 'a smith' from which derives *Gobannium* (Abergavenny), 'a smithy'. The first Gobhan, who was also called Mogopoc, was a follower of St. Ailbe and also his cook. He and two other disciples were sent by St. Ailbe from Ireland to Rome to bring back 'the correct form of the order of the Mass.' Upon his return Gobhan became an abbot in Ireland in Wexford. Ailbe died in about 530 and Gobhan found a new spiritual leader, St. Senan. He eventually took retirement in Pembrokeshire, where the well-known chapel is dedicated to him at St. Govan's Head, along with a holy well. The second St. Govan, or Gobhan, belonged to a later generation and was a disciple of St. Fursey or Fursa. They departed from Ireland, spent some time among the East Saxons, then left for Gaul. This Gobhan died in about 648, murdered by Vandals at his monastery or hermitage in a forest.[5]

The church at Llangovan is little used, and is leased by the Vincent Wildlife Trust as a bat reserve, so that the interior is not accessible for much of the year. The main structure is late medieval with a few lancet windows remaining of 13th century date. It was restored in 1888–90.[6]

The churchyard is quite small and slopes from west to east. It looks to be of an irregular square/rectilinear shape, with a curved eastern boundary. It is possible that extensions are incorporated, but subtle changes in levels are not clearly visible due to the tussocky grass. The churchyard boundaries are walled and the enclosure is very raised on the northern side, and there is a slope up to the main entrance gates. The drop to the lane is about 12 to 15 feet, especially to the north-east corner. The height difference reduces as one goes along the south-eastern boundary but is still quite significant. This is a striking site, redolent of an ancient past.

LLANGUA – St. James
(SO 390 258)

An idyllic site that was formerly dedicated to a 5th-century Irish female saint. The photograph shows the northern boundary and a possible filled in ditch.

This lovely church is about 1¼ miles south-south-west of Pontrilas. It sits alone in the midst of a field, sandwiched between the A465, the River Monnow and a railway line and is reached via a grassy drive.

The present dedication is to St. James but the original patron is considered to have been the female saint Ciwa, who is styled virgin and abbess, and who is also known as Cuach or Kewe. There is nothing recorded in the Welsh genealogies concerning her and it is likely she was an Irish saint who was part of a clan who lived on the northern slopes of Mount Leinster. This clan was converted to Christianity in about 430, but Ciwa's family was banished from their lands by a pagan king upon their conversion and probably moved to southern Munster. The exile lasted 20 years. It was during this time that St. Ciwa fostered St. Ciaran as an infant and he stayed with her until he was about 12 years old. Her family were called back when the crown passed to the king's son, who had been converted to Christianity by St. Patrick. St. Patrick handed Ciwa to a Bishop MacTail at Kilcullen where he was supposed to instruct her in religion 'but ugly reports circulated relative to his undue intimacy with her' and the bishop was denounced by his own clergy to St. Patrick. The outcome is not known. Nothing is known of Ciwa until Ciaran arrived at a place called Saighir in about 480 and became abbot of a monastery, when she sought his protection and became the abbess of two nearby nunneries. Life was never smooth — after Ciwa's family's lands were returned to them, local warfare started, and the new king was killed by his own grandson.[1]

Ciwa used to retire to a rocky islet to find peace at a hermitage, which was close to one of the monasteries at Ross Benchuir in Clare (the other establishment was at Kilcoagh [Cill-cuach] near Donard). Both Ciwa and Ciaran then moved to Cornwall where she founded a few churches, including Ladock, Lanowe and St. Kew(e). It is also likely that the church at Kew(e)stoke in Somerset was originally dedicated to Ciwa. She also appears to have had a monastery in Brittany near Cleguerec.[2] It is a telling fact that St. Ciwa seemed to prefer to be near water and this may have a bearing on the siting of Llangua which is immediately next to the River Monnow. It is thought that she died in the first quarter of the 5th century.

There is no explanation as to why Llangua in Monmouthshire is dedicated to this 5th-century Irish saint. In 1254 Llangua was spelt as *Lagywan* and it appears as *Lannculan* in the *Book of Llandaff*, and as *Llanguwan* and *Llangywan* in the book's 14th-century additions.[3]

There is a charter in the *Book of Llandaff* relating to the church in *c.*872 in which 'Cinuin ap Gwrgan gave *Lannculan*, with all its *ager* and three *modii* of land ... with sanctuary rights ... and with its *tellus* [land], to bishop Cerennyr, with king Brochfael's guarantee.'[4] It is interesting that this church had pre-Norman rights of sanctuary as few charters give such information.

The church is a delightful single-storey medieval structure, with a small timbered bell-turret, restored in the late 19th and mid-20th century.[5] The nave and chancel are well-lit and have decorated wagon roofs. There are old dark box-pews and simple panelling to the vestry at the west end.

The churchyard is very small and has a roughly rectilinear shape with curved corners — on the northern side the boundary has an hour-glass shape with a suggestion of a filled-in ditch outside the present churchyard boundary. There is some physical evidence of a hollow-way going to the river on the west, which was probably a fording point. The area would have been liable to flooding and alluvium deposits, which have probably levelled any hollows and embanking of boundaries within and around the churchyard. On the northern and eastern sides of the pasture surrounding the churchyard are humps and bumps in the field — the possible remains of forgotten buildings?

LLANGWM UCHAF –
St. Jerome (SO 433 006)
LLANGWM ISAF –
St. John (SO 429 007)

A pair of churches suggesting an early medieval monastic site.

There are two churches at Llangwm less than a quarter of a mile apart: Llangwm Uchaf and Llangwm Isaf which are dedicated to St. Jerome and to St. John respectively, but these are later dedications. In the Llandaff Charters, an 11th-century charter mentions 'the four Saints of Llangwm, Mirgint, Cinficc, Huui and Eruen.' Of St. Cinfic(c) he is styled as a confessor and his name may be remembered in a chapelry attached to Pyle, 5 miles west of Bridgend, in Mid-Glamorgan; there is a 'Kiffig in Carmarthenshire' which is called *Lann Ceffic* in the *Book of Llandaff*; it is also noted that the same name, written as Cinfic and Conficc, is borne by laymen on two occasions in the same source.[1] There are no further details on Eruen, Mirgint[2] or Huui, although the latter's name may survive in the Monmouthshire parish of Pen-how.[3]

There are two charters relating to Llangwm in the Llandaff Charters. The first is dated *c*.860 but it is not clear which church is meant. It states 'Cynfelyn freed *Lann Cum* and gave it with its *ager*, glossed *uncia*, of three *modii*, to bishop Grecielis.'[4] However Brook identifies this grant with Llangwm Uchaf.[5]

The second charter for Llangwm is identified by Brook and Davies with Llangwm Isaf[6] in which 'Caradog ar Rhiwallon, remembering his evil deeds on his sickbed and especially the killing of his brother Cynan, gave *Uilla Gunnuc* in *Guarthaf Cum* to the four saints of Llan-gwm — Mirgint, Cinficc, Huui and Eruen — and to bishop Herewald, with the guarantee of Roger fitzWilliam fitzOsbern, Count of Hereford and Lord of Gwent, in the time of William the elder.'[7] The grant of land comprised 100 acres. This is interesting as the present church is quite small and one would have thought a dependent of the larger St. Jerome's. A pair of churches, such as those at Llangwm, are usually considered to a indicate a monastic site.[8] The 'ruined little medieval church' of Llangwm Isaf was rebuilt between 1849–51, the only original feature remaining is probably the west porch with its arch carved with continuous hollow and wave mouldings.[9]

The churchyard of Llangwm Isaf is raised above the lane to the north and west, and farm buildings and domestic dwellings are next to the south-west of the enclosure. There are some slight undulations to the churchyard levels, although nothing definitive. A footpath connects this church with the larger church at

Llangwm Uchaf, and it is possible that this is an ancient track linking the two sites by the quickest route.

The churchyard at Llangwm Uchaf is quite sizeable, partly curved and bounded by a wall with a swift flowing stream, the Llan-Gwm-Isaf Brook, bounding the south. There is also a well marked on the Explorer OL 14 map close to the south-west but outside the churchyard. Such a water supply would have probably been one of the deciding factors in the choice of the site. To the north of the church is a female yew with a girth of 20 feet and an estimated age of 1,200 years,[10] which supports an early foundation date for the site.

The church is built of 'slabby Old Red Sandstone'. The nave and porch were mostly rebuilt between 1863–9 and the tower, which is tall, thin and battlemented, was restored with the chancel in 1869. However a 12th- or 13th-century origin for the present building is suggested. The church is rightly famed for its magnificent rood screen and loft, which Newman describes as a breathtaking sight, which indeed it is. The whole structure is surprisingly large, reaching almost to the ceiling and dates to c.1500, with sympathetic restoration undertaken in 1876–8. The chancel arch dates to the 14th century and the depictions of the Green Man on its corbels (an image with pre-Christian origins) are striking.

On view is a strange, carved cylindrical stone, about 2 feet tall and one foot wide, found in a wall in the church during the 19th-century restorations. It tapers to the middle from both ends to give a waist upon which is a wide central band. This band and the top half of the object are decorated with trellis carving in relief which indicate an 11th- or 12th-century date. It has been described as resembling a 'pillar piscina' — could it be a survivor from an earlier monastery? Indeed Brook notes that the early status of both Llangwm sites was monastic.[11]

The cylindrical carved stone found in the wall at Llangwm Uchaf during restoration in the 19th century that could be from the early monastery reputed to have been on the site

LLANHENNOCK –
St. John the Baptist (ST 354 927)

The original early dedication, the curvilinear, raised enclosure and an ancient yew indicate an early medieval foundation.

The church of St. John the Baptist is less than 2 miles north-east of Caerleon, on an elevated site with extensive views. It has a tall, slender tower of the 15th century, a medieval chancel and a nave which was rebuilt in the 19th century.[1]

The churchyard is of moderate size and is described as partly curved by Brook.[2] It is raised on the south-east and eastern sides by up to 5 to 6 feet in relation to the adjoining fields. There are some undulations in the level of the churchyard, and, around the church itself, the land appears lightly raised, perhaps indicating an earlier and much smaller enclosure. There is also a gentle rise on the eastern side of the churchyard from the boundary wall to the church, which is more apparent nearer the chancel. There is also a low roughly circular mound between 12 and 15 feet across, with a rise of about 3 feet overall opposite the porch on the southern side. In 2000 it was planted with a young yew. It is reminiscent of the mounds at Cascob and Llanlleonfel; at Llanlleonfel it is to the east of the chancel and is reputed to be the grave of a monk, but no legend is attached to those at Llanhennock or Cascob.

The presence of an ancient yew with a very wide bole in Llanhennock churchyard is an indicator of an early site. Another indication is given by the original patron saint being St. Henwg. He is styled a confessor, but there are few references to him and all of those are in the Iolo Manuscripts where the bard Taliessin is said to be the son of St. Henwg '(or Einwg Hên) of Caerleon on Usk ...'. In another entry he is called Henwg Fardd (the Bard) of St. Cadoc's monastery at Llancarfan, whilst another states that Taliessin founded the church at Llanhennock (Llanhenwg) in his father's memory — St. Henwg had apparently gone to Rome to fetch back the saints Garmon and Blieddan to Britain 'to ameliorate the Faith and renew Baptism', which latter statement Baring-Gould and Fisher dismiss.[3]

LLANHILETH – St. Illtyd
(SO 218 019)

The original patron of this church was a 7th-century princess of Powys and the site is mentioned in a 9th- or 10th-century Welsh poem. The church contains a pre-Norman font and is a most evocative site on a superb hill-top location.

Of all the sites in this book, this is one of the most extraordinary — its situation, high above the terraced mining valleys, and its lonely position on the edge of the wild Welsh hills makes the steep, winding ascent from Abertillery worth every second. The site would be difficult to find using any but the most recent maps because of a new main road, but the church is extremely well signposted on entering Abertillery — look out for the brown signs with 'St. Illtyd' which will direct you up a steep lane to the church.

An earlier church is thought to have been rebuilt in the 13th to 14th centuries by the Cistercians, possibly as a chapel for one of their granges or farms. Some parts of the structure survive from the Cistercian rebuilding, but a further rebuilding took place in c.1500 and it was restored in 1888–91. It closed in the 1930s because of subsidence from the local coalmines, was repaired and reopened in 1943, but closed again in 1957 because of open-cast mining in the area. When these operations stopped in 1962 the church was found to have deteriorated seriously and remained closed. Being the oldest standing building in their area, it was bought by Blaenau Gwent Borough Council after 1984 when it was restored and reopened to visitors and for concerts.[1] Inside there is a putative pre-Norman font comprising a square basin on a square pedestal. Although the top is damaged, having a severe chip to one edge, it is most unusual.

The shape of the present churchyard can be best described as irregular because of a large western extension, but the early enclosure was nearly circular. The interior ground level is noticeably raised above the exterior. In 1799 Archdeacon Coxe visited Llanhilleth and described a ring of yews around the church: 'The churchyard is planted with twelve old yews, which surround the church, and add to the solemnity of the scene.'[2] These yews have since gone.

Llanhilleth is unusual as it has two pre-Norman secular references. The first is to the alleged burial place of a Welsh prince, Owain, son of Urien. Urien was a 6th-century king of Rheged, a kingdom which covered the Solway Firth, Carlisle and Cumbria. Owain and Urien fought against the Anglo-Saxons and their actions were recorded by the poet Taliesin. Following his death, Owain became an heroic figure and the stories told about him worked their way into Wales; he became part of the legendary Arthurian stage and even figures in 'The Lady of the Fountain', one of the stories in the *Mabinogion*. In the *Black Book of Carmarthen*, written at the Priory of St. John in Carmarthen by a monk *c*.1250, there is a 'series of short verses known as *Englynion y Beddau* ('The Stanzas of the Graves') composed in the 9th or 10th centuries.[3] The graves of Welsh heroes are listed and most are identifiable as ancient burial sites, such as cromlechs and cairns. One of the stanzas reads:

> After things blue and red and fair
> and great steeds with taut necks,
> at Llanheledd is the grave of Owain.[4]

In another translation it is:

> After armour,
> red feathers,
> and finery:
> big, tight-lipped
> horses
> in Llan Heledd
> is the grave of Owain.[5]

The grave is considered to refer to the mound just west of the church. It is large, steep-sided and flat-topped, and probably dates from the 11th or 12th centuries. However it is thought that this medieval motte was built over a prehistoric barrow or cairn. The motte may have been constructed by the native Welsh princes of the kingdom of Gwynllwg, of which Llanhilleth was part, or it may be the work of invading Normans.[6] Quite why a prince of Rheged was thought to be buried so far south at Llanhilleth is not known.

The church is currently dedicated to St. Illtyd (Illtud) but before the 16th century it was dedicated to St. Heledd, as in the reference in the poem to Llanheledd. In the parish lists of the 16th and 17th centuries the church is spelt Llanhylledd and Llanhiledd, and in one manuscript the word 'vorwyn' is added, which means virgin. Baring-Gould and Fisher consider Heledd may have been one of the daughters of Cyndrwyn of Caereinion in Powys, and aunt to the saints Aelhaiarn, Cynhaiarn and Llwchaiarn (see entry under Guilsfield p.76). Cyndrwyn lived in the late 5th century, which means his daughter would have flourished in the earlier part of the 6th century. He was prince of part of the ancient kingdom of Powys which incorporated the Vale of the River Severn around Shrewsbury. He had eight sons, one of whom was Cynddylan, and most, if not all, were killed in battles with the Anglo-Saxons.[7] Cyndrwyn also had nine daughters which included Heledd. Their names are recorded in the elegy on the death of Cynddylan by Llywarch Hên, the second secular source, a poem that still has the power to move:

> The hall of Cynddylan is dark tonight, without fire, without candle; but for God, who will give me sanity? ...
> The hall of Cynddylan is dark tonight, without fire, without light; longing for you comes over me.
> The hall of Cynddylan is still tonight, after losing its chief; great merciful God, what shall I do? ...[8]

This is part of a series of poems called *Canu Heledd* — 'The Song of Heledd' — which were composed in the 9th or 10th centuries and are 'verse highlights of a lost prose saga' in which Heledd laments on the death of Cynddylan and her other brothers and the destruction of her home, and blames herself for what has happened. Yet, as the Site Report for Llanhilleth remarks, 'why this small church on a barren Gwent hillside should be dedicated to a 7th century princess of Powys is not known' and it is something of a mystery.[9]

However it seems that Llanhilleth was of some importance at least in the Middle Ages, for two further large mounds behind the Carpenter's Arms and the old Castle Inn mark the site of a substantial medieval castle. Excavations in the mid-1920s revealed the 'foundations of two large, stone-built towers'. One was a 'cruciform keep-tower' about 70 feet across, and the other, about 20 feet to the east, comprised the 'partly-destroyed base courses of a round tower' approximately 64 feet in external diameter. The latter was found to be much larger than any other round tower in south-east Wales and was comparable to that at Pembroke Castle and Morlais, near Merthyr. The castle had probably been abandoned by the 14th century.[10]

LLANISHEN – St. Dennis
(SO 475 033)

Mention in a late 10th-century charter and a previous dedication to a 6th-century saint imply an early foundation.

Llanishen is a ridge-top village about 7 miles south-south-west of Monmouth. The dedication to St. Dennis is a Norman alteration from the original dedicatee, St. Isan, one of the followers of Illtud who was with him when he foresaw his death. His parentage is unknown, but he is described in the Iolo Manuscripts as a monk or saint at Bangor Illtyd — Llantwit Major — where he was probably abbot. As St. Illtud died sometime between 527 and 537 this makes St. Isan an early 6th-century saint.[1] There is a note of *c.*970 in the Llandaff Charters which details the return of nine churches and their lands from King Morgan to a Bishop Gwgon in which Llanishen is referred to as *Lann Nissien*.[2]

The church was rebuilt between 1852–4 in a slightly ornate Victorian style, and no early work remains. Local sources recall that the new church was built whilst the old structure was still in use some 20 yards to the south and downhill from the present building.

Brook describes the churchyard as largely curved[3] and this is suggestive of an early site. The east end of the chancel is only a few feet away from a drystone wall above which is what appears to be a new extension. The natural topography has apparently limited the size of the site — even with the probable extension to the east, it is still a small enclosure. The churchyard to the south falls away quite steeply and it is looks as if the church is built on a platform. It is said that the previous church stood on a flatter area at the bottom of the slope on this side and there are indeed some flags (which look rather recent). There are differences in height between the churchyard and surrounding land of up to 15 feet on the north-east and eastern sides, but probably resulting from the natural topgraphy.

LLANLLOWEL –
St. Llywell/Llowel (ST 394 985)

An ancient yew and the dedication point to an early foundation.

The church of St. Llywel is 8 miles north-east of Newport. The River Usk flows just to the west and there is a small brook flowing along the southern boundary of the churchyard; a short distance to the north is a more sizeable stream.

The dedication is a contentious point, as the patron saint may be St. Hywel (the church was spelt Llanhowel in 16th-century parish lists) or St. Llywel. St. Hywel is styled knight and confessor and was the son of Emyr Llydaw. He was forced to flee from Brittany with his brothers for political reasons. The only notice of Hywel as a Welsh saint is found in a 17th-century document printed in the rather dubious Iolo Manuscripts. In this he is referred to as Hywel Farchog or Faig and he is said to have been buried at Llantwit Major — a connection with St. Illtud, abbot of Llantwit Major, is interesting as Illtud was soldier before taking up the religious life. Hywel is referred to as a knight at King Arthur's court in the *Triads* and the *Mabinogion*, in the former as one of three 'Royal Knights' of the Court who were 'invincible in battle', yet 'remarkable for their amiable manners and gentle speech that no one could refuse or deny them anything they asked.' In the story *Geraint and Enid*, Hywel is one of the knights who accompany Geraint to Cornwall. The medieval romancers, Geoffrey of Monmouth and Wace, make Hwyel a prince of Brittany who assisted King Arthur in his battles against the Romans but, as Baring-Gould and Fisher remark, it is doubtful if Hwyel ever returned to Brittany after fleeing the place in his youth. Llanllowel was spelt Llanlouel in a taxation record of 1254, supporting a dedication to St. Llywel[1] (see under Llywel p.238). Both of these saints are of early date and probably contemporary with St. David.

The church is basically a small, single-celled Norman structure built from Old Red Sandstone coursed rubble. An external lintel over the south door has geometric patterns of uncertain date. The church has a circular 12th-century font with an incised rim,[2] and a carved screen of perhaps 16th-century date.

The sloping churchyard is raised, of curvilinear-rectilinear shape and very small. The church may be built on a man-made or natural platform.

There is an ancient split yew to the south-east of the church that has a girth of 26 feet and an estimated age of 1,500 years.[3] There is another mature but not ancient-looking yew in the south-west part of the churchyard next to the brook. These south-east and south-west plantings may be deliberate, and the south-east yew dates to about the time that the saints Llywel and Hwyel were alive and may therefore poiny to an early foundation at this site.

LLANSOY – St. Tysoi
(SO 443 024)

A site with a charter dating back to *c*.725 and the sole dedication to an early British saint. It also has an ancient yew which has both male and female characteristics, a very rare occurrence.

Llansoy is 4 miles north-east of Usk, the church lying to the south of the small village. The early date of Llansoy is supported by a charter in the *Book of Llandaff* dated to approximately 725. In the charter, 'Conhae gave *podum Sancti Tisoi*, with its wood and pannage and hawking rights in the wood, which formerly belonged to Dyfrig, to bishop Berthwyn.' The land granted comprised about 500 acres, and Brook describes its early status as monastic. The *Book of Llandaff* describes St. Tysoi as a pupil of St. Dyfrig. Baring-Gould and Fisher consider that Tysoi is probably the Soy who was one of the clerical witnesses to a grant to Llancarfan monastery during the time of Abbot Paul. Nothing further is known of him.[1]

The church has some elements dating back to the 14th century and was lightly restored in 1858.[2] It has an attractive wagon roof with moulded timbers and some superb stained glass of modern design.

The churchyard has partly curved boundaries of which some are internally earth banked.[3] The site, although fairly flat within the enclosure, is somewhat raised above the surrounding land, particularly so at the front. There appear to be earthworks to the south and west outside the enclosure, but whether these are associated with the putative early monastery is questionable.

Within the churchyard is a particularly interesting ancient yew. It is said to be one of the oldest in Gwent, and in 1999 was examined by an expert and found to have both male and female features on the same branch — berries and pollen sacs — which are most clearly seen in autumn. It was the first yew found with such attributes in the 432 yews that had been studied in England and Wales. It could date back to the 8th century.[4]

LLANTILIO CROSSENNY
– St. Teilo (SO 398 149)

A foundation that dates back to *c.*600 which was a gift from a prince of Gwent to St. Teilo in gratitude for his prayers in battle.

The church of St.Teilo is about 6 miles east of Abergavenny on a low, wide hillock above the River Trothy.

In about 577, just after the battle of Deorham, the Anglo-Saxon forces crossed the River Wye and were destroying much in their path. Iddon, prince of Gwent, and son of King Ynyr, blocked their path at what is now Llantilio Crossenny. Iddon sought St. Teilo's help and found the saint praying at nearby Llanarth. Teilo accompanied him and bought his clerics. Climbing the hill where White Castle is now situated, about 1½ miles to the north-west of Llantilio Crossenny, Teilo and his men 'viewed the battle, shouting psalms of invocation and howling imprecations on the Saxons.' Iddon defeated the enemy and 'took much spoil', and in gratitude to St. Teilo granted him land on which was built Llantilio Crossenny church.[1] The transaction is recorded in a narrative in the Llandaff Charters dated *c.*600 where the church is called '*Lann Teiliau Cressinych*', thus incorporating an early spelling of Teilo's name. The king gave 'three *modii* of land around the mound in the middle of *Crissinic*.'[2] Does the mound refer to a man-made feature — a barrow perhaps? The charter bounds mention 'the ditch of Cinahi', the 'spring of the Grenin' (the Grenin was probably one of the streams) and 'Castell Mai'[3] which suggests a castle or more likely another fortification — might it refer to a stronghold on the site of White Castle? Another tradition suggests that the church was built on the mound on which St. Teilo prayed for Iddon's success, and that it was this mound and the land surrounding it that was given to Teilo with thanks by Iddon.[4]

Newman describes the church as 'an unusually grand cruciform church, built of roughly coursed Old Red Sandstone and crowned by a landmark shingled spire.' The crossing tower and aisled nave are of 13th- to early 14th-century date; the chancel is 14th century and the font of the 12th century. The church contains a vividly carved Green Man 'with lolling tongue' on the arch between the chancel and a chapel[5] — the Green Man has its origins in a pre-Christian fertility symbol. Brook observes that the early status of the site was as a church.[6] Adjoining the west and south-west of the churchyard are the ruins of a range of stone buildings (with some brick in evidence) — there are arched stone structures and sizeable areas of walls.

The current boundaries enclose a quadrangular area.[7] It has possibly been extended to the south, indeed the boundaries appear to have been much altered and there is some curving which may suggest an earlier, more circular site. There is a significant drop of up to 10 to 12 feet on the western and northern sides to the adjoining land, but less of a height difference on the other sides. The church is offset within the boundaries toward the north-east. This is a striking site where one can visualise the events in *c*.600.

The church from the south-west showing the ruins in the foreground
of the range of stone buildings

LLANTILIO PERTHOLEY –
St. Teilo (SO 312 164)

A deceptively early site, perhaps connected with St. Teilo personally, and home to an ancient yew on an earlier boundary within the churchyard.

Llantilio Pertholey is about 2 miles north of the centre of Abergavenny and has the feeling of being a satellite village. Its first mention is in *c*.600 in one of the Llandaff Charters where it is called '*Lann Maur*' and '*Lann Teliau Port Halauc*', which latter name incorporates an early spelling of Teilo and also helps to understand the present spelling of the place-name. The charter records that 'King Iddon gave *Lann Maur* ... with its *territorium*, to (archbishop) Teilo.' The area granted comprised 900 acres.[1] Brook states that its early status was as a church.[2] The fabric of the present church dates back in part to the 13th to 14th centuries, with later additions and modifications[3]

It is a low-lying site and the churchyard is not raised. The shape of the enclosure is quadrangular,[4] and there is a recent looking extension to the west. An ancient-looking yew is situated on this side against a low stone wall on what appears to be the earlier western boundary — from its girth and size it could well be of pre-Norman date. There are also two yews to the south-west corner of the church enclosure and although mature, they do not look ancient.

On first impression the site does not strike one as being particularly ancient, but the existence of the *c*.600 charter proves otherwise and demonstrates that some of the oldest sites have deceptively later medieval appearances.

LLANVACHES – St. Dubricius
(ST 434 917)

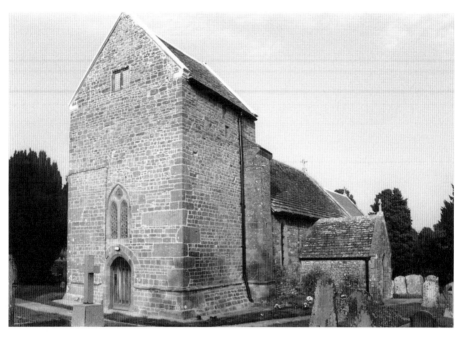

A possible early 'merthyr' or martyr church.

Llanvaches is about 2¼ miles north-north-west of Caerwent. Currently dedicated to St. Dubricius (Dyfrig), the church was originally dedicated to St. Maches or Machuta, who is styled virgin and martyr. She was reputedly the sister to St. Cadoc, daughter of Gwynllyw and Glywys and grand-daughter to Brychan, and an apparently very charitable person who always gave alms to any poor person who asked for help. There are two versions of her death. In the Iolo Manuscripts she is said to have been murdered by a pagan Saxon who knew where she gave out alms. Disguising himself as a beggar he stabbed her in the chest at Llanvaches, which was thereafter called Merthyr Maches. In the *Life* of St. Tathan she is referred to as Machuta and it relates how she met her death when shepherding a flock from which thieves planned to steal a three-year-old ram. They could not do so without her seeing them, so they lured her into a forest with her flock where they decapitated her before making off with the ram. They later confessed the murder to St. Tathan who built a church in her honour on the site of her murder, and then took her body to Caerwent where it was buried in the floor of the church.'[1]

If the Iolo Manuscripts are correct — and they are known for their inaccuracies — St. Maches/Machuta was already using the site at Llanvaches for distributing alms, thus she could be claimed as founder. Should the *Life* of St. Tathan be correct, and she was only shepherding a flock there, why not dedicate the site to Dyfrig? Perhaps she combined a pastoral and religious life. In any event, the site of her murder was referred to as *ecclesia Merthir Maches / Merthirmaches* in a charter of *c.*775.[2] One would have expected Dyfrig's name to have been substuted for Maches by the compiler of the *Book of Llandaff* — they were, after all, keen to claim as much land under Dyfrig's name as possible — but oddly it was not. In fact in a number of charters one suspects the very earliest saint's name was left intact.

The current church is an attractive building with an unusually shaped, rather squat tower with a short saddleback roof. Newman suggests a late medieval date and notes the massive quoins and finely-squared blocks of the lower half of the tower, whilst the upper half is more rubbly.[3]

The churchyard is indicative of an early medieval foundation but it is quite small. Brook describes the shape as quadrangular[4] and it is raised by about 3 feet on the southern side with an old yew against the boundary wall. It is not so raised on the south-west or western sides but, when viewed from outside, on the south, one can see how the external land slopes away from the boundary and the whole church site appears raised. There is some curving on the south-east perimeter near to a very old but healthy yew growing in this boundary. Some internal embanking exists along the wall on the north side. It certainly has the feel of a small, early medieval church site.

That the church originally had a merthyr place-name suggests it belongs to the earliest strata of early medieval church sites. There are ten merthyr churches named in the *Book of Llandaff* by *c.*950 and the place-name element 'merthyr' is considered to be of undoubted pre-Norman origin. The substitution of 'merthyr' by 'llan' was usual in subsequent centuries and this had happened at Llanvaches by 1254. Brook observes that 'as a group, virtually every merthyr–named place in Wales that can still be identified has some special feature, either historical or archaeological. This confers some importance on the few sites with such names without other special features.' However, by the 11th and 12th centuries it was assumed the merthyr element referred to a martyrdom, presumably on site, and thus the story of the murder of St. Maches was invented to 'explain' the name. As Brook notes, the distribution of 'merthyr place-names in Wales is strikingly south-eastern' and it is tempting to associate them with the survival of late Roman Christianity although the martyrdom of Aaron and Julius at nearby Caerleon is 'the only known evidence of such a link'.[5]

LLANVAPLEY – St. Mable (or Mabli) (SO 367 141)

There is charter evidence of the 9th century for the existence of a church which has the only dedication of an otherwise unknown female British saint, and is set in a significantly raised churchyard.

The church of St. Mable is about 4 miles east of Abergavenny in the centre of the small hamlet. One of the Llandaff charters dated *c.*860 states that 'Britcon son of Deuon gave six churches with their *territoria* to bishop Grecielis', one of these being named '*ecclesia Mable*'.[1] St. Mable is mentioned in the Iolo Manuscripts, but Llanvapley is her only dedication and nothing else is known about her.[2] From the pattern and frequency of dedications, it appears that, whereas male saints travelled far and wide setting up foundations en route, female saints tended to stay in one spot to practice their devotions. The evocative charter bounds are stated as:

> From the Glaswern to the ... deep black brook. Thence transversely between Jacob's river and Brynn Corne. Again through the wood from there it descends to the Manach rivulet. In a straight line to the Halannog, straight on through the wood to the Oncir as far as the further well. With the Ashwood for a guide it goes in a straight line between two castles to the long island of [blank] until it falls into the river Trothy.[3]

Once again, the use of the word 'castle' is interesting if this is indeed a genuine write-up of a 9th-century document.

The church is a handsome medieval structure built of Old Red Sandstone. The chancel is early to mid-13th century, the nave was remodelled in the 14th and 15th centuries, and the tower is basically 14th century with more recent additions and alterations. The font is 12th century. To the south of the church are the remains of a late medieval cross.[4]

The small, curvilinear churchyard is significantly raised for a good deal of its length above the surrounding land. For example there is a steep drop from the churchyard to the road level on the western side of up to 15 feet and 12 steps climb to the north-west entrance; on the southern side the height difference is about 8 to 10 feet. There is a light drop on the eastern side with a domestic outbuilding abutting the boundary, but no difference in ground level on the northern side between the churchyard and adjoining Vicarage garden. There is a large yew on the north-west corner of the churchyard with an enormous gnarled trunk which is starting to hollow. It has a sign stating it is over 400 years old, but its large girth suggests it is older still.

LLANVETHERINE –
St. James the Elder (SO 364 172)

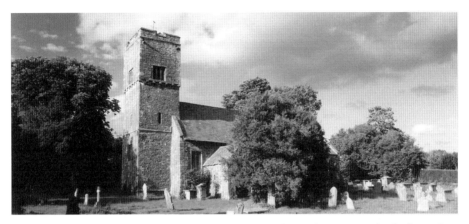

A pre-Norman foundation with written charter bounds previously dedicated to an obscure British saint, an effigy of whom probably exists within the church.

The church is 4 miles north-east of Abergavenny and 2 miles east of the dramatic, conical-shaped hill of the Skirrid. It is an attractive building built from slabby local red sandstone. The tower is of unusual design that has a top section that is wider than the bottom two-thirds. It is thought that the tower and nave were remodelled in the 15th and 16th centuries, whilst the chancel is 14th century.[1] Inside there is a life-size effigy of a priest with a right hand raised in blessing. No date is given for this effigy, but it is said to be a representation of St. Gwytherin, the original titular saint; it bears the inscriptions 'S. Vetterinus' (a derivative of the Latin Victorinus and considered to be the same name as Gwytherin) and 'Iacob P'sona'.[2] St. Gwytherin's parentage is not known.

The churchyard shape is deemed largely curved,[3] the church itself cut into the slope about half way down the enclosure. A moderately-sized stream (a tributary of the River Trothy) forms the southern boundary. Although there is nothing definitively early in the appearance of the site, there is a charter dated *c.*876 in the Llandaff Charters in which 'Cors and Morudd gave *ecclesia Gueithirin* with an *ager* of three *modii* around it.' Later Cors 'gave another three *modii* across the road beside the other *ager*, with its wood and *placitis*, to bishop Nudd, with king Hywel's guarantee.' Davies states that '*placitis*' normally means 'pleas' but here may refer to some associated rights — its use is unique in the Llandaff material.[4] The church appears in later lists as Lanwytheryn where details of the bounds of the charter are given. These mention the Trothy, the hind's ford (Rhyd yr Ewig), the spring of Colwyn, the Crug and a wood.[5] The earlier charter shows that the church was in existence by 876 and, by implication, was founded at an earlier time.

LLANWERN – St. Mary
(ST 371 878)

The shape of the church enclosure, the presence of a pre-Norman cross-head and 10th-century charter evidence indicate an early site.

The church of St. Mary is about 1½ miles east of the edge of Newport, and east of the settlement of Llanwern in an area criss-crossed by dykes and drainage channels. It is less than a third of a mile from the massive Newport steelworks and the main east/west railway, but remains undisturbed by modern development.

The church, then called '*Lann Guern Tiuauc*', is mentioned in a note associated with the Llandaff charters that records King Morgan as returning all lands and a number of churches to Bishop Gwgon of Llandaff in *c*.970.[1] The *Tiuauc* element appears to refer to the original patron saint, Tivauc.[2]

The church structure is largely of 14th- and 15th-century date with some later alterations, and contains what is thought to be a pre-Norman cross-head.[3] In front of the south wall of the tower outside is a part of a shaft to a cross on a small broached base which looks medieval.

The churchyard is not precisely circular but is strongly curvilinear to the southern western and eastern boundaries, with signs of internal embanking in places. The northern boundary is straight, but this looks as though it has been extended or altered, certainly the main entrance is in the north-eastern corner. If the churchyard is viewed from the adjoining field at the back, the curving boundaries can be seen to their best advantage. The ground levels within the enclosure are slightly raised above the exterior levels.

MAMHILAD – St. Illtyd
(SO 305 035)

Mamhilad is almost certainly an early medieval foundation. The earthen banks of the churchyard perimeter, the presence of the ancient yews and the curvilinear and raised nature of the enclosure are good physical evidence — the legend in St. Cadoc's *Life* is also excellent documentary proof.

Mamhilad lies about 2 miles north-east of Pontypool. The church is at the centre of the village and is a delightful, white-washed structure, mainly of 14th-century date. However the north wall of the nave and the lower part of the north and south walls of the chancel are built of 'slabby, slate-like stones, rather than blocks, [and] must belong to a building which pre-dated any of the existing openings.' There is a re-fashioned, possible 12th-century font, a 14th- to 15th-century screen and west gallery, the latter incorporating the bressumer and front of a rood loft.[1]

The churchyard is on top of a rise and is curvilinear with sizeable drops to the road to the west and also to the north-west. To the north there is only a small drop to the adjoining field which then falls away quite steeply. Brook notes that the there are earthen banks around most of the perimeter of the churchyard except on the side bordering the road[2] — a sign of an early church site in Gwent (see Bettws Newydd, p.315) A section of fairly low earth bank can be seen quite clearly on the northern side.

Mamhilad is renowned for its large, ancient yews. These include fine specimens in the north-west corner of the churchyard, another opposite the right-hand side of the porch and a further equally ancient one opposite the entrance to the south porch. Chetan and Brueton record that the yew to the south is female, has a girth of 31 feet and an estimated age of 2,000 years.[3] Even using Bevan-Jones' more conservative dating guideline of a yew with a girth of 23 to 33 feet dating broadly into the band of 1,200 to 2,000 years, it suggests the Mamhilad tree is still nearer 2,000 years old. We noticed at least five ancient yews in the churchyard. If the other yews are of approximately this age we may well have a pagan site which was re-Christianised, or have yews that were planted in the late Roman/sub-Roman period and possibly connected with the activity of early British saints.

The enclosure slopes from west to east with the natural contours, and the church is on a flatter area. To the east of the chancel is a scarp, but whether this is a previous boundary is not clear. The Welsh lords of Caerleon appear to have 'had some claim to the site or area' at Mamhilad, and a connection between high status religious sites and secular lordships is known in several other places. Mamhilad may at one time have been a high status monastic site, for Brook states that it is mentioned in the *Life* of St. Cadoc as a monastery (*Mammelliat locus*) which belonged to St. Cadoc's establishment at Llancarfan.[4]

In the *Life* of St. Cadoc, which was written in the late 11th or very early 12th century, a curious episode is related concerning Mamhilad. The *Life* states that 'a certain very powerful English viscount, named Eilaf' entered Glamorganshire with a large company of men 'for the purpose of plundering and destroying'. The clergy of Llancarfan hearing of the threat fled the monastery taking with them St. Cadoc's coffin 'and other relics, bearing the means for their protection, until they came to the place, Mammeliat, [Mamhilad] and there they hid themselves.' They had not been at Mamhilad long when 'a multitude of the Danish and English robbers came to them.' They saw Cadoc's fine coffin and tried to take it away and from 'four to one hundred men attempted with all their might to raise it' but they were unable to move it, which angered them. One, more mad with rage than the others, ran forward and grabbed a stout stick and struck the coffin, whereupon 'it produced a loud bellowing noise, like a bull, and greatly frightened the whole army, and immediately there was a great earthquake in those parts.' The men backed off except for 'one of them more unhappy than the others, being induced by greediness, cut off its golden pinnacle with a hatchet.' It fell into his lap and 'immediately like a fire burned his bosom; and stupefied, and excited by the pain of heat, he resolved to fix the pinnacle in its place; and being so fixed, it firmly adhered, as if it had been united by gold soldering.' With that done 'the unhappy violator of the coffin melted in the sight of the whole army, like wax before the fire.' Not surprisingly the army 'returned as exiles. Afterwards they had not a desire for plundering the before-mentioned places of the patron, and ceased to lay waste his territories.'[5] Although a date is not given for this episode, mention of the Danes and English imply a 9th-century or later date — that is if the use of these terms is not anachronistic. It is also interesting that the events relate to St. Cadoc and not the patron of the church, St. Illtud. Indeed the term 'patron' is used in the account with reference to St. Cadoc but whether this was meant to refer to Mamhilad is not clear.

MATHERN – St. Tewdric
(ST 523 908)

The site is of particular interest, as it contains the burial place of 6th-century St. Tewdric (also spelt Tewdrig), has a holy well nearby and one of the Bishop of Llandaff's palaces next door.

Mathern is less than a mile south-west of the outskirts of Chepstow, just south of the M4, the church lying at the far end of the old core of the village.

Most of what can be deduced of Tewdric is derived from the *Book of Llandaff* which was written up in the 12th century with the main purpose of strengthening Llandaff's claim over land against the dioceses of St. David's and Hereford. It therefore 'reflects the first half of the twelfth century, when it was written, far better than the sixth century which is its ostensible subject matter.'[1] It is said that Tewdric was king of Morganwg and, in old age, handed over the rule of the kingdom to his son, Meurig, and made a cell for himself in a rock at Tintern where he retired and lived as a hermit. He had had a reputation as a valiant warrior, and when the Saxons invaded Gwent, he took up arms again. He had a vision in which an angel told him that if he led an army to battle, the enemy would flee at Brockweir above Tintern Parva and not return for 30 years, although he himself would be mortally wounded at the ford of Tintern. This he duly did, but as the Saxons fled, one hurled a lance over the river and Tewdric was fatally wounded. At first he did not wish to move, but die where he lay and be interred on Flat Holm in the Severn Estuary. On the following day, however, two stags harnessed

373

to a wagon appeared and Tewdric, understanding that they had been sent by God, allowed himself to be lifted into the wagon. Baring-Gould and Fisher recount 'The wagon carried him to the bank of the Severn [at Mathern] and there stayed, and on the spot a sparkling spring began to flow. Then suddenly the wagon dissolved, and Tewdrig gave up the ghost.' Tewdric was buried here and Meurig, his son, built an oratory at the site, which was blessed by Oudoceus, bishop of Llandaff. The site and land around it was subsequently given to Oudoceus and, during late medieval times, the bishops built a palace there which was used for about three centuries. Bishop Godwin (1601–18) conducted an excavation at Mathern church, presumably to establish the burial place of Tewdric. A stone coffin with a skeleton in near perfect condition was discovered and was taken to be that Tewdric as there was a severe fracture to the skull. During restoration work in the chancel in 1881 the coffin was re-discovered with the bones still inside, beneath the tablet set in the south wall. In the *Book of Llandaff* the church is referred to as *Merthir Teudiric* or the *martyrium* or burial site of the martyr Tewdric.[2]

In a 17th-century document, sections of which may be inaccurate, we are told that beside founding several churches and colleges and supplying them with endowments, Tewdric founded a church at 'Llandaff on the spot where stood the church of Lles (Lucius) ab Coel, which was burnt down by the infidels ...'.[3] Tewdric is also credited with founding the churches of Merthyr Tydfil; Llandow (4 miles west of Cowbridge, South Glamorgan); and Bedwas (2 miles north-east of Caerphilly in Mid-Glamorgan).

There are three references to Mathern in the Llandaff Charters. The first is allegedly in *c.*620 when 'Meurig gave Tewdrig's *territorium* to bishop Euddogwy' (the latter is another name for Oudoceus). Although the *territorium* is not named, the bounds identify it as Mathern,[4] and give a wonderful sense of the place, purportedly from the 6th century, and include such references as Lybiaw's stone, the well of Elichguid, the pools of Rhinion, and ends with the directions which include 'Along the dyke as far as Lunbiw's Kiln. From the Kiln downwards along the dyke ... downwards to the ruins, to the pool. Along the pool to the mouth of the Hunger Pill on the Wye. Along the Wye and the Severn, with its wears and its landing-place for ships, as far as the mouth of the Merrick brook.'[5] Within a few lines a long distant landscape is wonderfully evoked, demarcated with dykes and busy with industry and communication. The reference to 'the ruins' has occasioned local interest. It is thought to refer to the Thornwell area just beyond the southern tip of Chepstow and perhaps describe a decayed Roman structure, if the bounds do indeed refer to the landscape in the 6th century and are not a later concoction to enable the see of Llandaff to collect its dues.[6]

A grant of *c.*900 details land given by March ap Peibio to Bishop Cyfeilliog as compensation for killing his cousin, which included 'part of the *territorium* of *Merthir Teudiric*'.[7] In a charter of *c.*1075, in a grant of land for Llangwm Isaf, one of the witnesses is *'iouan presbiter de merthirteudiric'* (Iouan, presbyter of Merthyr Tewdric, i.e. Mathern).[8] This documentation supports the early establishment of Mathern and its importance.

There is a legend in the works of the 9th-century historian, Nennius, of a holy well at Mathern who includes it in his 'Wonders of Britain'. He relates that there

> is a spring by the wall of Pydew Meurig [Meurig's Well], and there is a plank in the middle of the spring, and men may wash their hands and their faces, and have the plank under their feet when they wash. I have tested it and seen it myself. When the sea floods at high tide, the Severn spreads over the whole shore, and touches it, and reaches to the spring, and the spring is filled from the Severn Bore, it draws the plank with it to the open sea, and it is cast about in the sea for three days, but on the fourth day it is found in the same spring. Now it came to pass that a countryman buried it in the ground to test it, and on the fourth day it was found in the spring, and the countryman who took it and buried it died before the end of the month.'[9]

Nennius died in 809, and the earliest surviving copy of his history is a second edition dating to the year 828/9.[10] The source is rare as it is securely pre-Norman. The well is still in existence, and may be seen at the roadside about 400 yards north of the church and just south of the motorway bridge, surrounded by black paling. Above ground level it appears to be a modern reconstruction from 1977, but within the well the stonework looks much older.

The holy well

375

Mathern churchyard is flat, quite large and of curvilinear but irregular configuration. It is neither circular, nor particularly embanked around the edges and is wider to the northern side than the south. North of the church there is a remaining low medieval arch in the churchyard, but it is not known to what it belonged.[11] The churchyard boundary is mostly walled, and the interior is raised a little above the exterior ground levels, particularly to the long curving north-eastern boundary. However, considering the site's age, it is raised very little.

The church has a substantial tower of the late 15th century, and the structure was altered and enlarged during that time, but the main core of the building is 13th century.[12] The oldest visible section is at the west of the north aisle, and consists of a line of Romanesque arches on round pillars. The plaque above the reputed burial place of St. Tewdric is in the chancel.

To the south-west of the church is the former Bishop's Palace. It was 'one of three medieval palaces of the bishops of Llandaff' and the only one inhabited after the Owain Glyn Dwr rebellion.[13] This most attractive structure was rebuilt in the early 15th century and has been altered since.

The cult of Tewdric was very strong for a long time it seems, for example Miles Salley, Bishop of Llandaff from 1500–17, directed in his will that 'his heart and bowels [were] to be deposited at the High Altar of the Church at Matherne, before the image of S. Theodorick.'[14] There is an illegible incised slab in the centre of the chancel floor where these remains are said to have been buried.[15]

MONMOUTH – St. Mary
(SO 509 130)

There is some tentative charter evidence for an early medieval church in Monmouth, perhaps on the site of the present priory church.

The priory church, situated at the north end of the town centre, is built on a slight rise. The Benedictine priory of St. Mary was founded in *c*.1075 and the priory church was consecrated in 1101.[1] The church contains the remains of a massive early Norman pillar at the back of the nave and, intriguingly, it may have had an even earlier predecessor.

In *c*.720 there is a record of a grant in which 'King Ithel gave *Aper Menei*, previously given him by king Morgan, to bishop Berthwyn' and this is identified with Monmouth.[2] However it does not specifically mention a church. A charter dated *c*.733 does so when it states 'Elias gave a *podum* (with) four *modii* of land around it and its *census* to bishop Berthwyn, with the consent of king Ithel and his sons.' Whilst Davies tentatively identifies this with Monmouth, she notes that the wording of this charter, and another of the same date, give 'slightly more reason to suppose that the grant of an unnamed *podum* was made in Monmouth than that the *podum* itself was necessarily in Monmouth.'[3] Whichever way round it was, it shows Monmouth had some standing in the early medieval period. There is a further charter dated *c*.910 in which 'Brochfael ap Meurig gave *ecclesia Sanctae Mariae*, with three *modii* of land around it, to his daughter, a holy virgin.'[4] The title of the document is '*Lann Meiripenn Ros*' and Davies proposes an identification with Monmouth; Evans and Rhys go a step further and suggest it refers to St. Mary's at Monmouth. There followed a dispute between Brochfael and Bishop Cyfeilliog over the church and its land, with judgement being made in favour of the bishop.[5] There is also a rather confused narration attached in which Brochfael's daughter is said to have lived a 'holy life at the church till her death, but also how she was seduced by Edgar (son of *Leui*) and produced a son.'[6]

PENALLT –
dedication unknown (SO 523 107)

A hilltop church, home to an ancient yew and possibly mentioned in the 6th century.

The church of Penallt is an exciting site to visit. Situated only about 1½ miles south-east of Monmouth, the journey by road is nearer to 6 miles because of the wooded circuitous route that is necessary. The church lies at the top of a steep promontory above the River Wye and has extensive and superb views over the thickly wooded valley. There are a few scattered farms in the locality, but the church essentially sits alone on the hilltop and would have provided ample isolation and peace sought by any early British saint. It is still referred to as the 'old church'.

The church is imposing and is built from Old Red Sandstone that gives it a warm pinkish-brown hue. It has a tall and quite slender tower which probably dates to the 14th century. The porch and south aisle are of 16th-century date; the nave and chancel are of approximately 15th-century date and are not aligned to each other.[1] The interior of the church is most attractive. When viewed from the bottom of the slope, the church looks more like a collection of buildings rather than one structure because of the steep incline.

The churchyard boundaries are embanked and walled, and in the perimeter wall on the west are large, roughly-hewn boulders. The churchyard is large and has a rectilinear/squarish shape — termed quadrangular by Brook[2] — although the eastern side is curved with a significant drop to the field below. There is a very tall, female yew to the east of the chancel with a measured girth of 24 feet and an estimated age of 1,600 years,[3] which may have been an early saint's planting. Wells are marked on Ordnance Survey maps immediately east and north-west of the churchyard, and one wonders if they had any religious connotation.

Penallt appears in the later taxation lists of the *Book of Llandaff*, but is conjoined with Trelleck *'De ecclesijs de Trillek et Pennalth'*.[4] There is also a curious reference to Penallt in the *Life* of Oudoceus. St. Oudoceus had wanted to retrieve the body of his uncle, St. Teilo, that was preserved at Llandeilo Fawr. Baring-Gould and Fisher surmise that he went there and also carried off

> all the gold and revenue he could collect in that place and Penallt. The men of Penallt, and probably those also of Llandeilo Fawr, did not relish this; the prosperity of their churches depended on the possession of relics of their founder; as little were they pleased to be despoiled of the treasure in metal, and to have to pay dues and probably arrears, to the representatives of Teilo. A disturbance ensued, but a compromise was effected.'[5]

Is this Penallt in Monmouthshire? If it is, it would be a very early reference, albeit written in *c.*1150 but alluding back to the 6th century. It would also suggest that Penallt was an important and wealthy church in the early medieval period, something long forgotten, but it might explain the size and nature of the later medieval church building. However we wonder if it is in fact Penally that is meant; Penally was St. Teilo's ancestral home and the church at Penally was one of the claimants for the saint's body after his death.[6] However it would be strange that Baring-Gould and Fisher should mistakenly write Penally as Penallt, considering their careful and exceptionally high level of scholarship, although it might, of course, have been a scribal error in the 12th century. And yet, the possibility remains that Penallt in Monmouthshire was the place in question and gives the exciting thought that this church site dates back over 1,500 years — a date supported circumstantially by the estimated age of the yew.

PENRHOS – St. Cadoc
(SO 417 117)

There is no mention of Penrhos in the *Book of Llandaff* but the presence of an ancient yew and the remnants of an earthen-banked boundary suggest an early origin, supported by the dedication to the 6th-century St. Cadoc.

St. Cadoc's church is 3 miles north of Raglan in the centre of the small village of Penrhos. The church structure is basically of the 14th and 15th centuries, with a 16th-century tower with Victorian additions.[1] The area immediately surrounding the church is very slightly raised and this may be a possible earlier enclosure. There is also a very ancient-looking yew opposite the church porch on the southern side. This tree has a large girth and obvious hollowing, but despite its obvious age does not figure in Chetan and Brueton's list of ancient yews.

The tear-drop-shaped churchyard is fairly sizeable and has some curving to the northern and western sides. There are overgrown and weathered earthen boundary banks along all sides suggesting an early enclosure (see under Bettws Newydd, p.315). A section is clear on the western side when viewed from the lane and this side is about 3 to 4 feet higher than the adjoining road, although use of the latter may have accentuated the difference, otherwise there is not much height difference between the church enclosure and the adjoining land.

Three wells are marked on the large scale OS maps just north-west of the church. Other wells are marked to the south-south-east and east, with yet further wells slightly further to the north and running west/east — indeed the local area is rich in springs and wells.

The ancient and hollowed yew

ROCKFIELD – St. Cenedlon
(SO 482 148)

Probably dedicated to a very early but unrecorded saint with a 10th-century charter and bounds that record several wells within the vicinity.

The church of St. Cenedlon at Rockfield lies about 2½ miles north-west of Monmouth, on a sloping site close to the River Monnow. Of the dedication, Baring-Gould and Fisher discuss the possibility that St. Cynheiddon, daughter of Brychan, was the patron, her name having been corrupted in spellings over many centuries and appearing now as Cenedlon. She is described as a 'Saint on Mynydd Cymorth' in most late lists of Brychan's children, but the location of the mountain in question is not stated. She appears to have been the patron of the now vanished chapel on a hill at Capel Llangynheiddon (near Carmarthen), the place-name of which remembers the original spelling of her name. However Baring-Gould and Fisher conclude that, although she is said to have been the patroness of Rockfield, this is a mistake for St. Kenelm.[1] St. Kenelm was an Anglo-Saxon and reputedly a boy martyr, based in short-lived county of Winchcombeshire in Gloucestershire. In reality he lived into adulthood, but that is another story.

In a document in the Llandaff Charters dated *c*.970, Rockfield is apparently called *Lann Guoronoi*. The bounds begin with 'The Monnow, on one side, making for the pant in the Cecin towards the west on the north side of the church' and mentions 'the spring of Ffynnon Dioci.'[2] In a subsequent grant of *c*.1020 'The four *alumni* of Eil ... gave *Lannguronoi*, with a *modius* and a half of land, to Bishop Bleddri with king Rhys's guarantee.' The word 'alumni' refers to a type of legal ward. This charter also mentions bounds but Davies notes they are not the same as the ones recorded in the *c*.970 charter.[3] In the *c*.1020 document the bounds start 'From Rhyd y Cerr as far as the Cecyn, as far as the well of Guaidan' and include 'the well of the hazel.'[4]

The name *Lann Guoronoi* makes us question whether the original saint was ever St. Cenedlon or St. Kenelm. Brook lists Guoronoi as the patron, but quotes a listing of 'St. Kiniephant of Rokevill' in 1186.[5] If this latter is to be equated to St. Kenelm, why, one might ask, would he have a Monmouthshire dedication when he was an Anglo-Saxon saint? It sounds as though the original patron's name, Guoronoi, was displaced by the mis-spelt name of a daughter of Brychan, who somehow became mistaken for St. Kenelm. There is no St. Guoronoi mentioned in Baring-Gould and Fisher — the nearest spellings are St. Guorboe (see under entry for Garway, p.270) and St. Guordocui who was a disciple of St. Dyfrig and abbot of Much Dewchurch in the 7th century.[6] The identity of the original founder of Rockfield is therefore a mystery.

The well by the main enrtance to the churchyard

In front of the main churchyard entrance is a well set in a stone alcove with two stone seats. Francis Jones refers to a St. Michael's well within Rockfield parish but does not locate it. In this well there were stones with red spots said to 'be the bloodstains of "some saint" who was beheaded there.' The red stain is, in fact, more likely to come from iron found at chalybeate wells.[7] The Explorer series Ordnance Survey map shows two wells marked both north-west of the church, approximately a quarter of a mile away at SO 479 152 and SO 476 151. Which of these wells may be those mentioned in the charter boundaries: is it the well of Guaidan, the well of the hazel or the spring of Ffynnon Dioci?

The church tower is medieval, and the remainder rebuilt in 1859–60.[8]

The churchyard is irregular in shape,[9] and slopes downward from north to south with the church standing on a flatter area. There are slight undulations to the southern edge of this which may indicate that the enclosure was once smaller, but no clear indication is visible.

ST. ARVANS – St. Arvan
(ST 516 965)

Indications on the ground are that the site is early medieval, and documentary evidence supports this.

St. Arvans is 2 miles north of Chepstow. The church is an unusual building with dormer windows, an octagonal tower and attractive paintwork to the ceiling of the chancel. The south wall of the chancel is Norman as shown by its narrow priest's door, but the church has many later additions, mainly Victorian.[1]

The churchyard is of moderate size and is bounded by stone walls. The shape is curvilinear, and appears to have extensions to the north and east. There are slight undulations within the enclosure, but none so defined as to indicate earlier boundaries. To the south and west, where the churchyard is narrower, the internal ground level is a little raised above the exterior.

At the west end of the church on a window sill there is stone about 2½ feet long and 15 inches wide. On the front is a wheel-cross of Celtic type with interlace patterning which is flanked by two bird-headed angels. On the back is a plain Latin wheel-cross which is flanked by panels of interlace design. The form and decoration suggest a 10th-century date.[2] The stone is now in two pieces and the decoration is very eroded.

The church site is mentioned in a charter of *c.*955 where it occurs in the Llandaff Charters under the title of *'ecclesia sanctorum Iarmen et Febric'*[3] which suggests an early dedication to the saints Jarmen and Febric of whom nothing is known.[4] In the 14th-century additions in the Llandaff Charters it is called *'ecclesia de sancto Aruyno'*.[5] The charter actually relates to land in Penterry (ST 522 998) which is less than half a mile south-west of Tintern and is today represented by

The probable 10th-century stone, now broken, kept within the churrch

383

the area around Penterry Farm, about 2 miles north-north-east of St. Arvans church. There is a fascinating narrative with the charter in which Eli, a church deacon, accosted a reaper in a harvest field and they came to blows. The reaper cut off one of Eli's fingers with his hook, whereupon the deacon begged him to bind the wound, after which Eli stabbed him through the heart and ran to St. Arvans church for sanctuary. The murdered man's relatives broke into the church, ignored the right of sanctuary and killed Eli in front of the altar. Bishop Pater of Llandaff was furious that sanctuary had been broken and that the church had been desecrated, and told the local king that he would be excommunicated unless those responsible were caught. Six men were duly surrendered up by the king, and were held in chains at Llandaff for six months. They were only released on the condition that they paid a heavy fine and surrendered their possessions to the church. As these possessions were near to St. Arvans, Baring-Gould and Fisher consider there is no doubt that the church of St. Jarmen and St. Febric was St. Arvans church and they conclude that 'surely this was one of the most iniquitous judgements ever delivered' and one can only agree![6] Davies adds that the deacon's right of sanctuary was violated by members of King Nowy's *familia* and that the meeting between the king and Bishop Pater took place at Caerwent. She also adds that the bulk of the narrative is so unusual and detailed that 'it is highly unlikely to owe its origin to any late fabrication.' She suggests it was 'recorded shortly after the events described and represents at the least one sincere view of the events leading up to the settlement'.[7] It is rare to find such a drama applying to an early site.

ST. MAUGHAN'S –
St. Meugan (SO 461 172)
and LLANGYNFYL (SO 495 167)

St. Maughan's was abandoned in the mid-6th century and then re-dedicated in the early medieval period, whilst the lost church of Llangynfyl is the possible burial place of a forgotten British saint.

The church lies at the centre of a tiny settlement, about 4 miles north-west of Monmouth. The present patron of the church is St. Meugan, an early British saint, (see Llanfeugan, p.198) but he is not the person to whom the church was dedicated — that was to St. Malo. However the earliest church was actually dedicated to St. Dyfrig, but it was abandoned after the advent of the Yellow Plague in around 547. It was refounded by St. Malo, also known as St. Machu, Machutus and Maclovius. It appears from his various biographies that St. Malo was born in about 527, the son of a nobleman of Gwent; in other sources Malo's father is said to have been also the father of Ynyr Gwent, the king of Gwent. Malo's parents lived at Llancarfan and his mother, who was middle-aged when he was born, went into labour at the monastery where Malo was delivered on Easter Eve. Allegedly, on the night of his birth 33 other boys 'saw the light for the first time', and Malo's father had them all sent with his son to the abbot of Llancarfan for their education. The boys were to act as foster brothers and attendants to Malo. On reaching adolescence Malo's parents sent for him, requiring that he should leave the monastery and seek a secular life. The boy refused as he was set on a religious life and ran away, taking refuge on some distant islet until his parents agreed to his choice. Malo was ordained a priest and later left Llancarfan for Brittany, probably as a result of the Yellow Plague. He returned to Wales in about 550 but then departed for Brittany two years or so later and settled in Aaron, only returning to Llancarfan to gather assistants. He died in about 621 on his way back to Saintes in France.[1]

Not surprisingly most of St. Malo's dedications are in Brittany; in Normandy there are dedications to him in Picardy, Artois and Champagne and the Isle of France. Malo only appears to have had a few dedications in Britain — the one at St. Maughan's and possibly two adjoining churches mentioned in the *Book of Llandaff*: '*Lann Liuit Machumur*' and '*Lann Vannar de Machumur*' (Machumur means Machu Mawr or Malo the Great). These churches are thought to be Llanlliwyd/Llanllwyd (now vanished) which was at one time a chapel under Llanvannor/Llanfaenor, the other church mentioned.[2]

There are several charters relating to St. Maughan's. In a *c.*860 grant, 'Britcon and Iliwg gave *Lann Mocha* to (archbishop Dyfrig) with the consent of king Meurig, together with the gift of Caradog and Cincu, sons of Guoleiduc.' St. Dyfrig is named as the recipient because the grant was made to his church, clearly not to him in person as he died in the early 6th century. In another grant of the same year 'Britcon ... gave six churches with their *territoria* to bishop Grecielis ... which previously belonged to Dyfrig'. St. Maughan's is named as *Lann Bocha* in this instance. In the same grant a church called '*ecclesia Tipallai*' is mentioned, which Davies suggests may be near St. Maughan's.[3]

In *c.*1030 there is a record that 'Seisyll ... gave *Cecin Penn Ros*, on the Monnow on the other side of Llangynfyl, to bishop Joseph and to the church of Cynfyl, with king Gruffudd's guarantee.'[4] Llangynfyl (SO 495 168) lies about two miles east of St. Maughan's, but there is no trace of any church there, only Llangunville Farm at SO 495 166 and a small wood a short distance to the north called Llangynfyl Wood. One wonders at the identity of the saint Cynfyl. Baring-Gould and Fisher mention a St. Cynfall who is only known through the *Book of Llandaff* in which a *Merthir Cynfall* is recorded, otherwise known as *Lann Cinfall* and *Ecclesia Cinfall*. They identify the place with Llangynvil (Llangynfyl) near Monmouth[5] suggesting Llangynfyl (from the Merthir/Martyr reference) is the burial place for this otherwise unknown saint. There is also a charter boundary recorded for Llangynfyl which mentions a dyke or ditch, 'the spring of Evrdil's well', the River Monnow and the Pwll Rhud (? Red pool).[6]

Another charter adds an interesting human aspect. In *c.*1025 it is stated 'Rhiwallon ap Tudfwlch attacked St. Maughan's with his following, but was thrown from his horse and broke his arm when leaving; he therefore gave up the booty and gave his hereditary terra, Cecin Pennicgelli, to bishop Joseph'. Davies suggests that the land given was near St. Maughan's and that this event was probably recorded soon after the transaction.[7] It is significant in that it implies that the church or settlement of St. Maughan's was worth attacking for booty and that the early 11th century church or monastery was of some importance.

In the last charter to mention St. Maughan's dated *c.*1072, 'King Caradog gave *Uilla Tref Rita* in *Edelicion*, near Llangedfedd, to bishop Herewald, in penance for his *familia*'s consumption of the bishop's foodrent at St. Maughan's', and Davies believes this information was again recorded soon after the transaction.[8] The land given was somewhere west of Usk and it seems the king and his entourage had eaten their way through supplies at St. Maughan's which were due to the bishop, for which the king had to compensate him.

Although none of the church structure is early medieval, the interior is a rare survival especially the octagonal timber posts of the arcade which are said to have once been encased with plaster — there are rough tooling marks on the posts which may have been the key for this plaster. The font is 12th century and is a spherical tub of simple design. Most of rest of the structure is late medieval. To the back of the nave is a pre-14th century half-pillar/half-pier protruding from the wall which shows that the nave had a south aisle from the start.[9]

The churchyard is partly-curved[10] and farm buildings adjoin the eastern and north-eastern sides. The south-western boundary is next to the road and about 5 feet above it. Growing in the wall on the churchyard side — in fact almost forcing the wall apart — is an ancient yew, perhaps as old as the church site itself.

TREDUNNOCK – St. Andrew
(ST 379 948)

The church houses a Roman grave slab, its churchyard has indications of an early enclosure and there is a specific legend attaching to St. Cadoc and King Arthur.

This lovely church lies in the centre of the village of Tredunnock, 6 miles north-west of Caerleon. The nave and chancel are Norman and the tower is 14th century. There are small Norman windows to the chancel, and a blocked one to the northern wall of the nave, where there are also large, quite roughly squared stones in the lowest courses — are they evidence of a much earlier church foundation underlying the present building? There is a Roman grave-slab on the wall above the font with well-preserved lettering, commemorating one Julius Julianus, a soldier with the Second Augustan Legion at Caerleon[1] — the similarity of the name with that of Julius the martyr who was executed at Caerleon is striking.

The churchyard is basically quadrangular,[2] of moderate size and flat. In the south-east corner there is a very old-looking female yew with a girth which has been measured at 25 feet.[3] It has a squat bulbous trunk and looks as if it has been pollarded at a low level at some stage in its life. There are no visible earthworks within the enclosure to suggest the boundaries have been altered but there is an appreciable drop to the external ground level to the north. To the west side of the church is what appears to be a tithe barn which has been converted into a domestic dwelling — it is set in its own enclosure.

A stile in the north churchyard wall leads to a right of way down to the River Usk. It was near here that the famous dispute over sanctuary arrangements between Cadoc and King Arthur was resolved, with a compensation payment of cattle which had to be herded over the river to Arthur near this point (see p.62).

It is suggested that the original patron of Tredunnock was St. Cybi and that the church was called *Landauer Guir*. Cybi was the son of Solomon or Selyf, a Cornish king and military officer commanding the British, and was either grandson, or great-grandson to King Geraint, and also first cousin to St. David. St. Non, David's mother, was Cybi's maternal aunt. Cybi began his education at the age of 7, and lived in Cornwall until he was 27, setting up two foundations, then spending some years abroad on a pilgrimage to Jerusalem and France. On his return and his father's death, his subjects tried to elevate him to the throne, but he took ten disciples, including his uncle, Cyngar (who had earlier founded Llandough in South Glamorgan), and Maelog (Meilig of Llowes) and travelled to Wales, where they were badly received by the local rulers of Morganwg (roughly Glamorgan). Cybi was better received by St. Cadoc's uncle, Edelig, who was ruling as regulus in south-west Monmouthshire; he gave Cybi land for two foundations which were at Llangybi (Llangibby) and probably Tredunnock. After some time Cybi travelled through St. David's to Ireland where he remained for some years with his followers, but after friction with other religious leaders, left for Anglesey, where he set up further foundations. He died some time after the Yellow Plague of 547, possibly in 554.[4]

 # TRELLACK/TRELLECH GRANGE – dedication unknown (SO 492 017)

Charter evidence for an early monastery, of which the wider enclosure boundary perhaps remains.

The medieval church was restored between 1860–1.[1] The churchyard is small, stone-walled and squarish in shape. There is nothing in its appearance and size to hint at the site's age. However in the Llandaff Charters there is a record of a grant given in *c.*960 by King Nowy to one Bishop Pater. It was then called *Uilla Guidcon*. The charter is preceded by a short account of King Nowy's 'violation of the sanctuary of *podum Mainuon in medio Trilec*' and the subsequent synod held there.[2] Brook notes that Trellack Grange's early status was that of a monastery, and notes the presence of a possible outlying enclosure, which is pear-shaped and follows the contours of the site.[3] As the charter suggests a more important site, the presence of a larger enclosure makes sense.

TRELLECK – St. Nicholas
(SO 501 055)

Famous for its holy wells, and with evidence for a church in the 8th century.

St. Nicholas is in the centre of the village, about 5 miles south of Monmouth. The present church has an impressive nave and a large tower with spire, the whole dating from the early 14th century, with 19th-century alterations.[1] To the south of the church and in front of the remains of a preaching cross on five steps, there is a sandstone slab nearly 6 feet long and 3 feet wide for which we can find no suggested date. The whole is supported horizontally on two supports about 1 to 1½ feet tall and 9 inches thick, on the ends of which are carved circular crosses of an ornate design. The carving appears to be medieval, but the whole structure could be earlier. The church guide suggests that the preaching cross on the stepped based is believed to date from the 8th or 9th centuries.

The churchyard is large and curvilinear, with the road running around the northern and eastern edges, and could be indicative of an early medieval shape, but has probably been much altered as industry in the area led to expansion in the pre-Civil War period. The church guide states that in Roman times soldiers were garrisoned in the town on the site of the churchyard. In medieval times, apart from agriculture and forestry, the main occupation was iron smelting and the slag from these operations is often found when digging and is known as 'Trellech Treacle'.[2]

A charter relating to Trelleck dates to c.755. In it 'King Ffernfael, at Cemais, gave *ecclesia Trilecc*, with three *modii* of land, to bishop Tyrchan'. Davies considers that Ffernfael holding court at Cemais (Kemeys Inferior, 6 miles north-east of Newport) is suspicious in an 8th-century record, but Ffernfael is mentioned in a similar vein in another charter dated to c.755. That Trelleck church was already established in the mid-8th century suggests it was an even earlier foundation. A

The sandstone slab in front of the preaching cross in the churchyard

document of *c.*868 records King Meurig freeing Trelleck church in the presence of his sons and returning it to Bishop Cerennyr.[3]

There were traditionally nine wells at Trelleck, each fed by a different spring, of which four remain, and each supposed to cure different diseases including 'scurvy, colic, and other distempers' in the 17th century. In 1708 it was stated 'Treleg wells of late years have been found very Medicinal and of the Nature of Tunbridge waters, flowing from an iron-ore mineral.' On Midsummer Eve fairies were said to dance at the Trelleck wells and 'to drink the water from harebells which were found strewn around the wells on Midsummer morning.' A farmer tried to close the wells but 'an old little man' appeared to him at the edge of one of them and told him that as a punishment for this 'no water would flow on his farm' — not surprisingly 'he reopened the wells, and water was plentiful again'. One of the wells was used for divination. Jones reports how 'Pebbles were dropped into the Trelleck Well ... and if many bubbles appeared the wish would

be granted, if moderately few then the wish would be delayed, but if none the wish would not be gratified.'[3] The connection with fairies, divination and with healing may point to a pre-Christian past, a possibility strengthened by the presence of three prehistoric standing stones on the edge of the village. The two wells that are most visible today are a well in the village centre with an attractive stone trough into which water runs, with a further small access arch to the right, and the Virtuous Well, about one-third of a mile south of the village. This has a D-shaped walled enclosure around it about 3 feet high. There are also niches for offerings.

The Virtuous Well

The well in the centre of the village

USK - St. Mary
(SO 378 008)

Possible charter evidence for an early Christian site.

The church of St. Mary is a large, attractive priory church with many features of the 12th to 16th century. The nave, north aisle and crossing tower comprised a Benedictine nunnery founded by Richard 'Strongbow' de Clare, probably in the 1170s.[1] However Usk may have had a much earlier Christian foundation. Rees gives a translation of the grants of land given to St. Cadoc (or his church) at the end of the *Life* of St. Cadoc — one of them notes that 'Cynfelyn gave the field called *Lisdin Borrion* with his body, for the traffic of the heavenly kingdom, to God and Saint Cadoc, which would pay him annually six tierces of ale, with bread and flesh, and honey.' He notes that *Din Birrion* occurs in the *Book of Llandaff* and that it is possibly Usk, previously called *Burrium*.[2] Davies gives the date of the charter as *c.*765 but leaves an identification open.[3] Rees suggests that there may have been an earlier church at Usk either built by, or dedicated, to St. Cadoc.[4] Baring-Gould and Fisher, however, remark that St. Cadgyfarch is said to have been the original patron. He was the son of St. Cadfrawd, alternatively named Adelfius, for whom see p.319.[5] If this is the case, it makes Usk a very early foundation, comparable with Caerleon. This is quite logical as they are so close together and were in an area that had strong Roman influence and communications. On first arriving in south Wales the Romans had established a legionary fortress at Usk although it was soon superseded by a fortress at Caerleon. It would therefore be quite likely that there was early post-Roman Christian activity at Usk — unfortunately the evidence is equivocal.

WONASTOW – St. Wonnow
(SO 486 107)

A deceptively early site dedicated to a 6th-century Breton saint, and sold in the mid-8th century in exchange for two horses, a hawk and a hunting dog.

Wonastow lies 2 miles south-west of Monmouth. The Welsh name for the church, which was still in use at the end of the 19th century, is Llanwarw; Wonastow is the anglicised version. It is referred to as *Lann Gunguarui* in the *Book of Llandaff*.[1]

    The patron saint's correct modern name is considered to be Winwaloe, but there has been much confusion over his name as there are about 50 different spellings of it! Baring-Gould and Fisher suggest that St. Winwaloe was born *c.*457 and died *c.*532, in his mid-70s. He was the son of Fracan, who was a cousin of a Cornish duke, and of Gwen 'of the Three Breasts', and was born in Brittany after his parents had emigrated there. He was trained by Budoc, a British saint who had a school at Lavret in Brittany. He stayed at Lavret until he was 21 and then set up a monastery on an island in a wide creek, but finding the site too inhospitable, walked across the bay with his brethren during a neap tide and re-established his foundation at Landevennec, which became a famous monastery. He seems to have softened the previously cruel and rough king of the area and to have set up more sites, but it is likely that he looked to Britain for disciples, as the population of Brittany was so sparse.[2]

    St. Winwaloe is described by his biographer as a man of moderate height, with a bright and smiling countenance.' He was very gentle and patient in his dealings with others and lived a simple life, eating a diet with no meat; he was also very trusting. There is no direct evidence or well-known legend recording a visit by Winwaloe to Britain, although widely spaced dedications in Monmouthshire, Cornwall, Devon and East Anglia indicate that he either visited, or that his followers set up churches in his name. As well as Wonastow, there were said to have once been two other dedications to Winwaloe in Monmouthshire: one at Llandevenny near Magor and another at Llanwynny.[3]

In the *Book of Llandaff* a charter dated to *c*.750 confirms the early establishment of Wonastow, and records that

> Cynfor ap Iago bought *ecclesia Gurthebiriuc*, [identified with Wonastow] with one and a half *unciae* of land around it, from King Ffernfael, for a best horse worth twelve cows, a hawk worth twelve cows, a dog that killed birds with the hawk worth three cows, and another horse worth three cows; then, with Ffernfael's guarantee, he gave it the bishop Tyrchan.[4]

Trychan was bishop of Llandaff at the time. The purchase of the church and land from the king and its subsequent gift to the bishop of Llandaff does seem a rather a roundabout way of making a donation to the church. The fact that the church was sold on in about 750 also implies it was of an earlier foundation. The bounds of the grant are recorded as:

> The 'ford' on the Trothy. Along the high road upwards as far as the Ash-tree. From the Ash-tree across the road, straight to the Thornbush between the two lands, to the spring of Cwm Cedwin, along it as far as the road, across the road as far as Nant y Meneich, [the Monk's brook], along it as far as the Trothy. Along the Trothy upwards as far as the ford on the Trothy, where the boundary began.'[5]

The 'Monk's Brook' indicates the presence of a monastery at Wonastow although Brook states the early status of the site was as a church.[6] The Cwm Cedwin remembers St. Cedwyn see p.90)

The present church has received a good deal of restoration in past years. The chancel is 14th century, which unusually has a priest's door in the north wall, and the nave and tower are 19th century.[7] There is excellent stained glass in the nave and an attractive screen.

The churchyard is small and approximately rectangular and is surrounded by modern farm buildings on the northern and western sides. It appears to have been extended to the north but has been landscaped and planted with attractive formal rows of yew trees in fairly recent years which may mask any earlier boundaries. There is a steep drop to the farmyard along the southern boundary that it is likely to have been cut away in modern times.

Appendix

The sites given here have more tentative information as to their being early, so only a brief mention is given, with the exception of Llanddeusant. The latter is included for it is in Carmarthenshire, and therefore outside the scope of this book, but had an important role in the early development of the Celtic Church.

CASCOB – St. Michael and All Angels (Radnorshire) (SO 239 664)
The church lies 6 miles north of Presteigne and the tower is built into a large mound that stands up to 6 feet high. This was at one time viewed as a burial mound dating to the Bronze Age. However, Bleddfa church, some ten miles to the north-west, has a similar mound that was excavated and discovered to be the remains of an earlier collapsed tower, thus the burial mound theory for Cascob has now been largely discounted. There is a tump south of the porch which is about 3 feet high and 36 feet across thought to be made up, at least in part, of debris from when the church was repaired. To the west of the church is a large yew which we estimate from its girth as well over 1,000 years old. The shape of the churchyard is partly determined by the geography of the site which borders on to a stream to the south. On the north side there is an internal earthen bank ranging in height between about ½ foot to 3½ feet.[1]

CEFNLLYS – St. Michael (Radnorshire) (SO 085 615)
The church of St.Michael is 1½ miles east of Llandrindod Wells. Yew trees are irregularly spaced around the churchyard boundary and a male yew to the east-south-east has a girth of 19 feet hand an estimated age of 1,200 years.[1]

CWMCARVAN – St. Catwg/Cadog (Gwent) (SO 477 074)
Cwmcarvan is about 4 miles south-west of Monmouth. The elevated position of this church, the dedication, and the raised nature of parts of the churchyard above the surrounding land suggests this may have been an early foundation.

GWENDDWR – St. Dubricius (Breconshire) (SO 064 432)
Its dedication and the shape of the churchyard, five miles south of Builth Wells, are the only clues for this being an early site. However, the location is unusual for a Dyfrig dedication, as most of his churches were in Erging (approximately southern Herefordshire). The churchyard is considered possibly 'the shrunken remnant of a much larger oval enclosure,'[1] in keeping with a larger monastic enclosure, although the site is steep for the purpose. There are a number of middle-aged yews along the boundary of the churchyard.

HEYOP – St. David (Radnorshire) (SO 240 746)

5 miles west of Knighton, the churchyard has two mature yew trees, the largest of which has a girth that we estimate at 20 feet. It is hollowed through the centre.

LLANBADOC – St. Madoc (Gwent) (SO 376 001)

There is dedication evidence alone for an early site here, less than a mile south of Usk. The church is sandwiched between the main road and the River Usk. There are four St. Madocs on record, but the man in question is probably St. Madoc ab Gildas, another name for Aidan, son (or grandson) of Gildas.[1] Aidan was put into the charge of St. David for his education in Wales. Aidan went to Ireland after the death of St. Patrick to help spread the Christian faith. He died in the early 600s. There are no signs of early boundaries on this site which must have suffered from flooding and alluvial deposition over many centuries which would have levelled any subtle earthworks.

LLANDDEUSANT - St. Simon and St. Jude (Carmarthenshire) (SN 776 245)

In a late 9th-century biography of St. Paulinus (Paul Aurelian), which appears to quote a lost *Life*, it is said that he belonged to a noble family at Brehant Dincat which Doble identifies with Llandovery. Paulinus' cult can still be traced easily in the neighbourhood with two chapels dedicated to him at Capel Peulin and Nant y Bai, and a holy well, Ffynon Beulin, named after him. The place-name Llanddeusant means 'the Llan of the Two Saints.' An annual fair at Llanddeusant used to be held on 10 October, which is Paulinus' festival day, but was also the feast day of a pair of other saints. These were commonly said to be St. Simon and St. Jude, if only because they were the best known saints to also have feast days in October, but Doble suggests they were the rather more obscure brothers of Paulinus, Potolius and Notolius.[1]

Paulinus is said to have studied under St. Illtud at Llantwit Major. In his 9th-century *Life*, written in 884 by a monk called Wrmonoc in Brittany, it states that Paulinus resolved to leave Llantwit Major to live in solitude. Receiving the blessing and leave of his master

> he went forth and sought the seclusion of a certain desert place which adjoined his father's possessions. There he built some cells and a little oratory, which, they say, is now a monastic settlement containing numerous buildings bearing the names of his two brothers already mentioned. Here he received from the bishop (his name and see are not mentioned) the dignity of the priesthood, and lived for some time with twelve presbyters who desired to obey his precepts in everything relating to the monastic life.[2]

Wrmonoc states Paulinus was then aged 16 and that he was accompanied by his brothers Potolius and Notolius. At first they established a hermitage which 'developed into a considerable monastery', probably at Llanddeusant, which in the 9th century was called after the two brothers[3] — why not Paulinus as founder, one wonders? In 884 it was described as containing numerous buildings. The church notice board remarks that a cross-slab dating from the 7th to 9th centuries was found close to the present church and that it is similar to stones found at Pumpsaint (Dyfed) and Llantrisant (Mid-Glamorgan) which also owe their origins to early medieval religious settlements. The 12 presbyters of Wrmonoc's description are apparently also noted near Llangors — Paulinus' only other dedication in south Wales. In relation to the charter bounds for Llangors dated *c.*720 in the *Book of Llandaff* there is mention of 'the Well of the Twelve Saints on lake Syvadon' — which Doble identifies with All Saints' Well near Penllanafel — and not far away was a chapel called 'the Llan of the Twelve Saints'. Doble suggests the 12 saints are the same as the 12 presbyters who worked under Paulinus at Llanddeusant and who accompanied him to Brittany. He also considers that St. Teilo and St. David, who were said to have been disciples of St. Paulinus, studied at Llanddeusant, which adds even more weight to this once being a significant site with a monastic school.[4]

The present churchyard may belie this former importance as it is only a small to medium-sized enclosure, although it is significantly higher than the adjoining land — approximately 6 to 7 feet on the southern side and about 5 feet on the south-eastern and eastern sides. There is a steep drop to the north side but a recently renovated house with its associated landscaping may have accentuated this drop. The church notice board states that present churchyard walls are thought to enclose the 'classical oval shape' of the early *llan*, although, it has to be said, the exact site of the monastic school is not known for certain.

LLANDDEWI RHYDDERCH – St. David (Gwent) (SO 349 129)

This church is about 3 miles east of Abergavenny. On the northern side of the churchyard there is a grassy ridge running east/west which may indicate a former boundary. Close to the south-east corner of the chancel is a tall and old-looking yew, perhaps the remnant of an east/west Celtic alignment planting.

LLANDDEWI YSTRADENNI (Radnorshire) (SO 108 686)

The church is 9 miles north of Llandrindod Wells. The small cluster of David dedications 20 miles to the south-east lends some support to the idea that the dedication here is early, but it could be a late re-dedication during the Middle Ages. The churchyard is raised between 1½ feet and 2½ feet above the external land and is also banked internally up to a height of about 3½ feet on the eastern boundary.[1] The enclosure looks to have been extended to the west and north, and a scarp bank curves around the church to the north-west and west and may be an earlier boundary, which would make the original enclosure curvilinear. The church is built upon a low mound or platform. This may be either the remains of the earlier structure, a natural feature, or perhaps even a man-made mound pre-dating the church site.

LLANFAES – St. David (Breconshire) (SO 037 283)
St. David's church is within the busy suburb of Brecon by the side of the old A40. There is no evidence that the church is any earlier than Norman but its location near to the putative early mother church of Llanddew, and its position within the centre of the kingdom of Brycheiniog, opens the possibility that this may have been an early site.

LLANFIHANGEL NANT BRAN – St. Michael (Breconshire) (SN 944 343)
The church lies 7 miles north-west of Brecon in the centre of the village. The churchyard is embanked on the northern and western sides where it is 6 feet above the exterior ground level in places. To the south of the church there are several yews between the church and the boundary which may mark an earlier boundary line of a smaller enclosure.

LLANGATTOCK-JUXTA-USK – St. Cadoc (Gwent) (SO 330 096)
The church is 3 miles south-east of Abergavenny and is large in relation to the rather small churchyard. The dedication to St. Cadoc conforms with the geographical spread of his dedications.

LLANGATTOCK VIBON ABEL – St. Cadoc (Gwent) (SO 457 157)
The church is about 4 miles north-west of Monmouth. The church was first recorded in 1186 in the Episcopal Acts but the dedication to St. Cadoc suggests a much earlier foundation. Brook states that on 19th-century maps the enclosure is shown as partly curved and adds that in the Norman period the church had several dependent chapels which 'may reflect some importance in the pre-Norman [era]'.[1]

LLANGUNLLO – St. Cynllo (Radnorshire) (SO 212 713)
Llangunllo (also spelt Llangynllo) is about 3½ miles west of Knighton. St. Cynllo, described as a king and confessor and who may have been a brother of St.Teilo (see p.162), has a cluster of three dedications in the vicinity, Llanbister being the most important. Although reputedly a 5th- or 6th-century foundation, there are few medieval references to the church. The churchyard is walled, and there are steep drops to the external adjoining land.

LLANIDLOES – St. Idloes (Montgomeryshire) (SN 954 847)
Very little is known about the titular saint, St. Idloes, who is termed a confessor. His grandfather is celebrated as one 'the Three Tribe-Herdsmen of the Isle

of Britain [who] tended the kine of Nudd Hael, in whose herd were 21,000 milch cows'. He may have had a daughter Meddvyth who is remembered as St. Meddwid. His festival is recorded as being 6 September and a fair was once held at Llanidloes on the first Saturday in September. There is a holy well dedicated to him in Hafren Street.[1]

LLANSANTFFRAED (JUXTA USK) – St. Bridget (Breconshire)
(SO 122 235)
The church lies 6 miles south-east of Brecon. The dedication to St. Bridget (or Bride) is suggestive of an early foundation and of an area under Irish influence. In a map of 1817 there are slight indications that the church enclosure was more curvilinear and a slight curve is still visible to the south-east.[1]

TREGYNON – St. Cynon (Montgomeryshire) (SO 096 987)
Indications are that the site, about 4½ miles north of Newtown, is an early one because of the dedication and the original shape of the churchyard. The place-name Tregynon appears to mean 'the house of Cynon'. St. Cynon is reputed to have travelled from Brittany with St. Cadfan and St. Padarn. He was allegedly of the same family as Cadfan and was trained at Llantwit Major under St. Illtud and also at Llancarfan.[1] The churchyard is raised and was probably originally sub-oval, but is now extended to the north-west, a slight scarp in this direction indicating an early boundary.[2]

WHITTON – St. David (Radnorshire) (SO 271 674)
About 3½ miles north-north-west of Presteigne, the churchyard has several mature yews. The largest is a male tree to the south-west of the church which has a girth of 27 feet, and an estimated age of 1,400 years[1] — certainly old enough to be the planting of an early saint.

Bibliography

Andere	Andere, Mary *Arthurian Links with Herefordshire*, Logaston Press, 1995
Anderson	Anderson, M.D. *History and Imagery in British Churches*, John Murray, 1971 (1995 reprint)
Annett	Annett, D.M. *Saints in Herefordshire : A study of Dedications*, Logaston Press, 1999
Bailey	Bailey, Sir Joseph Russell – see under Jones, Theophilus
BGF	Baring-Gould, Sabine & Fisher, John *The Lives of the British Saints*, Facsimile Reprint. Produced as an eight volume set from the original four volumes which were published between 1907–1913, Llanerch, 2000
BE	Berresford Ellis, Peter *Celt and Saxon : The Struggle for Britain AD 410 –937*, Constable, 1993
Bevan-Jones	Bevan-Jones, Robert *The Ancient Yew : A History of Taxus baccata* Windgather Press, 2002
Bowen	Bowen, E.G. *The Settlement of the Celtic Saints in Wales*, University of Wales Press, 1954
Britnell	Britnell, William 'Capel Maelog Rediscovered' in *The Radnorshire Society Transactions*, Vol. LVI, 1986, pp.14-19
Brook (1988)	Brook, Diane 'The Early Christian Church in Gwent' in *The Monmouthshire Antiquary* Vol. V, Part 3, 1988, pp.67-84
Brook (1992)	Brook, Diane 'The Early Christian Church East and West of Offa's Dyke' in Edwards, Nancy & Lane, Alan *The Early Church in Wales and the West*, Oxbow, 1992
Chetan & Brueton	Chetan, Anand & Brueton, Diane *The Sacred Yew: Rediscovering the ancient Tree of Life through the work of Allen Meredith*, Arkana/Penguin Books, 1994
Children & Nash	Children, George; Nash, George *Prehistoric Sites of Breconshire*, Logaston Press, 2001
CPAT	Clwyd-Powys Archaeological Trust *Historic Churches Survey*. Various dates and sites, chiefly in the mid-1990s, the five or six digit number is the site report number
CPAT, TV	Clwyd-Powys Archaeological Trust *Historic Landscape Characterisation: The Tanat Valley - Funerary, Ecclesiastical and Legendary Landscapes*
CPAT, SMR	Clwyd-Powys Archaeological Trust - Regional Sites and Monuments Record
Coplestone-Crow	Coplestone-Crow, Bruce *Herefordshire Place-Names*, BAR British Series 214, 1989
Dark (1999)	Dark, K.R. *Civitas to Kingdom : British Political Continuity 300–800*, Studies in the Early History of Britain series, Leicester University Press, 1994 (1999 reprint)
Dark (2000)	Dark, Ken *Britain and the End of the Roman Empire*, Tempus, 2000
Davies (1979)	Davies, Wendy *The Llandaff Charters*, National Library of Wales, 1979
Davies (1982)	Davies, Wendy *Wales in the Early Middle Ages*, Studies in the Early History of Britain series, Leicester University Press, 1982 (1996 reprint)
Doble	Doble, G.H. (ed. D. Simon Evans) *Lives of the Welsh Saints,* University of Wales Press, 1971 (1986 reprint)
Doughty	Doughty, Audrey *Spas and Springs in Wales*, Carreg Gwalch, 2001
Dunn	Dunn, Marilyn *The Emergence of Monasticism : From the Desert Fathers to the Early Middle Ages*, Blackwell, 2000 (2003 reprint)

ECM	A Handlist of Early Christian Stones in *Brecknock : Later Prehistoric Monuments and Unenclosed Settlements to 1000 AD*, RCAHMW, 1997
Edwards & Lane	Edwards, Nancy & Lane, Alan (ed.), 'Archaeology of the Early Church in Wales' in *The Early Church in Wales and the West*, Oxbow Monographs 16, 1992
Evans	Evans, D. Simon — see under Doble
Evans & Rhys	Evans, J. Gwenogvryn & John, Rhys *The Text of the Book of Llan Dav : Reproduced from the Gwysaney Manuscript*, Oxford - Facsimile Edition by the National Library of Wales, 1979
Farmer	Farmer, David Hugh T*he Oxford Dictionary of Saints*, Oxford University Press, 1978 (1st paperback issue 1982)
Fenn (1968)	Fenn, R.W.D. 'Early Christianity in Herefordshire; in *The Transactions of the Woolhope Naturalists' Field Club*, 1968, pp.333-47
Fenn (1976)	Fenn, RW.D. 'The Age of Saints' in *A History of the Church in Wales* (ed.) David Walker, Church in Wales Publications/The Historical Society for the Church in Wales, 1976 (1977 2nd Impression)
Fenn & Sinclair (1988)	Fenn, F.W.D. & Sinclair, J.B. 'Old Radnor Parish Church' in *The Transactions of the Radnorshire Society* Vol. LVIII, 1988
Fenn & Sinclair (1990)	Fenn, R.W.D. & Sinclair, J.B. 'The Christian Origins of Montgomeryshire: An Interpretation' in *The Montgomeryshire Collections*, Volume 78, 1990
Fenn & Sinclair (2001)	Fenn, R.W.D. & Sinclair, J.B. 'Diserth Parish Church' in *The Transactions of the Radnorshire Society* Vol. LXXI, 2001
Fletcher	Fletcher, Richard *Who's Who in Roman and Anglo-Saxon Britain*, Shepheard-Walwyn, 1989
Geoffrey	Geoffrey of Monmouth (trans. & ed.) Lewis Thorpe T*he History of the Kings of Britain*, Penguin. 1966
Gerald of Wales	Gerald of Wales/Giraldus Cambrensis (trans.) Lewis Thorpe, *The Journey through Wales and The Description of Wales*, Penguin
Gill	Gill, M.A.V. 'Scheduled Ancient Monument R 100 (SO 192417) : The Cross-Slab in St. Meilig's Church, Llowes' in *The Transactions of the Radnorshire Society*, Vol. LXXI, 2001, pp.19-55
Granville Lewis	Granville Lewis, W.T.'Incised Cross-Stone at Ystafell-fach, Brecknockshire, and the Tradition of an Ancient Town' in A*rchaeologia Cambrensis*, Sixth Series, Vol. III, Part IV, October 1903, pp.293-7
Grinsell	Grinsell, LV. 'The Later History of Ty Illtud' in A*rchaeologia Cambrensis*, Volume CXXX, 1981, pp.131-39
Hardinge	Hardinge, Leslie *The Celtic Church in Britain*, S.P.C.K., 1972
Haslam	Haslam, Richard *The Buildings of Wales : Powys (Montgomeryshire, Radnorshire, Breconshire)* Penguin Books/University of Wales Press, 1979
Henken	Henken, Elissa R. *Traditions of the Welsh Saints*, D.S. Brewer, Woodbridge, 1987
Hoverd & Ray	Hoverd, T. & Ray, K. Herefordshire Archaeology Report No. 28. West Midlands Archaeology 43, CBA West Midlands, 2000
Howse	Howse, W.H. *Radnorshire*, E.J. Thurston, 1949
Jackson	Jackson, Kenneth Hurlstone *A Celtic Miscellany : Translation from the Celtic Literature* Penguin, 1951 (1973 paperback reprint)
James	James, Heather 'Early Medieval Cemeteries in Wales' in *The Early Church in Wales and the West*, 1992 (see under Edwards & Lane)
Jones, F.	Jones, Francis *The Holy Wells of Wales*, University of Wales Press, 1954 (1992 paperback edition)

Jones, T.	Jones, Theophilus *A History of the County of Brecknock*, enlarged by the notes collected by Sir Joseph Russell Bailey. Blissett, Davies & Co., 1911 edition
Knight	Knight, J.K. *et al.* 1977 'New Finds of Early Christian Monuments' in *Archaeologia Cambrensis*, Volume CXXVI, 1977
Leather	Leather, Ella Mary F*olk-Lore of Herefordshire*, S.R. Publisher Ltd, 1970 Reprint
Leland	Leland, John (ed.) Toulmin Smith, Lucy *The Itinerary of John Leland In or About the years 1536 – 1539*, Volume III, Centaur Press
Llanhilleth	Site Report for St. Illtyd's Church, St. Illtyd's Motte and Castell Taliorum (Llanhilleth Castle), 2000
Maude	Maude, J.H. *The Foundations of the English Church*, Methuen & Co., 1909
Morgan	Morgan, Richard 'An Early Charter of Llanllugan Nunnery' in *The Montgomeryshire Collections*, Volume 73, 1985
Morris J.	Morris, John *The Age of Arthur : A History of the British Isles from 350 to 650*, Phoenix, 1996 (reissue)
Morris R.	Morris, Richard *Churches in the Landscape*, Phoenix, 1989 (1997 reprint)
Morris T.E.	Morris, T.E. 'Capel Maelog, Llandrindod' in *Archaeologia Cambrensis*, October 1917, 17, pp. 397-404
Myles & Chadwick	Myles, Dillon & Chadwick, Nora *The Celtic Realms*, Weidenfeld & Nicholson, 1967
Nennius	*Nennius : British History and The Welsh Annals*, John Morris (ed. & trans.), Arthurian Period Sources Volume 8. Phillimore, 1980
Newell	Newell, Rev. E.J. *A History of the Welsh Church to the Dissolution of the Monasteries*, Elliot Stock, 1985
Newman	Newman, John *The Buildings of Wales : Gwent / Monmouthshire,* Yale University Press 2000, (2002 edition)
Pennant	Pennant, Thomas *Tours in Wales*, printed for Wilkie & Robinson *et al.*, 1810
Pennar	Pennar, Meirion *The Black Book of Carmarthen*, Llanerch, 1989
Pevsner	Pevsner, N. *The Buildings of England: Herefordshire*, Penguin, 1995 reprint
RCAHMW	Royal Commission on the Ancient and Historical Monuments of Wales *An Inventory of the Ancient Monuments in Brecknock (Brycheiniog) : The Prehistoric and Roman Monuments Part (i) :Later Prehistoric Monuments and Unenclosed Settlements to 1000 AD*, 1997
Radford	Radford, Ralegh & Hemp. W.J. 'The Cross-Slab at Llanraiadr-ym-Mochnant', *Archaeologia Cambrensis*, Vol. CVI, 1957
Ray	Ray, Keith 'Archaeology and The Three Early Churches of Herefordshire' in *The Early Church in Herefordshire*, Leominster History Study Group, 2001
Redknap	Redknap, Mark *The Christian Celts : Treasures of Late Celtic Wales*, National Museum of Wales, 1991
Rees (2000)	Rees, Elizabeth *Celtic Saints : Passionate Wanderers*, Thames & Hudson, 2000
Rees (1992)	Rees, Sian *A Guide to Ancient and Historic Wales : Dyfed*, HMSO, 1992
Rees (1853)	Rees, Rev. W.J. *Lives of the Cambro-British Saints*, The Welsh MSS Society, Llandovery, 1853
Salway	Salway, Peter *Roman Britain*, The Oxford History of England Series, Oxford University Press, 1981 (1987 reprint)

Sant	Sant, Jonathan *Healing Wells of Herefordshire*, Moondial Press, 1994
Shoesmith	Shoesmith, R. 'Llanwarne Old Church', *Transactions of the Woolhope Naturalists' Field Club* Vol. XLIII, 1981, pp.267-97
Simpson	Simpson, Jacqueline *The Folklore of the Welsh Borders*, B.T. Batsford, 1976
Stenton	Stenton, Sir Frank *Anglo-Saxon England*, Oxford University Press, 1971, 3rd Edition (1985 reprint)
Swanton	Swanton, Michael (Translated & Revised by) *The Anglo-Saxon Chronicles*, Phoenix Press,2000 New Edition
Thomas (1981)	Thomas, Charles *Christianity in Roman Britain to AD 500*, Batsford Academic and Educational, 1981
Thomas (1994)	Thomas, Charles *And Shall These Mute Stones Speak? : Post-Roman Inscriptions in Western Britain*, University of Wales Press, 1994
Thomas (2003)	Thomas, Charles *Christian Celts : Messages & Images*, Tempus, 2003 (Softback edition) (First hardback edition 1998)
Thornley Jones	Thornley Jones, T. 'The Llannau of Cwmdauddwr Parish', *The Transactions of the Radnorshire Society* Vol. XXXVI, 1966, pp.15-24
Utting	Utting, A.R. *Who Slew Tewdric? An historical review of his legend*, Mathern Parochial Church Council, 1998
Victory	Victory, Sian *The Celtic Church in Wales*, S.P.C.K., 1977
Watkins	Watkins, M.P. 'Lann Custenhinn Garthbenni', *Transactions of the Woolhope Naturalists' Field Club*, 1966, pp.196-203

References

Chapter 1
The Arrival of Christianity in Britain
1. BGF, Part 2, p.227
2. Newell, p.5
3. Fletcher, p.4
4. BGF, Part 3, p.147
5. Newell, p.5
6. BGF, Part 3, p.148
7. Thomas (1981), p.42
8. Maude, p.11
9. Thomas (1981), p.43
10. Rees (2000), p.12
11. Thomas (1981), p.42
12. *ibid.*, pp.48-9
13. Morris J., p.335
14. Rees (2000), p.12
15. Thomas (1981), p.48
16. Rees (2000), p.13
17. BGF, Part 1, pp.102-3
18. Thomas (1981), p.197
19. *ibid.*, p.197-8
20. Dark (2000), pp.18-20, 34-9, 124
21. Dunn, p.3
22. Morris R., p.93
23. Dunn, pp.7, 16-7
24. Morris R., pp.93-4, 96
25. see Dunn, pp.14-15
26. Morris R., p. 97
27. Dunn, pp.90, 139
28. *ibid.*, p.139; Morris R., p.100
29. Farmer, p.265
30. Dunn, p.63
31. Morris J., pp.335-6
32. Morris R., p.97
33. Morris J., p.336
34. *ibid.*, p.337
35. *ibid.*, p.339
36. Thomas (1981), p.54
37. Morris J., pp.340-1
38. Thomas (1981), p.57
39. Morris J., p.340
40. *ibid.*, pp.340-1
41. *ibid.*, pp.342-3
42. Salway, pp. 462, 465
43. Morris J., p.343
44. Dark (2000), p.42

Chapter 2
The Post-Roman Era
1. Myles & Chadwick, p.39
2. Dark (1999), pp.79, 81, 82-83
3. Myles & Chadwick, pp.38, 39-40, 54
4. Dark (1999), pp.78, 79
5. *ibid.*, pp.84-6
6. BGF, Part 1, p.46
7. Myles & Chadwick, p.42
8. Davies (1982), pp.169, 171
9. *ibid.*, p.141
10. *ibid.*, p.143
11. *ibid.*, p.143
12. *ibid.*, p.143
13. *ibid.*, p.143
14. Evans, p.12
15. Davies (1982), pp.143, 144, 149
16. *ibid.*, p.145; Ray, pp.113, 114
17. Davies (1982), pp.149, 152
18. *ibid.*, p.149
19. *ibid.*, pp.158-160
20. Fenn (1976), p.10
21. *ibid.*, p.10
22. Morris J., p.366
23. Fenn (1976), p.10
24. *ibid.*, pp.11, 12, 20
25. Victory, p.55
26. Davies (1982), pp.156, 157
27. *ibid.*, pp.150, 151, 154
28. Fenn (1976), p.19
29. Davies (1982), p.155
30. Brook (1988), pp.71, 79; Edwards & Lane, pp.5-6
31. Brook (1988), p.72
32. Chean & Brueton, pp.51, 52, 54, 56
33. *ibid.*, p.51
34. Brook (1992), p.79
35. Edwards & Lane, p.6
36. James, pp.93. 96
37. *ibid.*, p.101
38. Bevan-Jones, pp.22-25
39. Chetan & Brueton, pp.54, 55
40. Bevan-Jones, pp.5, 30, 31, 46
41. *ibid.*, p.50
42. Chetan & Brueton, p.57
43. *ibid.*, pp.58-9, 62
44. Bevan-Jones, p.45
45. Chetan & Brueton, pp.77-81
46. *ibid.*, p.82

47. *ibid.*, p.70
48. Davies (1982), pp.184, 185, 187
49. Victory, p.23
50. Davies (1982), pp.164-166
51. *ibid.*, pp.167-8
52. BGF, Part 1, p.3
53. BE, pp.120-121
54. BE, p.120
55. Hardinge, pp.85, 86
56. BE, p.121; Hardinge, p.100
57. BE, pp.121, 122
58. Fenn (1976), p.5
59. *ibid.*, p.5
60. *ibid.*, p.6
61. *ibid.*, p.7
62. Stenton, p.110
63. Fenn (1976), p.7
64. Morris R., p.10

Chapter 3
The Early Saints
1. Davies (1982), pp.163, 173
2. *ibid.*, pp.174, 176
3. Morris J., p.364
4. Davies (1982), pp.177, 178;
   Rees (2000), p.7
5. Bowen, p.39
6. Rees (2000), p.55
7. Bowen, pp.44-5, 48
8. *ibid.*, p.57
9. *ibid.*, pp.58, 63, 64
10. *ibid.*, pp.53-6
11. Ray, p.113
12. BGF, Part 4, p.360
13. Doble, p.86
14. *ibid.*, pp.56-8, 61
15. *ibid.*, pp.61, 86
16. Coplestone-Crow, p.139
17. Henken, p.101
18. *ibid.*, p.100
19. Doble, pp.65-6
20. BGF, Part 4, p.365
21. Davies (1979), p.102 charter 159a
22. *ibid.*, p.113, charter 192
23. Coplestone-Crow, p.139
24. Doble, p.66; Evans & Rhys, p.173
25. Davies (1979), p.107, charter 171b &
    p.190 under Ecclesia Cinfall
26. *ibid.*, p.94 charter 76a
27. Evans & Rhys, p.76
28. Doble, p.66
29. Fenn (1968), p.337

30. Doble, p.77
31. *ibid.*, pp.65-66
32. Coplestone-Crow, pp.14, 139
33. *ibid.*, pp.14-16
34. Fenn, (1968), p.338
35. *ibid.*
36. Doble, p.86
37. Farmer, p.114
38. Doble, p.86
39. Coplestone-Crow, p.100
40. Doble, p.62
41. *ibid.*, pp.62-3, 74
42. Anderson, p.11
43. Doble, p.67
44. Fenn (1968), p.330
45. BGF, Part 4, p.376
46. Geoffrey, pp.216, 320
47. Doble, pp.61, 68
48. BGF, Part 4, pp.370-1
49. *ibid.*, Part 4, p.371
50. *ibid.*, Part 4, p.371
51. *ibid.*, Part 4, pp.372, 374
52. John Tomes, "Blue Guide: Wales and
    the Marches" Benn, p.178
53. BGF, Part 4, p.382
54. *Book of Llandaff*, p.192 translated and
    quoted in BGF, Part 4, p.362
55. BGF, Part 4, pp.371, 380
56. Geoffrey, pp.198, 212, 227, 230
57. Doble, p.88, quoted from the *Life* of
    Samson
58. BGF, Part 6, p304
59. Rees (1853), pp.466, 467; BGF, Part
    6, p.305
60. *ibid.*, Part 6, p.306-7; Rees (1853),
    pp.471-2; Doble, p.106-7
61. Rees (1853), p.472; BGF, part 6,
    p.307-8
62. *ibid.*, Part 6, p.308
63. *ibid.*, Part 6, p.309 & n.1; Doble, p.108;
    Rees (1853), p.473
64. Doble, p.109; BGF, Part 6, p.309
65. *ibid.*, Part 6, p.310
66. Doble, p.106
67. Rees (1853), pp.483-4, 487-8; BGF,
    Part 6, p 310; Doble, p.115
68. BGF, Part 6, pp.311-3, 317
69. *ibid.*, Part 6, p.314
70. Doble, pp. 127, 139
71. Rees (2000), p.60
72. BGF, Part 4, p.287
73. *ibid.*, Part 4, p.286

74. *ibid*., Part 4, p.287
75. *ibid*., Part 4, p.287-9; Henken, p.32
76. *ibid*., Part 4, p.291-2; Rees (1992), p.192-3
77. Rees (1992). p.193; Rees (2000), pp.58-9
78. BGF, part 4, p.292, Henken, p.42
79. BGF, part 4, p.292; Rees (1853), p.420; Bowen p.59; Doble, p.169; Henken, p.42; Rees (2000), p.58
80. BGF, part 4, pp.295-6
81. Rees (2000), p.61, Rees (1853), p.431; BGF, Part 4, pp.299-300, 304; Henken, p.51
82. BGF, Part 4, p.300-3; Henken, p.53; Rees (1853), p.442
83. BGF, Part 4, pp.294-5
84. Bowen, p.51
85. BGF, Part 4, p.314
86. *ibid*., Part 7, p.226; Doble, pp.163, 164, 166; Bowen, p.57
87. BGF, part 7, p.227-8; Henken, p.128; Rees (2000), p.57
88. Doble, p.168; BGF, Part 7, p.230
89. *ibid*., Part 7, p.231, 237; Bowen, p.64
90. BGF, Part 7, pp.230-2
91. *ibid*., Part 7.p.233-5; Doble, p.185
92. BGF, part 7, p.235-6
93. *ibid*., Part 7, p.236
94. *ibid*., Part 7, p.227, family tree; Henken, pp.132-3
95. BGF, part 7, pp.239-40; Henken, p.134
96. BGF, part 7, p.242
97. *ibid*., part 7, p.238
98. Rees (1853), p.395, n.3
99. BGF, Part 3, pp.13-5
100. *ibid*., Part 3, p.15; Part 5, p.238
101. BGF, Part 3, p.16; Rees (1853), pp.317-9
102. BGF, Part 3, p.16; Rees (1853), pp.320-4
103. BGF, Part 3, p.17; Rees (1853), p.324-5; Rees (2000), p.55
104. Rees (1853), p.326; 328-9
105. BGF, part 3, p.19-20; Rees (1853), pp.333-4
106. BGF, Part 3, p.23
107. *ibid*., Part 3, p.23
108. Rees (1853), p.336; BGF, Part 3, pp.23-4
109. *ibid*., Part 3, pp.25-26
110. Rees (1853), p.340-2; Henken, p.90
111. Rees (1853), pp.343-4, BGF, Part 3, p.30
112. Rees (1853), pp.345-347; BGF, Part 3, p.30
113. Rees (1853), pp.348-9; BGF, Part 3, p.30
114. *ibid*., Part 3, p.31; Rees, p.367
115. BGF, Part 3, pp.33-5
116. *ibid*., pp.35-6
117. Henken, pp.96-7
118. BGF, Part 3, p.32, 35, 36; Rees (1853), pp.370, 372, n.1
119. Rees (2000), p.55
120. BGF, Part 7, p.39-43
121. *ibid*., Part 7, p.44
122. *ibid*., Part 7, p.40. Rees (1853), p.503-4; Henken, p.121
123. Rees (1853), p.502, n.2, 505, 506; BGF, Part 7, p.40-41
124. *ibid*., Part 7, pp.44, 49
125. *ibid*., Part 7, pp.41-2
126. Rees (1853), p.506-8; BGF, Part 7, p.41
127. Henken, p.122; Doble p.177; BGF, Part 7, pp. 41, 45; Rees (1853), pp.502 & n.2, 508
128. Rees (1853), pp.513-4
129. BGF, Part 7, p.42. Rees (1853), p.511
130. Rees (1853), pp.508, 509, n.1; BGF, Part 7, p.46
131. BGF, Part 2, pp.208-9; Doble, p.13; Bowen, p.81
132. Rees (2000), pp.63, 87; BGF, Part 2, p.209-10 & n.4
133. Rees (1853), pp.299-301, p.300 n.3; BGF, Part 2, p.220; Henken, p.84
134. BGF, Part 2, p.211; Henken, p.85
135. Rees (1853), pp.301-2; BGF, Part 2, p.211-2
136. BGF (1853), Part 2, p.220-1; Henken, p.88

MONTGOMERYSHIRE
Berriew
1. CPAT, 16709, p.1
2. *ibid.*, p.5
3. *ibid.*

Bettws Cedewain
1. BGF, Part 2, p.218
2. CPAT, 16711, p.1
3. *ibid.*, pp.1-2; Haslam, p.82
4. CPAT, 16711, p.5

Carno
1. CPAT, 16736, p.1
2. Pennant, iii, p.194
3. CPAT, 16736, p.1
4. CPAT, SMR, no.26644
5. Haslam, p.88

Guilsford
1. Haslam, p.105
2. BGF, Part 1, pp.109-110
3. John Ray dated 1760, quoted by BGF, Part 1, p.111
4. CPAT, 16786, p.2
5. Pennant, iii, p.216
6. CPAT, 16876, p.9
7. BGF, Part 1, p.112
8. Jones F., p.199

Llandinam
1. CPAT, 16832, pp.1-2; Haslam, p.120
2. BGF, Part 6, p.377, n.3
3. CPAT, 16832, p.1
4. BGF, Part 6, p.377-8
5. CPAT, 16832, p.7

Llandrinio
1. CPAT, 16836, p.2
2. BGF, Part 8, p.265
3. CPAT, 16836, p.2
4. *ibid.*, p.6
5. CPAT, SMR, no.1248
6. CPAT, 16836, p.7
7. CPAT, SMR, no.6038
8. Jones F., pp.197, 199

Llanerfyl
1. BGF, Part 4, p.464
2. CPAT, SMR, no.1741
3. Haslam, p.127
4. Fenn & Sinclair (1990), p.48

5. CPAT, SMR, no.1741
6. Chetan & Breuton, pp.54-55, 276
7. CPAT, 16409, p.5
8. *ibid.*
9. BGF, Part 4, p.464

Llanfair Caereinion
1. CPAT, 32637, p.1
2. quoted in *ibid.*, p.2
3. *ibid.*, p.7; Jones F., p.198
4. Jones F., p.198

Llanfyllin
1. CPAT, 16860, p.1
2. *ibid.*, p.5
3. BGF, Part 6, pp.487-489
4. CPAT, 16860, p.1
5. Jones F., pp.198-9

Llangadfan
1. CPAT, 16678, p.1
2. BGF, Part 3, pp.1, 4
3. *ibid.*, Part 3, p.4
4. *ibid.*, Part 3, pp.5-6, 7, 9
5. *ibid.*, Part 3, p.6
6. CPAT, 16678, p.4
7. *ibid.*

Llangedwyn
1. BGF, Part 3, p.98
2. CPAT, 16867, p.5
3. CPAT, SMR no.101768

Llangurig
1. CPAT, 16873, p.2
2. BGF, Part 3, pp.193-7
3. *ibid.*, Part 3, pp.198-9
4. *ibid.*, Part 3, p.193
5. quoted by BGF, Part 3, pp.193-4 from a Welsh translation of a Latin *Life* of St. Cyriacus
6. BGF, Part 3, p.194
7. *ibid.*, Part 3, pp.194-95
8. *ibid.*, Part 3, pp.195-6
9. *ibid.*, Part 3, pp.196-8
10. *ibid.*, Part 3, p.199
11. CPAT, 16873, p.2
12. *ibid.*, pp.7-8
13. *ibid.*, 16873, p.9

Llangynog
1. CPAT, 16482, pp.1, 4

Llanllugan

1. CPAT, 32541, p.1
2. Quoted in BGF, Part 6, p.378
3. *ibid.*, Part 6, pp.378-9
4. CPAT, 32541, p.1
5. Fenn & Sinclair (1990), p.57
6. CPAT, 32541, pp.1-2
7. CL/Deeds/I/3250
8. Morgan, pp.116-9
9. Leland, Vol.3, p.55
10. CPAT, 32541, p.5
11. Jones F., pp.131, 203

Llanmerewig

1. CPAT, 16404, p.1
2. BGF, Part 6, p.381 & n.2
3. *ibid.*, Part 6, p.382 & n.2, p.383
4. CPAT, 16404, p.6
5. Davies (1982), pp.26, 143
6. CPAT, 16404, p.5

Llanrhaeadr-ym-Mochnant

1. BGF, Part 4, p.347
2. CPAT, TV, p.5
3. BGF, Part 4, p.347
4. CPAT, TV, p.7
5. BGF, Part 4, pp.264-5, 346-7
6. CPAT, SMR no.101051
7. BGF, Part 4, p.347
8. CPAT, 101046, p.1
9. CPAT, SMR no.101048; notice board within church
10. CPAT, TV, p.5
11. CPAT, 101046, p.1

Llanwnog

1. Haslam, p.151; CPAT, 16403, p.1
2. BGF, Part 5, pp.242-246
3. *ibid.*, pp.243-6
4. CPAT, 16403, p.2
5. *ibid.*, p.1
6. *ibid.*, p.6
7. Chetan & Brueton, p.278
8. Bevan-Jones, p.22

Llanwyddelan

1. BGF, Part 5, p.218, n.3
2. CPAT, 16379, p.1
3. Quoted in BGF, Part 6, p.379; p.380
4. CPAT, 16379, p.1
5. Haslam, p.154

6. CPAT, SMR, no. 23173
7. CPAT, 16379, pp.1-3

Meifod

1. BGF, Part 5, p.219
2. *ibid.*, Part 5, p.220; Part 8, pp.296-8
3. *ibid.*, Part 8, pp.299-301
4. *ibid.*, Part 8, pp.302-3
5. *ibid.*, Part 5, p.219
6. CPAT, 75, p.2
7. BGF, Part 2, p.211
8. *ibid.*, Part 8, p.303; CPAT, 75, p.2
9. CPAT, 75, p.2
10. Pennant, iii, p.182
11. CPAT, 75, p.2
12. Pennant, iii, p.182
13. CPAT, 75, pp.7-8
14. Haslam, p.160
15. CPAT, SMR, no. 6049

Pennant Melangell

1. Pennant, iii, p.175
2. BGF, Part 6, p.463
3. Pennant, iii, p.173
4. BGF, Part 6, p.464
5. Pennant, iii, p.174; BGF, Part 6, p.464
6. CPAT, TV, p.5
7. CPAT, 19470, p.9
8. CPAT,TV, p.6
9. CPAT, 19470, p.9
10. *ibid.*, pp.2, 4
11. *ibid.*, p.1
12. CPAT, TV, p.6
13. Pennant, iii, p.174
14. CPAT short piece 'Penant Melangell Church and Valley'
15. CPAT, 19470, p.9
16. CPAT, SMR no.6342
17. CPAT, TV, p.8
18. BGF, Part 6, pp.464-5

Trelystan

1. BGF, Part 2,p.210
2. CPAT, SMR. no. 4500
3. CPAT, 16965, p.1
4. Radford, pp.112-115
5. CPAT, 16965, pp.1-2
6. *ibid.*, p.5
7. CPAT, SMR, No. 4500
8. CPAT, 16965, p.5

RADNORSHIRE

Aberedw
1. BGF, Part 3, pp.115-7
2. *ibid.*, Part 3, p.117
3. CPAT, 17243, pp.5-6

Boughrood
1. CPAT, 17716, p.1; BGF, Part 4, p.265
2. CPAT, 17716, pp.2-3; Haslam, p.222

Bryngwyn
1. CPAT, 17248. p.2
2. Haslam, pp.224-5
3. CPAT, SMR, no.385
4. Haslam, p.223; Howse, p.257
5. Howse, p.257
6. Children & Nash
7. Haslam, p.224
8. Information in Church
9. Howse, p.257
10. CPAT, 17248, p.5

Capel Maelog
1. Britnell, p.14
2. Quoted in Morris T.E., p.397
3. Britnell, pp.14-5
4. Morris, T.E. pp.400-1
5. Britnell, pp.15-16
6. *ibid.*, pp.16-7
7. *ibid.*, p.17
8. *ibid.*, pp.17, 19

Colva
1. Haslam, p.227
2. *ibid.*
3. CPAT, 16751, p.1
4. *ibid.*, p.5

Cregrina
1. CPAT, 16752, p.1
2. *ibid.*, pp.1-4
3. BGF, Part 4, p.317
4. The Rev. D.R. Davies 'St. David and Radnorshire', *The Transactions of the Radnorshire Society*, Vol. XLVI, 1976 referring to 'Welsh Saints', Rice Rees, 1836, p.164

Discoed
1. Haslam, p.229
2. CPAT, 16770, p.1
3. *ibid.*, pp.3-4

4. Bevan-Jones, p.192
5. Chetan & Brueton, p.269
6. Bevan-Jones, p.30
7. Chetan and Brueton, pp.59, 269

Disserth
1. Fenn & Sinclair (2001), p.142; Fenn & Sinclair (1990), p.62
2. Haslam, p.230
3. CPAT, 16771, p.1
4. *ibid.*, p.5
5. *ibid.*, p.6
6. Fenn & Sinclair (2001), p.142
7. Sant, p.32
8. Jones F., p.92

Glascwm
1. Leland, iii, p.42
2. BGF, Part 4, p.314
3. Henken, pp.66-68
4. Gerald of Wales, p.79
5. CPAT, 16782, p.1
6. *ibid.*, p.5
7. Henklen, p.46
8. CPAT, 16782, p.5

Llananno
1. BGF, Part 1, pp.165-6
2. CPAT, 16806, pp.3-4
3. Haslam, p.239

Llanbadarn Fawr
1. Howse, p.258
2. CPAT, 16810, p.2
3. Haslam, pp.240-1
4. CPAT, 16810, p.3
5. Howse, p.258
6. CPAT, 16810, p.4

Llanbadarn Fynydd
1. CPAT, 16811, p.1; Haslam, pp.241-2
2. CPAT, 16811, p.4
3. Howse, p.211
4. Jones F., pp.216, 218

Llanbadarn-y-Garreg
1. Haslam, p.242

Llanbister
1. CPAT, 16816, p.2
2. *ibid.*
3. Haslam, p.244

4. CPAT, 16816, pp.7-8
5. J.V.F. Davies, *Folk-lore of West and Mid-Wales*, Llanerch Press, facsimile 1992, pp.175-6
6. Jones F., pp.216, 218
7. BGF, Part 4, p.272

Llanddewi Fach
1. Haslam.p.244
2. CPAT, 16821, p.2
3. Information in Church
4. CPAT, 16821, pp.1-2

Llandegley
1. CPAT, 16829, p.1
2. BGF, Part 7, p.219
3. Pennant, ii, p.14
4. BGF, Part 7, pp.219-20
5. *ibid.*, Part 7, p.222
6. *ibid.*, Part 7, p.223
7. Doughty, pp.90-1
8. CPAT, 16829, pp.4-5

Llandeilo Graban
1. CPAT, 16830, p.5
2. *ibid.*

Llanfaredd
1. Haslam, p.252
2. CPAT, 16848, p.1
3. Bevan-Jones, p.191
4. Chetan & Brueton, pp.215, 260, 276
5. CPAT, 16848, p.4

Llanfihangel-Nant-Melan
1. Haslam, p.253
2. CPAT, 16855, p.1
3. Howse, p.260
4. Chetan & Brueton, pp.56, 276
5. Bevan-Jones, p.51
6. CPAT, 16855, p.1
7. *ibid.*, p.3
8. Chetan & Brueton, p.56
9. Howse, p.211

Llansantffraed Cwmdeuddwr
1. Thornley Jones, pp.20-22
2. *ibid.*
3. *ibid.*, pp.22-23
4. Haslam, p.228

Llansantffraed-in-Elvel
1. BGF, Part 2, pp.264-5
2. CPAT, 16888, pp.1-2
3. *ibid.*, pp.3-4
4. Chetan & Brueton, p.277
5. CPAT, 16888, p.1
6. Gerald of Wales, p.118 & n.162

Llanstephan
1. Haslam, p.255
2. CPAT, 16892, p.6
3. *ibid.*

Llanyre
1. BGF, Part 6, p.386
2. CPAT, 16898, p.3

Llowes
1. Davies (1979), p.99, charter no.149
2. BGF, Part 6, p.389
3. *ibid.*, Part 6, pp.401-2
4. *ibid.*, part 6, p.402
5. Gill, pp.37-8
6. BGF, Part 6, pp.403-5
7. Gill, pp.19, 21, 22
8. *ibid.*, pp.30-32
9. *ibid.*, pp.35, 36
10. Howse, pp.260-1
11. Gill, p.41
12. *ibid.*, p.43
13. *ibid.*, pp.43-4
14. CPAT, 16899, pp.3-4
15. Jones F., p.217
16. Howse, p.211

Nantmel
1. BGF, Part 4, p.263 and Part 7, p.44
2. CPAT, 16918, p.4
3. *ibid.*

Old Radnor
1. Fenn & Sinclair (1988), p.78
2. BGF, Part 8, pp.367-8
3. Fenn & Sinclair (1988), pp.78-9
4. Leland, iii, p.42
5. Howse, p.261
6. CPAT, 16929, p.2
7. Howse, p.249
8. CPAT, 16929, p.1
9. quoted in Fenn & Sinclair (1988), p.78
10. Haslam, p.264
11. CPAT, 16929, p.7

Rhulen
1. Haslam, p.274
2. CPAT, 16944, p.1
3. *ibid.*, p.3
4. *ibid.*, pp.3-4
5. Bevan-Jones, p.192
6. Fenn & Sinclair quoted in Bevan-Jones, p.49

St. Harmon
1. Fenn and Sinclair (1990), pp.49, 50, 54
2. BGF, Part 5, p.77, table
3. *ibid.*, Part 5, p.78
4. CPAT, 16957, pp.1-2
5. Gerald of Wales, pp.78-9
6. CPAT, 16957, p.3
7. Jonathan Williams quoted in BGF, Part 5, p.78

BRECONSHIRE
Capel-y-ffin
1. Haslam.p.307
2. Bevan-Jones, plate 6 & p.49; Chetan & Brueton, p.266
3. Jones T., iii, p.108

Cwmdu
1. Haslam, p.315
2. Jones T., iii, p.169
3. CPAT, 16757, p.7
4. *ibid.*, p.1
5. Evans & Rhys, p.279
6. Davies (1979), p.106, charter no.*167
7. Jones T., iii, p171 & Bailey in, p.180
8. ECM, p.287, nos. 41 & 42
9. CPAT, SMR, no.674

Defynnog
1. CPAT, 16764, p.2
2. Haslam, p.317
3. *ibid.*
4. *ibid.*
5. CPAT, 16764, p.1
6. *ibid.*, pp.6-7
7. Chetan & Brueton, p.269
8. CPAT, 16764, pp.6-7
9. Jones, T., iv, p.115
10. BGF, Part 4, p.268-9

Llanafan Fawr
1. BGF, Part 1, p.114
2. *ibid.*

3. CPAT, 16804, p.5
4. BGF, Part 1, p.115
5. *ibid.*, Part 1, pp.114-115
6. *ibid.*, Part 1, p,115
7. Knight, p.60
8. CPAT, SMR no.3005
9. Knight, pp.61-64
10. Chetan & Brueton, p.275
11. CPAT, 16804, p.5
12. *ibid.*, pp.4-5
13. Haslam, p.326

Llanafan Fechan
1. CPAT, 16805, pp.1, 3

Llanddetty
1. BGF, Part 4, p.325
2. CPAT, SMR no.647
3. Bailey in Jones T., iii.p.197
4. Haslam, p.328
5. CPAT, SMR no.647
6. CPAT, 16818, p.4
7. Bailey quoting Sir Stephen Glynne in Jones T., iii, p.197

Llanddew
1. Jones T., ii, p.163
2. Gerald of Wales, p.80 & n.50
3. Leland, iii, 109
4. CPAT, SMR no.484
5. RCAHMW, p.286 nos.30-1
6. Jones T., ii, p.162
7. CPAT, 16819, p.7

Llanddewi'r cwm
1. CPAT, 16823, p.5
2. Chetan & Brueton, p.275
3. Haslam, p.330

Llandefaelog Fach
1. Jones T., ii, pp.180-1
2. CPAT, 31233, p.1
3. Bailey in Jones T., quoting J.O. West-wood, ii, p.188
4. Jones T., ii, p.181
5. Thomas (1994), pp.139, 153
6. Jones T., ii, p.181
7. Bailey in Jones T., ii, p.188
8. CPAT, 31233, p.1
9. Haslam, p.331
10. CPAT, 31233, p.4
11. Chetan & Brueton, p.275

Llandefalle
1. Haslam, p.332
2. CPAT, 16827, pp.6-7
3. BGF, Part 8, p.290
4. CPAT, 16827, p.1
5. Jones T., iii., p.24
6. BGF, Part 8, p.290

Llandeilo'r Fan
1. Davies (1979), p.101, charter no.154
2. Evans & Rhys, p.370 & ns.11, 12
3. BGF, Part 5, p.157
4. CPAT, 16831, p.1
5. *ibid.*, pp.1, 4
6. Bailey in Jones T., ii, p.211

Llanelieu
1. CPAT, 16843, p.5
2. Haslam, pp.333-334
3. BGF, Part 4, p.448; Jones T., iii.p.73
4. Haslam, p.334

Llanelwedd
1. BGF, Part 4, p.419
2. CPAT, SMR, no.1601

Llanfeugan
1. BGF, Part 6, pp.478-81
2. Jones T., iv, p.26
3. BGF, Part 6, p.479
4. CPAT, 16850. p.1
5. Bailey in Jones T., iv, p.30
6. CPAT, 16850, pp.7-8
7. Bevan-Jones, p.51
8. Chetan & Brueton, p.276

Llanfihangel Tal-y-llyn
1. CPAT, 16857, p.1
2. Jones T., iii, p.57
3. CPAT, 16857, p.1
4. Haslam, p.339
5. CPAT, 16857, p.5
6. Davies (1979), p.124, charter no.237b;
   p.201 n.4
7. Haslam, p.339

Llanfilo
1. Haslam, pp.340-1; CPAT, 16858, p.1
2. Jones T., iv, p.7
3. CPAT, 16858, p.6
4. Jones T., iv, p.6

5. BGF, Part 2, p.204
6. *ibid.*, Part 8, p.440, n.
7. CPAT, 16858, p.2
8. BGF, Part 2, p.204
9. CPAT, 16858, p.2

Llanfrynach
1. CPAT, 16859, p.1
2. CPAT, SMR no.613
3. Haslam, p.341
4. BGF, Part 2, pp.321-2
5. *ibid.*, Part 2. p.325, re: Leland
6. CPAT, 16859, pp.4-5

Llangammarch Wells
1. CPAT, 16862, p.2
2. BGF, Part 3, p.67 under St. Cammab
3. *ibid.*, Part 4, p.247
4. *ibid.*, Part 3, p.68
5. *ibid.*, Part 4, p.247
6. CPAT, 16862, p.1
7. *ibid.*, p.2
8. Knight, p.62
9. Haslam, p.343

Llanganten
1. BGF, Part 3, pp.71-72
2. Jones T., ii, p.234
3. CPAT, 16863, p. 4

Llangasty Tal-y-llyn
1. BGF, Part 5, p.44
2. CPAT, 16865, p.3
3. CPAT, SMR, no. 17829

Llangattock
1. Haslam, p.345; CPAT, 16866, p.1
2. CPAT, 16866, pp.7-8
3. *ibid.*, p.2
4. Bailey in Jones T., iii, p.163

Llangenny
1. Jones T., iii, pp.145-6
2. BGF, Part 3, pp.105, 200
3. CPAT, 16868, p.1
4. *ibid.*, pp.1, 6
5. Jones T., iii, p.145
6. BGF, Part 3, p.105
7. Jones T., iii. p.145
8. BGF, Part 3, p.105
9. Jones T., iii. p.145

Llangors
1. Jones T., iii, p.65
2. BGF, Part 7, pp.72-73
3. Davies (1979), p.98, charter no.146
4. *ibid.*, p.124, charter no.237b
5. Jones T., i, pp.46-7
6. Jones T., iii, p.65
7. Haslam, p.348
8. CPAT, SMR no. 628
9. CPAT, SMR no. 629; Haslam, p.348
10. Bailey in Jones T., iv, p.128
11. Haslam. p.348; CPAT, SMR, no.636
12. CPAT, 16871, pp.5-6
13. Swanton, p.100 & n.9

Llangynidr
1. Haslam, p.349
2. Jones T., iii, p.188; Bailey in Jones T., iii, p.190
3. CPAT, 16877, p.1
4. *ibid.*, p.4
5. BGF, Part 4, pp.258-60
6. *ibid.*, Part 4, p.258
7. Jones T., iii, p.187

Llangynog
1. Jones T., iii, p.12
2. Bailey in *ibid.*

Llanhamlach
1. Jones T., iv, p.15
2. BGF, Part 2, p.305
3. CPAT, SMR no.620
4. *ibid.*, no.621
5. Haslam, p.350
6. CPAT, 16879, p.4
7. Henken, p.112

Llanigon
1. BGF, Part 4, pp.417-8
2. Jones F., pp.127, 144
3. BGF, Part 4, pp.416, 417 & n.4
4. *ibid.*, Part 4, p.418
5. Jones T., iii, p.106
6. BGF. Part 4, p.416
7. *ibid.* Part 3, p.218
8. RCAHMW, 1997, p.288, Lost Monuments (LECM 9)
9. CPAT, 16881, pp.1, 2, 5

Llanilltud
1. *What to See near the Mountain Centre on Foot* – Brecon Beacons National Park leaflet
2. Bailey in Jones T., iv, p.145
3. BGF, Part 6, p.315
4. Bailey in Jones T., iv, pp.144-5
5. see n.1 above

Llanlleonfel
1. Jones T. ,ii, p.238
2. BGF, Part 6, p.389, n.2
3. *ibid.*, Part 5, p.184
4. Haslam, p.353
5. Thomas (2003), pp.156-157
6. *ibid.*, pp.156-157
7. CPAT, 32166, p.1
8. *ibid.*, p.3

Llanspyddid
1. Rees (1853), pp,326-7
2. Haslam, p.354
3. Thomas (1994), pp.131, 153
4. CPAT, SMR, no.599, re:E. Lhuyd; Jones T., iv, pp.148
5. Jones T., iv, p.147
6. CPAT, 16891, pp.4-5
7. Chetan & Brueton, p.277

Llanwrthwl
1. BGF, Part 5, p.214
2. CPAT, 16894, p.1; Haslam, p.355
3. Jones T., ii, p.223; Bailey in Jones T., ii, p.224
4. Haslam, p.355
5. Jones T., ii, p.223
6. CPAT, 16894, p.3

Llanwrtyd
1. CPAT, 16985, p.1
2. *ibid.*
3. CPAT, 16985, p.5
4. Haslam, p.356
5. Granville Lewis, pp.293-6

Llanynis
1. CPAT, 16896, p.1
2. Jones T., ii, p.250
3. BGF, Part 6, pp.386-7
4. CPAT, 16896, p.4
5. Bailey in Jones T., ii, p.250
6. CPAT, 16896, p.1

7. Jones T.. ii, p.250 & Bailey in
8. CPAT, 16896, p.1

Llyswen
1. Jones T., iii, p.22
2. Davies (1979), p.106, charter no.166
3. Jones T., iii, pp.22-3
4. Bailey in Jones T., iii, p.23
5. Haslam, p.357
6. Jones T., iii, p.18
7. *ibid.*
8. BGF, Part 6, p.405

Llywel
1. BGF, part 6, p.387
2. *ibid.*; Davies (1979), p.96, charter no.*125b
3. RCAHMW, ECM 4, p. 284
4. Redknap, p.65; Haslam, p.360; Brecon Museum information boards
5. Haslam p.360; RCAHMW, ECM 3, p.284
6. CPAT, 16903, p.1
7. *ibid.*, pp.5-6
8. Chetan & Brueton, p.278

Merthyr Cynog
1. BGF, Part 4, p.264, n.2
2. Gerlad of Wales, p.86
3. *ibid.*, pp.86, 171
4. BGF, Part 4, pp.266-7
5. *ibid.*, Part 4, pp.266, 269
6. *ibid.*, Part 4, p,267-8
7. *ibid.*, Part 4, pp.265-6
8. *ibid.*, Part 4, pp.265, 268
9. CPAT, 16909, p.1
10. Jones T., ii, p.191
11. Bailey in Jones T., ii, p.195
12. CPAT, 16909, pp.1, 6
13. Thomas (1994), pp.139, 153

Partrishow
1. Haslam, p.362
2. BGF, Part 6, p.322
3. Jones T., iii, p.111
4. BGF, Part 6, p.322
5. Jones T., iii, p.111
6. Bailey in Jones T., iii, p.113
7. Haslam, p.363
8. CPAT, 16931, p.6
9. Jones F., p.145

Slwch Tump
1. Jones T., i., p.43
2. BGF, Part 4, p.419-20
3. *ibid.*, Part 4, p.420
4. Jones T., i, p.44 & n.; BGF, Part 4, p.420
5. CPAT, SMR, no.617 re: Cadw 1998
6. Gerald of Wales, pp.92-3

Talgarth
1. BGF, Part 5, pp.168, 203
2. Leland, iii, p.108
3. Jones T., iii, p.39
4. BGF, Part 5, p.168
5. CPAT, 16959, p.2
6. CPAT, 16959; Haslam, p.371
7. CPAT, 16959, p.8
8. Thomas (1994), pp.145-6

Trallong
1. Haslam, p.375
2. CPAT, 16963, p.4
3. Haslam, p.375
4. Bailey in Jones T., ii, pp.207-8
5. Haslam, p.375

Ty Illtud
1. BGF, Part 6, pp.315-6
2. Jones T., iv, p.17
3. Grinsell, pp.134-5
4. *ibid.*, pp.131-6
5. *ibid.*, p.133-5
6. *ibid.*, p.134
7. Children & Nash, pp.70-1
8. Jones T., iv, p.17
9. Grinsell, p.135
10. Jones T., iv, p.17

Waun Chapel
1. CPAT, SMR, no.5386

HEREFORDSHIRE

Ballingham
1. Coplestone-Crow, p.32
2. Davies (1979), p.104, charter no.164
3. *ibid.*, p.107, charter no.171b
4. Evans & Rhys, p.275
5. BGF, Part 2, p.328
6. L. Rollason dissertation quoted by Coplestone-Crow, p.32
7. Pevsner, p.71

Bredwardine
1. Davies (1979), p.93, charter no.73a
2. Evans & Rhys, p.364
3. Coplestone-Crow, pp.42-3
4. Hoverd & Ray, p.55
5. Ray, pp.130-131

Clodock
1. Pevsner, p.103; notice in church
2. BGF, Part 3, pp.153-154
3. Davies (1979), p.114, charter no.*193
4. *ibid.*, pp.114-5, charters nos.195 & *196

Cusop
1. BGF, Part 3, p.116
2. Coplestone-Crow, p.63
3. Pevsner, p.109
4. Chetan & Brueton, p.268

Dorstone
1. Davies (1979), p.94, charter no.73b; p.104, charter no.163a; p.113, charter no.*192
2. Coplestone-Crow, p.74
3. *A Brief summary of the History of St. Faith's Church, Dorstone*, no date, church guide
4. Annett, p.53

Foy
1. Coplestone-Crow, p.86
2. *ibid.*
3. Annett, p.54

Garway
1. Pevsner, p.135
2. Davies (1979), p.103, charter no.162a
3. *ibid.*, p.105, charter no.*165
4. *ibid.*, p.113, charter no.*192

5. Evans & Rhys, p.408 index
6. BGF, Part 5, p.155
7. *ibid.*, Part 1, p.109
8. *ibid.*, Part 4, p.414
9. Coplestone-Crow, p.91
10. Sant, pp.34-5
11. BGF, Part 5, p.155
12. Davies (1982), p.176
13. BGF, Part 5, p.155 & Part 1, p.109

Hentland
1. Andere, p.33
2. Hoverd & Ray, p.58
3. *Transactions of the Woolhope Naturalists' Field Club*, 1971, Vol. XL. Part II, p.281
4. Coplestone-Crow, pp.98, 100
5. Andere, pp.41-2

Kenderchurch
1. Evans and Rhys, p.407 index; BGF, Part 4, p.399, n.2
2. Coplestone-Crow, p.109
3. BGF, Part 4, p.258
4. Coplestone-Crow, p.109
5. BGF, Part 4, p.258
6. Davies (1982), pp.158-9
7. Pevsner, p.199
8. Thanks to Marge Feryok for most of the observations shared on a day church-yard spotting!

Kilpeck
1. Davies (1979), p.106, charter no.169b
2. Evans & Rhys, pp.169, 275
3. Church guide, p.1
4. Davies (1982), p.164

Linton
1. Pevsner, p.234
2. Chetan & Brueton, pp.25, 275
3. Bevan-Jones, p.30
4. Chetan & Brueton, p.275
5. Coplestone-Crow, p.130

Little Dewchurch
1. Davies (1979), p.107, charter no.170, & index p.190
2. Evans & Rhys, p.394, index
3. Coplestone-Crow, p.63

Llancillo
1. Pevsner, p.237
2. BGF, Part 8, p.304 & Part 7, p.202; Evans & Rhys, pp.30, 43, 90
3. BGF, Part 8, pp.307, 308
4. Davies (1979), p.103, charter no.160
5. Evans & Rhys, pp.371-2

Llandinabo
1. Chetan & Brueton, p.275
2. Davies (1979), p.197 index
3. *ibid.*, p.93, charter no.73a.
4. *ibid.*, p.105, charter no.*165
5. *ibid.*, p.113, charter no.*192
6. Annett, pp.63-64; Coplestone-Crow, p.42
7. Coplestone-Crow, p.131
8. Annett, p.64

Llangarron
1. Pevsner, p.238
2. *ibid.*
3. Ray, pp.123-4
4. *ibid.*, pp.124-5
5. Davies (1979), p.113, charter no.*192
6. Ray, p.124

Llanveynoe
1. Pevsner, p.240
2. Ray, p.120
3. *ibid.*, p.121-122
4. *ibid.*, pp.122-3

Llanwarne
1. Shoesmith, p.267
2. *ibid.*, p.270
3. Coplestone-Crow, p.136
4. Davies (1979), p.116
5. Shoesmith, p.269
6. *ibid.* after J.A. Bradney, p.269
7. *ibid.*, p.269
8. *ibid.*
9. Davies (1979), p.108, charter no.174a
10. Shoesmith, p.269
11. *ibid.*, pp.269-270
12. Coplestone-Crow, p.136

Michaelchurch
1. Pevsner, p.251
2. *ibid.*
3. Anderson, p.21

Moccas
1. Pevsner, p.253
2. Fenn & Sinclair (1990), pp.57-58
3. Morris R., pp.52-53
4. *ibid.*, p.56
5. Davies (1979), p.104 footnotes
6. Doble, p.87
7. Davies (1979), p.105, charter no.*165
8. Doble, p.87
9. Davies (1979), p.113, charter *192

Much Dewchurch
1. Davies (1979), p.104, charter nos.163b and 164 footnotes
2. *ibid.*, p.105, charter no.*165
3. *ibid.*, p.113, charter no.*192
4. Coplestone-Crow, p.65
5. Pevsner, p.258
6. Coplestone-Crow, p.68
7. Sant, p.32

Pencoyd
1. Davies (1979), p.94, charter no.*75 (6) A
2. Coplestone-Crow, p.161

Peterchurch
1. Chetan & Brueton, p.282
2. Pevsner, p.270
3. St. Peter's Church, Peterchurch, Church-yard Trail leaflet, 1999, notes by J.G.M. Jones; church guide
4. Simpson, pp.26-7
5. Sant, p.32
6. Leather, p.13; Sant, p.54
7. Leather, p.14
8. Sant, p.55
9. Davies (1979), p.104, charter no.162(b)
10. Coplestone-Crow, pp.162-3
11. Davies (1979), p.105, charter no.*165 (45)
12. Davies (1979), p.94, charter no.*76a
13. Coplestone-Crow, p.169
14. Davies (1979), p.103, charter no.161
15. *ibid.*, pp.104-105, list of names at foot of p.104 & charter nos.163b, 164 &165
16. *ibid.*, p.113, charter no.*192
17. Coplestone-Crow, p.169
18. Evans & Rhys, p.388, index

Peterstow
1. Ray, pp.114, 120
2. Davies (1979), p.111, charter no.184

St. Devereux
1. Coplestone-Crow, p.175
2. Doble, pp.72, 83

St. Weonards
1. Evans & Rhys, p.275
2. BGF, Part 5, pp.162-3
3. Annett, p.36
4. Pevsner, p.285
5. Pevsner, p.286
6. Bevan-Jones, pp.99-100

Sellack
1. Coplestone-Crow, p.179
2. Annett, p.35
3. Coplestone-Crow, p.130
4. Doble, p.85, n.74

Upton Bishop
1. Pevsner, p.304
2. Pevsner, p.304
3. Ray, p.107
4. *ibid.*, pp.107-8; *Historic Environment Today*, Herefordshire Council's Historic Environment Newsletter, Vol. 7 Issue 2, June 2004; Ray, pp.107-108

Whitchurch/ Huntsham/Welsh Bicknor
1. Watkins, p.197
2. Doble, p.78
3. Davies (1979), p.93
4. Watkins, pp.198-9
5. *ibid.*, p.201
6. Coplestone-Crow, pp.205-206
7. Ray, p.119
8. BGF, Part 4, p.365
9. Coplestone-Crow, p.33
10. Davies (1979), p.92, charter no.*72a; Doble, p.77
11. Doble, p.78

Winforton Chapel
1. Thomas Blount quoted in Annett, pp.14-15
2. Ray, p.119
3. Mrs. Dawson quoted from *Archaeologia Cambrensis*, 1898 in BGF, Part 4, p.259
4. BGF, Part 4, p.259, and n.2

Woolhope, Lower Buckenhill
1. Coplestone-Crow, p.213
2. Doble, p.84 & n.70

GWENT
Bettws Newydd
1. Brook (1988), p.77
2. BGF, Part 1, pp.127-8
3. Brook (1988), pp.72, 77
4. Newman, p.120 & footnote
5. Bevan-Jones, p.25; Chetan & Brueton, p.264

Bishton
1. Newman, p.121
2. BGF, Part 3, p.43
3. *ibid.*, Part 3, pp.43-46
4. Davies (1979), p.110, charter no.180b
5. Evans & Rhys, pp.373-4
6. Davies (1979), p.119, charter no.214
7. *ibid.*, p.123, charter no.235a

Caerleon
1. Brook (1988), p.74
2. Newman, p.141
3. BGF, Part 3, pp.10-11
4. Davies (1979), p.121, charter no.225
5. Evans & Rhys, p.377; BGF, Part 1, p.102; Davies (1979), p.121, charter no.225
6. BGF, Part 1, pp.102-3
7. Gerald of Wales, p.115
8. Leland, iii, p.44

Caerwent
1. BGF, Part 7, p. 211-2
2. *ibid.*, Part 7, pp.212-3
3. *ibid.*, Part 7, p.213-4
4. *ibid.*, Part 7, p.214
5. Davies (1979), p.120, charter no.218
6. Evans & Rhys, p.401, index
7. BGF, Part 7, p.213
8. *ibid.*, Part 7, p.214
9. Brook (1988), p.71
10. Newman, pp.149-150; Church Guide pp.5-6, 8-9

Caldicot
1. Newman, p.152
2. Davies (1979), p.123, charter no.235b
3. Evans & Rhys, p.378
4. Brook (1988), p.77
5. Newman, p.154
6. Evans & Rhys, p.378

Dingestow
1. BGF, Part 4, p.343
2. *ibid.*, Part 7, p.224 & Part 8, p.292
3. *ibid.*, Part 4, p.344
4. Brook (1988), pp.69, 78
5. BGF, Part 4, p.344
6. Davies (1979), p.121, charter no.227b
7. Evans & Rhys, p.377
8. Newman, pp.211-2

Dixton
1. Newman, p.216
2. Brook (1988), p.78
3. *ibid.*, p.78
4. BGF, Part 8, p.288
5. Davies (1979), p.110, charter no.183a
6. Evans & Rhys, p.231
7. Davies (1979), p.122, charter no.230b
8. Brook (1988), p.78

Gwernesney
1. Brook (1988), p.78; Davies (1979), p.125, charter no.*240
2. Evans & Rhys, p.380, n.22

Itton
1. BGF, Part 4, pp.325-332
2. Davies (1979), p.107, charter no.171b & p.165, index
3. Evans & Rhys, p.171
4. Davies (1979), pp. 107, 190
5. *ibid.*; Evans & Rhys, pp.372-3
6. Newman, p.257

Kilgwrrwg
1. Brook (1988), p.74
2. Davies (1979), p.110, charter 179c, – also in Evans & Rhys, pp.179-80
3. Brook (1988), p.69

Llanarth
1. Brook (1988), p.79
2. Davies (1979), p.95, charter no.121
3. Evans & Rhys, pp.365-6 – notes in brackets are theirs
4. Brook (1988), pp.72, 79
5. Davies (1979), p.121, charter no.225
6. *ibid.*, p.95, charter no.*123 & p.110, charter no.180a
7. Chetan & Brueton, p.275

Llandegfedd
1. BGF, Part 7, p.217
2. *ibid.*, Part 7, pp.217, 236
3. Davies (1979), p.115, charter no.199a
4. *ibid.*, p.129, charter no.272; Evans & Rhys, p.273
5. Brook (1988), pp.73, 79
6. *ibid.*, p.73
7. *ibid.*

Llandenny
1. Davies (1979), p.117, charter no.207
2. BGF, Part 8, pp.249-50
3. Davies (1979), p.118, charter no.208

Llandogo
1. BGF, Part 7, pp.33, 34
2. *ibid.*, Part 7, pp.33, 35
3. *ibid.*, Part 7, pp.32, 33, 35-6
4. Davies (1979), pp.101-2, charter no.156
5. Evans & Rhys, p.370
6. Davies (1979), pp.120-1, charter no.222

Llanelly
1. Jones T., iii, p.151
2. BGF, Part 4, p.447
3. Newman, p.279
4. Bailey in Jones T., iii, p.156
5. Chetan & Brueton, pp.56; 276

Llanfihangel Crucorney
1. Davies (1979), p.125, charter no.*240
2. Information at the church
3. *ibid.*
4. Newman, p. 286
5. Brook (1988), p.79
6. Chetan & Brueton, p.276

Llanfoist
1. BGF, Part 5, p.20
2. Newman, p.298
3. Chetan & Brueton, p.276

Llangattock Lingoed
1. Newman, p.305
2. Brook (1988), p.80
3. *ibid.*, p.80

Llangeview
1. BGF, Part 4, p. 247
2. Newman, pp.308, 309
3. Brook (1988), p.80

Llangibby
1. Newman, p.310
2. *ibid.*

Llangovan
1. Davies (1979), p.117, charter no.206;
   Evans & Rhys, p.375
2. BGF, Part 7, p.26
3. Davies (1979), p.117, charter no.206
4. BGF, Part 3, pp.201, 202
5. *ibid.*, Part 5, pp.143, 145-7
6. Newman, p.314

Llangua
1. BGF, Part 3, pp.139, 141, 142
2. *ibid.*, Part 3, pp. 142-5
3. *ibid.*, Part 3, p.139
4. Davies (1979), p.119, charter no.216a
5. Newman, p.316

Llangwm
1. BGF, Part 3, p.139 & n.1
2. *ibid.*, Part 6, p.487
3. *ibid.*, Part 6, p.286
4. Davies (1979), p.107, charter no.173
5. Brook (1988), p.80
6. Brook (1988), p.80
7. Davies (1979), p.129, charter no.274
8. Brook (1988), pp.74, 80
9. Newman, p.316
10. Chetan & Brueton, p.277
11. Newman, pp.316, 317; Brook (1988),
    p.80

Llanhennock
1. Newman, p.319
2. Brook (1988), p.80
3. BGF, Part 6, p.263

Llanhilleth
1. Llanhilleth, pp.1, 4
2. quoted in Llanhilleth, p.4
3. Llanhilleth, pp.2, 3
4. quoted in Llanhilleth, p.3
5. Pennar, p.103
6. Llanhilleth, pp. 3, 7
7. BGF, Part 6, pp.254, 255
8. Jackson, pp.251, 252
9. Llanhilleth, p.3
10. *ibid.*, p.9

Llanishen
1. BGF, Part 6, pp.313, 320, 321
2. Davies (1979), p.125, charter no.*240
3. Brook (1988), p.80

Llanllowell
1. BGF, Part 6, pp.288, 289, 387
2. Newman, p.324
3. Chetan & Brueton, p.277

Llansoy
1. Davies (1979), p.112, charter no.187;
   Brook (1988), p.81; BGF, Part 8, p.296
2. Newman, p.334
3. Brook (1988), p.81
4. Church information

Llantilio Crossenny
1. BGF, Part 7, p.236
2. Davies (1979), p.95, charter no.*123
3. Evans & Rhys, p.366
4. Information in church
5. Newman, pp.350-351
6. Brook (1988), p.81
7. *ibid.*

Llantilio Pertholey
1. Davies (1979), p.95, charter no.122
2. Brook (1988), p.81
3. Newman, p.355
4. Brook (1988), p.81

Llanvaches
1. BGF, Part 6, pp.392-3
2. Davies (1979), p.119, charter no.211b
3. Newman, p.360
4. Brook (1988), p.81
5. *ibid.*, p.69

Llanvapley
1. Davies (1979), p.107, charter no.171b
2. BGF, Part 6, p.390
3. Evans & Rhys, p.372
4. Newman, p.364

Llanvetherine
1. Newman, pp.364-5
2. BGF, Part 5, p.249
3. Brook (1988), p.81
4. Davies (1979), pp.121-2, charter no.228
5. Evans and Rhys, pp.320, 327, 377-8

Llanwern
1. Davies (1979), p.125, charter no.*240
2. Brook (1988), p.81
3. Newman, p.369

Mamhilad
1. Newman.p.378
2. Brook (1988), pp.73, 82
3. Chetan & Brueton, p.279
4. Brook (1988), pp.73, 82
5. Rees (1853), pp.372-3

Mathern
1. Canon E.T. Davies quoted in Utting, p.6
2. BGF, Part 8, pp.252, 253 & n.1
3. *ibid.*, Part 8, p.254
4. Davies (1979), p.97, charter no.*141
5. Evans & Rhys, p.369
6. Utting, p.5
7. Davies (1979), p.123, charter no.235a
8. Evans & Rhys, p.274
9. Nennius, p.42, no.72
10. *ibid.*, p.1
11. Newman, p.384
12. *ibid.*, p.382
13. *ibid.*, p.384
14. BGF, Part 8, p.254
15. Newman, p.384

Monmouth
1. Newman, p.395
2. Davies (1979), p.110, charter no.180a
3. *ibid.*, p.108, charter no.175
4. *ibid.*, p.122, charter no.231
5. Evans and Rhys, p.408 index; Davies (1979), p.122, charter no.122
6. Davies (1979), p.122, charter no.231

Penallt
1. Newman, pp.461-2
2. Brook (1988), p.82
3. Chetan & Brueton, p.281
4. Evans & Rhys, p.321
5. BGF, Part 7, p.32
6. *ibid.*, Part 7, pp.227, 237

Penrhos
1. Newman, p.466

Rockfield
1. BGF, Part 4, p.257
2. Evans & Rhys, p.379

3. Davies (1979), pp.125-126, charter nos.*240 & 246
4. Evans & Rhys, p.381
5. Brook (1988), p.83
6. BGF, Part 5, pp.155-6
7. Jones F., pp.39, 194
8. Newman, p.515
9. Brook (1988), p.83

St. Arvans
1. Newman, p.519
2. Church Information
3. BGF, Part 2, p.174; Davies (1979), p.120, charter no.218
4. BGF, Part 5, pp.3-4
5. Evans & Rhys, p.322, BGF, Part 2, p.174
6. BGF, Part 2, p.174
7. Davies (1979), p.120 charter no.218

St. Maughan's & Llangynfyl
1. BGF, Part 6, pp.419-420, 432, 480; Baring-Gould and Fisher suggested chronology table
2. *ibid.*, Part 6, p.433
3. Davies (1979), p.94, charter no.74, p.191 index
4. *ibid.*, p.128, charter no.264a
5. BGF, Part 4, p.241
6. Evans & Rhys, p.372
7. Davies (1979), p.128, charter no.264b
8. *ibid.*, p.129, Charter no. 272
9. Newman, p.523
10. Brook (1988), p.83

Tredunnock
1. Newman, p.572
2. Brook (1988), p.84
3. Chetan & Brueton, p.286
4. BGF, Part 3, pp.202-211

Trellack Grange
1. Newman, p.580
2. Davies (1979), p.120, charter no.217 – Davies gives the spelling Tryleg Grange but the same OS reference
3. Brook (1988), pp.72, 73, 84

Trelleck
1. Newman, p.576
2. Church guide
3. Davies (1979), p.115, charter no.199b
4. Jones F., pp.74, 95, 117, 125, 196

Usk
1. Newman, p.585
2. Rees (1853), p.390 & n.1
3. Davies (1979), p.118, charter no.210b
4. Rees (1853), p.390. n.1
5. BGF, Part 3, p.11

Wonastow
1. BGF, Part 5, p.164
2. *ibid.*, Part 8, pp.354-8, 360 – chronological table
3. *ibid.*, Part 8, pp.358, 361
4. Davies (1979), p.116, charter no.201
5. Evans & Rhys, p.375 – notes in brackets are theirs
6. Brook (1988), p.84
7. Newman, p.602

APPENDIX

Cascob
1. CPAT, 16700, p.5

Cefnllys
1. Cheton & Brueton, p.267

Gwenddwr
1. CPAT,16788, p.1

Llanbadoc
1. BGF, Part 1, p.116 & Part 6, p.394

Llandeussant
1. Doble, pp.150-151
2. Wrmonoc quoted in Doble, p.148
3. Doble, p.150
4. Evans & Rhys, p.369; Doble, pp. 152 & n.13, 169

Llandewi Ystradenni
1. CPAT, 16822, p.4

Llangattock vibon Abel
1. Brook (1988), pp.73, 80

Llanidloes
1. BGF, Part 6, p.291 & n.1

Llansantffraed (juxta Usk)
1. CPAT, 16886, p.3

Tregynon
1. BGF, Part 4, p.272
2. CPAT, 32492. p.6

Whitton
1. Chetan & Brueton, p.287

Index

Also from Logaston Press

Romanesque Architecture and Sculpture
in Wales

by Malcolm Thurlby

This is the first comprehensive study of Romanesque Architecture and Sculpture in Wales. As the project has progressed, so ever more Romanesque work was found to remain. Unsurprisingly some of the most lavish survivals are found in southern Wales (and to a lesser extent in central eastern Wales), where the Normans penetrated early on and where relative security allowed work to proceed. St Davids was rebuilt in 1182 in a very late Romanesque style after an earthquake largely destroyed the previous building erected some 65 years earlier.

Yet much survives in North Wales too, largely thanks to the patronage of Gruffudd ap Cynan and his aspirations on the European stage. In decyphering the work of Gruffudd ap Cynan, for example, there are few people better placed than Malcolm Thurlby, for he can bring his huge knowledge of the Romanesque to draw out the wider story — making comparisons with work across Europe in terms of overall design, and more locally and in the detail of the work to ascertain from where the masons and sculptors were drawn. Thus the book is not just about the individual examples of the style, but about why certain work has adopted the particular design and ornamentation that it has, with the ability to now read 'backwards' from what we can still see to the mind of the patron who was commissioning the work those centuries ago.

The book takes the building of Llandaff cathedral in 1120 as a juncture in the development of the Romanesque in Wales, its appearance being then on a massive and lavish scale for the country. Thus chapters deal with Romanesque work prior to 1120, the creation of Llandaff cathedral and its effect, notably in southern Wales, the work of Welsh patrons and then a chapter devoted to the unravelling of Romanesque St Davids, rebuilt when Gothic was well established in France and had been successfully introduced into England and Wales.

Malcolm Thurlby was born in England but is now the Professor of Visual Art at York University in Toronto and the author of countless articles in a variety of journals.

ISBN 1 904396 50 X (978 1 904 396 50 5)
400 pages, over 500 black and white photographs and 16 colour plates
Price £17.50

Also from Logaston Press

The Churches of Worcestershire
by Tim Bridges

Introductory chapters tell of the spread of Christianity across Worcestershire and the major events that affected church building in the county over the centuries. The core of the book is a gazetteer to the 270 Anglican churches in the county, detailing their building history, furnishings and tombs.

Tim Bridges lectures widely on church architecture and history and works as Collections manager for Worcester City Museums.

ISBN 1 904396 39 9 (978 1 904 396 39 0)
Paperback 288 pages, over 200 illustrations   Price £14.95

The Churches of Shropshire & their Treasures
by John Leonard

This book explores 320 parish churches of Shropshire, half of them medieval. Chapters guide the reader through changing architectural styles, from Anglo-Saxon origins to the 21st century and then detail the treasures of the churches, including towers and spires, porches roofs, sculpture, fonts, memorials and monuments, stained glass, rood-screens, pulpits, pews and chancel furnishings. The county is then divided into geographical areas, with descriptions of all the individual churches in each area.

John Leonard is a retired consultant physician who lives in Shropshire and has written numerous books on churches.

ISBN 1 904396 19 4 (978 1 904 396 19 2)
Paperback 336 pages, over 530 illustrations   Price £12.95

The Churches of Herefordshire & their Treasures
by John Leonard

This book adopts a similar approach to that for Shropshire noted above, but covering Herefordshire.

ISBN 1 873827 91 1 (978 1 873827 91 8)
Paperback 240 pages, 290 illustrations   Price £12.95

Also from Logaston Press

The Medieval Church Screens
of the Southern Marches
by Richard Wheeler

This richly illustrated book is the first major study of the church screens of the southern Welsh Marches. Despite being of unrivalled variety and including some of the finest medieval carving to be found anywhere in Britain, the screenwork of the region is little known and rarely seen, much of it lying in small churches hidden in the folded landscape of the Welsh borderlands. The book aims to increase understanding of this precious body of work, and encourage exploration of its treasures.

Early chapters examine the church screen in all its manifestations from its origin in pre-Christian times to the Reformation in the 16th century, and beyond. In Britain, the story of the church screen is traced through the 13th and 14th centuries—the formative period for the rood-screen in England—up to the 15th and 16th centuries, when the woodworker was at the height of his powers. The story of the rood loft—a disproportionate number of which remain in the Marches—is also told, as is that of the Great Rood: the once universal figure of Christ found at the head of the nave.

The second part of the book opens with the turbulent history of the March (the Welsh buffer zone ruled and administered by English feudal barons) which gave to Wales its status as the most densely fortified country in Europe. Against this background the screenwork of the region is examined: patterns of provenance and influence are charted, common workshops identified and aesthetic sources explored. The extensive gazetteer provides a detailed account and photographic record of the medieval screenwork in 112 of the region's churches.

Richard Wheeler combines work as a part-time conservation officer with professional photography and writing. Brought up in Herefordshire, he studied English and art history at university, and has from childhood been passionately interested in ecclesiastical art and architecture.

ISBN 1 904396 51 8 (978 1 904 396 51 2)
Paperback 320 pages, over 300 illustrations   Price £17.50

Also from Logaston Press

The Architecture of Death —
The Neolithic Chambered Tombs of Wales
by George Nash

The book details the background to the Neolithic, covering the climate and vegetation, the changing cultural influences and trade contacts, and comparing the scant evidence for settlements vis-à-vis the often dramatic remains of the monuments for the dead. The five different styles of chambered tombs are described   Portal Dolmens, the Cotswold-Severn Tradition, Passage Graves, Gallery Graves and Earth-Fast — with thoughts as to why the varied styles developed in the way and locations that they did. There follows a gazetteer to the 100 sites where there are significant remains, with copious details, plans and photographs. George Nash is a part-time lecturer at the Department of Archaeology and Anthropology, University of Bristol and Principal Archaeologist at Gifford (Chester).

ISBN 1 904396 33 X (978 1 904 396 33 8)
Paperback 256 pages, over 250 illustrations   Price £17.50

Prehistoric Sites of Montgomeryshire
Monuments in the Landscape • Volume XI
by Beth McCormack

Sections provide the background to each of the Stone, Bronze and Iron Ages in the area that became Montgomeryshire. Initial human contact was by hunter-gatherers but it is with the Neolithic, or new Stone Age, when farming is becoming an activity, that the evidence for man starts to really feature in the archaeological record. However, it is for the Bronze Age that Montgomeryshire deserves renown. The hilltops are littered with cairns, standing stones and stone circles, whilst there is aerial and excavational evidence for timber structures including henges and a cursus. It is towards the end of the Bronze Age that the Breidden hillfort is begun, it being further developed in the Iron Age, together with other sites. Throughout the text Beth McCormack explains what people were doing and why, with whom they were trading, and explains what was happening elsewhere in the British Isles. A gazetteer details many sites with information as to access.

ISBN 1 904396 32 1 (978 1 904 396 32 1)
Paperback 176 pages, 80 illustrations   Price £7.95